The
Elementary
Teacher's
Art
Handbook

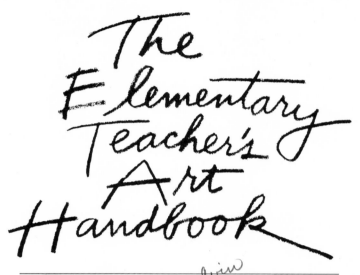

The Elementary Teacher's Art Handbook

KENNETH M. LANSING
ARLENE E. RICHARDS

University of Illinois at
Urbana-Champaign

Westfield State College

HOLT, RINEHART AND WINSTON

New York   Chicago   San Francisco   Philadelphia
Montreal   Toronto   London   Sydney   Tokyo
Mexico City   Rio de Janeiro   Madrid

To our parents and grandparents, who gave
each of us the basis for a satisfying life.

Publisher: Ray Ashton
Senior Acquisitions Editor: David P. Boynton
Developmental Editor: Lauren Procton Meyer
Administrative Editor: Jeanette Ninas Johnson
Project Editor: Harriet Sigerman
Design Supervisor: Renee Davis
Production Manager: Patrick Sarcuni

Library of Congress Cataloging in Publication Data

Lansing, Kenneth Melvin, 1925–
    The elementary teacher's art handbook.

    Bibliography: p.
    Includes index.
    1. Art—Study and teaching (Elementary)—
United States—Handbooks, manuals, etc. I. Richards,
Arlene E., joint author. II. Title.
N362.L36   372.5′044   80-27116
ISBN 0-03-048211-9

CBS COLLEGE PUBLISHING
Holt, Rinehart and Winston
The Dryden Press
Saunders College Publishing

PREFACE

In our opinion, an outstanding art program in the elementary school necessitates instruction in art history, art appreciation, and art production. Experience has shown, however, that production has consumed almost all of the time devoted to art in the schools. We believe that more instruction in history and appreciation is needed, but we disagree with those who would substitute such teaching for all instruction in the making of art. In fact, we believe that teachers and administrators should continue to emphasize artistic production because of its high but frequently unrecognized educational value and because children clearly consider it to be the most interesting aspect of art. We believe that the wise teacher should capitalize on that interest and bring history and appreciation into the program by relating it to the creation of art. Consequently, we have written this book to help the teacher with that task.

Although we have provided more information about art and artists than textbooks in art education normally do, the amount of such information is still restricted. There are two reasons for this: first, student teachers cannot absorb much more material in the short time given to art in their teacher-training programs, and secondly, when student teachers begin work in the schools, they will find that they do not have time to offer significantly more information because most school systems devote no more than an hour a week to art in the elementary grades.

We have tried to encourage teachers to integrate the creation of art with history and appreciation without telling them exactly what to say about art, artists, and other matters. After all, teachers are intelligent people capable of deciding what to teach in relation to a given activity, and they are likely to be more comfortable and effective if they act in their own natural manner without trying to imitate our style or the teaching techniques of others.

Although teachers should know about child development in art, we have not covered the topic in this book. Such information can be provided by college professors of art education who are usually experts on the subject, or it can be found in almost any standard textbook on art education. Instead, our arrangement permits us to deal with history, appreciation, and other information more difficult for teachers to acquire.

We have also reduced the usual theoretical content in favor of more practical material because student teachers as well as experienced instructors perceive the latter to be more crucial to their success and survival. Greater attention to theory, both philosophical and psychological, is likely to be more effective after experience in the real world of the public schools.

The photographs appearing throughout the text are of finished works of art. However, the emphasis on finished products should not lead to the erroneous conclusion that we are more interested in art production than we are in art history, appreciation, or the total development of the child. We simply want the reader to see what can be learned and accomplished through the educational activities we have explained, and finished products are one excellent source of information about growth and development. Naturally, they do not reveal everything that has been learned about history and appreciation, but evidence of such learning is not likely to be captured in a photograph. The reader is asked to note that the photographs appearing at the beginning of the chapters are all referred to in the body of the text.

The authors wish to thank the numerous but unnamed individuals who assisted so graciously in the preparation of this book. Most of all, perhaps, we are indebted to our students, who have provided the stimulation for our growth and development in art and education. We are also deeply grateful to Professor Eleese Brown of the University of Massachusetts and Professor Hazel Koenig of the University of Washington for their careful reading of the manuscript and their helpful criticisms. We appreciate and admire the understanding and skillfulness of the editors and designers at Holt, Rinehart and Winston, and we are thankful for the kind assistance of Suzanne Chamberlin, who translated numerous documents from French to English and vice versa. The manuscript, of course, was typed and retyped by Alice Lansing, who managed to accomplish the task while raising a family of two fine girls and managing other activities too numerous to mention. Finally, we wish to accept full responsibility for any weaknesses the book may have. We have tried our best to achieve perfection, but we know from experience that it is an elusive goal.

K. M. L.
A. E. R.

CONTENTS

PART 1

Introduction

The primary purposes of this book are four in number. The first is to help teachers integrate a small but realistic amount of art history and art appreciation with productive art activities. History and appreciation have been neglected in art education for many years because teachers have placed a major emphasis on making art. They have done so because of their children's own interests and because the time for offering art instruction in schools has been seriously limited. Furthermore, the education of teachers has not provided them with a background in art history and appreciation, and the available educational resources do not make it easy for teachers to find and apply such information.

The second purpose of this book is to help teachers develop an artistic vocabulary in youngsters from 5 to 12 years old. Participants cannot learn about art through intelligent discussion if they do not know the meaning of words that refer to various aspects of the subject. And they cannot develop an understanding of appropriate words or concepts without repetitive use of those words.

The third goal is to assist teachers with the task of building an art curriculum in the elementary school. It is difficult for beginning instructors to build an art program when they lack experience with children and with the subject. They need a brief introduction to the media of art, and they need to know a few things that will work successfully at each grade level. After that, instructors can proceed to build their own programs and give them the refinement that only time can produce.

The fourth aim of the book is to help teachers do all the foregoing things on the basis of a point of view about art and education that has proved to be successful for a quarter of a century. A point of view is necessary if a meaningful, coherent program of art education is ever to develop, and in our opinion, it is helpful for young instructors to begin with a model of thought and practice that has enjoyed a measure of success. Then, as they gain experience, they can gradually alter that model and build a philosophy that is truly their own. The model gives them a framework with which to begin, and it speeds their learning.

The text is intended for those who already work in the schools, as well as for teachers in training. In the second instance, professors of art education will undoubtedly determine how to employ the book. The possibilities are numerous, so instructors should do whatever they consider natural and reasonable for their courses and their styles of teaching. In the public schools, however, teachers are advised to read and reread the first chapter because it offers a logical basis for making judgments about the teaching of art. The next step is to give careful consideration to the number of lessons likely to be taught during the year. Then return to pages 28 through 37 and use the information contained in those pages to build an art curriculum.

As the teacher builds his program, he should select a few activities from prior experience. This will give him more time to prepare for unfamiliar projects. Preparation time is essential for doing well with the lessons recommended in this book, and it is especially important to use that time for trying unfamiliar activities before introducing them to children.

Finally, it is important to understand that the concepts listed for development throughout the rest of the book are merely suggestions. There are other worthwhile ideas to be taught, and many of them are embedded in descriptions of lessons as well as in discussions of various artists. Furthermore, teachers are not expected to build all the recommended concepts in a few sessions with their students, but they should make an effort to teach at least one or two artistic concepts in each of their lessons. The concepts might fall within one or more of the following categories:

1. Life. The teacher might try to build students' visual knowledge of themselves and the world around them, because such knowledge is the content of art.
2. Artistic procedures. The teacher might develop concepts of the techniques used in drawing, painting, printmaking, sculpture, and crafts.
3. Composition. The instructor might teach concepts related to visual structure, arrangement, organization, or design.
4. Art history. The teacher might build a modest understanding of artists, their works, and the environment in which the works were developed.
5. Art appreciation. The teacher might develop a knowledge of the unique qualities that characterize certain works of art.

More information about why and how these concepts should be developed is offered in Chapter 1, but concepts are mentioned at this point to emphasize the fact that art education is not a matter of providing play time. It involves solid content and genuine instruction. And if we are to facilitate the learning of conceptual material, we have to make certain that concepts receive reinforcement from one lesson to another. In other words, we have to repeat them again and again, as we do in mathematics, if we expect children to learn them.

CHAPTER 1

A FOUNDATION FOR THE TEACHING OF ART

Figure 1-1.   *Self-Portrait.* Brush drawing.

All teachers of art must have a point of view about the nature of the subject. Without such a view there is no logical basis for deciding what to do with students, no way of judging their success, and no standard for the evaluation of instruction. Consequently, most instructors develop ideas about art if they are required to teach it. The trouble is that their views are often established without much thought, discussion, and the criticism that discussion creates. The result is that many teachers unknowingly hold erroneous ideas about art, and they teach the subject on the basis of those ideas.

To avoid instruction based on false assumptions, it seems logical that teachers should turn to authorities for guidance in developing an accurate definition of art. The difficulty with that approach, however, is that although experts have made unmistakable progress in illuminating the nature of the concept, they have not constructed a view or definition of art upon which they can all agree. Perhaps this is to be expected when the things we call art have changed significantly through the years. The inability of experts to fashion a perfect definition of art, however, does not relieve the teacher from the necessity of having a point of view, and it does not eliminate the need for a view that is reasonably free from serious weaknesses. After all, it is impossible to teach while remaining either vacuous or neutral about the subject, and it is equally impossible to do a good job while basing educational efforts on ideas that are clearly unsound.

THE NATURE OF ART

To help teachers meet the need for a reasonable view of art the authors of this text recommend a workable definition that has served them successfully for many years. The view that we propose is as follows: Art is the presentation of concepts and emotions in an original public form that is structurally pleasing and intended to satisfy human needs. It is obvious, of course, that concepts and emotions cannot be presented publicly in the form they possess as elements of a person's mind. Consequently, the presentation of concepts and emotions is really the creation of substitutes for those mental entities. We create such substitutes continually as we bring new form into existence, but the factor that separates artistic form from other instances of creativity is its pleasurable structure, a structure that is not irritable to perception.

Sometimes we try to make a distinction between applied art and fine art, but if there is a difference, it is small and subtle. In a sense, all art is applied; it is put to use in the satisfaction of human needs. The processes and products normally referred to as applied art are simply those that are at least partially involved in meeting commercial and scientific needs while the fine arts are concerned with the fulfillment of other human requirements. Artists engaged in the production of fine art are occasionally commissioned to make works of art according to specifications, and such artists also sell art objects they were not hired to make. In both instances, their actions are not unlike those of artists who apply their art to the gratification of commercial needs, but, in general, the producers of fine art present their own ideas and feelings more frequently than do the practitioners of applied art.

Henceforth, when we speak of art we mean fine art. We believe that fine art is more appropriate as a vehicle for general education in the public schools. If our view of art is correct, what are the characteristics that separate works of high quality from those of low quality?

To put it simply, great art is more *complex* in

its content and its composition. It is more novel in its content, more individualistic in its style, and more appealing in its structural organization. This means that experiences with great art will be more captivating, more intense, and more moving than experiences with works of lesser quality. But what does all this mean for art education and for classroom teachers? What should teachers do if they want children to produce art that is high in quality?

The nature of art, as we have described it, indicates that teachers must begin by helping children to develop and clarify their concepts of themselves and of the world around them. Teachers must try to make these concepts as complex as the physical, mental, and emotional maturity of a particular child will allow, and they must do all they can to encourage originality and the formation of novel ideas. Teachers must also try to inspire the child by helping her to develop ideas that are so interesting and exciting that she will want to present them in a visual form.

The second major task for the teacher is to offer instruction in composition. The purpose, of course, is to help the child to present his concepts and emotions in a form that is pleasing to the senses. If the configuration can be made highly attractive and captivating, so much the better. But truly masterful works should not be expected from children.

Finally, teachers must strive to have their students produce artifacts for the satisfaction of human needs that are neither commercial nor scientific.

THE VALUE OF ART

Before proceeding with suggestions about how to teach art, it is important to explain why art should be experienced. In other words, it is essential to indicate the worthiness of art if it is to be offered as a part of the curriculum in the elementary school. The value, if it exists, must come from the product, the process, or both, and it must be a unique value that cannot be obtained elsewhere. In what way does the art product offer distinctive benefits to the individual?

THE VALUE OF THE PRODUCT

In essence, the art product is valuable because it fosters intellectual and emotional growth. It does so because it is a model of the human condition, a model of concept and emotion that can be perceived and interpreted meaningfully by an observer. This is simply another way of saying that the art product is a vehicle of communication; it permits the observer to perceive and to understand the ideas and feelings of another human being. And it makes a contribution to self-fulfillment because it causes a person to become aware of things that he might otherwise miss; it helps him to learn and grow.

Art products are especially effective as sources of information because they are organized in a pleasing or beautiful way. Beautiful form is persuasive. It attracts and holds the observer's attention, thereby allowing the content or the meaning of the work to reach the observer. If the content is not extensive or profound the work can still be valuable because the beauty of artistic structure contributes to our sense of emotional well-being.

The products of each of the individual arts are worthwhile in their own special way. The products of visual art, for example, are uniquely valuable because they offer information to the observer that cannot be transmitted through other modes of communication. They offer highly *particular* visual information about life as it is conceived by the artist, and they offer it in a *presentational* manner. To communicate ideas and feelings presentationally is to communicate them all at once, instantaneously. This is different from offering information sequentially over a period of time, and it means that the visual artist can transmit certain visual relationships that cannot be communicated except in the form of an image. In Figure 1-2, for example, the exact visual relationships within and among the woman, the dog, and the fire hydrant cannot be communicated except by way of a visual image.

Figure 1-2. Kenneth Lansing. Woman Walking a Dog. 1974. Terra cotta, 14" x 35" x 70".

Furthermore, the products of visual art give us information about particular colors, shapes, sizes, and textures; they let us know about emotion and specifically how it reveals itself in a given person or group. And, they help us to understand the visual particularities of nature, of imagined forms, and of all the other aspects of life that are interesting and important to the artist.

THE VALUE OF THE PROCESS

The process of making visual art is as valuable as the product because of the unique contributions the process makes to the growth of the individ-

ual. It helps her to grow perceptually, for example, because it causes her to pay attention to the sensuous dimension of experience and to the sensuous aspects of her own visual creations; it forces the individual to practice attentive perception. And because of the concentrated study that she gives to the subject matter, the content, and the structural organization of her work, the individual learns about those elements. The resultant intellectual growth is clearly unique because it includes knowledge of the particularities of visual experience that cannot be obtained through talking, writing, dancing, or other kinds of communication.

As the individual goes through the process of making a painting, a print, a piece of sculpture, or some other form of visual art, he also learns about the tools, materials, and procedures that are involved. And, because these things are peculiar to the visual arts, he learns something that he would not learn through spelling, writing essays, and solving mathematical problems.

In addition to its contribution to intellectual development, the art process aids emotional growth, and it does so in more than one way. It allows a person to release tension, hostility, or feelings of aggression in a socially acceptable way, and it often serves as a vehicle for discovering and facing personal problems. The fact that the art process can do these things is especially evident in the work of children, where it occurs regularly. But more importantly, perhaps, the process of making art can provide young and old alike with a great deal of pleasure and joy. Working with art materials can be pleasing to the senses; it can be relaxing; and it can give the participant a feeling of personal accomplishment. She can see, hear, touch, and smell things that are new, different, and stimulating, and she can put them together and say, "I made that; it's mine." Only the most insensitive person could fail to see that the making of visual art helps to make the school a place where youngsters are eager to spend the day. To remove such an activity from the schools is to remove one of the most exciting and emotionally satisfying educational enterprises that the schools can offer to children.

At a time when educators are asking youngsters to spend more and more time in front of television sets, computers, teaching machines, tape recorders, workbooks, and programed readers, the making of visual art is a veritable oasis of humanism. It is one of the few remaining activities in which the individuality of a child's work is still encouraged and highly valued.

Having shown that the making and studying of art objects can be uniquely valuable in the mental and emotional development of the individual, it is important to indicate how the classroom teacher can get his students to create and appreciate works of art. The first step, as we have already suggested, is to inspire children and develop their knowledge of themselves and the world around them. Stimulation is the key.

STIMULATION

The teacher's purpose in stimulating children is to build children's concepts and to arouse their emotions. Stimulation effectively accomplishes these goals by attracting and holding the children's attention and by focusing that attention on the objects, events, and ideas about which we would like them to learn. There are four kinds of incitement that are especially useful in art education. They are direct experience, verbal stimulation, audio-visual aids, and art materials. Let's discuss them individually.

DIRECT EXPERIENCE AS STIMULATION

To use direct experience as a stimulus to the development of artistically relevant concepts is to put youngsters in contact with real objects or events prior to having the children engage in art. By doing this, the teacher helps his students to learn about those objects and events, and he increases the chance that the concepts and emotions brought on by the experience will be fresh and clear. The sharpness and clarity of ideas and feelings will obviously make it easier to draw and paint.

Field Trips. There are at least five kinds of direct experience that a teacher can pro-

vide for his students. One of these is the field trip which can be taken either inside or outside the school. Trips to distant places are excellent, when possible, but they are often more difficult to arrange than teachers believe. Consequently, it is more feasible to plan outside trips that can be taken in the immediate vicinity of the school. Some of the things that youngsters might observe, draw, or paint on such a trip are houses, trees, bicycles, automobiles, telephone poles, fire hydrants, windows, doors, play equipment, men working, children playing, pedestrians, and silhouettes against the sky. Inside the school, students might be taken on a visit to the furnace room, the kitchen, the principal's office, or the nurse's room.

To make field trips successful as a means of building visual concepts and creating the desire to make art, there are a number of things the teacher can do. These things are listed below, and they apply to trips both inside and outside the school:

1. Plan beforehand. If permission is needed from administrators or parents, make sure that local regulations are carefully followed, and be certain to make an appointment with anyone you intend to visit.
2. If tools and materials will be necessary, prepare them ahead of time.

3. Let the children know why they are going on a trip, what they will be expected to do, and how they are to behave.

4. Keep the group reasonably quiet and under control. A noisy, chaotic group will not only make itself undesirable to the community, but will not learn.

5. Don't show the students too much, and don't spend an equal amount of time on each of the things you observe. Seeing too much can mean that nothing is observed thoroughly, and it can cause youngsters to be overwhelmed and confused. The result is that the children may have a hard time deciding what to draw or paint, and the subject matter and content of their work are likely to be more superficial than they should be.

6. When children draw and paint on field trips, they have a tendency to produce panoramic scenes composed in essentially the same way. By urging the creation of close-ups as well as distant scenes, however, it is possible to obtain products that differ significantly in their visual organization.

7. If students have trouble deciding where to begin a drawing or painting, suggest that they start with a large or important part. When finished, they can draw whatever is next to that part, and so on until they have completed their drawings.

8. Help the students to see patterns, colors, and textures. Ask them to compare heights, widths, thicknesses of lines, and light and dark areas. Call their attention to horizontals, verticals, diagonals, curves, and points of intersection.

Still-life Arrangements. A still life is an arrangement of one or more inanimate or nonmoving objects. By placing a still life in the classroom, the teacher provides direct experiences with a wide variety of objects. It is appropriate to do so at any grade level. Whenever the still life is employed, however, it is important to use interesting, unusual objects and to provide

more than one arrangement. By placing several groupings around the room, the teacher makes it easier for the children to get close to one of them and to see it clearly. This, in turn, produces drawings and paintings with more detail, better composition, and fewer distant views which tend to look alike.

In the first three grades, it is wise to keep the arrangements simple; one to three objects would suffice. It works well, in fact, if youngsters are divided into groups of four with each group receiving one item to draw or paint. Objects useful for that purpose are coffee pots, lanterns, plants, shoes, toys, fly sprayers, hand drills, musical instruments, hand mixers, roller skates, skulls, bicycles, projectors, typewriters, and other such items. In addition, the following suggestions should be helpful when children are drawing or painting a single object:

1. Encourage the students to search for details such as screws, wires, rivets, or washers. Urge them to include those details in their work.

2. Children tend to draw the whole object in the middle of their paper, and this causes the products to look alike. Explain, therefore, that the whole object need not be drawn. Part of it can go off the page.

3. Sometimes youngsters might be encouraged to draw the object smaller or larger than life size. There is no reason why a coffee pot, for example, should not be made an inch tall or six feet tall. By varying the size of the art work, the teacher gives variety to his program and produces striking differences in the final products.

4. It is clear that changing the size of a drawing may also involve a change in the size of the drawing paper. Remember, also, that changing the type and color of the paper will make an ordinary activity seem different.

5. On occasion, it would be good to have the children include patterns in their work (polka dots, stripes, and so on). The patterns could be used in the background or they could be placed on the objects, even if such designs do

not appear in the still life itself. Patterns help to make drawings interesting to perceive.

6. In grades four through six, it would be appropriate to have the students shade their drawings occasionally.

7. Don't forget that the use of single-object, still-life arrangements need not be limited to drawing and painting. Try using them for collages and prints.

In grades four through six, it is appropriate to continue using the single-object still life, but it is also fitting to use arrangements that are larger and more complicated. Ideally, there should be three or four groupings of objects in a classroom containing thirty children, and each of the groupings should receive considerable care in its organization. The time and effort involved will be repaid by the high-quality art that a good still life generates.

To make a stimulating still life it is advisable to employ objects of different heights and to place some of them in front of others. Arrange the objects so the eye will move from one to another following a visual path. A mixture of plain and patterned things will help to make each still life more effective, and will help to avoid the boredom or confusion that might occur if the whole still life were either plain or patterned. A mixture of hard and soft objects or a combination of natural and man-made items will also add variety to the grouping. And fabrics are always helpful in adding color and pattern.

Working with a still life can be varied if the teacher occasionally constructs a large one. It might reach from floor to ceiling, and it might occupy an area in the center of the room so children can sit around it. Another idea is to use objects that are all the same color, such as white. And the degree of contrast from light to dark will be significantly increased in the finished art products if a floodlight is used on the still life.

Portraits and Self-Portraits. The human figure has always been a popular subject for artists, and it is one of the easiest to use in the classroom. Self-portraits are usually less trouble than portraits, because they eliminate the friction that occasionally develops between youngsters who draw and paint each other.

To increase the educational value of making self-portraits, give each student a small, inexpensive mirror. It will allow her to see and learn about details that the student might overlook otherwise, and it will permit her to study the various parts of the face as the teacher discusses them. Remember that a portrait can be made of part of the head, the whole head, the head and shoulders, the torso, or the whole figure. Highly unusual and beautiful work can also be produced by making portraits of hands, arms, feet, or legs.

Creating portraits can be varied if the instructor, the principal, the janitor, or some other teacher does the posing. By getting colleagues to participate as models, the teacher helps to build good relations with them, and he helps to create espirit de corps in his school.

If one of the children should serve as a model, visual interest can be increased by dressing the person with a fancy hat or some other colorful article of clothing. It also helps to use drapery in the background, and it is especially advantageous to urge the children to work carefully to finish whatever they start. Some portraits might require two hours to complete; consequently, the children must be given support and encouragement.

Animals. The instructor can arrange direct experiences with animals by asking children to bring their pets to school. Rabbits, kittens, puppies, fish, caged birds, and hamsters make excellent subjects for art. The children will enjoy touching, feeding, and watching the animals, and these experiences allow them to build concepts and excitement. The teacher's job is largely a matter of calling attention to distinctive features and urging the students to include them in their work. Such features might be straight or curly hair, tails, cloven hooves, erect or floppy ears, whiskers, short and long feathers, scales, claws, eyes, and other special parts.

Physical Activity. By having youngsters act out the activity they are about to portray, the teacher helps to build knowledge of the human figure, and he assists in reducing the stiffness with which the figure is frequently depicted. It is especially beneficial to call attention to the way body parts bend, to the angles they take, and to how it feels to be in that particular position. Sometimes, this kind of muscular involvement is helpful to those who are not sensitive to things they see.

The children can take turns demonstrating the activity to be portrayed, or the whole class can act simultaneously. Furthermore, the best results are likely to be obtained if the students depict the event immediately after it is acted out. If they wait too long or if too many activities are demonstrated, the educational value of the experience is drastically reduced. A few of the activities that have proved successful are:

Jumping rope	Arm wrestling
Doing exercises	Touching toes
Bouncing a ball	Blowing nose
Marching	Chewing gum
Pitch-and-catch	Tying shoes
Tug-of-war	Hula-dancing

If the teacher selects blowing the nose as a topic to act out, his comments might proceed as follows (in grades one to three):

How many people in the class have had a cold?

How do you feel when you have a cold? Does your nose get sore? What else bothers you?

I'm going to give each of you a piece of facial tissue. When I count three, we will all blow our noses. Notice how you hold your hands and arms. Notice if they bend and where they bend.

Pass out the tissue, and let the children act out the activity. Have the children discard the used tissue.

Now show me how you blow your nose in class, and show me some of the things that bother you when you have a cold: Make the drawing large enough to fill the paper.

VERBALIZATION AS STIMULATION

From what has already been said, it is clear that verbal stimulation is often used in conjunction with direct experience. It helps to make that experience more meaningful by focusing attention on things to be learned. But verbal stimulation is also worthwhile when used all by itself. It aids the teacher in directing attention to objects and events that cannot be experienced directly. Hence it can be used to focus on the past, the future, things that are far away, and on imaginative materials of all kinds.

Telling stories, reading stories or poems, and conversing with students are all forms of verbal stimulation. Reading is probably the easiest, and for that reason the teacher should not overdo it. The best practice is to alternate the different kinds of verbal incitement, and it is also advisable to keep stimulation relatively short. Anything that goes beyond fifteen minutes is likely to bore or confuse students and leave them without sufficient time to draw or paint.

A good stimulation is one that builds and clarifies concepts; it refreshes the memory; or it excites and inspires the student. To have this effect, the teacher must project interest, enthusiasm, and conviction. If the opposite attitudes are projected, children will sense them and respond negatively. This suggests that teachers must know and enjoy their subject matter if they are to exhibit the self-confidence and enthusiasm that successful stimulation requires.

Another important factor in stimulating children is making certain that the topic to be covered is suitable for the ages of the students. In general, this means that youngsters less than nine years old should be given topics involving concrete objects or events, aspects of everyday life, relatively uncomplicated spatial relationships, and things that their experiences will permit them to imagine. Topics that require shading, linear perspective, or knowledge that youngsters are not likely to possess are not appropriate. Further suggestions about suitable topics can be found in subsequent chapters of this book.

To make stimulation successful it is important to talk about the visual characteristics of an object or an event, but it is also helpful to talk about sounds, smells, odors, or other sensuous elements. In addition, it is advisable to discuss how, when, and where something occurs. This means that if brushing teeth is the topic, it is wise to talk about how, when, and where they are brushed, and it is helpful to have one or more children demonstrate how the job is done.

Finally, it would be unfair to give the impression that good verbal stimulation is easy. It is not. It takes practice and constant self-examination to develop one's ability. When effective topics and techniques are developed, however, there is no good reason why they should not be used year after year.

AUDIO-VISUAL AIDS AS STIMULATION

Audio-visual aids offer an excellent means of building the child's concepts and arousing his emotions. By taking advantage of the unique characteristics of artistic reproductions, photographs, films, and other aids, the teacher can provide stimulation that cannot be offered through direct experience or pure verbalization.

Probably, the most useful aids are reproductions and photographs. They can be displayed for any length of time; they do not require a darkened room or special equipment to serve their purpose; they make it possible to see great works of art approximately as they are in their original form; they help to make the classroom attractive; and they can be used in a wide variety of ways. If the class is making portraits, for example, reproductions of famous drawings or paintings of the figure can be used for one or more of the following:

1. To illustrate and explain style in art and to show that excellent portraits can be made in many different ways.
2. To indicate that certain qualities, effects, or meanings could not be achieved if artists were restricted to one way of drawing or painting.
3. To show that there are as many correct styles in art as there are people.
4. To illustrate the effects that can be achieved through different procedures and to encourage the use of different techniques.
5. To illustrate the principles of composition.
6. To show children that their work often resembles the work of great artists.
7. To explain perspective, shading, proportion, and other technical matters.
8. To show the difference between art and non-art or great and mediocre art.
9. To explain what different artists were trying to do and what caused them to do it.
10. To illustrate the effects of the natural and cultural environment on art.

Photographs of animals, insects, birds, people, buildings, vehicles, and other objects are extremely helpful for remembering or learning about things that cannot be experienced in the classroom. Like many professional artists, young people can work directly from the photographs, but we must be careful not to overdo the practice. We do not want children to become dependent upon photographs, and we do not want youngsters to get the impression that we favor highly naturalistic art or that such art is superior to other art. But photographs are an excellent means of bringing the world inside the classroom.

Films offer still another way of providing vicarious experiences to children, and they are especially successful as stimuli for art because they eliminate extraneous elements and cause the observer to focus on the most important and most interesting aspects of a particular topic. They might concentrate on the life of a beaver, on transportation, on doctors and nurses, or on some other appropriate subject. And they often do so within ten to fifteen minutes, which means that the stimulation is highly efficient and that adequate time is left for making art.

Films not only help to build ideas for subject matter and content, but many of them do an excellent job of demonstrating artistic procedures. In other words, they indicate methods of making paper sculpture, linoleum prints, and other artistic products, and they make children eager to try those methods. This is one of the outstanding contributions of the loop film, which comes in a cartridge that simply plugs into a projector. The average loop is about four minutes long; consequently, it can be shown two or three times before the children begin working. Like anything else, however, films should not be used too often or they lose their effectiveness; they become boring.

Slides, filmstrips, tape recordings, and other aids can also be helpful in stimulating children, but they are not quite as useful as reproductions, photographs, and films. The important point, however, is to use audio-visual aids for the unique contributions they can make and for the variety they can introduce in the art program.

MATERIALS AND TOOLS AS STIMULATION

Artists and teachers have known for a long time that tools and materials are exciting, especially if they are new and different. And it has also been known that materials serve as a source of ideas for creative expression. A piece of scrap paper, for example, might suggest the shape of an animal while new crayons might create an eagerness to develop the imagined animal into a fine work of art. Obtaining ideas in this way and experimenting with new tools and materials are among the most provocative adventures of life in the early years, and they are educational. Hence, it is important to introduce new tools and materials in each of the grades. This does not mean, however, that teachers should overdo the effort by introducing a wide variety of scrap materials. Scrap can be useful, and teachers should be alert to the possibilities that it provides. But they should also realize that projects begun with scrap often end as scrap.

Without a doubt, the best tools and materials for use in the school are those that have already demonstrated their fitness for making art and their suitability for young people. Most of these items are listed in Table 1-1, and they are listed according to the grade level where they might be introduced. The recommendations are not meant to be followed rigidly or without thought or common sense. Much depends upon the abilities and past experiences of the children in any given class. But teachers who do not plan the introduction of new tools and materials from grade to grade are likely to lose the stimulating benefits that sequential and carefully planned programs can provide, and they are likely to create spontaneous curricula with all the missing relationships that such courses of study are destined to have.

Table 1-1.

SUGGESTED INTRODUCTION OF TOOLS AND MATERIALS BY GRADE LEVEL*

K	1	2	3	4	5	6	7
Wax Crayons			Oil Crayons	Conté Crayons	Pressed Crayons		
Graphite Pencils							Colored Pencils
Ball-point Pens	Felt-tip Pens			Nylon-tip Pens		Reed Pens and India Ink	Metal Pens
					Chalk and Charcoal		
Bristle Brushes				Hair Brushes			
Finger and Tempera Paint							Watercolor
Manila Paper	White Drawing Paper	Kraft Paper and Cellophane					Charcoal Paper
Newsprint Paper	Colored Poster Paper	Aluminum Foil	Colored Construction Paper	Tissue Paper			
Clipped-point Scissors				X-Acto Knives	Razor Blades		
Paste		White Resin Glue	Rubber Cement and Metylan Paste				
Wood and Hand Tools			Papier-Mâché		Plaster	Jigsaws	Wire
		Vaseline	Printmakers' Plate	Linoleum-cutting Tools		Wood-cutting Tools	
		Soft Brayers	Oil-based Ink				
Corregated Cardboard		Oak Tag				Three-ply Chipboard	
Cotton Roving			Rug Yarn				
Finger Looms			Needles				
Clay				Limited Glazes			

*Once a material or tool has been introduced, it can be used in all subsequent grades.

PROCEDURAL INSTRUCTION

In addition to helping students develop their concepts and emotions through stimulation, it is the teacher's job to offer instruction in artistic procedures. This means that she must provide information about the use of tools and materials, and indicate the steps to be followed in making different kinds of art objects. To ignore this type of instruction and to rely instead on the child's ability to discover appropriate procedures in art is to waste an enormous amount of time. Furthermore, it makes the teacher's background of training and experience almost worthless, and it inevitably leaves the child frustrated and disgusted with art.

A good job of procedural instruction requires that teachers go through the same steps or processes that they expect to teach to their students. This helps them anticipate and avoid the problems children will encounter; it helps them to become aware of the tools and materials that will be needed; and it provides them with a finished product or a model to show their students. Examples are helpful because they give children a better idea of the object they are attempting to make. But the children should be discouraged from trying to copy the model because efforts to do so can cause the youngsters to lose confidence in themselves and to become overly dependent upon the teacher. To discourage copying, simply tell the children that you are interested in their ideas and in the work they do by themselves.

When a procedure is introduced for the first time, it is wise for the teacher to give a demonstration as the process is being explained. Students find it much easier to understand and retain procedural information if they can see how something is done as well as hear about it. And, if the procedure is especially long, youngsters are able to work without repeated explanation if the information is also presented in writing. In other words, writing the steps of the process on the blackboard or on a chart helps the students and relieves the teacher from the strain of excess repetition. Charts are the most efficient because they can be saved and used from year to year.

Procedural demonstrations also offer an excellent opportunity to build a craftsman's attitude and a good citizen's sense of responsibility toward tools, materials, and equipment. In short, the craftsman's attitude is one of care and respect for tools and materials because he knows that their condition determines the work that he can do and the ease with which he can do it. To keep his tools in good condition, he makes it a rule to use them only for those tasks that they were meant to perform, and he keeps them clean, properly maintained, and carefully stored. Like a good craftsman, good citizens take care of their tools and materials, and do not waste them or destroy them. Good citizens know that the tools and materials are furnished by the taxpayers of the state and that they are not personal property. The teacher who can build these ideas in children will be doing a great service to art education, to the school, and to society at large.

In addition, teachers should not be too critical of themselves or of their students if high quality art products do not result from the experiences with a new procedure. It takes time and experience to develop skill and to become familiar with any artistic process. Consequently, it makes sense to be patient and understanding and to plan an art program that allows for repeated experiences with basic procedures. This does not necessarily mean that processes should be repeated several times in one semester, but it indicates that repetition must occur from semester to semester or from year to year if skill, learning, and self-confidence are to flourish.

Finally, it is good to remember that procedural instruction in art must be correlated with classroom management if instruction is to be successful. In other words, the classroom has to be organized in a way that will permit the procedure to be implemented easily. Suggestions about classroom management appear on pages 22 to 24.

COMPOSITIONAL INSTRUCTION

The third major task in teaching art is to offer instruction in composition. The object, of course, is to teach children how to recognize and produce visual configurations that are pleasurably organized. To be successful, this must be done without placing too much emphasis on it and without offering an excess of formal instruction. The reason for saying this is that too much formal instruction in composition can be boring and frustrating. It can cause children to dislike art by thwarting their natural desire to concentrate on the presentation of ideas and feelings; it can make them too self-conscious; and it can reduce the enjoyment that comes from uninhibited manipulation of tools and materials. If this is true, it is fair to ask why composition should be taught at all.

Actually, composition need not be given much attention below the fourth grade. It might help to make occasional suggestions about balance, about using the whole paper, or about the use of patterns and repetition. But children in the lower grades usually pay attention to composition intuitively, and their products are almost always pleasing. Unfortunately, cultural habits, attitudes, and values soon cause children to become preoccupied with photographic naturalism, with the idea of art as a vehicle for the communication of literary information (a means of telling stories), and with truth in art. The effect is that youngsters from the third or fourth grade upward pay less attention to visual organization than they did when they were younger, and their creations are structurally less pleasing. It is appropriate, therefore, to redirect their attention and improve their art through a certain

amount of compositional instruction. We suggest that the instruction be given occasionally through formal lessons presented to a whole class, but we also recommend that most compositional teaching be offered informally on an individual basis. Excessive formal lessons on structural organization are likely to be dull, and more importantly, they cannot be made to deal with composition as it relates to the highly individualistic concepts and emotions presented by each student. And it is vital for youngsters to see that information about visual arrangement is relevant to their own personal success or the information will be ineffective.

Throughout subsequent chapters of this book we make practical suggestions about compositional instruction in the different grades, but, for obvious reasons, we cannot tell the teacher what to say to each child individually. We can only recommend that instruction focus on the production of balance, unity, and variety in each piece of work.

Balance is equality in opposition of any sort; it is a state of equilibrium or stability; and it is achieved by making one side of a visual configuration equal to the other side in its visual weight and in its capacity to attract attention. Making the sides approximately equal is a matter of adjusting the elements of visual form. The elements include color, line, shape, texture, direction, and volume. They can be manipulated in an infinite number of ways to create weight and to attract attention, and the effect they have depends to a great extent upon their context. Consequently, it is difficult, if not impossible, to give advice about balance that will be accurate in all instances. We can say only that visual weight in child art is probably achieved most often through the use of dark colors, large shapes and lines, the downward direction of shapes and lines, large volumes, and large numbers of shapes, volumes, or lines. Attention is attracted by bright colors, by contrasts of any kind, by active shapes and lines, by strong directional movements, and by the concentration of shapes, lines, colors, or volumes.

Unity is a state of oneness, wholeness, or coherence. Without it, a visual configuration is chaotic, disintegrated, and difficult to perceive. To assist children in creating unity, it helps to suggest the following:

1. Repeat colors, shapes, lines, textures, or patterns throughout your work. The repetition contributes to unity because similar elements tend to be perceived as a group rather than as single, discreet parts.

2. If objects or visual units are so far apart that they compete for attention, put them closer together or put more objects or units into the configuration. The reason for this is that separate visual entities tend to be perceived as a group if they are placed close together.

3. Make sure that all parts of the visual image appear to be finished. Unfinished areas look as if they do not belong; they look weak and uninteresting compared to the completed areas; and they often produce visual busyness that makes the perception of form difficult.

4. Avoid lines or shapes that tend to cut off corners or divide the configuration into two or more parts. Once this has been done it is difficult to make the separated parts into one coherent whole.

5. As color is added to forms within the configuration, make sure that it does not destroy the form or break it up so thoroughly that the form is difficult to perceive.

6. As depressed areas are produced in sculpture, be careful about making them too deep. Sometimes, such areas destroy the overall form of the sculpture by breaking it up so completely that it cannot be seen as a whole.

7. Be careful about placing too much emphasis on detail. If detail becomes too overpowering it can cause the artist to lose sight of the fundamental form underlying the work. When that happens, the form can be lost easily.

8. Try to arrange lines, shapes, and other elements so the observer's eye will move easily from one place to another within the configuration. A visual path of this kind helps to tie the parts together.

The last of the three compositional characteristics that we must try to develop in student art is variety or diversity. It is exemplified by differences among the parts which combine to make the whole. A visual configuration that lacks variety can be extremely dull, but too much variety can destroy the unity of a work. It is important, therefore, to maintain a balance between unity and variety by altering the sizes, colors, or textures of shapes as they are repeated for unity. Or a person might vary the size, texture, or shape of a color as it is used throughout her work. She might also employ detail in several places while altering the amount of that detail from place to place. The possibilities for working out similar accommodations between unity and variety are too numerous to mention here, but the general idea should be clear.

In addition, it is a good idea to create variety by using several different colors, shapes, textures, patterns, and linear qualities and by arranging lines and shapes so they do not divide a product into equal parts. Art objects segmented in that way are frequently very dull; it is unfortunate that works are so often divided in half by placing objects in the middle of the paper.

Variety can also be achieved by making one part of a work attract more attention than other parts. This can be done by making the area different from the rest of the composition in some significant way. More specific suggestions about the creation of variety can be found in the remaining chapters of this book.

INSTRUCTION IN ART HISTORY AND ART APPRECIATION

The fourth of the art teacher's major tasks is to offer instruction in art history and art appreciation. It is an important task because the full value of art cannot be realized until people know about great works of art and appreciate the unique contributions that such masterpieces have made to the advancement of civilization. Furthermore, the education of nonprofessional, child artists is aided considerably if they are given the opportunity to use historical works as sources of information about techniques, composition, and so on.

One way to bring history and appreciation into the art program of the elementary school is to correlate it with instruction in the productive aspect of art. Most children are interested primarily in making art not in talking about it. It makes sense, therefore, to take advantage of their interest by involving them in productive activities that have proved to be exciting as well as educational. The next step is to select major artists who have engaged in those same artistic processes and to talk to the students about those artists and their works.

The topics listed below give an indication of the topics that might be discussed with children. Obviously, the list is not exhaustive; nor is it intended to be a prescription for subjects that must be discussed in every lesson. The amount of material covered and the words used in cover-ing it depend upon the maturity of the students, the time available for the lesson, and the primary purpose of the lesson.

1. What was the artist's philosophy of life and of art? In other words, what did he believe?
2. Describe the artist's personality, his appearance, his mannerisms, and his friends. How and where did he live?
3. What were the characteristics of the culture in which the artist lived? What was most of the art like at that time? Who bought it? Did the buyer affect the art?
4. What effect did the culture have upon the artist and vice-versa?
5. What did the artist do that was new and different? What was distinctive about his style, subject matter, content, or the composition of his work?
6. Did the artist invent any new techniques or procedures for making art? What was new about them?
7. What were the characteristics of the tools and materials that the artist used?
8. Did the artist have any major effect upon the world of art? If so, in what way?
9. How was the artist received by the people of her time? How is she received today?
10. Can we learn anything worthwhile from this particular artist? What can we learn?

DEVELOPING RELEVANT ATTITUDES

As we have indicated, part of the teacher's job is to develop in his students the knowledge needed to create art, but the pursuit of such a goal remains insufficient by itself. If children are to make art and judge it with taste, they must have attitudes to support their behavior. What are those attitudes, and how can they be fostered by the teacher?

INTEREST

Clearly, students are unlikely to acquire the knowledge necessary for success in art if they have no interest in making art or in judging it, and it is equally clear that teachers will stand no more than a meager chance of building that interest if they do not have it themselves. Possessed with the necessary excitement and concern, however, the teachers must also gain the respect of their pupils. After all, experience indicates that students are not likely to accept the attitudes and values of persons whom they hold in low esteem.

Know Your Subject.

To gain the necessary respect and to encourage interest in art, there are a number of interrelated things the teacher must do, and the first of these requirements is to learn as much as possible about the subject to be taught. Equipped with knowledge and skill in art the teacher is able to speak with authority and conviction, and she is able to answer questions and solve technical problems as they arise. If she cannot do these things, she is likely to be faced with disciplinary problems which are indications of disrespect.

Maintain Control.

Numerous disciplinary problems are an indication that the teacher cannot control his class, and learning more about his subject is only one way of avoiding such a problem. The teacher must also develop routines for doing things, and he must organize his classroom for efficiency, comfort, and peacefulness. Good classroom management reduces stress and strain on students and teachers alike, and it helps to make them more congenial (see pages 22 to 24).

Friction among the students and between the teacher and her students can also be reduced or avoided by eliminating distractions that interfere with concentration and communication. Too much noise, too much movement, and too many competing activities not only divert the student's attention but they contribute to feelings of anxiety and insecurity.

Insecurity and anxiety are also increased by classes that are too large. Unfortunately, the average class size in America is about 29 students, which is four more than the number favored by most teachers. This produces overcrowding, and it causes the teacher to spread himself too thin. The result is that students compete in one way or another for the teacher's attention. Some succeed, but many feel neglected and unappreciated. And unequal treatment, whether real or imagined, intentional or unintentional, is one of the primary antecedents to trouble with classroom control and with interest in school. Hence, it is essential for the teacher to avoid even the impression of favoritism, and it is equally important for him to strive for classes that do not exceed 25 pupils in size.

Offer Suitable Activities.

Needless to say, interest in art and other subjects cannot be generated and maintained unless learning activities are adapted to the physical, mental, and emotional maturity of the students. Hence, the remaining chapters of this book describe successful projects that have proved to be stimulating for children in the designated grades. If more art lessons are needed, the teacher is advised to consult the writings of Laura Chapman, Edmund Feldman, Pearl Greenberg, Al Hurwitz, Pauline Johnson, Hazel Koenig, Dorothy McIlvain, Chandler Montgomery, Spencer Moseley, Edward Mattil, Earl Linderman, Frank Wachowiak, and other authors of standard texts. All are experienced art educators who offer a wealth of good advice to their readers.

Provide Enough Time.

Appropriate learning activities lose their educational value if enough time is not provided to complete them properly. Consequently, things that cannot be done well in the time allotted should not be done at all. And many, if not most, worthwhile art activities cannot be done well in less than an hour. In fact, the projects in this book often require more than two hours to be completed satisfactorily. The daily or weekly schedule, therefore, must be sufficiently flexible to allow for large blocks of time to be spent on art, and there must also be enough flexibility to permit the occasional teaching of art during a favorable part of the day or week, because interest is more difficult to develop at the end of the day or late on Friday afternoons. Furthermore, interest and enthusiasm are precious characteristics that must be sustained whenever they develop. If the daily schedule is so rigid that it cannot be changed to provide more time and better time, then art will not be the only subject that suffers.

As we have already indicated, the activities in this book often require larger blocks of time and more effort than teachers and students normally give to art in the elementary schools. But improvements in any subject require favorable time allotments and hard work. The question is, "How much time can we reasonably expect for art education, and how many art activities can we expect to offer in the course of a school year?" This is a difficult question, but we believe that forty to fifty hours a year should be the minimum amount of time devoted exclusively to the visual arts. Roughly translated, this comes to about one to one-and-a-quarter hours a week, two to two-and-a-half hours every other week, or four to five hours a month. The number of activities that the teacher should offer will necessarily vary depending upon the nature of the lessons and the maturity of the children, but ten to twenty a year would probably be acceptable as a minimum. Ten activities would mean approximately one a month, and twenty would be about one every two weeks. The teacher who chooses to offer the minimum number, however, should be expected to do an *outstanding* job with each of the projects. If he does only ten, for example, he should devote at least five hours of class time to each of the tasks, and he should make them *memorable*.

Having argued that forty to fifty hours per year should be devoted exclusively to visual art, we also recommend that visual art be correlated with other subjects whenever feasible. The time spent on correlated activities, however, should not be deducted from the forty to fifty hours allotted entirely to visual art.

SELF-CONFIDENCE

If an individual is to make or appreciate art, she must feel confident of her ability to do so. Without such confidence, she is likely to lose interest and turn her attention to things that offer a greater feeling of success or security. Consequently, one of the most essential actions that a teacher must pursue is to build self-esteem in his students. In practice, however, the tendency has been largely in the opposite direction. How can we avoid such mistakes in the future; how can we develop self-confidence in art?

The first step is to make it possible for each student to enjoy a measure of success. This is done by offering appropriate tools, materials, stimulations, and procedural instructions, as well as opportunities to practice.

The second step is to recognize success when it occurs and to make that success known to the child by complimenting him. Unfortunately, this is not always easy for a busy teacher to do because success often occurs in small and unspectacular ways, making it difficult to detect. On the other hand, it is almost always possible to see achievement if teachers are willing to spend a little time looking for it. It might appear as an appealing use of line, color, or texture; it might occur as a distinctive style or a different way of making a nose; it might consist in subject matter different from that employed by other students; it might take the form of superior craftsmanship; or it might appear in a number of other ways. It is not possible, of course, for the teacher to recognize all the achievements in the class and point them out to the achievers whenever they happen, but an attempt should be made.

Furthermore, it is extremely important to avoid things that destroy self-confidence, which brings us to the subject of criticism. Criticism is essential in teaching, but it has to be positive. In other words, it must leave the child with a clear understanding of where and how he can improve his work. And it must leave him with the feeling that he is still liked and appreciated by the teacher and capable of making the necessary improvements. Such criticism is offered most effectively in private discussions and not in front of his peers.

Unfortunately, teachers give a large amount of destructive criticism. Much of it is unintentional, but that does not reduce its destructiveness. It hurts, for example, to have your work compared with that of another for purposes of showing how the other work is superior. More indirect and subtle, but equally destructive, is the practice of having students color dittoed drawings, copy or trace the work of others, or follow step-by-step instructions for making identical objects of some kind. These actions are destructive because they clearly imply that the child is incapable of doing her own work; they make her dependent upon the teacher; they build erroneous ideas about art; they foster intolerance toward a variety of styles in art; and they cause the child to become dissatisfied with her own natural way of working. And when such habits, attitudes, and values are established at an early age, they are almost impossible to change.

TOLERANCE TOWARD STYLE

Style in art is the manner in which a work is done; it is one of the qualities that gives distinctiveness to the work. To be tolerant of style is, therefore, an attitude of openness and acceptance toward the many distinctive forms that art might take. It is an attitude that is not essential for the making of art, but it certainly is helpful because it gives the artist additional freedom. It permits her to deal with almost any subject matter or content, and it allows her to adopt the mannerisms most conducive to the expression of her concepts and emotions.

To build in children a tolerance toward style, we must first help them understand that different styles actually exist. Then we must proceed to show that certain ideas and feelings could not be expressed if the artist were re-

stricted to only one way of working. The impressionists, for example, could not have communicated their concepts of light and atmosphere if their attitudes toward style had restricted them to working in the neoclassic manner of Ingres or David. By the same token, the expressionists could not have communicated emotion so powerfully if their attitudes toward style had kept them working in the same fashion as the impressionists.

Exposing youngsters to a broad selection of styles and explaining how stylistic flexibility increases freedom of communication is excellent, but it must also be supplemented by the acceptance and encouragement of stylistic differences in the work of the children themselves. Discovering and showing delight in the stylistic character of each child's work is indeed one of the most important things a teacher can do because it builds self-confidence and tolerance at the same time.

In addition, it is good for children to express their likes and dislikes for different forms of art especially if the youngsters are required to justify their opinions. This allows the teacher to uncover faulty reasoning as well as the kind of narrow-mindedness that limits creativity and intellectual growth. It also offers an opportunity to show that there are other points of view and that there are reasonable explanations underlying the different styles of art. The object is not to make a child feel that his taste is wrong (because taste is never wrong), but to move the child toward an appreciation of art that approaches more closely the taste of experts. In other words, the object is to move the youngsters toward an appreciation of the works that are generally regarded as the masterpieces of history and of our own time.

A WILLINGNESS TO WORK HARD

It is possible to produce art occasionally without discipline and hard work, but most of the time it requires substantial effort, especially if a person is to grow in and through the process. The old saying that a person gets out of an activity whatever she is willing to put into it certainly applies to the making and judging of art. Art is rarely produced during fits of inspiration or insight. Such occurances might initiate creative activity, but the task of realizing the inspiration in material form is plain, ordinary work. Or to phrase it differently, art is not something that a person produces only when she feels the urge. It involves effort that extends well beyond the moment of insight. And, without a doubt, the effort itself often provides the inspiration for more art.

Getting youngsters to work hard for their own good is not always easy because it requires that the teacher be successful with all the things we have discussed so far. And products acceptable to children must be forthcoming if the youngsters are to feel that their efforts were justified. Consequently, it is important for the teacher to identify and admire the accomplishments of students after they have been through a session of extra hard work. While they are in the midst of the effort, of course, it is equally necessary to provide interest, encouragement, understanding, and appreciation. Children are, after all, like everyone else. They will do almost anything if they are given encouragement and other forms of feedback.

Experience indicates, moreover, that teachers have been too willing to accept slap-dash, half-finished products from students. They have been afraid to urge longer, more intense efforts from their pupils because they have concluded that it would harm the youngsters in some way. The result has been work that provides little satisfaction either to viewers or to the children themselves. This leads to self-condemnation, a loss of self-confidence, and a feeling that art is frivolous and a waste of time. Naturally, it is possible to work children too long and too hard, but it is also possible to expect too little, and we believe that the tendency in the recent past has been toward the latter.

DEVELOPING SKILL

Skill in art is the ability to manipulate tools and materials efficiently and it is the ability to judge art effectively. If skill does not develop along with a knowledge of life, composition, artistic procedures, and art history, the child will not become especially capable as a nonprofessional artist and connoisseur. And, if that happens, he will not receive the full value that comes from making art and from studying art objects. The development of skill is, therefore, one of the major tasks that the teacher of art must undertake.

There are three things that must be done to develop technical facility. First, we must build a knowledge of the procedures for making and judging art. Secondly, we must develop the attitudes necessary to keep the child involved in those procedures. And, thirdly, we must give her ample opportunity to practice.

For a long time, practice has been recognized as one of the essential ingredients in the teaching of reading, writing, and arithmetic, but educators seem to have overlooked its importance in art. They rarely give children an opportunity to practice artistic procedures because they constantly introduce new ones without providing for systematic repetition. Certain procedures are, by nature, easier to repeat than others, but repetition must occur if youngsters are to learn those processes and become skillful with tools and materials. The repetition of the more involved procedures need not occur in a single semester, and in some cases it need not occur in a single year. But it should take place no less often than from year to year.

CLASSROOM MANAGEMENT

Classroom management is the supervising, organizing, coordinating, and handling of the furniture, equipment, tools, materials, lighting, and ventilation normally associated with a school classroom. Skillful management can help to make the room an inviting place to spend the day; it can increase efficiency in teaching and learning; it can contribute to the physical and mental health of teachers and students; and it can help to reduce disciplinary problems.

Classroom management is the teacher's responsibility, and it can require a considerable amount of effort, especially during art lessons, because art often involves movement by the students as well as a wide variety of tools, materials, and equipment. The job is complicated by the fact that a conscientious teacher always tries to do what needs to be done without using more or better tools, materials, and equipment than the job requires. And he always does his best to keep the classroom and its contents clean and in good condition. To do otherwise would be to waste money and betray the responsibility invested in the teacher by the people of the community.

Although classroom management can be time-consuming, there is no reason why it should be handled entirely by the instructor. Much of the work can and should be done by the students under the teacher's direction. Students should help with the storage, preparation, distribution, collection, and cleaning of tools and materials; they should assist with the display of finished art; they should help to keep the room neat and clean; and they should take some responsibility for the avoidance of waste, theft, and vandalism. We say that students *should* do these things for at least six reasons: 1) it helps them to develop a sense of responsibility; 2) it helps them to build positive working habits; 3) it gives them a sense of belonging; 4) it promotes cooperative behavior; 5) it assists in bringing the teacher and his pupils closer together; and 6) it

provides satisfaction and pleasure. If anything, teachers do not allow youngsters enough to do with classroom management. As a consequence, they lose one of the easiest and most effective ways of helping young people to enjoy school.

FURNITURE AND ITS ARRANGEMENT

Classrooms differ in size and shape from one place to another and so does the furniture. But if we had our preferences we would choose a plain room that is clean, comfortable, uncrowded, and cheerful. The furniture would include two sinks, plenty of bulletin board space, a small blackboard, a movable workbench, storage space for tools and materials, storage space for products produced in all subjects, a teacher's desk, and tables large enough to seat at least four students comfortably. Tables are superior to desks because they allow more open space for moving around and working, and they make it easier and less expensive to supply every student with tools and materials. If tables are not available, it is possible to create them by moving four desks together and placing plywood or Masonite on top. By arranging the tables carefully, the teacher can free a large open space to be used as a teaching station. Such a space is extremely useful because it provides room for a workbench, for giving demonstrations, and for getting youngsters together for an intimate conversation. If they stay at their tables during discussions, they are often distracted by interesting tools and materials, and they miss the essence of the lesson.

Sinks are most useful if they can be approached from two sides, because more children can use them at one time. The sinks should be equipped with hot and cold water, soap, and paper towels, and they should be at least 16 x 26 inches in size.

The blackboard space might be 4 x 10 or 4 x 20 feet in size, while the bulletin board could easily occupy the remaining wall space. We recommend a large amount of bulletin board space because we believe that it is important to display art work as well as instructional materials from all subject areas. Such displays make the room attractive, educational, and exciting, and they help to make the school pleasant and cheerful. In addition, bulletin boards are useful in constructing still-life arrangements; they make the creation and display of murals much easier; and they lead to more variety in the size and kind of art produced.

A movable workbench or sturdy table is useful in teaching almost any subject because it provides space for giving demonstrations, displaying educational materials, and constructing things. Along with the countertops that usually cover storage areas, the workbench offers a good place to put supplies for immediate use by students, and it is ideal for building still-life arrangements. If workbenches are not available, they can be constructed by starting with school desks. See the instructions on page 276.

STORAGE

Many teachers find it advantageous to have a central storeroom in each elementary school for storing extra materials as well as tools and materials that must be shared. At the same time, each classroom must have a considerable amount of space for the storage of paper, glue, paint, brushes, pencils, crayons, chalk, scrap, and other items that need to be kept handy. Such space is most useful if it has adjustable shelving with dimensions large enough to accommodate 18-x-24-inch sheets of paper. It should be located and organized so tools and materials can be obtained easily by either the students or the teacher. And, as far as art materials are concerned, it is most efficient if drawing, painting, printmaking, sculpture, and craft materials are stored in their own separate areas.

Perhaps the biggest weakness in most contemporary classrooms is a lack of storage space for work in progress. If such space is not included in the room at the time of its construction, it is not easy to provide. Work may be stored on the floor, on counters and workbenches, and on inexpensive metal shelving purchased (little by little) from discount stores. Unfinished art work can often be hung from wires stretched across the room, and three-dimensional items can be kept on shelves made of inexpensive lumber.

PREPARATION, DISTRIBUTION, AND COLLECTION OF MATERIALS

As with other aspects of classroom management, the efficient preparation, distribution, and collection of tools and materials can do much to reduce the physical and emotional strain of teaching, and it can free time for genuine educational activities. To reap these benefits it is essential to: 1) develop routines; 2) teach the systematic methods to students; and 3) let children help with the work.

Young teachers occasionally frown on routines because they think that habitual practices give too much stiffness to teaching. But they soon learn that survival until retirement depends to a large extent upon the elimination of unnecessary or relatively unimportant work. Furthermore, they discover that children like a certain amount of routine because it offers the kind of security that comes from knowing what is to happen next. Children are unhappy, anxious, and even fearful in the midst of disorganization, lack of direction, and continuous change.

Throughout the remainder of this book suggestions are made about the preparation and distribution of materials connected with specific art activities. Therefore, the recommendations listed below are general in nature; they apply to almost all activities.

1. Let students help in filling glue bottles, paint bottles, ink bottles, and paste containers.
2. Allow students to assist you in organizing crayon boxes and in cleaning and straightening the boxes of scrap paper and scrap wood.
3. Seek help from students in mixing clay, papier-mâché, and printing ink.

4. Make sure that you have enough tools and materials for the job at hand.
5. Place materials on counters, workbenches, or tables in such a way that children can get them quickly and easily. It helps to keep items well-separated.
6. Make sure sufficient time is allowed for cleaning up. Organize the job so children know exactly what to do.
7. If a big cleaning job is needed, divide the class into small groups and assign a job to each group.

EXHIBITING CHILD ART

Exhibitions of child art are important because they help to create a pleasant, supportive environment. Children are honored and pleased to see their work on display; the display acts as a reinforcement of things they have learned, and it gives them a measure of self-confidence. Exhibitions are also highly educational. Children are able to see how others have handled a given topic; they observe techniques and styles different from their own; and they learn that art can take many different forms. Teachers and parents can also learn from art displays. They can discover the things that children think about; they can obtain an estimate of concept development in individual children; they can get ideas about what is needed in the way of instruction; and they can see the extent to which previous teaching has been successful.

If exhibits are to be educationally worthwhile for all children, however, it is imperative that the work of all children be displayed. Unfortunately, this is not always possible because of spatial limitations. But, in those instances, teachers should make every effort to see that each child gets a regular turn at having his work displayed. The practice of showing only the best

work must be stopped because it deprives the youngsters who are most in need of encouragement from getting the support they require.

From a practical standpoint, displays of two-dimensional child art are most likely to be created by fastening drawings, paintings, and other products to bulletin boards without matting, framing, or mounting them. The practice makes sense because special handling takes time, and it is more expensive. On the other hand, a little embellishment can improve the appearance of finished products by a considerable degree, and there are times when a more elaborate display is highly desirable. How can such exhibitions be produced with a minimum of time and money?

Matting and framing are usually out of the question because they require an unjustifiable amount of effort and expense. But mounting is well within reason. It simply requires that drawings, paintings, and prints be glued to another piece of paper or cardboard. Probably the most economical material upon which to mount two-dimensional art is construction paper of the same size. The mounting can be done most easily by trimming the original drawing, painting, or print with a paper cutter before gluing the work to construction paper. The trimming should be enough to allow one-fourth to one-half an inch of construction paper to show around the edge of the work. Make sure that the border is the same width on all sides. If it is crooked or uneven, it will look distasteful so it is important to do the job carefully.

Sometimes people try to do an elaborate job of mounting by making a wide border and bend-ing it into the shape of a picture frame. Practices of this kind should be avoided because they call too much attention to the border when the at-tention should be directed toward the work of art. The border should be no more than a nonob-trusive transition from the work of art to the wall. Sometimes it helps if the color of the bor-der is the same as one of the colors in the work that is being mounted.

ECONOMY IN ART EDUCATION

Funds for art are rarely plentiful. Consequently, we must spend wisely if we hope to get maxi-mum value from every dollar in the budget. The unhappy fact, however, is that many school sys-tems spend money foolishly, especially for art materials. One of the primary reasons for such waste is that school systems choose to get along without professional art teachers and supervisors who might be helpful in making economical purchases.

Administrators and teachers are constantly saying that school systems cannot afford electric kilns, printing presses, India ink, oil crayons, colored Kraft paper, oil-based printing ink, lino-leum, wood-cutting tools, portable jigsaws, wood-working equipment, and other expensive things. But almost any school can afford these items if common sense is applied to the purchas-ing of materials. For example, it is not unusual for a system serving 3,000 elementary school chil-dren to spend a thousand dollars or more per year on watercolors. By eliminating the purchase of watercolors for one year it would be possible to buy two electric kilns or one kiln and four tons of clay. Watercolors are not especially suit-able for the elementary school anyway, so their loss for one year would not be disastrous. Yet, the addition of a kiln would open a new realm of experience to children. Equally dramatic im-provements can be made easily with other changes in the management of money and mate-rials. Therefore, let us turn our attention to the business aspects of art education.

To get maximum value from funds spent on art materials, it helps to know how much money will be allocated to art from year to year. With-out this information the art educator may lose the incentive to plan purchases wisely and im-prove the program. This happens occasionally in systems which do not assign specific budgets to different instructional units. The argument for not assigning budgets is that it gives administra-tors more flexibility in meeting current needs, and it saves money because it permits the shift-ing of funds from a well-stocked department to one that is in need of new materials or equip-ment. The idea is fine so long as it does not disrupt or destroy departmental efforts to im-prove programs through planned purchasing. For example, it would be destructive if an adminis-trator were to veto the purchase of two kilns on the basis of their high cost if the acquisition had been made possible by the elimination of water-color purchases for one year. Such an action would discourage careful planning. Therefore, it is important for administrators and all persons making claims on the budget to be reasonable people who care about the welfare of the whole school system rather than the advancement of certain selected departments. It is also important for administrators to maintain communication with all units so the needs and plans of those departments are not overlooked or thwarted. And another good practice is for administrators to assign a minimum but dependable budget to each department while withholding additional funds from each unit for the purpose of handling emergencies or special needs. Then if the emergencies or atypical needs do not develop, the extra funds can be disbursed to the departments. This allows responsible planning to take place because the department heads know that they can expect at least the minimum budget from year to year, and the administrators can maintain enough fiscal flexibility to meet unexpected problems.

To get the full value from every dollar in art education the art educator must also have control over the art curriculum. Unfortunately, many school systems do not have an organized program in art. Things just "happen" according to the whims of the teachers. And, the result is that those school systems do not have as much as they could have in the way of tools, materials, and equipment. The children are shortchanged in more ways than one.

By exercising control over the art activities to be offered for two to five years, the art educator can make better decisions about what to buy and when to buy it. To make this clear, let's assume that an art educator is able to plan the art program for five years. During the first year he could emphasize inexpensive activities such as drawing, certain kinds of printmaking, papier-mâché, collage, and a little painting. The money saved on such projects could be used to buy two kilns and several tons of clay. During the second year, a few small clay projects could be introduced in place of collage, and the excess funds could be spent on printing presses and other kinds of printmaking equipment. The third year

could then be devoted to projects in printmaking, sculpture, and drawing, and the excess funds could be used to replenish all the basic expendable materials. During the fourth and fifth years, the program might emphasize highly inexpensive activities of all kinds, and the money saved by such projects could be used to purchase more tools and equipment. With careful planning, many of these tools and pieces of equipment could be moved from school to school as needed. And, as the schools gradually acquire their own pieces of equipment, the money spent on such expensive items could be diverted to the enrichment of basic materials, the addition of teaching aids, and the maintenance of tools and equipment. The idea is to gradually acquire expensive items through carefully planned inexpensive activities and through yearly emphases on certain selected projects.

Before leaving the subject of economizing through the control of educational offerings, it seems worthwhile to call attention to the fact that some school systems are decentralizing the management of the curriculum by allowing each school to develop its own independent program. The idea is to give teachers and administrators in the separate schools more freedom to individualize programming. But the system is likely to increase expenses because tools, materials, and equipment may vary from school to school and a system-wide emphasis on certain learning activities becomes more difficult to implement. This means that the most economical methods of buying supplies cannot be put into effect.

Purchasing tools, materials, and equipment in the most inexpensive way means buying them in large quantities, all at the same time, for the whole school system, and it means that the school system gives its business to the supplier who offers the lowest bid. Usually, it is most economical to buy art materials in large sizes because of the lower cost and increased flexibility. Recommendations of a more specific nature are listed below:

1. Buy a medium grade of liquid tempera in quart sizes. When each classroom has eight colors, buy the paint in gallon containers and place them in the storerooms of the various schools. Teachers can then refill the quarts, when necessary, from the gallon containers. The quart bottles should not be thrown away.

2. Purchase construction paper in 18-x-24-inch sizes. The large size allows the creation of big paintings and constructions, and it can be cut into smaller sizes. Hence, it gives greater flexibility.

3. If considerable cut-paper work is to be done, buy 12-x-18-inch poster paper instead of construction paper. It cuts more easily, and it costs about half as much.

4. Buy glue in 4-ounce bottles until each classroom has at least one bottle for every two children. Then purchase the glue in gallon containers, and use them to refill the bottles.

5. Buy white shellac, turpentine, mineral spirits, alcohol, media mixer, and paste by the gallon. Keep these materials in a storeroom in each school.

6. Purchase India ink by the quart.

7. Buy white drawing paper of high quality in 18-x-24-inch sizes.

8. Buy medium- or high-grade pastels or chalks.

9. Clay should be purchased dry and in large quantities. It can be mixed in plastic bags. See page 258.

10. In general, it is best to buy tools of medium or high grade. Inexpensive tools and equipment are often a poor bargain.

11. The best practice, from both an educational and an economic standpoint, is to buy the standard tools, materials, and equipment that have been used in art for a number of years. Exotic or unusual items are often expensive and rarely appropriate. The things listed below, for example, are not recommended for purchase:

glitter	candle wax
spray paint and spray varnish	prepared papier-mâché
pipe cleaners	self-hardening clay
macaroni	play-dough
seeds, beans, and peas	pudding for finger painting
wood-burning sets	prepared strips of plaster and cloth

origami paper
styrofoam balls
exotic papers or fancy crayons
special printmaking paper
raffia

looms for finger-weaving
beads
cork sheets
liquid metal
craft kits and molds of all kinds

12. Before preparing orders to submit to the business manager of the school district, it is wise to take an inventory of the materials on hand. This is usually done in the spring. Orders are then prepared and submitted to the business manager, who consolidates them and obtains bids from school supply houses. In the late spring the orders go to the lowest bidders, and the supplies begin to arrive during the summer. Then, before classes begin in the fall, it is important to check the newly arrived materials to make sure that everything has arrived in good condition and as specified. Money is often lost if this step is not properly carried out.

13. Do not order so much that things spoil in storage.

14. Avoid throwing away scrap, construction paper, paint, glue, or any other usable material. An enormous loss occurs in many school systems because of carelessness in this matter.

15. Certain tools should be expected to last at least three years. Scissors, rulers, brushes, clay tools, X-Acto knives, blades for linoleum-cutting tools, drills, needles, and similar items fall in this category. But hammers, brayers, looms, saws, barens, hand drills, and other sturdy tools and equipment should last much longer. Plan on it!

16. Teachers should find out what art materials are available to them in their school as well as materials available to them in the school district.

Without a doubt there are other things that can be done to foster economy in art education. For the good of everyone, it is imperative that we do the best work we can with a minimum expenditure of funds. Remember that a good art program is not necessarily indicated by a high budget.

CURRICULUM DEVELOPMENT

The art curriculum in the elementary school is the sum of all the educational offerings in art. Planning those offerings and organizing them into sequences that promote smooth, efficient, relevant, and logically progressive learning can be complicated and confusing for the most experienced teacher, and the task is even more difficult for the person with a limited instructional background. It is especially hard for inexperienced persons simply because curriculum-building requires a thorough knowledge of children, teachers, classrooms, art materials, the goals of education, the goals of art education, and numerous art activities with high educational potential. Nevertheless, inexperienced teachers are required, more often than not, to devise their own programs in art. Consequently, we have attempted to help them by presenting the material in the remaining chapters of this book. The material includes information about artists, representative examples of their work, and a large number of highly educational art activities that should be helpful in integrating art history and art appreciation with the making of art. We have divided the art experiences into two groups; those suitable for the primary grades (ages six through eight) and those appropriate for the intermediate grades (ages nine through eleven). But we have not organized the activities into a sequential curriculum because teachers and students do not all have the same needs, interests, and abilities. We believe that teachers should be given assistance, but we also believe that they should put together their own programs because they are in the best position to know their own strengths and weaknesses as well as the needs and abilities of their students. How should they proceed; how should they use the information contained in subsequent chapters of this book?

First, it helps to know what a person should do if she were building a curriculum from the beginning. The work falls into approximately six categories which include: 1) the determination of objectives; 2) the selection of content; 3) the choice of activities through which the content is to be presented; 4) the selection of teaching techniques or strategies; 5) the organization of lessons into a sequence for learning; and 6) the decision about how to evaluate individual lessons as well as the whole curriculum. The work need not proceed according to the order in which the foregoing categories have been listed, and it need not be done one category at a time. In fact,

the work from one category is often so closely related to work from another that both jobs can be done simultaneously, and that is exactly what happened as the authors attempted to prepare the curricular materials for Chapters 2 through 21. To make this clear, let us turn our attention to the work done by the authors in each of the foregoing categories and to the work that remains to be done by the reader.

DETERMINING OBJECTIVES

The same general objectives that have traditionally guided education in America are the objectives assumed by the authors as they began to develop the art activities outlined in subsequent chapters. These objectives may be found in any standard text that deals with the goals of education in America.[1] But to summarize them in a single sentence, one might say that the primary purpose of education is the development of the good citizen; the free and civilized person; and the person of wisdom, virtue, and taste; the person with a sense of beauty and style.

Like other educators before us, we also assumed that the study of art could and should make a unique contribution to the attainment of the general aims of education through the development of nonprofessional artists and connoisseurs. Naturally, we concluded that the level of artistic ability and the level of aesthetic judgment to be expected from children at each of the various grade levels should be in accordance with the commonly accepted developmental characteristics of children.

To produce nonprofessional artists and connoisseurs we had to determine the knowledge, attitudes, and skills necessary for the production and appreciation of art. These were the charac-

---

[1]See, for example, Kenneth M. Lansing, *Art, Artists and Art Education* (Dubuque, Iowa: Kendall-Hunt Publishing Co., 1976).

teristics we would try to develop in children through the lessons we intended to organize. Clearly, this was not only a matter of identifying specific objectives in the areas of knowledge, attitude, and skill, but it was also a matter of selecting the content to be covered in art education. We shall say a little more about the nature of that content in the next two or three paragraphs, but first, let us add one or two more thoughts about objectives.

As the reader organizes the activities in the remainder of this book, we strongly recommend that he try to determine the objective or objectives that we were attempting to reach through each lesson. In other words, he should attempt to find out what we wanted children to know and what we wanted them to be able to do after being exposed to each lesson. We also recommend that specific behavioral objectives be written for each lesson so they can be used later on as a basis for evaluation.[2] Furthermore, the most important objectives are those that have to do with knowledge and skill. The teacher should be interested in attitudinal objectives, of course, but they seldom reveal themselves through our description of a given activity.

A teacher should also feel free to alter the objective of a lesson at any time. He may discover that such a change is advantageous while the lesson is underway; if so, he should not hesitate to make the change.

SELECTING CONTENT

Selecting content is a matter of choosing the concepts, ideas, or knowledge to be taught through carefully developed lessons at each

[2]It is hoped that students and teachers will refer to one of the following texts for advice as they think about and write objectives:

Robert F. Mager, *Preparing Instructional Objectives* (Palo Alto, California: Fearon Publishing Co., 1962).

Norman E. Gronlund, *Stating Behavioral Objectives for Classroom Instruction* (New York: Macmillan Co., 1970).

grade level. From what has already been said in earlier portions of this chapter, it should be clear that the authors believe in developing five kinds of knowledge. First, we consider it important to build the child's concept of *herself and the world around her* through stimulation. We also believe it is necessary to develop an understanding of *composition* and of *artistic procedures*, and as we work at fostering these forms of knowledge we must also build an understanding of *art history* and *appreciation*. The amount of knowledge that can be developed in these areas during six years of elementary schooling depends to a large extent upon how much time is given to art instruction. We all know that considerable time is devoted to mathematics in the elementary school curriculum, yet we do not expect youngsters to enter junior high school as youthful versions of Albert Einstein. We expect them to know how to add, subtract, multiply, and divide, and we think they should know something about fractions and decimals. By the same token, we should not expect young people to be highly accomplished artists and connoisseurs by the time they reach seventh grade, especially if their education in art has been limited to a minimum of ten to twenty lessons a year. To be more realistic, we might expect the graduates of our elementary schools to know some of the visual characteristics of ordinary objects and events in their daily lives; we might expect them to know the fundamentals of visual artistic composition; we might anticipate a knowledge of the basic procedures involved in drawing, painting, printmaking, sculpture, and crafts; we might expect youngsters to know a little about several artists who have achieved a place in the history of art; and we might anticipate some appreciation of the work of those artists as well as an appreciation of their own artistic products and the products of their peers.

Because of the large number of specific concepts that might conceivably fit into the categories of knowledge mentioned in the preceding paragraph, we cannot list the concepts here. But each of the lessons developed for this book is intended to get across to youngsters at least one of those concepts, and it would be good for the reader to ask himself what the content of each lesson is before he uses the lesson. This can be the same as identifying the objectives of each exercise, but it is not always the same thing. If the goal of a particular educational experience is to have students learn the meaning of a given concept, we might say that the objective and the content of the lesson are one. But a lesson that teaches a concept for purposes of achieving a larger goal is a lesson in which the objective and the content are different. An example of the latter would be a lesson in which the teacher explains the meaning of Expressionism so the student will be able to detect the difference between an Expressionist painting and an Impressionist painting.

Needless to say, we recommend that the curriculum planner design his program so it includes all five kinds of knowledge we consider relevant to making and appreciating art. And if he builds his program from a broad selection of the lessons contained in the remainder of this book, it is likely that he will cover the five kinds of knowledge.

All the lessons in the book make a contribution either to the child's knowledge of himself or to his knowledge of the world around him (especially the latter). But the lessons that stress the development of such knowledge for purposes of preparing mental materials to be used as content and subject matter in the child's art are the lessons that involve stimulation by the teacher. Lesson 3 in the section devoted to brush drawing for the primary grades is a good example of this. It causes the child to focus attention on himself before drawing a self-portrait; thus it helps him to build a concept of himself which is reinforced as he makes the drawing. Other lessons at the primary level which focus on the concept of self are Activities 1a and 5 under pencil drawing, Activities 2 and 4 under crayon drawing, Activity 2 under relief printing, and Activities 1 and 2 under ceramic sculpture.

Numerous activities cause the student to concentrate on aspects of the world around him. They might deal with family, friends, or people in general; they might cover animals, birds, insects, buildings, mechanical objects, flowers, trees, vehicles, weeds, or other tangible subjects too numerous to mention. Abstract concepts such as love, sadness, fatigue, and happiness are also involved in some of the activities, especially in the intermediate grades. And in several instances the authors have not suggested any content or subject matter for the art work. This means that the teacher is completely free to help a student develop a knowledge of any topic he chooses.

Although we assume that teachers will work to build a knowledge of composition in almost all the activities described in this book, we have given more emphasis to composition in some of those activities than we have in others. At the *intermediate* level, for example, composition has a prominent place in Activities 1 and 2 under pencil drawing; Activities 2, 3, 4, 5, 7, 11, and 12 under crayon drawing; Activities 3 and 7 under charcoal drawing; Activity 4 under chalk drawing; Activities 2, 3, 4, and 7 under brush drawing; Activities 1 and 12 under painting; Activities 1, 2, 3, 4, 9, 10, and 11 under collage; Activities 1, 2, and 6 under ceramic sculpture; Activities 2, 4, and 5 under wood sculpture; and Activities 1 and 4 under paper sculpture. These activities contain important fundamental concepts; therefore, we would expect to see them sprinkled liberally throughout any art program. In fact, some of them would be excellent lessons with which to begin the year. Activities 1 and 2 under pencil drawing, for example, would fit that category because they introduce several concepts which can be reinforced through other lessons during the rest of the year. And the learning experiences used for such reinforcement need not be the ones listed below. The reader is completely free to introduce compositional instruction into any lesson she chooses.

A large number of lessons in the remainder

of the book offer assistance in developing a knowledge of artistic procedures. In fact, there are so many that we cannot list all of them here. Some of those experiences emphasize the development of procedural knowledge while minimizing other kinds of artistic knowledge; when they do, they are usually meant to be introductory lessons for students who have not experienced those procedures before. We have found, through many years of teaching, that students exposed to wholly new procedures have enough trouble trying to master those procedures without trying to cope with compositional information and content at the same time. So we tend to minimize our comments about composition and content when we introduce new procedures.

Lessons intended to develop a knowledge of art history or art appreciation clearly relate information about artists and their works to the productive art activities of the students. Lessons of this kind constitute one of the unique features of this book. But the reader need not confine art history and art appreciation to those lessons. He should read the accounts of artists and their works which precede each series of art activities, and use this information in any lesson where it seems appropriate. He should also feel free to say more about the artists and exemplars than we have said in the lessons.

CHOOSING ACTIVITIES AS VEHICLES FOR CONTENT

An examination of the activities described in Chapters 2 through 21 will show that they include drawing, painting, printmaking, sculpture, and crafts. The authors have prepared educational activities in all those areas because the education of a nonprofessional child artist and connoisseur is best served through broad rather than narrow exposure to the media of art. A lack of care in the development of art programs, however, can easily result in too much variation from medium to medium and therefore a signifi-

cant deficiency in both knowledge and skill. Hence, it is important for the reader to include enough activities in each medium to permit students to grow intellectually and technically through that medium.

Because the usefulness of a curriculum depends upon the selection of activities that involve readily available tools, materials, and equipment, the projects in this book must meet that requirement. Nothing unusual or prohibitively expensive has been employed, and no activities have been included which cannot be done by children in the elementary school. Some projects are more difficult than others simply because we expect children to grow from the time they enter school until the time they leave, and this growth can be encouraged through the sequencing of activities and content.

SELECTING TEACHING TECHNIQUES

The selection of teaching strategies goes hand in hand with the tasks already mentioned. Consequently, the activities presented in Chapters 2 through 21 include such techniques. We have recommended demonstrations, discussions, exhibitions, stimulations, and other teaching behaviors for each of the projects in the remainder of the book. But there is no reason why the reader should not alter or supplement those strategies to meet his own needs.

Incidently, the instructor should never feel that there is anything rigid about the techniques of teaching. If one way of working does not seem to be achieving the desired goal, there is no reason why the strategy should not be changed, even while the lesson is underway.

ORGANIZING LESSONS INTO SEQUENCES

The portion of curriculum development in art which the authors have left largely to the reader is the organizing of the lessons into sequences for learning. We have done so for four reasons. First, each teacher knows his own strengths and weaknesses better than anyone else, so he is in a better position to select lessons that take advantage of his strengths. Secondly, the teacher knows more about the unique needs and past experiences of his students than we do, so he should be the one to select the lessons they are to receive. Thirdly, there are numerous ways to organize lessons for learning, and a prepared sequence might be interpreted as the only way to order the lessons. And, fourthly, the experience of arranging lessons in a meaningful educational sequence is a worthwhile learning activity. It causes a person to think more carefully about what and why he is teaching.

Perhaps one of the best ways to begin sequencing the art lessons is to place them in order from the easiest to the most difficult. In doing so, think about the difficulty of the skills and concepts involved in each lesson, and consider the ability of your students to master those skills and concepts. This will help you to decide the order in which the lessons should be arranged from September to June, and it also will help in determining the grade level at which the various learning activities should occur. Keep in mind the fact that some concepts and skills logically precede others. It is logical, for example, to teach the meaning of different compositional terms before expecting students to manage compositional elements thoughtfully in their art. Similarly, it makes sense to develop the skill for making collagraph prints with one color before getting involved with the complications of multiple colors.

Naturally, a teacher's objectives can also be expected to influence the sequencing of lessons. If a major objective is to produce a student who has an understanding of drawing, painting, printmaking, sculpture, and crafts, the teacher will obviously offer lessons in all those media, and he will arrange them so the concepts covered in one will carry over into another. The number of lessons in each medium will necessarily be fewer than one would expect if his objectives were less ambitious. In other words, an instructor who intends to develop an understanding of drawing, painting, and sculpture has a different sequencing problem from the person who chooses to develop a knowledge of printmaking and crafts as well.

Space does not permit us to indicate all the ways in which our lessons can be sequenced, but we can mention a couple of possibilities. A teacher could select several lessons that have to do with line in composition, for example, and he could place them in order from the easiest to the most difficult. He could do the same with color, light and dark, shape, pattern, or other compositional elements. Or he could sequence a group of lessons which deal with the same topic in different mediums. The possibilities are numerous.

When organizing the lessons into a sequence the teacher needs to consider the connection or continuity between them. This is important because efficient learning cannot occur unless the lessons build one upon the other. And, by the same token, permanent knowledge is not likely to develop unless teachers plan for the repetition of learning at frequent intervals.

EVALUATION

Evaluation is an important aspect of curriculum development. Without it, there is no way of knowing whether efforts to educate are succeeding or failing. However, the necessity of evaluating does not make it any easier. It involves judgment about the development of children as nonprofessional artists and connoisseurs, and the judgment must focus on their achievements in knowledge, attitude, and skill. It is possible and desirable, moreover, to go beyond the evaluation of individual students to judge the achievement of specific classes and grade levels. How can it be done?

EVALUATING INDIVIDUAL STUDENTS

There are no widely accepted standards which can be used as a basis for judging achievement in art. Hence it is necessary for teachers and school systems to decide for themselves what children might be expected to know and do as a result of specific lessons, a series of lessons, and years of instruction. Some educators believe, however, that any effort to formulate objectives is antithetical to creativity and to art because the essential feature of both is that which is original or unexpected. To predict results, in other words, is to produce them before they have been achieved, and when that happens the teacher's predictions may thwart creativity. But the authors of this text take the position that the original or unexpected aspects of art are only half of its essential character—the subjective half. We agree with Herbert Read, who argued that there is also an objective aspect to art which he regards as the compositional portion of the work. In addition, we contend that artistic procedures and a significant portion of art history and art appreciation are also objective aspects of art. This means that the things students are expected to know and do in the areas of composition, artistic procedures, art history, and appreciation are things that teachers can predict through formulating objectives, without restricting creativity or artistic innovations. If these predictions were to be avoided on the grounds that there are no objective aspects of art, teachers would have no logical basis for justifying the things they teach. Furthermore, there could be no education in and through art if there were nothing objective about the subject that could be passed on to students.

We also contend that the unpredictable or subjective aspect of art can be given its proper recognition in the formulation of objectives, without placing any restrictions upon it. Simply indicate that one of the objectives of art education is for students to produce works of art that are original. Originality results from imagination, and imagination is a function of the total personality. To expect originality in art, therefore, is to predict that indications of the idiosyncratic personality of the artist will be evident in the art product.

Assuming, therefore, that the formulation of objectives is perfectly reasonable, we recommend that teachers compare student achievement to the behavioral goals each lesson was supposed to achieve and ask themselves if the aims were actually realized. Perhaps the evaluation can proceed as follows:

1. If there were attempts, through stimulation, to develop the child's knowledge of a given subject, the art product should provide evidence of the knowledge the child possesses. If no evidence of the subject is discernible, or if the student's symbols are stereotyped or lack visual distinction and interest, it is likely that he has little visual knowledge of the subject. It is possible, of course, that a child may know more than his work reveals, but until evidence of that visual knowledge can be provided, we have to assume that it does not exist. However, it seems safe to say that a person does not know less than his art work reveals.

2. If the purpose of a lesson is to build knowledge of an artistic procedure, evidence of that knowledge may be seen in the student's behavior and in the art product. Was the child able to go through the procedure successfully subsequent to instruction? To what extent did he require the instruction to be repeated? Can he explain the procedure verbally? Can he explain or go through the procedure successfully after a significant period of time has elapsed, or does the instruction need to be repeated?

If the lesson is aimed at developing an understanding of how to use a medium effectively (for example, the ways of manipulating charcoal), does the art product reveal that efforts were made to use the medium properly? Remember that skillfulness in such matters often requires many opportunities to use the medium and to try the various techniques. Do not expect high degrees of skill if these opportunities have not been provided.

3. If the objective of the lesson is for youngsters to learn certain compositional concepts, look at the art products for evidence of their knowledge. Does the product indicate that efforts were made to employ those compositional ideas? The product may reveal a general understanding of the concept, but the quality of the composition depends to a large extent upon sensitivity to the nuances of a formal arrangement. Such sensitivity takes time to develop. Consequently, it would be a mistake to expect a high degree of sensitivity to develop in one or even a few lessons. Certainly it is likely to develop much more slowly if the teacher does not make a habit of calling attention to compositional relationships.

Although improvement in composition is largely an intellectual enterprise, skill also has an effect upon it. Consequently, it would be a mistake to expect compositional sophistication in the elementary school. A general knowledge of compositional fundamentals is about all we can hope to attain.

4. If a knowledge of art history is to be expected from a given lesson, it might be revealed in the art product. Using broken color in the manner of the impressionists or composing in the way of the cubists, for example, could indicate an understanding of the techniques employed during the heyday of those styles. But a knowledge of art history is likely to be evaluated more accurately through written examinations, essays, and verbal presentations. Be careful not to expect more information than your teaching has provided. How long is the information retained? Is it ever used or applied beyond the lesson in which it was covered?

5. If the goal of one or more lessons includes an appreciation of the works of master artists and children, this appreciation should reveal itself in oral or written comments and tests or in the recognition of styles and artistic qualities. Children might be expected to explain how styles differ, the value of differing styles, and the contributions those styles have made to civilization. Assuming that instruction warrants it, children might be expected to explain the value of art products, and they should be able to justify their own preferences. In other words, they should demonstrate the ability to make critical judgments or evaluations. Their sophistication will depend to a large extent upon the number of opportunities they have had to practice these visual and verbal activities. Remember that appreciation involves the recognition of certain qualities in art, the understanding of values associated with those qualities, and the ability to make critical judgments. It is possible to appreciate and evaluate composition, style, subject matter, content, technical proficiency, and the nature of individual sensuous elements.

6. Skill is technical proficiency. The ability of the nonprofessional artist to manipulate tools and materials efficiently can be detected in art products, and the ability of the nonprofessional connoisseur to make judgments about art can be sensed from oral and written expression and from the act of making judgments. The degree of skill that we can expect depends upon the opportunities the child has been given to develop facility with a given medium or with a certain judgmental situation.

7. The assessment of attitudes is no less complicated than the judgment of knowledge and skill. Look for the amount of interest that the student shows in his art work; check the level of confidence that he displays in his art activities and the satisfaction that he shows in response to his own products; watch for the

degree of effort he is willing to put forth in art; and note the amount of tolerance that he has toward different art forms.

8. Since original work of all kinds is what we always seek in art education, it is an important element to look for in evaluation. Novelty is even more desirable, but it may be less likely to occur in child art. Both factors can be judged through an examination of subject matter, content, composition, and style.

9. The factors listed above are the logical elements to judge in evaluation, but certain kinds of growth and development may occur which have not been accounted for in an examination of those logical elements. Check to see if any unexpected educational benefits have accrued from your lesson or lessons. But be careful! Educators have the habit of claiming remarkable educational gains of a vague nature that are difficult to measure even for those who make the claims.

If it appears, after evaluating the foregoing elements, that the objectives of a lesson were not achieved, the teacher must decide what went wrong. Perhaps the objectives were too difficult to attain, or perhaps there was a flaw in the teaching. It is well to consider that success in art can never be fully assured, especially if the art activity or lesson is really worth doing from an educational and artistic standpoint. Activities of little value can often be done again and again with guaranteed results, but truly worthwhile ones usually involve a risk. Failure is possible, and it sometimes occurs. If it does, the teacher must not throw up her hands in despair and refuse to try again. She must work to figure out what went wrong and eliminate the factors that caused the problem.

Although all of us should evaluate the student after his participation in a single activity or lesson, we should also evaluate the effects of a year's work. This can be done by keeping a record of the child's achievements on each lesson and checking to see if the achievement has been consistently high, average, or low. To evaluate *growth* from the beginning to the end of the year, however, one has to compare achievement on comparable lessons or projects. Drawings must be compared with drawings, sculpture with sculpture, criticism with criticism, and so on. To make this comparison meaningful there should also be a number of products to compare. But the number of art lessons offered in the course of a year is often so small that meaningful evaluation is difficult. Perhaps one of the best things we can do is to develop a series of tests (studio, written, and oral) to measure the knowledge, attitudes, and skills which have been covered during the whole instructional period. As art curricula become more sophisticated and carefully sequenced, the last activities or lessons of the year may serve as tests, and they may require the application of material covered during the rest of the year. The evaluation of achievement over longer periods of time, such as three-year intervals, might be handled in the same ways we have suggested for yearly judgments, but different teachers may be involved and they may use different standards or objectives as a basis for estimating achievement. Efforts should be made to see that teachers eventually use the same standards.

EVALUATING INDIVIDUAL CLASSES

There are times when a teacher can justifiably rejoice over the successful achievement of three or four students, but most of the time it is better for the instructor to judge *his own accomplishment* by the achievement of students as a group. A few students usually do well even under the guidance of the worst teacher, but whole groups seldom advance significantly unless their instruction has been effective. Furthermore, it is important to avoid judging individuals or groups on the basis of criteria that have not been covered by the teacher's lesson or by instruction in previous classes. Yet this is one of the most prevalent mistakes in art education today. Teachers frequently offer instruction in artistic procedures, for example, and then evaluate final products (and students) on the basis of composition, originality of subject matter, or some other factor unrelated to their teaching. Instructional efforts to develop specific kinds of knowledge, attitudes, or skills cannot be expected, however, unless directions or goals have been established by the school system. Perhaps the lessons provided in this book can assist in providing some of that direction.

To evaluate the group (which is really to evaluate the instructor) after a single lesson or a year's work, the teacher may average the evaluations of individuals in that group. It would also be worthwhile to compare the achievements of two or more classes at a given level. Making comparisons can be enlightening if the evaluator observes the instruction as well as the behavior and products of the students. If behavior and products consistently indicate low achievement, instruction is likely to be inadequate. High-quality products by themselves, however, do not necessarily indicate superior teaching because products can be made to look good through excessive teacher input during the creative process. That is why it is important to observe instruction and to examine the behavior of students. Perhaps carefully developed tests (studio and academic) administered outside the influence of the teacher would provide the best basis for comparing the achievement of groups and the quality of instruction.

EVALUATING GRADE LEVELS

Evaluating the achievement of large groups, such as grade levels, is useful because it indicates the effectiveness of the total art program more successfully than does the evaluation of individual students or classes. It can be achieved by averaging the achievement of all individuals at a given level. We must emphasize once again, however, that achievement cannot be measured accurately simply by looking at products even if the products are produced apart from the immediate influence of instructors. This is because art education is concerned with the development of nonprofessional connoisseurs as well as nonprofessional artists. Consequently, a testing mechanism must measure verbal as well as visual knowledge and skill, and it must indicate attitudes. Unfortunately, at the moment, adequate testing or measuring devices or procedures in art are not available. Until they are, school systems will have to develop their own.

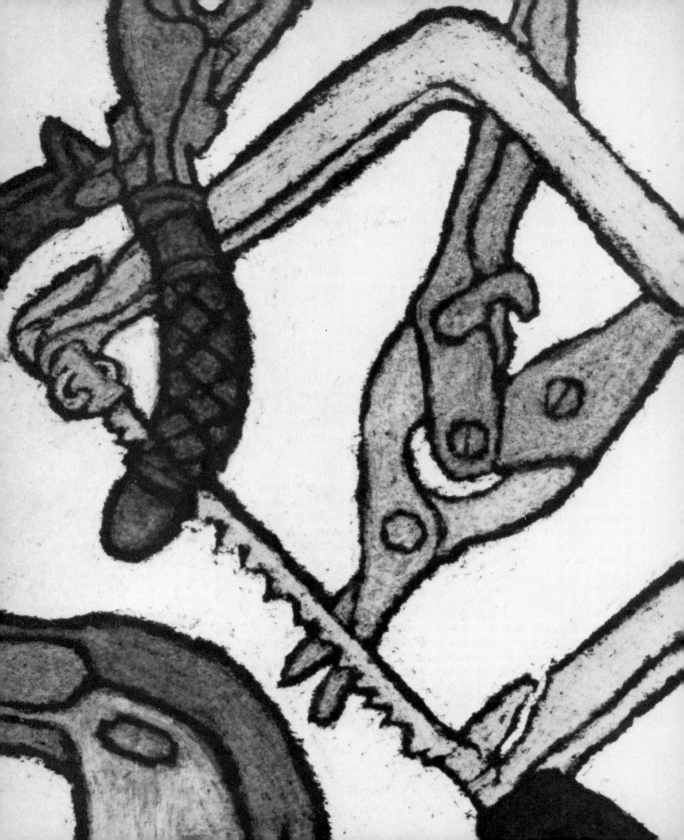

PART 2

Drawing

Drawing is the act of making an image, usually of a linear character, by marking directly on a surface. People have been creating such images since prehistoric times when their first representations were made on bones, flat rocks, and cave walls. Eventually, the images or drawings also appeared on wood, clay tablets, pottery, wax tablets, and other smooth materials. One of the most satisfactory of the early drawing surfaces was papyrus which was sliced from the pith of the papyrus plant and pressed into flat sheets by the ancient Egyptians, Greeks, and Romans. Papyrus was widely used from the fourth century B.C. to the fifth century A.D. when it was replaced by parchment.[1] But papyrus and parchment were scarce and expensive. For that reason, drawing as we know it today did not begin in the Western Hemisphere until the introduction of paper in the early part of the fifteenth century.[2]

Basically, there are four kinds of drawings: sketches, studies, cartoons, and finished works of art. A sketch is a pictographic notation, a device for aiding the memory, or a partially developed plan. A study, on the other hand, is an attempt to clarify or define something more fully. Hence, an artist might make a study of the human figure to define more carefully the skeletal or muscular structure. Or, he might make a drawing of a proposed painting to clarify the composition of the work. In certain instances, such a study may also be called a cartoon. A cartoon is a full-scale drawing of a proposed work of art. If it proves to be satisfactory, it is carefully reproduced on another surface where it is developed into a finished work of art in a different medium.

---

[1]Parchment is the whitish skin of a goat or sheep. It is cured and polished to smoothness before it is used. Vellum is high-grade parchment, and it is made from the thin, finely textured skin of a calf, lamb, or kid.

[2]Paper was used in China more than a thousand years before it became available in Europe.

A cartoon allows the buyer to see what the product will look like, and it sometimes acts as a contract to which the artist must adhere if he expects the buyer to pay for the art when it is done. A finished drawing is, of course, complete as it is. It is not intended as preparation for something else.

Obviously, drawings can be made with anything that makes a mark. However, the tools most commonly used by artists have been metal points, charcoal, chalk, pen and ink, brush and ink, pencils, pastels, and crayons. Most of these tools can also be used by children. Consequently, we shall turn our attention to ways in which the appropriate drawing instruments can be used by youngsters in elementary schools, and we shall also indicate how the same tools have been used by master artists.

CHAPTER 2

PENCIL
DRAWING

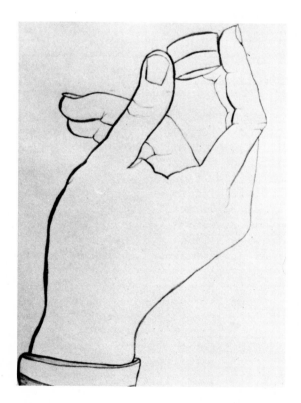

Figure 2-3.   Hand. Note line variation.

A pencil is a piece of graphite or black carbon encased in wood. It was invented in 1795 by Nicholas Conté, a Frenchman. After combining natural graphite with clay, Conté shaped the mixture into thin rods and subjected them to intense pressure. The rods were dried, baked in a kiln, and enclosed in strips of straight-grained wood that would not warp. Unlike earlier instruments, the new pencils could be manufactured with different degrees of hardness permitting the artist to create both light and dark lines. They also allowed him to draw on nearly any surface and in almost any location.

Prior to the invention of the pencil, artists produced pencil-like drawings by using a piece of natural graphite in a holder of some kind. During the Middle Ages and the Renaissance, however, they used a stylus or a metal point, which was a slender shaft having a point of silver, gold, lead, or some other metal. The chief limitation of the tool was clearly its lack of flexibility. It did not permit the making of lines that were dark, textured, or variable in width; and it had to be used on specially prepared surfaces. Consequently, it is easy to understand why the pencil replaced the metal point as one of the primary tools for drawing.

EXEMPLARS OF PENCIL DRAWING

Probably pencils have been used more frequently for sketching and for making studies than they have for creating finished works of art. One reason for this is that pencils do not lend themselves to the creation of large or powerful images. They produce thin, gray, and comparatively delicate lines which lose their visual impact when surrounded by a large amount of space, which is what happens in large drawings. Thus, it is apparent that artists who make finished works of art with a pencil are likely to be those who are satisfied to work on a small scale. Jean Auguste Dominique Ingres was such an artist.

JEAN AUGUST DOMINIQUE INGRES (Ann'gr), 1780–1867

Experts usually agree that Ingres, a Frenchman, was one of the greatest draftsmen of all time. He recorded the appearance of his subjects deliberately and flawlessly, with a minimum of lines and of shading. He believed that, in art, lines are more important than color, and by emphasizing lines and reducing them to their most pure and elemental form, he made highly articulate and restrained visual statements with a strong sculptural quality. Because this was his style, he is called a neoclassic artist. A neoclassic artist produces art similar to the clear, logical, and highly simplified art of Greek and Roman times.

Although Ingres was successful in simplifying lines and making each of them count, he also added to the visual complexity of his drawings by including many details. In the portrait of Paganini, for example, he drew with great precision the smallest parts of the violin, the coat, and the cravat (Plate 2-1). The inclusion of such detail is fascinating because it reveals the remarkable perception and skill of the artist, but if it is overdone, it does not always result in a satisfactory composition. Perhaps that can be seen in a few of Ingres's group portraits which exhibit the same linear quality and the same degree of minute detail in each of the figures. The result is a unified drawing that lacks visual variety. Furthermore, too much detail can serve to focus attention on the parts instead of the whole, and that can weaken the unity of a composition. Thus it is probably correct to say that details can add visual enrichment to art but they must be handled with care and restraint.

Like most neoclassic artists, Ingres preferred

Plate 2-1. Jean Ingres. *Portrait of Paganini.* 1819. Pencil, 11⅝" x 8½". The Louvre. Photo from La Réunion des Musées Nationaux.

the shading is placed on the right and bottom sides of the nose, lips, face, and violin. This tends to separate the side planes of those objects from the front planes, and it gives the figure a three-dimensional quality.

The horizontal shading in the middle of the arm holding the bow is also effective. It helps to locate the position of the elbow, and it indicates the presence of the forearm in the upper half of the horizontal sleeve. The shading, or the change in value (lightness or darkness) from one finger segment to another, adds further clarification to the figure because it shows that the fingers bend and change planes at the knuckles.

Notice also the white spot or highlight on the iris of each eye. It represents reflected light, and serves to make the eye seem spherical and sparkling.

Finally, it is important to see that Ingres has not given the same amount of emphasis to all parts of the drawing. He has placed more detail, more shading, and more variation from light to dark in the face, hands, and violin than he has in the rest of the drawing. The result is a greater density of pencil marks in those areas and a greater visual variation in the drawing as a whole. This makes it more interesting and exciting to the eye.

JUAN GRIS (Wahn Gree), 1887–1927

Jose Victoriano Gonzales, better known as Juan Gris, was born in Madrid, Spain. At the age of 19, he moved to Paris where he worked as a newspaper illustrator and designer until 1910. The building housing his studio also served as a home and workshop for Pablo Picasso, so it is understandable that Gris soon became friendly with one of the most important artists of modern times.

Between 1907 and 1910, Picasso and Georges Braque developed the artistic style known as

the representation of historical and mythological events to the drawing and painting of portraits. However, he produced more portraits and they have become more famous than his other works. His portrait of Paganini, for example, is a renowned masterpiece which reveals the form of the figure with a minimum of lines and shading. Notice how the curving lines in the cravat indicate the cylindrical shape of the neck. If the lines had been drawn straight, the neck would appear to be flat. Observe also how shading helps to clarify the form by separating one plane from another. The location of the shading depends upon the source of light, and the light in the Paganini portrait comes from above, in front, and slightly to the left of the figure. Consequently, cubism, and Gris proceeded to individualize and perfect the style for the rest of his short, productive life. The cubists tried to depict the essence of objects by reducing them to their most elemental forms (cylinders, cones, pyramids, and cubes). They also attempted to present those objects more fully by showing them from more than one point of view in a single drawing or painting, and they made an effort to unite objects with each other and with the surrounding pictorial space. The result was a dramatic break from naturalistic representation. Objects were simplified and their shapes distorted; planes from one object were made to penetrate and overlap the planes of another and to extend into space; lines, shapes, and patterns were repeated throughout a picture; and paintings were made with less depth than before.

In Plate 2-2 evidence of the overlapping and penetrating of planes can be seen. The upper right edge of the dish seems to penetrate the fruit and become the edge of its frontal plane. The same line spirals through the drawing for quite a distance, outlining both the plate and fruit on its way. The effect is a visual tying-together of the parts of the drawing.

Unity was also achieved through the repetitive use of firm, precise, fluent, and curving lines. The repetition does not become boring because Gris created mild visual excitement or variety at the same time by varying the width as well as the lightness and darkness of the lines.

Plate 2-2.   Juan Gris. *Still Life.* 1920. Pencil, 9⅞″ x 12⅞″. © by ADAGP, Paris 1981.

Still more coherence and variety were created by repeating shapes while changing their size. An oval with a pointed end, for example, can be seen in the top and middle of the goblet, the top and handle of the pitcher, the top edge of the plate, and the slices of fruit on the plate. The cubists believed that such repetition also produced a pleasurable visual rhythm similar to the auditory rhythms in music, and they made a conscious effort to achieve it.

The drawing in Plate 2-2 also shows that Gris made images that were structurally simplified. Like Ingres, whom he admired, he was economical with lines; he did not put them on paper unless they had a definite purpose. As a result, his drawings are sharp, precise, hard, and highly controlled. The forms or shapes of his subjects are always clear, and his compositions are stable. In fact, his work is frequently described as cerebral or intellectual because it does reveal a flawless understanding of form, a propensity toward essential rather than superficial elements, and a high degree of planning and control. Certainly it is not emotional.

CHARLES BURCHFIELD, 1893–1967

For many years American artists considered themselves uneducated and relatively incapable until they had gone to Europe, especially to Paris, for training. During the first half of the twentieth century, however, attitudes began to change. American art became more respectable, and artists felt less inclined to make the traditional pilgrimage to Paris. Charles Burchfield, for example, never left the United States. After graduating from the Cleveland School of Art in 1916, he began his career as a professional artist by drawing and painting in his spare time. He began that way because he earned his living by working in an auto-parts company and by designing wallpaper.

By 1929, Burchfield was able to give up designing wallpaper and devote himself full time to painting. He liked to portray the changing of seasons and the changing of the weather, and he had a special fondness for old buildings and trees. Unquestionably, he gained inspiration from the American scene, especially from the unpretentious rural and small-town landscapes of Ohio and New York. Thus he is often regarded as a regional painter, a person who concentrates on a limited portion of the country and captures its character in his work.

Burchfield once said that painting was not all unalloyed joy; it was a continuous battle in which advances were followed by regressions and periods of complete frustration. Drawing, on the other hand, was different. If a mistake were made, the drawing could be tossed aside. There wasn't so much at stake; consequently, the whole activity could be more enjoyable.

The study in Plate 2-3 is an example of Burchfield's work. Probably it was made in preparation for a painting because notes about color are evident in several parts of the drawing. Burchfield was in the habit of making these preparatory drawings as a way of solving the basic composition of his paintings ahead of time. He felt that drawings helped him to avoid numerous changes while he was painting.

Notice that Burchfield used shading liberally and that his drawing has a spontaneous, sketchy quality not found in the work of Juan Gris. This is because Burchfield was interested in capturing moods, the effects of light, changes in the weather, and feelings of fantasy, while Gris was largely concerned with form and composition. Gris imposed an organizational structure upon the objects in his drawings, whereas Burchfield allowed the nature of the subject matter to affect his composition. Gris was highly intellectual in his approach while Burchfield was more emotional.

The drawing in Plate 2-3 indicates that an artist need not show whole objects in his drawings; he can show parts of them. This is important be-

Plate 2-3.   Charles Burchfield. *Store Front, Late Afternoon*. 1935. Pencil, 17½" x 12¼". From the collection of Andrew Goodman.

and frequently leads to symmetrically balanced arrangements which are visually less dynamic and less interesting than asymmetrical arrangements.

Notice that the most important object in Burchfield's drawing is slightly to the left of center and that the major lines divide the paper into unequal segments both horizontally and vertically. If the paper had been divided into equal segments, the drawing would have lacked variety in its spatial organization, and it would have been dull.

In addition, Burchfield has used shading to make a high degree of contrast between light and dark. This not only produces more visual variety but it creates a more powerful visual impact than he could achieve with less contrast. This means that in drawing it is good to pay attention to the degree of variation from light to dark because it can affect the amount of subtlety or power in the finished product.

ADDITIONAL EXEMPLARS

Since the eighteenth century, most artists have drawn with pencils. Hence, it is relatively easy to find additional exemplars for use in the classroom. The following artists are a few of those whose work might be displayed and discussed: Philip Evergood, Amedeo Modigliani, Edouard Vuillard, Maurice Utrillo, Jean Corot, Diego Rivera, Eugene Delacroix, George Grosz, Andrew Wyeth, Fernand Léger, and Larry Rivers.

cause a person who always feels compelled to draw a full and complete object will inevitably draw single items in the center of the paper surrounded by blank space. Isolating and centering things produces drawings that tend to look alike

PENCIL ACTIVITIES FOR THE PRIMARY GRADES (AGES 6 THROUGH 8)

In the primary grades, it is important to provide regular opportunities to draw with pencils. By using tools that permit the making of details the child can develop his visual concepts of those details and thereby grow intellectually. The pencils appropriate for young children are primary pencils, sketching pencils with wide leads, or ordinary number two pencils. Additional necessities are pink pearl erasers, small sheets of paper (no larger than 12 x 18 inches), drawing boards (12-x-18-inch Masonite), small mirrors, and still-life materials.

CONCEPTS FOR POSSIBLE DEVELOPMENT

The following terms should be associated with different kinds of lines and different types of drawings:

light	wide	fuzzy	simple	clear
dark	narrow	sharp	complex	sketchy
long	strong	straight	portrait	gray
short	weak	curved	self-portrait	black
thick	hard	vertical	landscape	heavy
thin	soft	horizontal	still life	shape
details	firm	miniatures	shading	outline

SUGGESTED ACTIVITIES

It is possible to build the foregoing concepts and to relate exemplars to the work of students in numerous ways. The following lessons indicate only a few of the possibilities:

1. Display the exemplars of pencil drawing and pen and ink drawing. Discuss the meaning of details and self-portraits. See if the children can locate the drawing with the most details, and offer a *little* information about the person who made the drawing. Then do the following:

   a) Distribute inexpensive mirrors and 9-x-12-inch paper. Ask the children to draw a self-portrait containing as many details as they can see in the mirror and ask them to make their drawings fill the paper. The drawings may be of the head alone or the head and torso. Then, using a child as a model, point to several little things that might be drawn (eyelashes, ear lobes, nostrils, eyebrows, and so on). When all are finished, display the drawings, and call attention to the details that have been shown. It is not necessary to talk about each drawing.

   b) After emphasizing the fact that details can help to make a picture interesting, ask the class to make a full-length portrait of you with as many details as they can find. If you pose by standing on a chair or a desk, they will be impressed. Ask them to look carefully for things that others may not see. Do not criticize or make fun of unnaturalistic drawings. Praise the work, and display it in class instead. See Figure 2-1.

Figure 2-1. *My Teacher,* by a second-grader.

c) Distribute paper and drawing boards and take the children outside to draw the school, a house, an automobile, a bicycle, or a landscape. Have them identify the details they can see, and ask them to put those details into their drawings. If they have trouble getting started, suggest the outlining of a large part. Then they can draw another part that goes next to the large one, and they can add the details last. Tell them that Matisse worked that way (see page 82). Then praise the unique features in their drawings.

If the activity seems too long, too painstaking, or too frustrating, simply ask your students to draw a small portion of the subject, and give them small sheets of paper.

d) Explain that Ingres made many famous drawings of families. They were small but full of eye-catching details such as jewelry, buttons, neckties (cravats), ruffles, and curly hair. Then give the children some sharp pencils, erasers, and 9-x-12-inch white paper. Ask them to draw their families and to include details. Perhaps pets and friends could also be added.

2. Following the suggestions on pages 7, 8, and 9, create three or four still-life arrangements in different parts of the room. Display the exemplars (pencil plus pen and ink), and call attention to those made with a small number of lines (the Gris and the Matisse). Explain that the artists did not believe in making lines that were not needed. Then ask the children to draw one of the still-life arrangements by employing as few lines as possible. Use pencils with wide points, and expect the project to go quickly. Perhaps several drawings can be made. When they are finished, praise them and point out any similarities to the work of Gris and Matisse.

3. In discussing the exemplars by Gris and Burchfield, ask students if they can see and describe differences among the lines. Hopefully, they will say that some lines are dark, heavy, and wide while others are light and thin. If they fail to do so, point out the differences yourself. Then divide the class into groups of two and give each group an object to draw (an old coffee pot, an iron, a shoe, a pocketbook, a weed, and so on). Ask them to use wide and narrow lines as they include numerous details. The idea is to produce linear variety, but if the children fail to vary the thickness of the lines, don't bother them about it. Furthermore, let them know that the object can be made to go partially off the paper, like the automobile in the Burchfield drawing. Indicate also that the drawing should be large enough to fill most of the space on the paper.

4. Review the information on verbal stimulation in Chapter 1. Then engage in an animated discussion about one of the topics listed below (or something similar). Talk about color, texture, pattern, position of body parts, sizes, and shapes, but not necessarily all of those things. If appropriate, let the children act out the activity they are discussing, but do not allow the stimulation to last more than 15 minutes. Then ask the children to show you in their drawings what the experience was like and make an effort to find something unique in each of the finished drawings. Let it be known that you like the differences among the drawings and point out any similarities to the exemplars. This activity can be repeated several times.

Drinking a bottle of pop	Birds eating
Blowing my nose	Playing leapfrog
Jumping rope	Washing windows
Sawing wood	Walking with my mother
Eating a hotdog	The carnival
Landing on the moon	Swinging in a swing
My grandmother	A scary person
My favorite animal	Watering the plants

5. Take the children to the playground or gymnasium to play a game. When they return, give them pencils and 9-x-12- or 12-x-18-inch drawing paper. Then spend about five minutes discussing the game they have been playing. Talk about the equipment they used and how people were running, jumping, stretching, throwing, or standing still. Ask about parts of the environment that might be included in drawings, and urge them to make pictures that show you what it was like to play that game on the playground or in the gymnasium.

6. Ask each of your students to bring to class a weed, a flower, or a twig with a leaf on it. Explain that pencil drawings are often very small and that you would like some small drawings for the classroom. Then give each child three or four pieces of 3-x-4-inch white paper, and ask him to draw an interesting part of his weed, flower, or twig. The drawings will be made quickly, so each child will be able to make three or four. Exhibit all the drawings and call the show an exhibition of miniatures.

7. For other ideas about drawing in pencil, see the lessons involving crayons, and pen and ink.

PENCIL ACTIVITIES FOR THE INTERMEDIATE GRADES (AGES 9 THROUGH 11)

It is important for pencil activities to continue through the intermediate grades, and it is advisable to use the same materials recommended for the primary grades. Do not use paper larger than 18 x 24 inches, and when paper that large is used, give the children pencils with soft, wide leads.

CONCEPTS FOR POSSIBLE DEVELOPMENT

The concepts covered in the primary grades can and should be reviewed, but new concepts should also be introduced. Some of the most suitable are listed below:

contour line	abstract	controlled	unity
proportion	contrast	plane	variety
shading	highlight	structure	composition
visual emphasis	reflected light	repetition	three-dimensional
cylindrical	shadow	volume	two-dimensional
value	precise	sketches	intellectual drawing
naturalistic	delicate	studies	emotional drawing
		cartoons	classical drawing

SUGGESTED ACTIVITIES

Lessons recommended for the primary grades can be used again in the intermediate grades, but students can be expected to make drawings that reveal greater eye-hand control and a more naturalistic appearance. Most students will be able to draw more details and understand suggestions about composition. Consequently, they will be able to profit from the advanced lessons listed below.

1. Repeat Activities 3 and 6 from the primary grades, but emphasize the fact that Gris made his drawing compositionally attractive by varying the width of lines as well as their lightness and darkness. The variation often occurred within a single line as well as between lines. Encourage your students to produce those variations in their own drawings.

    Probably students will wonder where to make lines thick and where to make them dark. Therefore, it is helpful to put the following information on the blackboard.

    a) Dark, wide lines have more visual weight than light, thin lines. Consequently, it often works well to put the heavy lines on the bottom sides where the weight seems most natural and satisfying. Thick, dark lines on the top of something are likely to make it seem top heavy.

    b) On light paper, dark lines come forward while light lines recede. This means that parts close to the observer might be made darker and thicker. As lines move away from the observer, make them lighter and thinner.

    c) Since dark lines have considerable visual weight, it is important to distribute them in such a way that the drawing balances.

    d) When several lines converge, they might be made thicker at the point of convergence.

    It may take two hours to do a drawing of this kind. It is essential therefore, to give encouragement, praise, and support. Let students know that you appreciate their patience and hard work. If they tire excessively, stop and allow them to finish at a later time. See Figure 2-2.

2. Arrange six small vases of flowers or dry weeds with approximately three stems in each vase. Then discuss the exemplars, and stress the way Ingres emphasized certain parts of his drawing. Call attention to the fact that Burchfield drew parts of objects and that he did not draw single objects in the center of his paper.

    Distribute ordinary pencils and paper (about 6 x 9 inches in size). Then write the following suggestions on the blackboard, and explain them.

    a) It is not necessary to draw the whole vase of flowers or weeds; part of the drawing can go off the paper.

    b) Avoid placing the vase and its contents in the center of the paper.

    c) Vary the width and darkness of lines. Let this variation occur within lines as well as between lines.

    d) Vary the density of lines, or put more details in some places than in others. Together with the darkening of lines, this will give the kind of emphasis created by Ingres in his drawing of Paganini.

    e) Avoid shading. Keep the drawing completely linear.

    f) Avoid large areas of unused space.

Figure 2-2. Twig made larger than life.

As the children work, let them know that a successful drawing is not necessarily one that looks exactly like the flowers being drawn. A successful drawing is compositionally attractive, and *one way* of achieving that end is to follow the suggestions on the board. Give considerable encouragement.

If children become discouraged with their work, explain that this is only one way of drawing, and it may not suit their personalities. Urge them to do their best, and assure them that many different activities and drawing techniques will be offered in the future.

3. As an alternative to flowers and weeds in the foregoing activity, have each student draw his hand or a small twig with leaves. The twigs can be cut from different trees and bushes, producing a variety of drawings. See Figure 2-3 at the beginning of the chapter.

4. Explain that artists develop the ability to capture the essence of a pose or they learn to grasp the direction of various body parts (head, arms, legs, back, feet, and the like) by making hundreds of quick sketches. Distribute sketching pencils with wide leads, and let students make sketches of you standing on a table. Change your pose every 15 seconds, every 30 seconds, or every minute. Ask everyone to forget details and to concentrate on sketching the direction of the body parts and the angles at which the parts meet. Supplement your comments with the views of Matisse (see page 82). If questions indicate a need for information about proportions of the human figure, provide the necessary help. It can be found on page 90. Use newsprint and ask each student to submit a favorite sketch for display.

5. Some of the exemplars contain shading and others do not. See if the children can explain why artists use shading. They use it, of course, to produce the illusion of three dimensions, of curving surfaces, of differing planes, and of volumes, Therefore, you might call attention to the portrait of Paganini by Ingres and show how the shading helps to separate the front plane of the face from the side plane. Shading gives depth to the drawing, and it indicates a source of light above and slightly to the left of the figure.

Following such discussions, pass out paper, mirrors, and sketching pencils (wide points), and have students make portraits or self-portraits. Ask them to decide where the light is coming from in their portrait and to put shading on the plane of the figure that does not receive the rays of light. If someone models for the class, clamp a floodlight on a chair and turn it on the model. It will make the shaded parts of the figure easier to see.

Do not stress naturalism, perfection, or polish in these drawings. Treat the activity as a skill-developing experience to repeat in the future. If portraits do not seem appealing, try shading drawings of a still life, a small object, or a building.

6. Provide verbal stimulation by discussing with your class one of the topics listed below. Mention the visual characteristics of objects that might be included in a drawing of that subject. Then ask the class to produce such a drawing either with numerous or limited details. Make the visual units or objects close together (or overlapping) to increase unity, and begin with a light sketch. Later on, appropriate lines can be darkened and widened to produce depth, or certain areas can be pencilled in solidly. See Activities 1 and 2 plus Figure 2-4.

A crowded elevator	Disco-dancing
The store on main street	A gang of tough kids
My house	A frightening experience
Cooking hamburgers	During the storm
Working in a florist shop	Working in a garage

7. Show the exemplar of crayon drawing by Seurat, and explain that shading makes the parts of the figure seem cylindrical. Then distribute newsprint and let students practice drawing cylindrical forms by shading with a sketching pencil. After about five minutes, discuss one of the topics listed in the foregoing lesson. As the children make drawings about the topic, ask them to use shading of the kind used by Seurat. Ask them to make body parts look rounded or cylindrical. Use 12-x-18-inch drawing paper.

Figure 2-4.   *My House,* by a fifth-grader.

8. More ideas for pencil drawing may be obtained by reading the lessons devoted to crayon, charcoal, and pen and ink.

CHAPTER 3

CRAYON DRAWING

Figure 3-2.   A large painting based on a 9"-x-12" crayon drawing of the same color.

A study of the history of drawing will quickly reveal the ambiguous nature of the word "crayon." The uncertainty of the term comes from its long use as a name for chalks, pastels, graphite sticks, pencils, and rods of color held together with fatty or waxy adhesives. However, in an effort to be more precise, contemporary writers commonly use the word "crayon" only when referring to a solid coloring stick having a waxy or fatty binder.

Three of the most popular crayons in current use are lithographic crayons, Conté crayons, and wax crayons. The lithographic variety is employed most often in the production of lithographic prints, but Conté crayons are used extensively for drawing on paper. They are made of chalk, and they come in black, brown, white, and reddish colors. The chalk is fastened together with a slightly greasy binder that helps to hold the color on paper and reduce smudging. Although Nicholas Conté, who also invented the pencil, was not the first to fabricate such a crayon, he was the first to give the instrument a trade name. He did so about 1790, and the tool he created has been in use since that time.

Apparently, the modern wax crayon originated in the 1880s when Charles Bowley, a salesman, attempted to develop a material for writing on leather. As he watched children playing with sticks of the substance, he concluded that it had other uses, but he was not successful in selling the idea. Before long, however, the manufacturing of the new marker was taken over by the American Crayon Company, and a popular drawing instrument was born.[1]

EXEMPLARS OF CRAYON DRAWING

Because crayons are capable of making wide, dark, and colorful lines, they can be used successfully to make large drawings. This means that school children can work on paper as large as 18 x 24 inches or 24 x 36 inches. The following exemplars are approximately that size:

GEORGES SEURAT (Su-rah'), 1859–1891

Like most artists, Seurat began drawing when he was young, and at the age of 15 entered the municipal drawing school in Paris. This was the beginning of his formal training in art which continued later at the Ecole des Beaux-Arts.[2] As a result of this training, Seurat became skilled in traditional techniques, but his independence did not allow him to adopt those techniques as his own. Instead, he developed the unique drawing style for which he is universally recognized. The novelty of the style can be seen in *Seated Boy with Straw Hat* (Plate 3-1). The drawing was created with a black Conté crayon on thick-grained, white paper. The roughness of the paper and the careful application of the crayon combine to produce a sparkling overall texture which helps to unify the work. The darkest areas are a rich, velvety black; the lightest are the color of the paper; and the gray areas are a mixture of white paper and crayon. There are no lines, no details, no sharpness of outline. Instead, the figure is reduced to a clear, three-dimensional form with hazy edges. It is a soft and quiet form although it possesses strong contrasts between light and dark. The sensitive shading or modeling serves to clarify the form and give it solidity, stability, and volume. The shaded side of the boy is placed against a light background; the light side is pro-

---

[1]Thelma R. Newman, *Wax as Art Form* (South Brunswick, N.J.: Thomas Yoseloff, 1966), p. 75.

[2]The Ecole des Beaux-Arts was the official French school for the training of artists and architects. It was tradition-bound with great power to award commissions, grant honors, and exhibit art.

vided with a dark background. However, on the bottom, the color of the figure blends with the color of the ground and helps to unite the two. By varying the way the edges of an object relate to the surrounding space, an artist can create a more interesting image, and Seurat has certainly done so.

Seurat was one of the most methodical and scientific artists in history. He seemed to know what the final product would look like before he painted it. This was probably due to the numerous preparatory drawings that he produced before he began painting. The study in Plate 3-1, for example, was made prior to creating *Une Baignade, Asnières* (The Bathers at Asnières), one of the masterpieces of modern times. Ironically, the painting was rejected for exhibition by the artistic authorities of 1884. The rejection caused Seurat to join with other innovative painters in forming the Society of Independent Artists which henceforth sponsored exhibitions of art by persons who worked in nontraditional ways. These unconventional artists often had difficulty exhibiting their work, and, as a consequence, they had trouble earning a living. Seurat, however, was more fortunate because his father, as a minor legal official, was able to support him while he experimented with his drawing and painting.

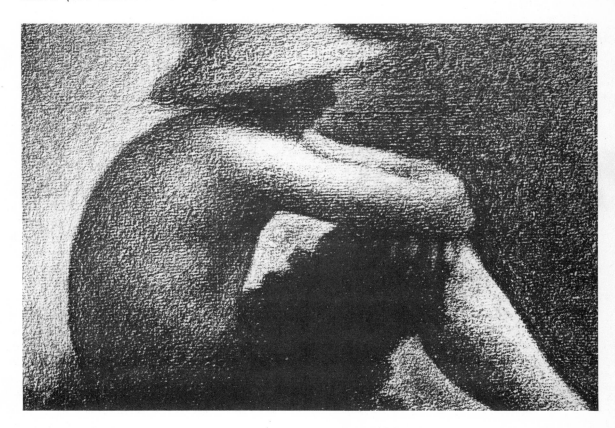

Plate 3-1.   Georges Seurat. *Seated Boy with Straw Hat.* 1882. Conté crayon drawing, 9½" x 12¼". Yale University Art Gallery (Everett V. Meeks, B.A 1901, Fund).

OSKAR KOKOSCHKA (Kuh-kosh'-kah), 1886–1980

The art of Oskar Kokoschka is often described as a form of expressionism. This means that it is an attempt to depict subjective feelings that have been aroused by certain objects or events. Frequently, the subject matter and composition are of less importance to the artist than the presentation of that emotion. And, in an effort to have a strong impact on the observer, the artist often distorts or exaggerates the form and color of visual reality. Expressionism, therefore, is not likely to appeal to those who consider photographic naturalism to be the epitome of art.

Because of the vivid, intense nature of his expressionistic work, Kokoschka, as a student, was discharged from the Arts and Crafts School of Vienna. In fact, he was characterized as a "public terror" and advised to leave town. He did depart from Austria on numerous occasions. He spent extended periods of time in Germany, England, and Switzerland, and in 1924 he embarked on a seven-year trip to many of the great cities of the world. The trip resulted in several remarkable paintings of those cities, and it probably contributed to Kokoschka's reputation as the most influential of all expressionist painters in making expressionism an international phenomenon.

Today, it is difficult to understand how Kokoschka's work could have caused so much animosity. The drawing in Plate 3-2, for example, is strong and bold, but it is not likely to arouse hostility in anyone. Taste in art has obviously changed since 1920, and the qualities associated with expressionism have become highly acceptable. Notice how the Kokoschka portrait differs from the exemplars discussed previously. The lines are more active, more turbulent, and less precise in defining the form of the figure. They have the free, uninhibited appearance of a scribble, which makes the drawing look as if it has been executed quickly, like a sketch. Furthermore, the marks on the face not only serve as

Plate 3-2. Oskar Kokoschka. *Hugo Erfurth.* 1920. Green crayon, 22⅛" x 19⅜". Collection, The Museum of Modern Art, New York.

shading which gives a three-dimensional form to the figure, but they also make the skin seem rough and irregular rather than smooth and taut. The total effect, therefore, is a lifelike figure. It also seems more human, less mechanical, and less perfect or proper than figures made with precise and flawless lines. Hence, the drawing appears to be more emotional than the previous exemplars. It is expressionistic; it is probing for the human qualities that lie beneath the physical exterior.

Finally, it is important to recognize that expressionism is different from abstract expressionism. Expressionism makes use of representational elements while abstract expressionism does not.

PABLO PICASSO (Pee-kah'-so), 1881–1973

Picasso was influenced by many other artists, but he always managed to maintain his individuality and add original elements to his work. He was impressed by Cézanne, for example, who believed that painting should be an attempt to give permanence and solidity of form to visual experience.[3] Consequently, Picasso worked to achieve clarity of form and solidity of structure in his own work. And one of the results was cubism, a style of painting which many authorities believe to be the most influential of modern times. It was an attempt to record the basic form of objects (cylindrical, conical, spherical, etc.) while uniting them with each other and with the surrounding pictorial space.[4]

Cubism, however, was not the only style of painting that Picasso used. He worked successfully in so many different ways that he became one of the most stylistically flexible artists in history. His flexibility was due in part to the fact that he found numerous things to express, and he realized that different concepts and emotions inevitably require different modes of visual expression. Furthermore, Picasso maintained that all art is essentially the same in spite of the fact that diverse expressive motives necessitate a variety of artistic styles or mannerisms. For example, the same artistic elements and principles of composition are used in all works of art. Certainly, these views, together with immense technical skill, must have helped Picasso to make stylistic changes with relative ease.

The drawing in Plate 3-3 indicates the artist's flexibility, because it was made with wax crayons. Probably, most artists have ignored the wax crayon because they associate it with children. But Picasso's status as an artist was such that he did not need to worry about associations of that kind. If a material had potential as an artistic medium, he exploited it. In the drawing of *The Family Album*, for example, he took advantage of the strong color of the crayons to make a lively, lighthearted statement. And he also capitalized on the blending qualities of the medium as well as its suitability for placing one color on top of another.

Notice the frilly gray lines in the faces of the grandmother and grandfather. They produce the effect of wrinkles and age, while similar lines in the bonnets and dresses of the grandmother and the daughter give the impression of fussiness and frilliness. Coupled with the straighter, scribbly marks found elsewhere in the drawing, the lines produce a liveliness similar to that found in the Kokoschka drawing. The effect is given further support by the bright colors and the wide variation from light to dark. The repetition of the same linear quality throughout the picture also helps to unify the work while the alternation of light lines against dark background and dark lines against light background provides some of the visual variety that makes the work interesting to perceive.

In the hands of an inexperienced person, the use of a large number of hues could lead to a jumble of color, making the figures difficult if not disturbing to see. Picasso avoids this by repeating colors as well as linear elements throughout the drawing. He also puts one color on top of another, which helps to unite them, and he does not allow an excess of uncolored space to exist. If he had left many places uncolored, there would have been too many broken areas, too many attention-gathering contrasts, and too much visual busyness for comfortable perception.

Picasso also distributes his dark colors in such a way that the drawing balances. One side has as much visual weight and as much capacity to attract the eye as the other. And he keeps the colors that he does not choose to repeat in the most important part of the picture. All these things

---

[3] Cézanne was reacting against the impressionists who had made an effort to capture in paint the momentary effects of light and atmosphere. Cézanne thought their efforts had led them to neglect form and pictorial composition. He also believed that the artist's task was not to imitate nature but to reconstruct nature in paint or some other medium.

[4] See page 44 for further information about cubism.

Plate 3-3.   Pablo Picasso. *Family Album.* 1962. Crayon, 22" x 29⅞". ©S.P.A.D.E.M., Paris/V.A.G.A., New York, 1980. Photo from La Réunion des Musées Nationaux.

help to stabilize the drawing and make it easy to perceive.

Finally, it is important to observe the uninhibited way in which Picasso applied the crayon. He did not worry about the exactness with which each stroke was made. Consequently, the drawing has freshness and life. It is different from the work of Seurat who worked in a more tightly controlled, painstaking manner.

ADDITIONAL EXEMPLARS

To show more examples of drawings done with Conté crayons, an instructor might use the work of numerous artists, including Charles Sheeler and Charles White. Wax crayon drawings, however, are more difficult to find. We recommend the works of Henry Moore, Mirko Basaldella, and Lyonel Feininger.

CRAYON ACTIVITIES FOR THE PRIMARY GRADES (AGES 6 THROUGH 8)

Crayons are excellent tools for drawing in the elementary school, and they are widely used. Sometimes they are used so often that children get tired of them. And there is a chance that such boredom will increase if the teacher does not provide a choice of crayons, a variety of crayon activities, and an adequate level of instruction in the use of the medium.

In the primary grades, the most suitable crayons are the ordinary wax type and the kind that contains a little oil, such as Cray-pas. The latter are most appropriate for children who are eight years of age or older, because oil crayons are more difficult to use without smearing. Art educators occasionally recommend heavy, thick crayons for the primary grades, but we do not agree. Thin crayons are easier to hold, and they allow for more details to be produced. By making details, the child learns about them; consequently, the use of thin crayons is more educative than the use of thick ones.

CONCEPTS FOR POSSIBLE DEVELOPMENT

It is always worthwhile to study crayon drawings made by other children and by adults. As they are discussed and compared, try to develop an understanding of the artistic concepts mentioned in connection with pencil drawing. Then introduce terms such as the following:

names of colors	scribble	quiet lines
bright and dull	wax crayons	happy and sad colors
overlapping	oil crayons	weak and strong colors
warm and cool colors	busy lines	hard and soft colors
solid color	agitated lines	naturalistic colors
pattern	lively lines	unnaturalistic colors
	active lines	

SUGGESTED ACTIVITIES

When using the exemplars by Seurat, Kokoschka, and Picasso, you might relate your discussion of the drawings to your students' work in some of the ways listed below. And if you wish to discuss more than three exemplars, you might use the rest of the drawings in Part Two as well as the exemplars of painting.

Children occasionally feel more secure if they are allowed to draw in pencil before adding crayon. Let them do so, but urge them to draw lightly, quickly, and without a lot of detail. The idea is to keep them from using all their time on the pencil sketches.

Some of the following drawings are to be done in line while others are to be done in solid color. The latter require more time, and if it is not provided, the drawings will be lightly and partially colored. They will look weak and unfinished, but they can be improved by letting the children work on them again. Have them add more color.

1. Show students the crayon exemplars and the charcoal drawing by Gauguin (page 97). Ask if they can see any differences among the drawings. Hopefully, they will observe that the Seurat, the Gauguin, and the Kokoschka were made with one color while the Picasso was made with several. Perhaps they will notice that the Gauguin and the Kokoschka are the only drawings made almost entirely with lines, while the Seurat is the only one produced with no lines at all. They may also see that the Seurat contains the most shading, and it is the drawing most thoroughly covered with crayon. If the youngsters fail to see these things, help them to do so and call their attention to the fact that none of the drawings looks unfinished. Then try one of the following activities:

a) Invite the custodian to pose for 10 to 15 minutes. Give each child either a black crayon and white drawing paper or a white oil crayon and black construction paper. Ask that a *line* drawing be made of the custodian. If 12-x-18-inch paper is used, the drawing could include everything from the waist up, but if 9-x-24-inch paper is employed, the whole figure could be drawn. Urge the youngsters to draw belts, buttons, glasses, eyebrows, teeth, pockets, and other details, and emphasize the importance of using the full sheet of paper so the drawing will not look unfinished. If the lines are so light that they cannot be seen easily, ask the children to go over them again and to press harder with their crayons. This could conclude the lesson, or you could continue by displaying the exemplar by Picasso. Have the children pay attention to the way he filled the background with scribbled lines drawn close together. Urge them to fill the backgrounds in their own drawings with the same kinds of lines, using a colored crayon. If the lines are not scribbled closely together, the drawing may look too busy. Help students to recognize that fact.

When the work is finished, display the drawings and add a sign that says something like this: "Our friend, Mr. Williams. We appreciate the things he does to make our school so nice."

b) In the second or third grade, invite the principal to pose for about 15 minutes, which is long enough for students to draw basic shapes and details in pencil. If the principal can stay longer, encourage him to do so; it will help. Distribute packages of oil crayons and wax crayons, and ask the youngsters to make a portrait something like the Seurat drawing. By this we mean that the drawing should be fully colored and it should not be made with lines alone. Coloring all parts of the drawing, however, takes time and hard work. This means that you will have to encourage the children, and praise them warmly for their efforts. Explain that the task will be easier if they make their drawings fill the paper, which should be about 12 x 18 inches in size. Compliment them if they include details, color combinations, patterns, or color mixtures that add to the visual richness of their drawings. Display the finished products, and call attention to the beauty and uniqueness of individual works. Emphasize that drawings are often beautiful partly because they are completely colored or finished. When the paper shows in numerous places, it may create the unpleasant feeling of visual busyness.

2. As you discuss the exemplars, indicate that Seurat must have paid careful attention to seated figures, because his drawing accurately indicates how the body bends in a seated position. Some artists take the position of the person they are drawing, because it helps them to learn about the placement and movement of body parts (see Matisse, page 82). Try the same technique by leading your class through a series of exercises while calling attention to the location, movements, and angles of arms, legs, heads, and backs. Pay special attention to the places where bending occurs. When finished, ask the children to make a drawing that shows how they did one of the exercises in class. Display the products and praise the way the action of the body has been shown. Call attention also to those drawings which make use of the full sheet of paper.

3. Do the things indicated in the foregoing lesson, but instead of having the class exercise, have them march around the room raising their knees high. Have a few of them jump rope. Or, take them outside to play dodge ball before they draw themselves playing the game.

4. Talk with students about one of the topics listed below. Try to move, touch, or inspire them with your words. Try to say things or get them to say things that will build images or visual concepts in their minds. Then ask the children to make a drawing about the topic. Further suggestions about stimulation can be found on page 10.

Swatting flies in summer	Sewing buttons on my clothes
Blowing out the candles	Crossing a busy street
Visiting the school kitchen	Putting on makeup
Blowing bubbles	Fishing from a rowboat
Washing a big, big dog	Toasting marshmallows
The time I was afraid	An animal visits our class
The fire hydrant cools us	Watching the steamroller

This project can be repeated many times using a different subject on each occasion. Show the exemplars each time, and try to have your students do the following things: 1) color parts of their drawings solid, like Seurat did; 2) color other parts in a tightly-packed, scribbly fashion, as Picasso did; 3) repeat colors in the Picasso manner; 4) finish everything that they start to color; 5) include the characteristic features of animals and special people; and 6) avoid large areas of unused space.

If the students do not have time to finish their drawings adequately in one hour, have them complete the work in the near future. The extra time and effort will tend to improve the drawings.

5. Crayon resist is a mixed-media activity suitable for the primary grades. It requires that a drawing be made on 12-x-18- or 18-x-24-inch white paper by pressing hard with a wax crayon. After that, the whole paper is painted with watercolor. The paint does not stick to the parts colored with crayon, but it does adhere to the uncolored paper. The effect is especially striking if the drawing is made largely with lines rather than areas of solid color, and it helps if dark paint is used over light, bright colors.

Try doing flower gardens, underwater scenes, and exotic birds. Have the children draw patterns in their flowers, insects, fish, plants, and birds. Then have them paint over the drawing with one dark color, or have them paint the different parts of their picture with different colors. In the latter case, urge the children to paint the background with a color that has not been used elsewhere in the picture. See Figure 3-1.

6. Beginning in the second grade, ask each of your students to pick a piece of colored scrap from a box of leftover construction paper. Have them look at the scrap to see if it resembles a living creature (animal, bird, fish, and so on). Then

Figure 3-1. Note how the patterns contribute to the attractiveness of the drawing.

tell them that they can tear the paper to make it look more like the creature it resembles. As they finish, talk about patterns, and urge them to cover their creature with a pattern made with crayons. Encourage them to use imaginative, unnaturalistic colors to make their products cheerful or fantastic. Finally, have them glue their creatures to 12-x-18-inch sheets of colored construction paper, and see if they can use their crayons to make backgrounds for their imaginative figures.

This activity is helpful to children who lack confidence in art. It gives them something to start with, and a high degree of naturalism is neither required nor possible.

7. Ask your class to collect a variety of insects (moths, butterflies, grasshoppers, crickets, lady bugs, etc.). Have them examine the insects using a magnifying glass if necessary. Then ask the class to draw the insects lightly with pencil on 9-x-12-inch black paper. Two or three of the creatures should fill the sheet, and they should be different sizes to create variety. The children can then color the insects and background with oil crayons, leaving the pencil lines uncolored. As they do so, remind them that they can put one color on top of another as Picasso did.

As an alternative, have the children draw four or five insects as well as weeds and flowers. This will require more than one sheet of paper. Then all the insects, flowers, and weeds can be cut out (leaving a narrow black margin around them), and they can be mounted on a sheet of 12-x-18-inch colored construction paper. Suggest that they be made to overlap.

CRAYON ACTIVITIES FOR THE INTERMEDIATE GRADES (AGES 9 THROUGH 11)

At this level, it is advisable to continue with the use of wax and oil crayons, but it is also important to introduce Conté crayons and pressed crayons. The combination adds variety, and it offers a broader range of color and texture than any one type of crayon can provide.

Comparing exemplars of crayon drawing is always advisable, and at the intermediate level it is fitting to discuss the expressive qualities in each of the drawings and to show how they differ. The Seurat, for example, projects calmness, softness, gentleness, mystery, voluminous form, simplicity, stability, and the concept of a seated boy. The Kokoschka, on the other hand, presents ruggedness, vitality, and the notion of a man's head, while the Picasso offers cheerfulness, lightheartedness, frilliness, and the concept of three human figures. In each case, the expressive quality of the work is due largely to the way the crayon was applied. The monochromatic, precise, and studied technique of Seurat, together with his modeling, is responsible for the unique meaning communicated by his work. The same may be said for the brisk, bold, loose, and totally linear method used by Kokoschka. And the fact that Picasso used bright colors and active lines without inhibition is responsible for the import conveyed by his drawing.

CONCEPTS FOR POSSIBLE DEVELOPMENT

In building an understanding of artistic concepts, terms from the preceding paragraphs may be useful, as well as terms from the list that follows:

pressed crayons	wax binder	uninhibited
sketches and studies	contour	scratchboard
expressionism	contrast	background
monochrome	style	foreground
mixed media	Conté crayons	shading or modeling

SUGGESTED ACTIVITIES

Some of the lessons for the primary grades can be repeated successfully with slight variations at the intermediate level. However, listed below are lessons of a more advanced nature that are especially appropriate for the fourth, fifth, and sixth grades:

1. As a home assignment, ask your students to make pencil sketches of at least ten objects commonly found along the streets of their community. This means fire hydrants, telephone poles, street signs, traffic lights, mail boxes, parking meters, park benches, telephone booths, street lights, trash cans, barber poles, gasoline pumps, and other such objects.

   When the children return, give them sheets of 18-x-24-inch gray drawing paper, some oil crayons, wax crayons, and pressed crayons. Have them select a few of their favorite sketches, and ask them to combine those sketches as they redraw the objects on gray paper. The drawing can be done lightly with pencil, but the objects should be drawn much larger in the process. Urge the youngsters to use objects of different heights, widths, and shapes, and advise them to make some of the objects tilt and overlap.

   With the preliminary pencil work finished, the next task is to apply color with crayons. Encourage the children to repeat colors and to use lines in the manner of Picasso. Stress the importance of using dark and light colors, bright and dull colors, thick and thin lines, and plain and patterned areas. Then discuss the expressive effects in the finished drawings. Do they express the feeling of a city? If so, what contributes to the communication of that feeling? Look at the exemplars. Which ones employ techniques that could suggest most easily the busy nature of a city? Try this activity in paint. Cut the street objects out, and mount them on the wall.

2. Display the exemplars of crayon and chalk drawing as well as the exemplars of painting. Call attention to the fact that each is unique in its style. This uniqueness is desirable because it shows that the artists are being themselves, and it means that a broad range of ideas and feelings can be expressed and ultimately understood and appreciated.

Select one of the following topics and discuss it briefly with your students. Remember that the purpose is to get them enthused and to build their mental images or concepts of the topic.

An insect's view of a beautiful field	Paradise
Riding on a crowded bus or subway	Working hard
A long line of old stores or houses	Helping to build a fire
The accident	An elderly friend
Cooking with my friend	The city I know
Life on a skateboard	Kindness

As students deal with the topic in their drawings, encourage them to be themselves and to draw in a natural way. Let them know that you expect each of their drawings to be different. If a child's technique or style is similar to the style of one of the exemplars, point out the similarity. Perhaps there are features in the exemplar that can be used by the child in his own work.

This project can be done with one type of crayon, a mixture of crayons, or a combination of crayons and chalk. The project offers an opportunity to talk about the effect of color in creating mood, depth, or a pleasing composition. To help with composition, ask yourself some of the following questions, and then offer constructive suggestions to your students:

a) Does the drawing balance?

b) Are units (objects) within the drawing close enough to each other to be seen as a coherent whole, or are they so far apart that they seem like separate pictures competing for attention?

c) Does the drawing appear finished? Has the paper been fully used or has much of it been left blank?

d) Is there too much visual busyness? Could it be eliminated by reducing the number of colors, contrasts, or uncolored spaces?

e) Would more colors, patterns, or lines make the picture more interesting by increasing visual variety?

f) Would the drawing be more appealing if the sizes or shapes of things were more varied? Could the distance between things be varied?

g) Could objects and their relationships be made clearer by coloring an area with one consistent color?

h) Are the right and left sides of the drawing too similar?

3. Show your class the exemplar of pencil drawing by Burchfield and the exemplar of chalk drawing by Degas. Discuss the composition of those works paying special attention to the automobile and ballerina which are cut off by the edge of the paper. Then make the following points:

a) An artist does not have to draw a whole object; he can draw part of it. If people felt that they had to draw whole objects, drawings would look so much alike that they would be boring.

b) If you do draw a whole object, place it a little off center. This will create a more interesting division of space on the paper.

c) Avoid letting the edge of a form touch the edge of the paper. If it does touch, it will produce an unpleasant, crowded effect. Let forms go off the paper instead, or make them stay well away from the edge of the paper.

d) To produce visual variety, artists often try to keep the lines in their drawings from dividing the paper into equal segments (halves, quarters, thirds, and the like).

Following your discussion, take the class outside to draw in pencil all or part of an automobile, a bicycle, a motorcycle, a fire hydrant, a street light, or any object of a similar nature. Ask them not to draw anything in the background. Then distribute 9-x-12-inch sheets of white drawing paper, and explain that the students will go over the pencil lines with pen and ink or black nylon pens when everyone returns to the classroom. Explain further that the whole paper will eventually be colored with oil crayons, and the coloring will be kept approximately one-eighth of an inch away from the lines. Consequently, the students should not make their lines too close together. The only reason for keeping the color away from the lines is to show that such a technique produces a unique effect in crayon drawings. It gives extra emphasis to the linear elements.

When the children begin coloring, urge them to select a limited number of colors and to repeat them within the object. This will help to produce unity; if the object is broken up by too many colors it is likely to lose form and be difficult to perceive. Finally, you might suggest that the background be colored with a hue different from those used in coloring the object. The difference will make the object separate clearly from the background. See Figure 3-2 at the beginning of the chapter.

4. Repeat Activity 3, but have the students draw on 12-x-18-inch white paper, and have them put backgrounds in their pictures. See if they can create pleasing compositions and make the object in the foreground separate visually from the background. Some of the following suggestions may help:

a) Study the Burchfield exemplar to see how he places background objects so they divide the paper unevenly.

b) Put more contrasts and details in the object in the foreground.

c) Make the background colors duller, cooler, and lighter than the foreground colors.

d) Let the foreground object overlap things in the background, and make it larger.

5. Display the Burchfield pencil drawing and conduct essentially the same discussion on composition that was covered in Activity 3. Then distribute some

12-x-18-inch black construction paper, and give an assignment to do at home. Ask students to draw an interesting door or window in pencil on their black paper. Encourage them to draw part of the area around the door or window, and explain that the drawing will eventually be colored and that you would like them to create a pattern of some sort in their pictures. Patterns help to give visual richness to art. See Figure 3-3.

When the youngsters return with their pencil drawings, write the following suggestions on the board, and let them begin coloring with their oil crayons:

a) Color the whole sheet of paper, but allow the black paper to show in certain places. If you want a dark line between forms, for example, let the paper show in that area.

b) Color lightly at first, and work all over the drawing. If you finish one area before moving to another, you may commit yourself too soon, and you may not be able to change what you have done.

Figure 3-3. Take enough time to make the pencil sketch carefully.

c) Do not attempt small details. The crayons are too large to do them properly.

d) Sometimes it is helpful to color large areas first.

e) Include a pattern in your work. Bricks, windowpanes, and clapboards make patterns. What else could do so?

f) Try creating interesting colors in at least one place by putting one color on top of another.

g) Repeat some color, pattern, or linear elements.

As an alternative to doors and windows you might have students draw mechanical objects inside the school (door latches, typewriters, tape recorders, record players, fire extinguishers, faucets, soap dispensers, etc.). And, as a follow-up to this activity, you might pick a slightly different topic and ask the students to use their color and line expressively. To see what is meant by the word expressive, read the material that follows.

6. Display the exemplar of printmaking by Kirchner as well as the Kokoschka and Picasso drawings, and discuss the meaning of expressionism. Let the children know that artists express character and feeling by manipulating visual elements such as color, line, shape, texture, and volume. Then give them pencils, mirrors, oil crayons, and some 9-x-12- or 12-x-18-inch black construction paper. Ask them to make a self-portrait (head, or head and shoulders), and remind them that they need not draw the whole head, and it need not be in the center of the paper. Most importantly, indicate that they should try to use their color or lines expressively. Perhaps some of the following questions will help them to see how colors and lines can be used to produce character and feeling:

a) What colors might be used to make you look sickly, weird, gentle, lively, old, cool, or hot? What meanings are attached to yellow-green, white, pink, red, gray, blue, and orange?

b) Will naturalistic colors create character and feeling as strongly as unnaturalistic colors? What will high contrast do?

c) What kind of line did Kokoschka use in his drawings? What effect was produced? Do the lines in the Picasso drawing contribute to the character of the people in the picture? How?

d) To make a person look strong, loud, or tough, what kind of lines would you use? If you wanted him to look kind and gentle, what would you use?

As the students begin working, urge them to make use of the black paper by letting it show in many places. Perhaps the information in Project 8 will help to give more suggestions for working on black paper.

7. A collage containing drawings of human figures in action is an excellent thing to make in the intermediate grades. The first portion of the activity involves painting several figures, and it requires that each child be given four or five sheets of newsprint, a ¼-inch bristle brush, a number 12 and a number 7 hair brush, and some black, brown, orange, or yellow tempera paint.

After distributing the materials, stand on a desk or table and assume an action pose. Hold the pose long enough for the children to complete a quick painting of you; then change to another pose, and continue until 10 or 11 figures have been painted. Make the following suggestions while you pose:

a) Try to capture the main movement of the figure (the curve of the back, bending of elbows, tilt of head, angle of legs, and so on).

b) *Do not outline the figure.* Paint it solid black or solid brown, etc.

c) Eyes, ears, noses, and other details should be left out.

d) Make the figures different sizes. Some might be a foot tall; others might be as small as three inches.

e) Look carefully at the figure.

The second portion of the activity requires that each child look at his painted figures to decide what they could be doing (loitering on the street, dancing, enjoying a picnic, playing at the beach or on the playground, and the like). The next job is to put clothing on the figures with oil crayons. The clothing should be appropriate for whatever the figures are doing. Recommend that patterns be used on some of the clothing, but remember that patterns are most effective if combined with plain areas. When the clothing is finished, the figures are cut out and glued to a sheet of colored construction paper.

The third part of the activity requires that the students create a background for the figures with oil crayons by drawing on the colored construction paper (12 x 18 or 18 x 24 inches). Perhaps the suggestions listed below will be helpful.

a) To create depth in the picture, make your color change from foreground to background; have the closest objects overlap the ones in the distance; create contrasts of various kinds in the foreground; reduce contrasts in the background; put bright colors in the front and duller colors to the rear.

b) Do not let your figures become isolated spots that compete for attention.

c) Distant figures do not always have to be near the top of the page.

d) In general, the objects in the foreground will be larger than those in the background.

8. In the fifth or sixth grade, arrange a still life composed entirely of white objects. You might use drapery, a pitcher, two or three eggs, an old window frame with panes, a vase with carnations in it, and two or three old boards of unequal length (painted white and standing on end). Make sure the objects are of different heights and that some are placed in front of others; then shine a floodlight on the arrangement.

Call attention to highlights, shaded areas, and shadows. Show that some places appear much whiter than others even if all the objects are white. Point to places where the whiteness changes gradually from light to dark (for instance, across the body of the cylindrical pitcher), and ask if anyone can find a place where the whiteness changes from light to dark more rapidly (such as at corners or across the surface of a thin cylinder, like the handle of a pitcher).

Point to the Seurat drawing and show how the artist has caused the shading to go from light to dark on the human figure. Then give the class black paper and white Conté crayons and ask them to make a drawing of the still life showing how the color changes across the surface of the objects. Explain that they must press heavily where they want highlights, and they must ease up on the crayon when they want the color to be darker. Suggest that they begin by sketching the whole arrangement *very* lightly with their crayons or with pencil. You might also suggest that they fill the whole paper with their drawing.

If you do not have Conté crayons, use white pressed crayons or oil crayons. And the first time you do this project use small sheets of paper, about 9 x 12 or 12 x 18 inches.

9. For a very different effect, try the foregoing project with black Conté crayons on white or gray paper, or use both white and black Conté crayons on gray paper. Suggest that the white be used for highlights, the black for shades and shadows, and the untouched gray paper for middle values between the light and the shade.

10. Try some of the charcoal activities with black Conté crayons. Activities 4 and 5 would be especially worthwhile.

11. In the fall, bring to class a collection of flowers, branches from trees and bushes, cornstalks, and dry weeds. Let each student select a stem or two, and give each person a 9-x-24-inch sheet of black paper and some oil crayons. Have the students draw the stems lightly with pencil before coloring the whole picture, including the background, with their crayons. Make sure that they let the paper show in and around the object they are drawing.

The beauty of the result depends to a large extent upon the placement of the stems on the paper. Keep them slightly out of the center; do not allow them to divide the paper into equally proportioned segments; be careful of strong diagonals; and avoid stems that go off both ends of the paper. See Figure 3-4.

12. Display the exemplar of pencil drawing by Burchfield and the exemplar of pen and ink drawing by van Gogh. Discuss the composition of the drawings. Explain that the objects in the foreground were made to appear close to the observer by having them overlap things in the background and by making them larger than similar objects in the distance.

Give the students a variety of 12-x-18-inch colored construction paper, some pencils, and drawing boards, and go outside to draw the front or side of an automobile or a truck. Make the drawings fill the paper, and have the students select different vehicles to draw. Then return to the classroom; ask the children to cut the vehicles out of the paper; and show them how to col-

Figure 3-4.   Stems of bushes or dry weeds.

or the drawings with oil crayons. The idea is to let a small amount of paper show around the edges of the auto and around all the pencil lines.

When the vehicles are fully colored, glue them to a piece of 12-x-18-inch construction paper that is different in color from the piece that was taken outside. Have each student draw in pencil a simple background for his vehicle. Then have him color the drawing with oil crayons, allowing the paper to show around pencil lines and in other choice places. Mount the finished products on 12-x-18-inch sheets of colored construction paper. See Figure 3-5.

The purpose behind this activity is to make foregrounds and backgrounds, and it also is to show that artists often make drawings and paintings on colored surfaces or grounds. Sometimes the color of the ground (or working surface) is changed from one part of the picture to another.

13. Scratchboard drawings often appear in advertisements. The artist begins with a clay-coated piece of lightweight cardboard painted with India ink. He scratches away the ink with a pointed tool producing a white drawing on a black background. To simulate the foregoing process, give your students some 9-x-12-inch white paper, pencils, and wax crayons. After having them draw large insects or birds in pencil, have them double all their lines leaving about 1/16 of an inch between the lines. The drawings must then be colored heavily

Figure 3-5.   Three different ground colors are
visible in this drawing—collage.

with the crayons. The children should be careful not to color the narrow spaces
between the lines.

Take the colored drawings to an inking area and paint the whole paper
with India ink containing a few drops of liquid detergent. When the ink
dries, all parts of the drawing will be visible through the ink. Show your pupils how to scratch lines in the India ink, revealing the crayon underneath.
The scratching can be done with needles, razor blades, metal pen points,
round toothpicks, X-acto knives, and the points of scissors. Encourage your
students to create designs in parts of the figure as they scratch away the ink.

Figure 3-6.   Note the attractive patterns.

14. Prepare still-life arrangements composed of fruits and vegetables resting on a patterned fabric. Display the pencil drawing by Ingres and the chalk drawing by Rubens, and show how the two artists give form to the human figure by making their lines follow the contour of the figure. Then, following the procedure outlined in Activity 13, have students produce a scratchboard drawing. But when they are ready to scratch away the India ink show them how to make their lines follow the contour of the objects in the still life. Also, show them that they can give fruits and vegetables a three-dimensional form by scratching away more ink in the areas that are closest to the source of light. Then they can gradually scratch away less in the areas that move away from the source of light. See Figure 3-6 on page 74.

CHAPTER 4

PEN
AND INK
DRAWING

Figure 4-1.   *Housewife.* Black and gray crayons were
used in addition to ink.

Probably no drawing instrument has been more popular than the pen. It has been used for at least six centuries, and practically all the well-known artists in the Western Hemisphere have worked with it. Its popularity, undoubtedly, can be traced to two factors. First, it is flexible enough to produce different kinds of lines, and, second, it is adaptable to the idiosyncratic styles of individual artists. These characteristics are due largely to the existence of five or six different kinds of pens, each with its own peculiarities. However, the quill, the reed, and the metal pen are the kinds most often used by artists. The reed was introduced well before the Middle Ages, making it the oldest of the three, but it is also the least popular because it lacks flexibility. It is made from canelike, hollow-stemmed grasses which are hard and nonpliable. As a result, the reed produces coarse, powerful lines. And, in many instances, they are short lines, because the nature of the reed requires that the pen be given a broad point which releases its ink quickly, producing short lines.

From the late fourteenth century to the end of the eighteenth century, the quill pen was clearly the favorite. It was more versatile and adaptable than the reed; it could make lines of variable thickness and length; and it could glide over the surface of the paper more easily than pens with metal points. Consequently, it was used for calligraphy and illustrations in medieval manuscripts, as well as for larger drawings. The best quills were made from the feathers of geese, swans, ravens, and crows; and, according to Watrous, the most desirable feathers came form the leading edge of the wing.[1]

Apparently, numerous efforts had been made to create metal-point pens, but it was not until methods of mass production were invented in the early part of the nineteenth century that metal points came into widespread use. Furthermore, the first varieties were not immediately

---

[1]James Watrous, *The Craft of Old Master Drawings* (Madison, Wis.: University of Wisconsin Press, 1957), p. 48.

useful because their sharp, stiff points caught the fiber of the paper and cut or tore it. In time, however, paper was made harder with less fiber projecting from its surface. This meant that metal points were able to function more satisfactorily, and the result was that reeds and quills were almost completely replaced by pens with metal points. The new tool lasted longer; it came in a variety of widths; the quality was always good; and it made sharp, clear lines. But it never has produced marks with the same primitive attributes of reed lines or the same soft, variable qualities of quill lines.

Pens require ink, of course, and there were four kinds that were used most frequently by the old masters. The darkest and strongest was carbon black, or Chinese ink, which was invented in China about 2700 B.C. Ordinary lampblack was mixed with a solution of glue and allowed to dry in the shape of a small stick. By adding water to the stick, the artist obtained his medium for drawing.

Iron-gall ink was made from the growths or galls commonly found on oak trees; sepia was made from the bladders of cuttlefish; and bistre was made from the soot of burned wood. Iron-gall was a black liquid which turned brown with age, but sepia and bistre were brown from the start.

Today the most commonly used drawing inks are India ink and brown ink similar to the sepia of long ago. Occasionally, liquids of a more colorful nature are used, but artists seem to prefer the contrast obtained with darker substances.

EXEMPLARS OF PEN AND INK DRAWING

Like pencil, pen and ink lend themselves most successfully to the creation of small drawings, but it is possible to combine them satisfactorily with other materials to produce large configurations. When an art object has been made with more than one material, we say that it has been done with mixed media.

VINCENT VAN GOGH (van Gogh'), 1853–1890

Vincent van Gogh died at the age of 37, yet many persons consider him to be the greatest and most revolutionary Dutch artist since Rembrandt. One of the most astonishing facts about him is that he did such an enormous amount of superior work. To appreciate his achievement, consider that he produced approximately 900 drawings and 800 paintings during his ten years as an artist. This means that he created a little more than one drawing and one painting every week for ten years. Rubens and Picasso, among others, may have created more art objects in the course of a lifetime, but no one to our knowledge has produced more drawings and paintings in one decade.

To be as prolific as van Gogh, a person has to dedicate himself to his work, and he has to be willing to sacrifice the pleasures and responsibilities that most people accept as necessary elements in their lives. The fact that van Gogh was inclined to do so is a sign that his background and personality were different from those of an average man. These differences were evident almost from the beginning.

Vincent, as he liked to be known, was a sociable, affectionate, and gentle child with plenty of patience and sympathy, but he was constantly rebuffed in one way or another by his family and other people. Or, to put it differently, he was a sensitive but socially awkward person whose youth lacked trust and tenderness.

As he grew older, he worked as a clerk in an

art gallery; he served as a minister in the poor, coal-mining district of Belgium known as the Borinage; and he made three or four proposals of marriage. In all these instances, he was unsuccessful, and these constant rejections and failures in his associations with people were a source of great unhappiness. They caused him to devote all of his time to his art, which he had begun while serving in the Borinage.

Van Gogh's drawings and paintings were more colorful, more active, and more alive than anything produced before his time, and they offended almost everyone. People were simply unaccustomed to art that was so emotional and so powerful. Consequently, only one of van Gogh's paintings was sold before his death. Together with his other failures, this may have contributed to the mental breakdown that ultimately ended in suicide.

By studying the image in Plate 4-1, it is easy to see the distinguishing features in van Gogh's

work. The trees, hills, fields, and stars seem healthy, alive, and moving. The drawing looks vigorous, crude, strong, heavy, earthy, and emotional. These are the meanings embodied in the image; they are the communicative elements or the content of the work. Without a doubt, they are the concepts and emotions that van Gogh developed as a result of his exposure to the countryside in southern France. To embody these concepts and emotions in his work, he created formal elements to match his expressive intentions. He used short, stubby, repetitive lines which were broad and dark. Many of them were made to curve and swirl in an undulating manner, and sometimes they lined up parallel to each other in a way that made them seem to spin or sway. Furthermore, the lines did not vary from thick to thin, because van Gogh's reed pen did not permit such flexibility.

A sense of depth was achieved in Plate 4-1 by using comparatively long lines for the trees in

Plate 4-1. Vincent van Gogh. *The Starry Night.* 1889. Reed pen, brush, and ink, 18½'' x 24⅝''. (Whereabouts unknown).

the foreground and short lines for the objects in the background. Depth was also achieved by making the closest tree large and by making it overlap the things in the distance.

By using all the space on the paper, by placing lines close together, and by repeating the same type of line throughout the drawing, van Gogh was able to produce a highly unified picture. If he had not done these things, the drawing could have been spotty, unfinished, and excessively busy. In short, it could have been unpleasant to look at.

Notice also that van Gogh did not bother with shading or shadows. He was not, after all, a classical draftsman in the tradition of Ingres. He was more closely akin to Delacroix, Courbet, and Millet. His drawing was more emotional than cerebral, more dynamic than placid, more rough than smooth, more hot than cold, more handsome than pretty.

GEORGE GROSZ (Gross), 1893–1959

George Grosz was born and educated in Germany, where he studied at the Dresden Academy and the Berlin School of Arts and Crafts. Like some of the other young artists of his era, he was bored with his classes because they required that he copy ancient works of art and perform other dull, repetitive exercises. As a result, he avoided his classes and gave attention to the more exciting work of avant-garde artists such as the expressionists and the proponents of art nouveau.[2] He was especially interested in car-

tooning, and, when he was 16, one of his cartoons was accepted for publication in a prominent magazine. World War I intervened, however, and Grosz was forced to postpone his experiments in cartooning. Instead, he gained a firsthand knowledge of service as a combat soldier. After the war he observed the economic chaos of his country as well as the moral degeneration of the ruling class. His experiences filled him with disgust and moved him to express his bitterness against the causes of world conflict. In this respect, he was not unlike the artists of the dada movement, who used their art to rebel against war, militarism, and the uninspired academic art of postwar Europe.

Critics have also associated Grosz with the artistic style known as *neue sachlichkeit* (new objectivity), a hard-hitting, brutally objective form of social commentary. This is an accurate association because the drawings for which Grosz became famous were vitriolic social documents. They expressed a profound disgust with society as he knew it, and he drew it at its worst. His drawings were peopled with inhumane militarists, gamblers, drunks, prostitutes, murderers, and mindless people of all kinds. In fact, the drawings were so shocking and so clearly aimed at specific groups that Grosz was convicted and fined two or three times for libeling the army and for blasphemy. Strangely enough, before the whole affair ended, Grosz developed a worldwide reputation as a powerful social critic, and he made a lot of money. Apparently, his drawings were in great demand by the people he criticized.

It was in disgust, therefore, that George Grosz left Berlin in 1932 to accept a teaching position at the Art Student's League in New York. He had always admired the United States, and he was determined in his desire to become a full-fledged American. The desire was fulfilled, but some critics feel that in the process he lost a little of his expressive power. They expected him to attack the unpleasant aspects of American society in the same way he criticized German soci-

---

[2]The German expressionists were revolting against academic art, and their work tended to be highly emotional and unconventional in color, texture, and form. In short, they were very intense in their expressiveness (see page 216). Art nouveau was a stylized, decorative way of drawing and painting that was characterized by serpentine or undulating linear elements and flat areas of color.

ety, but he simply could not do it. Instead, he turned his attention to the presentation of other ideas and emotions, and this necessitated a change in the style and subject matter of his drawings and paintings. They became more naturalistic, peaceful, and pleasant. There were drawings of still-life arrangements, landscapes, portraits, and nude figures, cityscapes, and animals. And they were all the work of a master draftsman.

The drawing in Plate 4-2 is an example of the work Grosz did before coming to America. It is a caustic piece of social commentary; it depicts middle-class Germans as degenerates who spend too much of their time drinking and gambling in the cafés. The people were made to look stupid, dissipated, vulgar, and ugly, but what is it that makes them look that way? Notice that the

heads were made with wrinkles, thick necks, tufts of disagreeable hair, dull eyes, toothy grins, and other unpleasant features. The bodies were placed in uncomplimentary positions, were given an excess amount of fat, and were sloppily dressed. Furthermore, the lines made by the pen were crude, bold, hard, and unrefined. They tend, therefore, to give the figures those same characteristics.

By comparing the Grosz drawing with the one by Vincent van Gogh, similarities and differences are immediately apparent. Both drawings can be described with the same adjectives, but the subject matter and the style are different. It is the style, however, that is most important in differentiating the work of the two men, because both utilized some of the same subject matter on other occasions. The Grosz style is characterized by longer, sketchier lines that seem to touch and cross each other more often than the van Gogh lines. They also appear to occupy less of the picture space, and this makes the drawing seem less compact and more airy. But if this is true, what is the importance of bringing these stylistic differences to your attention? The significance is that nuances of style embody much of the unique content or meaning in a work of art. These expressive qualities cannot be framed in words. Consequently, the adjectives used to describe what is seen in a work of art are only indicative of its generalizable content or meaning. They cannot indicate what its particular or unique content happens to be. It is possible, therefore, to describe the meaningful qualities in two works of art with essentially the same adjectives and, at the same time, remain fully aware that the two works say something different that cannot be put into words.

HENRI MATISSE (Ma-teess'), 1869–1954

Henri Matisse was one of the leading artists of the twentieth century. He was innovative in

Plate 4-2.   George Grosz. *Cafe.* 1916. Pen and ink. Estate of George Grosz, Princeton, New Jersey.

drawing, painting, printmaking, and sculpture. Thus, is should not be surprising that we refer to his work in more than one place in this book (see pages 165–166).

In addition to being original and productive as an artist, Matisse was influential as a commentator on art and artists. His ideas affected both art criticism and teaching. And one of the most surprising of those ideas, to persons unfamiliar with art, is that studying ancient works can be beneficial in the development of an artist. Probably, the idea is surprising to most laymen because they can see no connection between the works of antiquity and the drawings and paintings produced by Matisse. The connection is that Matisse concentrated on the totality of the image he was creating and did not restrict his attention to the parts. He believed that the artists of antiquity had succeeded in doing the same thing.

In addition, Matisse agreed with the priority that artists of antiquity had given to large masses and relationships. They solved the problems connected with those elements first, and then proceeded to the consideration of details. In Matisse's opinion, it was only during decadent periods of art that artists put their chief interest in details, and this view is widely accepted today, along with the notion that studying the antique can be useful.

Matisse was also in favor of using and studying a model. He recognized the artist's need for knowledge that comes from contemplating subject matter, and he suggested that artists gather such knowledge by occasionally assuming the pose of the model. Once the necessary information has been obtained, the artist can use his imagination to enrich it. The enrichment may involve exaggeration, and if it does, Matisse would contend that it should be done in accordance with the character of the model.

In studying the model, Matisse believed that it was important to grasp the basic proportions of the figure and to absorb the fundamental linear movements of the body and its major parts. The axis or angle of the shoulders, for ex-

ample, is an important linear movement to observe, and so are the axes of the pelvis, the back, the legs, the arms, the neck, and the head. If these are not fully understood, it is difficult, if not impossible, to produce the character of the pose in a work of art.

Matisse believed that every line in a drawing or a painting should have a function, or it should not be there. He also maintained that all lines should close around a center, which probably meant that they should lead the eye in and around the picture but not out of it. Lines that make the eye leave the picture help to destroy the unity of the work and make it unpleasant to perceive.

Still another of Matisse's ideas about line and its effectiveness in art was that the nature of a given line can be made most obvious if the line is placed among other lines that have a different character. In other words, the essence of a curved line can be established most easily if it is placed in the presence of a straight line. If it is placed among more curved lines, it tends to lose its distinctiveness and its force.

The drawing of the young woman in Plate 4-3 probably was done with a metal point because the lines are fine, precise, and uniform in width. When an artist keeps the width of his lines the same everywhere, he runs the risk of making a boring image. But Matisse has avoided boredom by making lines that differ in character. There are straight lines, zigzag lines, slowly curving lines, rapidly curving lines, lines that close upon themselves, and lines that do not. Because of these differences there is considerable variety in the drawing, and the essence of each line comes through more forcefully.

By comparing the Matisse drawing with those of Vincent van Gogh and George Grosz, it is easy to see that the Matisse is different. It seems more open and airy than the van Gogh, and it is less emotional than the Grosz. The lines appear to be softer, quieter, more gentle, and delicate. That is probably caused by their thinness and curvature. On the whole, the Matisse

Plate 4-3. Henri Matisse. A Lady with a Necklace. 1936.
Pen and black ink on white paper, 21⅗" x 18".
Courtesy of the Fogg Art Museum, Harvard
University (Bequest—Meta and Paul J. Sachs).

drawing is also more decorative, which means that it possesses certain embellishments or ornamental elements. These decorative features are characteristic of Matisse, and they usually take the form of patterns in drapery, clothing, wallpaper, or floor coverings. In this case, a floral pattern appears on the woman's blouse.

By keeping some of Matisse's ideas in mind, it is possible to make some educated guesses about how he proceeded to make the drawing in Plate 4-3. He probably started by defining the large masses of the head, the draped chest, and the arms, and he must have established the axes of those parts as well as the axis of the shoulders. After that, he probably added details such as the eyes, nose, mouth, floral pattern, necklace, and so on.

ADDITIONAL EXEMPLARS

Because of the popularity of pen and ink as drawing implements, numerous reproductions of graphic work by master artists can be obtained for instruction. Among those reproductions could be the work of Raoul Dufy, Edouard Manet, Paul Klee, Pieter Brueghel, Ben Shahn, Wassily Kandinsky, Honoré Daumier, Rembrandt van Rijn, Antonio Canale (Canaletto), Saul Steinberg, and Alexander Calder.

PEN AND INK ACTIVITIES FOR THE PRIMARY GRADES (AGES 6 THROUGH 8)

Bottled ink is not suitable for the primary grades because it spills easily; children drag their hands and arms in the wet marks; and it leaves a permanent stain on clothing. Consequently, it is far better to make pen and ink drawings with ball-point pens and felt-tip pens in grades one, two, and three. Small sheets of paper, no larger than 12 x 18 inches, are also recommended.

CONCEPTS FOR POSSIBLE DEVELOPMENT

The artistic terms or concepts to be developed with pen and ink are the same as those to be built while working with pencil. The concepts listed below, however, are also worthy of development:

vacant or empty space	parallel lines	calm lines
an unfinished drawing	cartoon	quiet lines
dots	depth	active lines
decorative patterns	vague lines	hazy edges

SUGGESTED ACTIVITIES

Many of the activities recommended for pencil and crayon drawing are equally appropriate for pen and ink. The suggestions that follow are therefore not extensive.

1. When the projects discussed under pencil drawing are completed in pen and ink, you might do the following:

a) Show the children how van Gogh used dots and hundreds of short lines to fill spaces in his drawings. Urge them to do the same in some of the spaces in their drawings. Make the drawings on 9-x-12-inch paper. Use either ball-point or felt-tip pens.

b) Display the exemplar by Matisse; talk about his use of decorative patterns; and ask the children to put one or two decorative patterns in their work. Use 9-x-12-inch paper and ball-point pens.

c) Before having children draw pictures involving people (Activities 4 and 5, page 49), show them the drawing by Grosz and talk about the way he made people look funny or ugly. The drawing looks a little like a cartoon from a magazine, but it does not contain words. Explain that Grosz made cartoons when he was young. Then encourage the children to make some of their people look funny or ugly without using words in their pictures. Use 9-x-12-inch paper and ball-point pens.

2. Let us assume that your class is studying the workers in their community. Give each person about ten sheets of white drawing paper, 4½ x 6 inches in size, and ask him to draw ten people in a way that will show the different occupations of the workers. This may lead to a brief discussion about the identifying characteristics possessed by certain workers, or it might cause someone to comment on the tools and materials commonly used by such persons.

When finished, each child can place his drawings in a folder made from 9-x-12-inch colored construction paper. After stapling the edge, he has a booklet to take home. Before beginning this project, however, it might be advisable to compare the effects of a ball-point pen with the effects of a felt-tip pen. The former produces lines similar to those in the exemplar by Matisse while the latter makes heavier marks of the kind seen in a crayon drawing by Kokoschka. Let the children choose the pen they would prefer to use. Urge them to avoid large empty spaces and the appearance of an unfinished drawing. Remind them that marks made by pen are permanent and cannot be erased. Mistakes are, therefore, left on the paper, and the job of the artist is to ignore them or make the best of them. See Figure 4-1 at the beginning of the chapter.

3. Booklets of the kind mentioned in the foregoing project can be made using a variety of themes. Instead of drawing community workers, the children can make farm animals, vehicles for transportation, fish, parties, imaginary beasts, and other such things. They can make their drawings with one color or with many colors.

4. Exhibit all the exemplars of drawing. Ask if anyone can find ways in which the drawings differ. Can they find similarities? If they have difficulty finding similarities or differences, ask the following questions:

a) Which drawings are landscapes? Which are figure drawings? Are there any still-life arrangements?

b) Which drawings have lines in them that look busy, active, or alive? Which contain lines that look calm or quiet? What makes them look that way?

c) Which drawings contain lines that have soft, vague, or hazy edges? Which contain lines with sharp, hard edges?

d) Which drawings make things look natural? Which do not?

e) Which drawings look like they were made with a sharply pointed tool? Which look like they were made with a relatively blunt tool? Why?

  f) Which drawings were made with ink? How can you tell?

  g) Which drawings have depth to them? Which have only a little depth?
What makes some things look far away?

PEN AND INK ACTIVITIES FOR THE INTERMEDIATE GRADES (AGES 9 THROUGH 11)

By the time youngsters reach the fourth grade, they are capable of using reed pens, pens with nylon or metal points, and India ink in bottles. Ball-point pens and felt-tip pens continue, of course, to be useful drawing instruments, and paper no larger than 12 x 18 inches is still the preferred drawing surface.

CONCEPTS FOR POSSIBLE DEVELOPMENT

The artistic concepts to be developed with pen and ink drawing are the same as those recommended for pencil drawing. There are, however, a number of other concepts that are especially appropriate for use with pen and ink exemplars. They are listed below:

calligraphy	iron-gall ink	repetitive lines
reed pen	sepia	avant-garde artists
quill pen	bistre	art nouveau
metal point pen	prolific	German expressionism
Chinese ink	art gallery	social commentary
India ink	foreground and background	exaggeration
lampblack	content	

SUGGESTED ACTIVITIES

The activities recommended for pencil drawing are also fitting for pen and ink. There are, however, certain projects that are sufficiently different from the pencil activities to deserve special mention. They are discussed in the following paragraphs:

1. It is possible to create landscapes by drawing directly from nature or from memory or imagination. In any case, it can be educationally profitable for youngsters to see and discuss at least one exemplar of landscape drawing before they begin their work. By showing them the van Gogh, for example, it is possible to indicate that skies need not remain empty or passive. They can become full, active, and dynamic spaces if the artist chooses to make them that way. Instead of leaving the sky blank, he can draw the sun, the moon, and the stars. Or, he can indicate clouds, the movement of the wind, the direction of light, and the darkness of the heavens. He can fill the sky with dots, parallel lines, multi-directional lines, long lines, short lines, swirling lines, vertical lines, horizontal lines, or other marks too numerous to mention. By manipulating these elements in different ways, he can create skies that differ in character from one drawing to another.

As you look at the van Gogh, ask the children what the artist has done to make the tree in the foreground look alive and growing. What did he do to the hills and fields to make them look equally alive? It may help to know that vertical lines create the impression of stability, dependability, nobility, quality, and rigidness; horizontal lines suggest peacefulness, calmness, and quietness; and diagonal lines produce the feeling of speed, instability, and action. Curved, circular, and wavy lines produce the effect of softness, joyousness, effervesence, growth, and movement. Zigzag, jagged, or crisscrossing lines project the feeling of hardness, action, terror, explosiveness, and chaos. Perhaps you could ask your students to name other kinds of lines (thick, thin, light, dark, etc.) and then indicate the effect they create upon the observer.

After talking with the children, give each of them a black nylon-tip pen and some 9-x-12-inch paper, and take them outside. If there is an interesting street, field, or vacant lot nearby, ask them to draw it showing things in the foreground as well as in the background. Urge them to make use of the techniques seen in the van Gogh, but if they do not choose to do so, do not force them. Furthermore, if they hesitate to begin drawing with a pen, let them start with pencil.

If it is not possible to go outside, discuss a landscape or a scene you know they have witnessed. Then ask them to show you in their drawings what the place is like. See Figure 4-2.

Figure 4-2. *Illinois Landscape,* **by a fifth-grader.**

To obtain drawings that are not spotty, urge the children to put their lines and dots close together, and if certain areas need to be made more distinct suggest that one section be given more lines or marks than another section. This will make one area darker than another.

2. Try having the children use the van Gogh technique on underwater scenes, kitchen scenes, street scenes, vehicles, and portraits. Sometimes you can encourage them to fill all the space on their paper with lines and dots, and other times you can ask them to fill only portions of the paper. The van Gogh technique requires time and patience. Consequently, it is wise to use small paper, and to give support and praise for the effort put forth.

3. At a store that sells gardening supplies, buy a package of the reeds used to support flowers in a garden. Have students cut four or five of the reeds into seven-inch pieces with a small saw. Show them how to use a sharp pocket knife to cut the end of the reed into the shape of a pen point. If the children are to cut their own pens, make sure they are given instructions on safety and that they are carefully supervised. If you expect to make pens by yourself, plan to spend about three hours at the task. In either case, the directions for cutting the point are as follows:

a) Cut the end of the reed until it looks like Figure 4-3A from the side and Figure 4-3B from the top.

b) With a 3/32 inch drill point in a hand drill, make a hole through the pen point as shown in Figure 4-3C.

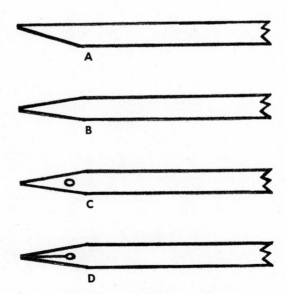

Figure 4-3. Steps in making the point of a reed pen.

c) Place the sharp edge of the knife at the point of the pen and press gently in the direction of the hole. Stop when the reed splits as far as the hole. At that point the pen is finished (see Figure 4-3D).

When the pens are complete, display the pen and ink drawing by Grosz. Describe his life and his contribution to social criticism in Germany. Explain the difference between social commentary and other forms of expression; discuss the way that Grosz made his drawings so powerful. Then ask the children to make drawings commenting on some aspect of the current social scene. One of the following topics would be suitable:

Crime	School	Automobile accidents
Pollution	Gangs	Violence in sports
Poverty	Conspicuous consumption	The cost of living
Strikes	Totalitarianism	Living conditions
Famine	War	Dull moments

If the children feel happier making a light sketch in pencil before drawing in ink, let them use pencil. Then give each of them a bottle of India ink, and let them begin. Pens with a nylon tip may also be used. See Figure 4-4.

Figure 4-4.   *Dull Moments.*

4. In our recommendations for pencil drawing, we suggest that children be given objects to draw (page 49). As a variation on that activity, we recommend that youngsters be given black nylon-tip pens and asked to draw an object at home. It might be a typewriter, an umbrella against a chair, a telephone, a desk and chair, a window with curtains, a pencil sharpener, a shoe, a tape recorder, a person, or any other object. Advise them to increase the visual richness or attractiveness of their drawings by varying the width of lines as Juan Gris did or by using dots and swirling lines as Vincent van Gogh did. Or, they might be urged to use crosshatching, parallel lines for shading, and other such elements.

5. Display all the portrait drawings, including the pen and ink portrait by Matisse. Compare the ideas about drawing that were offered by the various artists. Remember that Ingres, Gauguin, and Matisse were all inclined to use a minimum of lines. Why?

   Place special emphasis upon the ideas of Matisse. In accordance with those ideas, urge students to begin portraits of a posed classmate or family member by concentrating on the delineation of major forms. As they draw those forms, stress the importance of observing the primary directions, angles, or axes of the forms. This is especially important when drawing the figure, and it is also important to give the children information about the proportions of the figure if their questions and comments indicate that they want such information. The average proportions of the human figure are approximately as follows:

   a) The eyes are about halfway between the top of the head and the bottom of the chin.

   b) The bottom of the nose is about halfway between the eyes and the bottom of the chin.

   c) The center of the mouth is about one-third of the distance from the bottom of the nose to the bottom of the chin.

   d) The ear reaches from the level of the eyebrow to the level of the bottom of the nose.

   e) The distance between the eyes is about the width of one eye.

   f) The height of the human figure is about seven and one-half times the length of the head.

   g) The hip socket is about halfway between the top of the head and the bottom of the feet.

   h) The knee is about halfway between the hip socket and the bottom of the feet.

   i) The width of the shoulders is about equal to the width of two heads.

   j) The elbow is about halfway between the wrist and the top of the shoulder.

   k) The elbow is on the same level as the waist or belt.

   l) The length of the hand is about equal to the length of the face (not the whole head).

6. As part of their education in science, children may use microscopes. This offers the perfect opportunity to correlate science and art. Simply ask that the children study leaves, insect wings, moss, sand, and other materials under the microscope, and ask them to pay particular attention to the beauty of what they see. Then have them draw things they consider attractive. The result might be a design covering a 9-x-12-inch sheet of paper. The design could be made with reed pens and India ink. And, if color seems desirable, it could be

added with nylon-tip pens, crayons, colored pencils, or watercolor. See Lesson 3 under crayon drawings.

7. Moisten a 9-x-12-inch sheet of white drawing paper with a sponge. Touch the paper in several places with brushes full of watercolor or diluted tempera paint. The color will seem to explode in different directions on the paper, producing an accidental configuration. When the paint is dry, show the children how they can draw on top of it with pens and crayons. Then ask them to follow the same procedures and to use their pens to make the accidental shapes look more like something they experience in everyday life (flowers, crowds, pebbles, and so on). Or, the drawing can be made highly imaginery or fantastic. See Figure 4-5.

8. To combine ink drawing with chalk drawing, see page 120.

Figure 4-5. *Grasshopper.* Watercolor, ink, and crayon.

9. Try some of the foregoing activities with a felt-tipped pen instead of a reed or nylon-tipped pen. Use white drawing paper and make it larger than the sizes recommended. It could be as large as 18 x 24 inches. See Figure 4-6.

Figure 4-6.   *Making a Cake,* by a fourth-grader. Felt pen and crayon.

CHAPTER 5

CHARCOAL DRAWING

Figure 5-1.   *My Teacher,* by a second-grader.

Charcoal is one of the oldest drawing materials. Hence, it has been used extensively by professional artists, especially in creating sketches, studies, and cartoons. It has been particularly serviceable for the preparation of cartoons because it does not adhere stubbornly to the drawing surface. It can be dusted off, leaving a faint gray mark which can then be covered with watercolor, ink, or oil paint.

Although the impermanence of charcoal made it adequate or even desirable for sketches, studies, and cartoons, that same characteristic caused it to be unsuitable for finished works of art until the nineteenth century. It was then that artists discovered how to preserve their charcoal drawings by spraying them with a fixing solution (fixative). Once that discovery was made, charcoal became a popular medium for creating finished works of art. It is inexpensive, it is effective for making large drawings, and its tonal range extends from deep, rich blacks to warm, light grays.

Charcoal is made by heating thin pieces of wood in a closed container until they are thoroughly carbonized. The kind of wood that is used partially determines the hardness of the charcoal and therefore the lightness or darkness of the marks it can make.

Contemporary *compressed* charcoal, on the other hand, is different. It is similar to fabricated chalk, and it is always very black. It is made by fastening particles of carbon together under high pressure, and the result is a nongritty drawing instrument that is especially beneficial in producing broad, evenly-textured strokes.

EXEMPLARS OF CHARCOAL DRAWING

Charcoal is often used rapidly to capture fleeting impressions or to produce effects that look spontaneous. But it can also be used in a slower and more painstaking way to achieve accurate details, varied textures, and other characteristics requiring maximum control over the drawing instrument. The following exemplars illustrate these two different approaches to the use of the medium.

JEAN-BAPTISTE CAMILLE COROT (Ko-roe'), 1796–1875

Corot was perhaps the most notable French landscape painter of the nineteenth century. Yet, he began his professional life not as an artist but as an apprentice in the drapery business. In fact, he spent seven years of his life in the trade before breaking away, with parental support, to become a professional artist. The financial assistance provided by his father was unquestionably helpful because 30 years went by before Corot was able to sell a painting. His lack of success was due to the fashionable status of neoclassical figure paint-ing during the first half of the nineteenth century (see Ingres, pages 42 to 43). Corot, at the time, was engaged in the creation of small, highly poetic landscapes. Before long, however, the landscapes became extremely popular, and Corot emerged as one of the most imitated artists in history.

He drew and painted outdoors most of the time because he felt the need to see the scene he was trying to depict. This was contrary to the habits of most of his contemporaries, and it meant that he traveled widely in his quest for desirable natural settings. He went to many parts of France and Italy, and he tried to make faithful imitations of nature as he found it. But he also injected his own feelings into his work. Evidence for this can be seen in numerous landscapes which have the same mood no matter what location is represented. They are vaporous, sentimental, bathed in silvery light, and composed of delicate trees, misty fields, shimmering ponds, and young people enjoying nature. They portray life in a highly favorable light, so it may be accurate to describe them as happy, idealistic, or noble works.

As far as Corot was concerned, two elements should receive primary consideration in making a work of art. One is form, and the other is value (light and dark). Color and polish should receive secondary attention, because they add no more than charm to the work. Considering these views, it is easy to understand why Corot said that he was never in a hurry to work on details. He began by indicating the large masses and values to establish the general character of the picture. Only then did he proceed to work on refinements or subtleties of form and color.

Keeping Corot's methods in mind, it is possible to make a reasonable guess about how he drew the charcoal landscape in Plate 5-1. Probably, he started by indicating the large masses that represent the ground, the tree trunks, and the foliage. As he did so, he undoubtedly established the major areas of dark and light. Then he probably drew the limbs of the trees and finished by adding details such as individual leaves, human figures, and the boat.

The light gray portions of the foliage might have been made by applying the charcoal lightly and rubbing it with a paper stump.[1] The light figure at the right, however, was probably made by removing the charcoal with a kneaded eraser. Notice that the tree trunks and limbs have been

---

[1]A paper stump is a small, tightly rolled stick of paper. It can be purchased from an art store, or it can be made with a piece of newspaper about one inch wide and six inches long. The rubbing is done with the point of the instrument.

Plate 5-1.   Jean-Baptiste Camille Corot. *Landscape with Tree and Lake.* c. 1865. Charcoal, 14¾" x 21⅘". Copyright The Frick Collection, New York.

made with broken lines which give the impression that leaves are in front of the trunks and branches as well as behind them. The woody parts of the trees wiggle and grow thinner as they move up and away from the bases of the trees. This makes the limbs seem natural rather than artificial; additional naturalness and depth have been given to the foliage by making it vary from light to dark. If the foliage had been made with one shade of gray, the trees would seem flatter and the effect of distance would be reduced.

Lastly, it is important to consider the significance of the figures and the boat. If nothing had been drawn in that area, the picture would lack visual interest at the focal point of the whole composition, and the observer would lose a useful benchmark which helps him to judge the scale of other objects.

PAUL GAUGUIN (Go-gann'), 1848–1903

When Gauguin was three years old, his father died leaving his mother to raise three children. She took them to Peru for four years before returning to France where Paul completed his schooling. Then at the age of 17, he went to sea in the merchant marine, and in 1871 he began a twelve-year career as a stockbroker in Paris. He was very successful at the work, and before long, he was established as a well-to-do financier with a wife and five children. Two years after entering the bank, however, he began to paint in his spare time. Soon he discovered that painting meant more to him than banking or raising a family. So he gave up the life of a stockbroker; he deserted his wife and children; and he pursued his artistic interests under conditions of poverty for the rest of his life.

Gauguin knew that he was a talented artist, and he bitterly resented a society that did not appreciate his work or allow him to exist and practice his craft without money. Consequently, he traveled throughout the world in a never-ending search for inexpensive places to live where people were pure, unsophisticated, and untouched by the materialistic struggles of European life. Therefore, primitive societies were attractive, and their appeal led him to places such as Panama, Martinique, Tahiti, and to the Marquesas Islands, where he died in 1903.

Although Gauguin admired the impressionists and collected their paintings, he developed his own unique style based on a new theory of art. The theory evolved out of his association with Emile Bernard, who probably contributed a major share of the ideas upon which the hypothesis was founded.[2] The theory is called *synthetism*, and it is based on the idea that the elements of art (line, shape, texture, and color) have expressive meanings that must be taken into account in making a work of art. If they are not given sufficient attention, the synthesis of form and content, or the unification of visual structure and meaning, will be less than satisfactory.

The theory of synthetism was also founded on another principle which Herbert Read explains as follows:

> It is based on the idea that the imagination retains the essential form of things, and that this essential form is a simplification of the perceptual image. The memory only retains what is significant—in a certain sense, what is symbolic. What is retained is a "schema," a simple linear structure with the colours reduced to their prismatic purity.[3]

In other words, the essential meaning of visual experience is embedded in the artist's imagination or in his memory images. Any other meaningful material existing in the perceptual image is merely superfluous and should be disregarded in the creation of a work of art.

---

[2]Emile Bernard was an artist, but he achieved greater prominence as a critic who promoted the work of Cézanne and van Gogh.

[3]Reprinted from *The Philosophy of Modern Art* by Herbert Read, copyright 1952, by permission of the publisher, Horizon Press, New York.

As a result of the foregoing ideas, Gauguin believed that artists should not copy from nature. They should rely, instead, upon imagination as a source of visual imagery. By doing so, they stand a better chance of matching form with content, because they would not be troubling themselves with insignificant details. Naturally, these ideas led Gauguin to the creation of drawings and paintings that were different from works produced by other artists of his era. He used heavy contour lines, simplified shapes, and little or no detail. He avoided shadows, used a minimum of modeling; and employed broad, flat areas of intensified color together with bold, decorative patterns. The result was highly decorative and representational art, but it was less naturalistic than the popular art of the time.

The charcoal drawing in Plate 5-2 shows some of the salient characteristics of Gauguin's work. Details such as tear ducts, eyelashes, ear parts, individual hairs, buttons, and fingers are eliminated. The outline and the shape it describes are simple and bold. Only the slightest amount of modeling is evident, producing a relatively flat, patterned effect instead of depth and volume. Compared to the work of Ingres, the drawing is primitive, bold, crude, and unsophisticated. But those are exactly the effects that Gauguin was trying to obtain, and charcoal lends itself beautifully to the achievement of those effects.

Plate 5-2.   Paul Gauguin. *Woman of Arles.* 1888. Charcoal, Conté crayon, red crayon, white chalk; 22⅖" x 19⁷⁄₁₀". The Fine Arts Museum of San Francisco (Dr. T. Edward and Tullah Hanley Collection).

KAETHE KOLLWITZ (Koal'-vitts), 1867–1945

Kaethe Kollwitz was one of the greatest graphic artists of all time, as well as being a dedicated wife and mother. Her husband, Karl Kollwitz, was a doctor who devoted his life to helping the poor, working-class people of North Berlin. This meant that Kaethe Kollwitz was close to laborers and to their problems for most of her life, and she was pleased with that relationship. She was attracted to workmen for the first time when she was still a young girl in Köenigsberg. It was not pity or sympathy that drew her to them; it was the plain, straightforward beauty of their lives and gestures. Later, as the wife of a doctor, she became much more aware of the difficulties and tragedies that filled their lives, and she became an unrelenting champion of their cause. Indeed, the work of Kaethe Kollwitz was devoted exclusively to the common man and to the classic tragedies of his existence.

The drawing of the man in Plate 5-3 clearly expresses the weariness and despair that is so deeply felt by those who work terribly hard without hope of improving their social and economic condition. Because of its visual power and strength, the drawing communicates clearly and

Plate 5-3.   Kaethe Kollwitz. *Portrait of a Young Man.* n.d. Charcoal, 26⅜" x 20½". National Gallery of Art, Washington D.C. (Rosenwald Collection).

forcefully. It gains its power and strength from the fact that the artist has drawn the gestures or movements most intimately associated with sadness or despair, and has subordinated everything else. In other words she has eliminated all unnecessary detail, and stressed fundamental forms through the use of simple, bold, and heavy lines. The shading gives additional weight and compactness to the figure, and it makes the figure seem heavier and sadder.

To the average observer all this may seem simple and easy, but to Kaethe Kollwitz it was not. She often worked for long periods of time to get the angle of a head, the curve of a back, or the fold of a cloak just right. It is this careful attention to basic shapes and forms that makes her work so magnificent and so enduring.

ADDITIONAL EXEMPLARS

Charcoal drawings by any number of artists might be used as extra exemplars, including some or all of the following: Charles White, Jean Millet, Gustave Courbet, Edward Hopper, John Sargent, Fernand Léger, and Oskar Kokoschka.

CHARCOAL ACTIVITIES FOR THE PRIMARY GRADES (AGES 6 THROUGH 8)

Charcoal is a lot like chalk. It produces a soft, powdery line that does not adhere tightly to the drawing surface until it is sprayed with fixative. For that reason, it is not a good medium for youngsters in the primary grades. They tend to drag their hands and arms across their drawings as they work, and they are not pleased with the results. It is better, therefore, to reserve charcoal for the intermediate grades.

CHARCOAL ACTIVITIES FOR THE INTERMEDIATE GRADES (AGES 9 THROUGH 11)

Vine charcoal, compressed charcoal, and charcoal pencils are all suitable for the intermediate grades. Vine charcoal tends to fracture or shatter more easily than the other types, and it produces a rougher line that is not as evenly textured. Compressed charcoal and charcoal pencils are alike, except that the charcoal in the pencil is encased and therefore cleaner to use. It cannot be used on its side, however, which makes it less versatile than the uncased variety.

Charcoal paper is too expensive for the elementary school, but newsprint, Kraft paper, and manila drawing paper can be used satisfactorily. Paper stumps are also useful, and kneaded erasers and fixative are necessities.

CONCEPTS FOR POSSIBLE DEVELOPMENT

compressed charcoal	center of interest	synthesis of form and content
vine charcoal	simplification	flat, patterned effect
poetic landscape	mural	compact shape or figure
value	abstraction	cartoon
focal point	synthetism	highlights

SUGGESTED ACTIVITIES

Charcoal activities that work nicely with children are outlined in the paragraphs that follow, but once again it is important to remember that some of the pencil, crayon, and chalk projects can also be done in charcoal. By keeping this in mind, the teacher can widen the scope of the art program without much trouble.

1. In the spring or fall it is nice to give children a treat by taking them outside to draw. But first, it helps to give a demonstration, especially if charcoal is being used for the first time. You can indicate how to create an even tone of gray by applying the charcoal and rubbing it with a paper stump; you can show how to create light lines or spots within that tonal area by using a kneaded eraser that has been given a point or a knife edge; and you can explain how to add dark spots to give the impression of holes. Perhaps you can also show your students the Corot drawing so they can see the relationship between the demonstration and the foliage created by Corot. Explain Corot's ideas at the same time.

After the demonstration, give the class some newsprint, erasers, drawing boards, paper stumps, and vine and compressed charcoal. Let them experiment with the making of foliage, and explain that bushes and trees can be made to appear cylindrical by darkening the sides away from the source of light. Then challenge your students to make a bush or tree that seems farther away than others. This effect can be created by overlapping and making the distant object smaller, lighter, and free from strong contrasts between light and dark.

After about 15 minutes of experimentation, take the class outside to observe bushes and trees. Have them concentrate on making four or five pieces of foliage with some farther away than others. Call attention to the different values that can be seen in the foliage, and urge the inclusion of that lightness and darkness.

2. It takes many attempts before a person can become proficient at drawing charcoal landscapes. Consequently, it would be wise to repeat the previous activity more than once. And with each repetition, something new can be added to the lesson. The teacher can demonstrate how background features such as houses and land forms can be drawn before the foreground objects are drawn on top of them. He can call attention to the unique shapes of certain trees, and he can point to trunks, limbs, and twigs to show that they become thinner as they move up and away from the base of the tree. He can explain that artists do not draw everything they observe because it would make their drawings too confusing; hence, they simplify in an effort to make their drawings clear. Objects are often made bigger or smaller for the same reason, and when artists make these distortions from visual reality, we say they are creating abstractions.

3. It is common for some students to finish an art project before others. When they do, the time is opportune for the creation of a charcoal mural. It can be started by fastening a 10- to 20-foot piece of yellow, tan, white, gray, or cream-colored Kraft paper to the blackboard. The students can then be divided into groups, if necessary, and each group assigned to a three-foot segment of the mural.

If the mural is to be a landscape with land forms in the background, the first available students can sketch them lightly across the whole paper. This helps to give unity to the work. Then, as students begin to draw objects in the foreground and background, the sizes of those objects will determine the scale that other students are to follow. The things to be drawn could grow out of the charcoal projects already described. In other words, the children could use what they had learned about the drawing of foliage by putting trees and bushes in the mural. Then they could add buildings, animals, people, crops, fences, telephone poles, and other objects that might be found in a rural landscape. Listing these objects ahead of time may help.

A cityscape could also be produced. It could be done in line alone, or in solid tones of gray. Windows could be left uncolored; they could be made by erasing; or they could be made dark, depending upon the effect desired. Consider that an object in the foreground could reach from the top of the mural to the bottom, and it could overlap things in the background. It could also be made in silhouette.

Spray the mural with fixative at various stages of its construction. This will reduce the chances of spoiling parts made in the beginning, and if the students decide to paint their mural, the fixative will keep the charcoal from mixing with the paint. Be sure the room is well-ventilated when using the fixative.

Finally, discuss the finished mural with your class. Do the objects intended for the foreground appear to be in front of other things? Could the proportions of anything be changed to make it more consistent with other objects? If certain things were made lighter or darker would they be easier to separate visually? Do the dark colors come forward or recede? Why? Do they always do the same thing? Look at the Corot once again. Can anything be learned from his drawing?

4. Have your class compare the Gauguin exemplar with the drawings in pencil, crayon, and chalk. Whose work is most like the Gauguin? Is it Kokoschka's? Why? Whose work is least like the Gauguin? Ingres'? Seurat's? Rubens'? Why?

Clearly, the Gauguin is highly simplified and bold. What does this do to the woman in the drawing? Does it make her more like a fairy princess or a working woman? Why did Gauguin draw in such a simplified way, without detail or shading? Explain his reason for doing so to your class. Then give each student a sheet of 18-x-24-inch gray paper, charcoal, white chalk, and a kneaded eraser. Ask them to make a portrait of you with as few lines and as little shading as possible. Explain that the chalk is for highlights. The drawing in Figure 5-1 at the beginning of the chapter was made in response to this kind of stimulation.

5. Show your class the drawings by Kollwitz and Seurat. Call attention to the sculptural or three-dimensional nature of the figures. This is caused by the shading which moves from light to dark across the cylindrical body parts. A transition from light to shade occurs on any cylindrical object, which can be demonstrated by shining a light on a cylinder in front of the class. Then, ask a pupil to pose in a seated position on top of a table. Shine a floodlight on him, and show how to give volume to the figure by drawing with the side of a piece of compressed charcoal. If you place your fingers near one end of the stick, you will find that the marks you make are darker on one side than they are on the other. Allow the dark side to outline those portions of the body that are away from the source of light. You will see immediately that the body parts begin to look three-dimensional.

Give the class some charcoal and newsprint and ask them to draw the same figure. Forget details and concentrate on making the body look three-dimensional. Change the pose of the model two or three times, and urge that the drawings be made as large as possible on an 18-x-24-inch sheet of paper.

6. Compressed charcoal is excellent for rudimentary exercises in figure drawing. The drawings can be made on old printed newspapers, because the purpose is not to produce finished works of art. It is to help youngsters become aware of the position, size, and direction of parts of the human figure. The work goes quickly, so the pose of the model should be changed every 30 or 15 seconds. Relate the exercise to the ideas of Matisse.

7. Arrange a big still life in the middle of the room, and shine a floodlight on it. Make sure the arrangement contains objects with different shapes, textures, heights, widths, values, and patterns. Explain that artists nearly always exclude things when they draw and paint the world around them. They do so to eliminate confusion and to make their visual statements strong and clear.

Give the children some 18-x-24-inch gray paper, and ask them to make simplified drawings of the still life. Tell them that you know charcoal is a difficult material with which to work. Suggest that they stand as they draw to avoid getting their arms or sleeves in their work. Walk around the room encouraging and praising the children. Compliment them for their patience and effort, and make certain that you give equal attention to all the children.

The Corot drawing has a focal point or a center of interest. Encourage your students to produce such a focal point in their drawings by adding a little more detail or contrast to the area where they want to focus attention. Have them balance their pictures asymmetrically, and avoid dividing the paper into equal segments. See Figure 5-2.

Figure 5-2. An hour's work. Grade five.

8. Show your class the drawing by Kaethe Kollwitz and tell them about the artist and how she devoted her life to depicting the condition of poor and oppressed people. Then fasten some 1½-x-3-foot pieces of Kraft paper to the walls and blackboards of the classroom, and ask your students to make drawings of a full figure (head to foot). See if they can make the figure look sad, tired, starving, full of grief, or frightened, and discuss the things that make a person look that way (lowered head, stooped and rounded shoulders, wrinkled face, head in hands, and the like). Urge students to use the side of the compressed charcoal in the manner of Kollwitz, and see if they can give a three-dimensional appearance to the figure as well as an indication of the source of light. If it would be helpful to the children, pose for them in several tired or grief-stricken positions. See Figure 5-3.

9. A variation on the foregoing project can be created by fastening a twenty-foot piece of Kraft paper to the blackboard. Then have the class draw a long line of people waiting for food in a war torn country. Some of the people could be young and strong, some could be children, and some could be old and tired. Each child could make one of the figures in the line. Study the figures of Kollwitz before you begin. See Figure 5-3.

Figure 5-3.   One portion of a twenty-foot mural. Three feet high.

10. If there are any automobiles or trucks in the vicinity, take the class outside to draw them. Use drawing boards, 18-x-24-inch sheets of gray paper, and compressed charcoal. Ask them to create bold, strong, powerful pictures that make the vehicles look as if they were strong enough to plow through a brick wall without being dented. See Figure 5-4.

Figure 5-4.   Charcoal silhouette of an automobile.

11. To do something unusual, have your students add details to their charcoal
drawings after the drawings have been sprayed with fixative. The details
could be added with India ink and a reed pen. Use the fixative in a well-ventilated room.

CHAPTER 6

CHALK
OR PASTEL
DRAWING

Figure 6-2. A *Weird Dream.* Pastel drawing.

During the fifteenth and sixteenth centuries, natural chalk came into common use as a graphic medium. It was taken from the ground in black, white, and reddish colors, and it was sawed into sticks suitable for drawing. Toward the end of the eighteenth century, however, natural chalk became less and less popular. Its decline was caused by the invention of the pencil and by the gradual disappearance of high quality supplies. Furthermore, fabricated or synthetic chalk had been developed to the point where it was equal or superior to the natural kind.

The Conté crayon is a fabricated chalk in which the natural powder has been glued together with a fatty or greasy binder. Pastels, on the other hand, are composed of chalk and finely ground pigment pressed together with a weak, nongreasy binding agent such as gum tragacanth or methylcellulose.

Pastels were employed consistently for the first time during the early half of the eighteenth century when they were widely used in portraiture. They were popular because they produced bright, fresh lines and because they came in a variety of colors. Unlike the fragile natural chalks, pastels were relatively strong, and they could be used to color large as well as small areas. This made possible the creation of sizable drawings. Consequently, by the time of the French Revolution, it was not unusual to see pastel portraits as large as life. Drawings of such proportion were different because the older portraits in natural chalk were typically small enough to fit on a page of this size.

The disadvantage of pastels, however, has always been their susceptibility to smudging, and the only way this can be avoided is to cover the drawing with glass or to spray it with a fixing solution. It has been said that spraying tends to reduce the strength of the color, but Degas, Renoir, Redon, Cassatt, and others sprayed their work, and they still produced pastel drawings in brilliant, long-lasting color.

EXEMPLARS OF CHALK OR PASTEL DRAWING

The popularity of chalk as a drawing medium has been so great that it is especially difficult to select exemplars without omitting works of unquestionable merit. Drawings by Leonardo, Michelangelo, Raphael, and other Renaissance masters are especially conspicuous by their absence in this text, but they have not been included because children seem to prefer works that contain more color.

PETER PAUL RUBENS (Roo'-bens), 1577–1640

Peter Paul Rubens was a remarkable man. He spoke six languages fluently, and he distinguished himself both as an artist and as a Flemish diplomat.[1] In the latter capacity, he participated successfully in several important missions to Spain, France, and England, but his fame rests largely upon his artistic accomplishments.

By the time he was 21, Rubens had become a master of his trade. He opened a studio, and immediately employed apprentices to help him. In addition, his diplomatic missions and his associations with scholars and European dignitaries were immensely helpful, because he succeeded in winning a large number of commissions almost from the beginning. His lifetime output of drawings, paintings, and prints is still one of the largest in the history of art.

The enormous volume of Rubens' work can be explained in part by his long life and by the way he operated his studio. He made the preparatory sketches and cartoons for finished works of art, but his pupils and employees took over from

there. Some specialized in painting animals while others concentrated on landscapes, human figures, or other subjects. Then, when the work was nearly complete, Rubens added the finishing touches. The whole enterprise might be called an art factory. At the very least, it was one of the largest school-workshops ever developed.

The drawing in Plate 6-1 reveals the skill of a superb draftsman. It was limited to red, black, and white colors, because pastels had not been invented. Yet the figure seems surprisingly colorful and lifelike. Perhaps it could be described as warm, soft, gentle, quiet, pensive, dreamy, tender, or graceful. These qualities are part of the expressive content of the drawing. How were they achieved?

Observe the black lines. They are not heavy, straight, or angular. Instead, they are thin, supple, fluttering, fluid, and weblike, and they seem to have been made in a free and effortless manner. They give the drawing much of its expressive character. In addition, the red chalk tends to provide a great deal of warmth. This is supplemented by the relatively warm gray lines of the dress and the light tan paper. If blue, green, or violet had been used in place of the reds, tans, and grays, the total effect would have been different.

Although many of Rubens' drawings contain bold contrasts in value (light and dark), this one does not. As a result, it is less active, less dynamic, less emotional than some of his other work. It is quiet and gentle. Of course, the pose of the figure also adds to this feeling of delicacy, tenderness, and grace. The eyes seem to stare dreamily at nothing in particular, and the hands are crossed in a calm and restful manner.

Still another element that contributes to the unique expressiveness of the drawing is the shading. The white chalk on the sleeve at the left, on

---

[1] Although Rubens was born in Germany, he spent most of his life in Antwerp, the largest city in Flanders. Flanders was roughly the area now known as Belgium.

Plate 6-1. Peter Paul Rubens. *Young Woman with Crossed Hands.* 1630. Red, black, and white chalk; 18⁹⁄₁₀" x 14 ⅕". Museum Boymans-van Beuningen, Rotterdam.

the side of the head, and on the nose indicates that the source of light is to the left of the figure. A delicate but slightly darker tone of reddish chalk has been given to the front plane of the face which is turned away from the light, and the tone is strongest on the cheeks, giving them a warmish bloom. The shading gets slightly darker as it moves further toward the side away from the light, but it lightens again as it nears the right side of the face. The lightness at that point represents reflected light, and it helps to give the

figure fullness, roundness, and solidity. In like manner, the shading on the hands tends to give them direction and three-dimensional form. It is done with the hatching technique; that is, with lines placed close to each other. And the lines are carefully made to follow the contour of the hand as they move across its surface. Success with such a technique requires considerable practice, but characteristically Rubens makes it look easy. Nothing in his work ever looks labored or strained. He was indeed a master of his craft.

EDGAR DEGAS (Day-gah'), 1834–1917

It is probably correct to say that Edgar Degas was conservative in appearance and in social philosophy, but in art he was anything but unprogressive. It is true that he is often called "the last of the old masters," but that is because he made drawings and paintings that dealt with the objective world around him. It is also true that he was a great admirer of Ingres and a believer in Ingres' dictum that drawing is the foundation of all great art. But these characteristics hardly made him a conservative. Furthermore, Ingres would not have approved of Degas' work because of its numerous innovative features. The subjects of his drawings and paintings, for example, were ordinary people rather than aristocrats. He tried to portray these people as active, performing human beings who strain at their work, yawn, assume uncomplimentary poses, and collapse wearily at the end of a hard day. Or, it might be said that the figures dominating his work were captured in poses that were assumed unconsciously and momentarily by common people in the daily activities of life. This was not the kind of subject matter used by the accepted artists of the day.

Another way in which he differed from the traditional was in his use of broken color. This means that he used several colors in areas that conventionally had been made with one hue. Instead of creating faces with gradations of a single flesh color, for example, he made them with juxtaposed tones of red, yellow, blue, brown, and white. The result was one of dazzling or luminous color, which was strikingly different from the dark and comparatively drab effects found in the fashionable art of the time.

A third way in which Degas' work departed from the conventional was in the view presented to the observer. His figures were often drawn or painted from unusual angles, or they were cut in half by the frame. Depicting people from above or below was certainly not the normal procedure, and cutting off their heads, faces, legs, backs, and other body parts with the frame was equally unusual.

The unexpected angles of vision, the cropped effect produced by the cut-off figures, the bright and broken color, and his way of capturing transient characteristics are features that help to identify Degas as one of the original impressionists. The others are Monet, Renoir, Pissaro, Sisley, Berthe Morisot, and Bazille. They were interested in presenting their momentary impressions of the effects of natural light on objects, but their use of broken color in obtaining such effects was responsible for making the form of the objects slightly vague.

Despite the foregoing similarities, Degas was different from his fellow impressionists. They often worked outdoors while Degas worked almost exclusively in his studio. He made sketches and photographs outside on certain occasions, but he went indoors to develop the notations into finished works of art. He did so because he felt that art was a product of the imagination and not a copy of nature. He believed that the artist had to falsify what he saw to make other persons see what he wanted them to see.

Degas began using pastels in 1881, and in the 36 years that followed, he produced the drawings that earned him his reputation as one of the supreme masters of the pastel medium. An example of his work can be seen in Plate 6-2. It shows ballet dancers adjusting their costumes prior to going on stage. The rich, shimmering, and iridescent colors were achieved by placing different hues next to each other in a given tonal area. In the blue dress at the left, for example, the artist used light blue, dark blue, green, dull orange, black, and yellow. The technique may seem easy, but those who attempt it are likely to find that the first layer of color mixes with layers placed on top, and that makes it difficult to achieve the rich coloration evident in Plate 6-2. Degas did it by spraying the first layer of color with a fixing solution which held the pigment in place. Subsequent layers of color were then added without disturbing the first. And, by keeping his strokes separate, he allowed the colors underneath to show through.

Notice that the view of the dancers is from above and that the figure on the left is partially cut off by the frame. Notice also how the broken color tends to soften the edges of the forms and make them less distinct. Degas, at this stage in his life, was nearly blind. Consequently, he did not concern himself with details and with sharp definition of form. He concentrated instead on the richness of color relationships. Therefore, it is not surprising to find that the only modeling in the drawing occurs on the arms and faces and that the hues in the background do not describe forms; they simply enhance the coloration of the total picture.

Finally, it is interesting that observers occasionally describe Degas' work as spontaneous. In all likelihood they do so because the drawing appears to have been done in a free and inexact manner. However, Degas himself said, "No art is less spontaneous than mine." If it looks spontaneous, it is probably because the artist deliberately tried to make it look that way. In other words, it is a case of studied spontaneity.

Plate 6-2.   Edgar Degas. *The Dancers.* 1899. Pastel. 24½" x 25½". The Toledo Museum of Art.

ODILON REDON (Rey-don'), 1840–1916

Although Redon was a contemporary of the impressionists, the postimpressionists, and the cubists, he followed his own instincts and produced an art form that was both original and influential. Unlike other artists of his time, he tended to emphasize his own inner reality instead of the reality of external objects and events. In other words, he consciously allowed his own subjective feelings, intuitions, and dreams to affect his work and to be captured in it. This suggests that he was similar to the artists of our own era, and, of course, he was. He was ahead of his time.

Redon believed that there were three influential factors that combined to produce a work of art. The first was the artistic tradition, which no artist could fail to observe and feel. The second was nature or objective reality, and the third was personal inventiveness or the inner spirit of the artist. Redon also believed that there were certain universal laws of life or nature, and he felt that works of art should be organized in accordance with those laws if the art were to be visually bearable. Today we know that shells, honeycombs, skeletons, and other natural objects are structurally arranged according to certain natural laws, but Redon sensed the truth long before it was revealed by science. And he came to the logical conclusion that art must be put together with the same basic proportions or relationships if it is to be as appealing as nature. The idea is certainly persuasive.[2]

On at least one occasion, Redon was asked if he went to his easel with a predetermined concept to present in his work. He refused to answer the question, but his writing suggests that an artist might conceivably begin with such a concept. According to Redon, however, a sensitive artist would still respond to the medium and to the image as it develops, and he would alter his original goal or concept accordingly. This is the kind of statement that might be uttered by an artist of our own generation.

Redon produced a large number of lithographic prints, charcoal drawings, pastel drawings, and paintings. Plate 6-3 is an example of his work in pastels. It has the mysterious, dreamy quality so characteristic of his drawings, and it contains flowers and human figures which he used again and again as subject matter. The mysterious nature of the work is probably caused by the absence of clearly defined forms, the lack of detail, and the vagueness of the heads in the upper corners. In other drawings, he produced even more of a dreamy or supernatural effect by depicting unrecognizable objects or by placing familiar objects in unnatural surroundings. He seems to have let his drawings grow and unfold with the flow of his imagination and with his intuitive response to the medium.

Redon loved black, and he used it with great effectiveness. In this instance, it enhances the other colors in the drawing; it makes them sparkle as if they were jewels. Apparently, Redon perceived forms as sparkling or vibrating areas of color rather than as immobile shapes with clearly defined outlines. His teachers at the School of Fine Arts in Paris, however, did not appreciate the uniqueness of his perceptual abilities, and they urged him to adopt their methods of outlining and modeling. But Redon did not do so. He remained independent and true to his own convictions. As a result, we are able to enjoy drawings, such as the one in Plate 6-3, that are almost totally free from outlines and traditional shading and modeling.

ADDITIONAL EXEMPLARS

It would be helpful to show and discuss chalk and pastel drawings by artists such as Jean

---

[2]For a view that is remarkably similar, see Herbert Read, *Education Through Art* (New York: Pantheon Books, Inc., 1958), Chapter 2.

Antoine Watteau, Thomas Gainsborough, August Renoir, Alfred Sisley, Philip Evergood, Mary Cassatt, Michelangelo, Henri de Toulouse-Lautrec, Francois Boucher, and Edvard Munch.

Plate 6-3.   Odilon Redon. *Flowers.* n.d. Pastel, 24" x 17¾". The Solomon R. Guggenheim Museum, New York. Photo credit: Robert E. Mates.

CHALK ACTIVITIES FOR THE PRIMARY GRADES (AGES 6 THROUGH 8)

Chalk is not the best drawing material to use in the primary grades. It smudges if touched, and it sticks to anything that comes in contact with it. This means that little children often spoil their drawings accidentally, and they get themselves covered with chalk, because they have a hard time keeping their hands and arms off their drawings.

However, there is one good chalk activity for the primary grades; it is blackboard drawing. Simply set aside a section of the blackboard that children can use whenever they have time. White and colored chalk, made especially for blackboards, should always be available together with erasers and sponges. The children can work on their drawings individually or in small groups, and they can relate their drawings to the seasons, the holidays, or the materials studied in class. To do this in an orderly fashion, it is best to make a schedule for the drawings on a monthly basis.

CHALK ACTIVITIES FOR THE INTERMEDIATE GRADES (AGES 9 THROUGH 11)

The best chalk for the elementary school is high quality chalk. The inferior type, although inexpensive, is costly in the long run. It is gritty, powdery, easy to break, and weak in color. This means that it is less appealing and more difficult to use.

Sometimes, children find paper stumps to be helpful in making flat, even tones of color. A paper stump is a stiff rod of tightly rolled paper. It can be purchased from art supply houses, or it can be made by rolling a 1-x-6-inch piece of newspaper into the shape of a solid stick. By rubbing the freshly applied chalk with one end of the stick an even tone is obtained, and the chalk adheres more satisfactorily to the paper. No amount of rubbing, however, will keep chalk from coming off. That can be prevented only by treating the finished product with a fixing solution that glues the chalk to the drawing surface. Such a solution can be purchased, or it can be made by mixing equal parts of white shellac and alcohol. The mixture is sprayed on the finished drawing with an ordinary fly sprayer. Do the spraying in a well-ventilated room.

CONCEPTS FOR POSSIBLE DEVELOPMENT

While developing an understanding of the following terms, the teacher will find that he can also teach the concepts associated with pencil, crayon, and charcoal drawing.

natural chalk	fixative	smudging
fabricated chalk	reflected light	artist's apprentice
pastels	impressionism	supple lines
binder	medium	cropped effect
hatching technique	broken color	objective reality
subjective reality		

SUGGESTED ACTIVITIES

Several crayon activities can also be done in chalk, but the result will be different. Crayons, especially oil crayons, produce a thick, heavy, solid, opaque mark, while chalk makes a softer line that is frequently open textured. The activities described in the following paragraphs are especially suitable for chalk:

1. Display the chalk drawing by Degas. Explain the purpose of impressionism, and call attention to the use and effect of broken color in the exemplar. Describe the way Degas produced broken color, and demonstrate his technique. To do so, bring to class a drawing that has been given one layer of color and a coating of fixative. Then show how a second layer of color is applied on top of the first, using the hatching technique (short marks with spaces between them). Then spray the drawing once again with fixative. And, if you have time, show what happens when one layer of color is placed on top of another without a coating of fixative between them. The two colors will mix, and the vibrating effect so evident in Degas' work will be missing.

   After your demonstration, give the class some colored construction paper (18 x 24 inches) and pastels. Ask them to try the Degas technique as they draw one of the colorful still-life arrangements that you have already prepared. When the first layer of color has been applied to all parts of their drawings, the work can be stopped, and the drawings can be sprayed with fixative. On the following day, the children can apply a second layer of color, using the hatching method; they can spray the drawing again; and they can continue until they are satisfied that enough layers of color have been applied.

   Clearly, a still life is not the only subject that can be used in this project. Portraits, landscapes, animals, sporting events, buildings, portions of the classroom, and many other topics are suitable, but it is advisable to urge the children to make their objects large rather than small. Small shapes are difficult for children to delineate with chalk. Landscapes can also be troublesome, unless they contain large elements such as buildings, trees, fences, telephone poles, or people. A wheat field or a seascape frequently does not have enough in it to make it visually interesting when drawn by a child. See Figure 6-1.

2. Display the drawing by Rubens and talk about its singular qualities in much the same way that they have been discussed in this text. Give each student a piece of 18-x-24-inch gray drawing paper and pieces of white, reddish brown, and black chalk. Then ask them to draw a portrait of a fellow student whom you have asked to pose in a white, frilly blouse with a ribbon in her hair. Urge the students to combine colors, to include highlights and shaded areas, and to show reflected light. See if they can capture some of the girlishness in the model. But, if some students naturally produce drawings that are harsh or crude, accept those characteristics and make suggestions, if any, that help the students to maintain the same style throughout their drawings.

Figure 6-1.   The hatching strokes and broken color add considerable richness to this drawing by a fifth-grader.

3. When we say that an artist deals with objective reality, we mean that she depicts objects and events that we can recognize as parts of our environment, and presents them in a way that may or may not be naturalistic. In other words, she represents objects and events in a fashion similar to the way we perceive them. She may depict them in a highly naturalistic or photographic manner, or she may offer them in a more abstract form by distorting them.

　　The artist who deals with subjective reality, on the other hand, is a person who presents visions of the inner life. This means that she deals with figments of the imagination, dreams, emotions, and sensations. The content of these experiences is no less real than the things we experience outside the human body, but it is extremely personal or idiosyncratic. Consequently, we speak of such aspects of reality as being subjective.

　　Confusion can arise easily when discussing objective or subjective reality in art because it is possible to combine both dimensions of reality in one product, and it is difficult to tell if certain works of art are concerned with objective reality, subjective reality, or a combination of the two. When an artist deals with nothing except nonrepresentational line, shape, color, and texture, for example, we might say that the medium is the message, and it is difficult to tell whether such content is objective or subjective.

　　Unfortunately, most people have been trained to believe that the only good art is the kind that deals with objective reality. As a result, they teach their children to value naturalistic art at the expense of work devoted to dreams, fantasies, emotions, sensations, and imaginative topics of all kinds. This means, for example that they probably teach their children to value the work of Rubens and Degas over the art of Redon, because Redon frequently presented subjective reality in his work. To build such restrictive values, however, is to deprive children of the opportunity to learn about the subjective realm of life. And the child who fails to understand and appreciate the inner world of dreams, fantasies, and so on is likely to be less humanistic than we would prefer him to be because he lacks some of the knowledge that makes a human being different from the lower animals, insects, and machines.

Display the exemplars by Rubens, Degas, and Redon, and discuss the characteristics that make the Redon appear to be based on subjective reality. It looks dreamy, mysterious, or other-worldly. At least it does not appear to be a representation of objects and events as they occur in the environment. But, why does it appear that way? Is it because the forms are vague and imprecise? Is it because the recognizable forms are not arranged in the way we ordinarily perceive them? Could the artist have done anything to make the work seem even more subjective or more inwardly oriented?

After completing your discussion, suggest a topic for students to manipulate in their drawings, and talk with them about it. Perhaps one of the following would be suitable:

Paradise	Vision from closed eyes
Feelings of despair	The mind
A vision of impending disaster	Tension
Thoughts of bygone days	Soaring spirits
A crazy dream	Wishful thinking

Urge your class to use lines and colors that will contribute to the particular subjective idea or mood the students are trying to convey. What could be done with color to create the appearance of weirdness, peacefulness, anxiety, or vitality? Would contrast, brightness, dullness, lightness, or darkness in the color of the work have any effect on the meaning it conveys? Look at the exemplars. How has color contributed to their impact upon you? Compare the Rubens and the Redon. How do lines contribute to the concepts and emotions expressed by each of them? Are lines necessary? See Activity 6 under crayon drawing and Activity 1 under pen and ink drawing.

In this instance, ask your class to work in the manner of Redon (except that they may use more lines if they wish). Urge them to draw their objects large and to overlap them. This will improve the composition of their work. If 18-x-24-inch paper seems too large, use 12-x-18-inch paper. Black or colored construction paper is excellent for this activity. Let the students begin with pencil if they wish. See Figure 6-2 at the beginning of the chapter.

4. Try the foregoing activity, but instead of having students work in the manner of Redon, have them use the hatching technique employed by Degas. To provide variety and contrast, however, recommend that some parts of the drawing be filled with solid color. See Figure 6-3. Then write the following suggestions on the blackboard:

a) Make a list of all the objects that could appear in your drawing, and indicate which ones are most important for conveying the meaning you have in mind.

b) Make a quick pencil study on scrap paper to help you clarify the organization of your drawing. Remember that the objects in a subjective drawing need not be arranged in a natural way.

c) Make your objects large to avoid spottiness.

d) Make some objects larger than others to produce variety and to emphasize the elements that convey your meaning most effectively.

e) Overlap the objects to avoid spottiness and to avoid the boring effect of having all of the objects against a flat, plain background.

f) Arrange the objects in a way that will make the observer's eye move from place to place through the drawing.

g) Transfer the pencil study to colored construction paper; do it very lightly. Begin drawing in chalk.

h) When one color area is finished, spray it with fixative and begin another. Continue until finished. Spray in a well-ventilated area.

Figure 6-3.   A *Vision from Closed Eyes.*

5. Sometimes, chalk drawing is offensive to teachers because chalk dust gets on floors, desks, and clothing. This can be reduced by drawing on wet or moist paper. Gray bogus paper and colored construction paper are both good for this purpose. Soak the paper in a sink full of water prior to drawing, or wet the paper with sponges. Make sure that both sides of the paper get wet, and remember that a place will be needed to store wet drawings without placing them on top of each other.

While the 12-x-18-inch paper is soaking, display the pencil drawing by Gris, the pen and ink drawing by Matisse, the crayon drawing by Kokoschka, and the chalk drawing by Rubens. Explain that the kind of line an artist uses will determine much of the meaning communicated by his drawing. Call attention to the hard, precise, controlled, mechanical nature of the drawing by Gris. Compare it with the soft, spontaneous, and decorative work of Matisse and Rubens. See if the children can find the rough, active, loud, and exuberant drawing in the group (the Kokoschka), and see if they can detect the effect that color has on the mood of a drawing. How does it contribute to the mood or temper of the Rubens, for example?

After the discussion, distribute the wet paper and pastels, and ask your class to draw a few of the faces in a crowd. The crowd could be angry, cheerful, tired, or frightened, and the students could use colors that would help to establish one of those moods. Have them begin by drawing large head shapes

Figure 6-4. Pastel with ink added.

with the sides of their pastels. Then they can add hair and facial features little by little, being careful not to add too much. As they add such things, remind them that the lines they use can contribute further to the mood or meaningfulness of their drawings. When the work is finished and dry, discuss the results. What could be done to improve the drawings?

6. Consider the possibility of combining chalk with another medium. When the foregoing project is dry, for example, students could draw on top of the chalk with crayons, felt pens, or with India ink and reed pens. The class might also begin a flower garden by creating amorphous color areas with chalk on wet paper. Then, when the drawings are dry, they might draw over the flowers with ink to add detail and to define the shapes more clearly. See Figure 6-4.

7. Discuss the exemplar by Redon, putting special emphasis on the way Redon created mysterious and other-worldly effects in his work. Did he create these effects occasionally by making his figures vague? See if your students can create similar effects in drawing a face on a 12-x-18-inch piece of wet colored construction paper. Try having them begin with a vague shape not unlike a doodle. Then they can add subtle lines and colors to suggest a face. When the drawings are dry, assemble them and discuss the results.

CHAPTER 7

BRUSH DRAWING

Figure 7-2.   *Still Life.*

Brushes are used for both drawing and painting. As a result, confusion often arises about the difference between these two modes of expression. Sometimes it is difficult, if not impossible, to distinguish one from the other, but in general, brush drawing is more linear than painting, and is usually more limited in color.

Brush drawings can be made with a variety of liquids, and they can be produced on almost any surface. The most popular of the liquid mediums, however, has always been ink, and it has been used most frequently on absorbent surfaces such as paper. The artist can use carbon black, sometimes called Chinese ink, or he can use iron-gall, sepia, bistre, or a wide assortment of other colored products. For further information about these liquids see page 78.

Brushes can be flat or round, blunt or pointed, and they can be made of different kinds of hair. The type of brush determines the kinds of lines and textures that can be made. And, compared to the pen, a good brush is extremely versatile because its springy character permits making highly variable lines. By applying pressure to the instrument, for example, the artist can make a heavy, wide line, and by releasing that pressure, he can make the mark thinner. An open-textured or speckled line can be produced by removing most of the ink from the brush before dragging the instrument across the surface of the paper. This is known as the dry-brush technique.

Like ink and brushes, paper has been around for a long time. It was invented in 105 A.D. when T'sai-Lun, a Chinese officer of the Imperial Guard, discovered a substitute for silk, which had previously been used as a surface for painting and writing. The new paper was made from bark, linen waste, fishing nets, and old rags. The art of making the paper spread quickly throughout China, but it was kept a national secret until the eighth century. During that time, the basic process remained the same, but ingredients such as bamboo, moss, cocoons, and stalks of corn and rice were substituted for T'sai-Lun's original materials.

Paper became known outside China in the eighth century when Arabs at Samarkand learned the process of making the substance from captured Chinese craftsmen. The Arabs carried the knowledge to Baghdad, Mecca, Egypt, Morocco, and by the twelfth century to Spain. Although paper mills were erected in Italy as early as 1276, the product was not used extensively in Europe until the fifteenth century, when printed books and engravings came into being.

EXEMPLARS OF BRUSH DRAWING

Almost all artists have engaged in brush drawing, but the Chinese are considered to be masters of the process. After all, they were the inventors of ink, paper, and brushes, and they have had hundreds of years to perfect the tools and techniques of the craft.

MU CH'I (Moo Chee), 1210–1275

Each Chinese artist has several names, one of which is his *hao* or pen name. Mu Ch'i is the *hao* for Fa Ch'ang. Unfortunately, little is known about Mu Ch'i, but he lived during the Sung Dy-

nasty, and was active as an artist between 1210 and 1275 A.D..

Mu Ch'i's works were not appreciated by the Chinese during his lifetime, but they were highly valued by the Japanese. This is why his drawings are found in Japanese collections. Apparently, one of the reasons for the lack of appreciation on the part of his countrymen was that he did not belong to the Academy, nor did he paint in the conservative academic style. Today, however, he is considered to be one of the great Ch'an artists.

The Ch'an, or "contemplation," sect of Buddhism is better known as Zen, and the beliefs of that sect greatly influenced the Ch'an artists. Long periods of intense meditation supposedly prepared the Ch'an artists to sense Buddha inhabiting all natural objects including themselves. Each object, whether animate or inanimate, was then interpreted by the artist as a living thing. In the small album piece called *The Six Persimmons*, for example, the fruit seems to have an inner life (Plate 7-1). Each persimmon is different from the others in its own subtle way. It may be different in shape, tone, or placement on the paper. But whatever the difference, each fruit has its own identity or its own life.

In addition to presenting subject matter as the embodiment of Buddha, the Ch'an artists produced other identifying characteristics in their work. One of those traits is an emphasis on rapid calligraphiclike brush strokes which are sometimes called "ink splashes." And, because of these brush strokes, the style of the Ch'an artist is said to be "spontaneous." It is different from the mannerisms of other Chinese artists, just as the

work of one dynasty is different from that of another. But traditional characteristics are still present in all Chinese art. The way in which time and space are represented, for example, is one conventional trait, while subject matter is another.

Although scientific perspective had been used by a Chinese artist as early as the fourth century, the Chinese did not consider it to be appropriate for the representation of three-dimensional space. Scientific perspective is based on a fixed point of view, and, according to Chinese artists, a fixed view did not allow their drawings to move and change for the observer. Furthermore, Chinese works of art were not an end, but a means to an end; they were meant to serve as a vehicle for the observer's meditation. To allow for such periods of thought on the part of the observer, the artist carefully organized the positive and negative space (or the objects and empty areas) in his drawings. In his landscapes, he divided the picture surface into three separate

Plate 7-1.   Mu Ch'i. *The Six Persimmons.* n.d. Brush and ink, 11" x 13". Courtesy of Nanrei S. Kobori, Kyoto, Japan.

sections, each of which contained objects or land forms, and all of the sections were drawn from the same angle of vision. As a result, the observer's eye passes from one positive area through a negative space, or interval, to the second positive area, and continues through the drawing. The interval between objects, or the negative space, allows the observer's imagination to soar. This is evident, to a small extent perhaps, in the still-life drawing by Mu Ch'i. Each persimmon has been carefully placed to create varying intervals or voids between the pieces of fruit, and these intervals allow the observer's eye to rest while his mind begins to work.

Two other traditional artistic devices, isolation and the "law of five," were also used by Chinese artists to create interesting effects.[1] Isolation, or the separation of an object from a group, allowed the artist to point out the importance of selected forms. In *The Six Persimmons*, for example, Mu Ch'i has isolated the smallest piece of fruit. It has been placed below the horizontal row formed by the other five persimmons. Our attention is drawn to this particular fruit because of its placement and isolation. If it were not placed there, our eyes might remain on the largest, darkest fruit in the middle of the row. Furthermore, the two fruits on the right and left of the darkest persimmon have been made to overlap. Overlapping was restricted to minor forms so the important figure or figures could be left alone to capture our attention.

The "law of five" originated with the idea that people are unable to grasp visually more than five things at once. In most Chinese works of art, the five items were divided into groups of two and three, and in Plate 7-1, the five fruits in the horizontal row have been arranged that way. When using such a device, the artist was compelled to say much with little. The meaning had

to be conveyed simply and clearly with a few forms and with the help of intervals or voids.

Another major characteristic of traditional Chinese art is the nature of the subject matter. The Chinese valued orderliness, simplicity, and quiet more than loud, active, displays of emotion. Consequently, there is no violence, brutality, or ugliness represented in their art. In describing their work, one author says, "Keep everything quiet; never shout but whisper your emotions."[2] In other words, the Chinese whispered their emotions through drawings of landscapes, animals, and plants.

REMBRANDT VAN RIJN (Rem'-brant van Rine), 1606–1669

Rembrandt was the eighth of nine children born to Harmen and Neeltje van Rijn. His father was a miller, and the family lived near the Rhine River. His full name was Rembrandt Harmenszoon van Rijn, which means that he was Rembrandt, son of Harmen of the Rhine. At the age of 15, Rembrandt was apprenticed to an architectural painter, Jacob Isacszoon van Swanenburgh. He also studied with Pieter Lastmen and Jacob Pynas, and it is interesting to note that his artistic training, in certain respects, was similar to that of Mu Ch'i. He was required to copy or imitate old masters and "borrow" their ideas.

From the age of 19, however, Rembrandt worked independently. In 1631, he went to Amsterdam, which had become the economic, cultural, and artistic center of the northern countries. Three years later, he met and married Saskia van Uylenburgh, a woman whose social rank was much higher than his own. For about ten years after the marriage, he sold a number of paintings, and lived a life of luxury. But his wealth never seemed to affect his behavior or his appearance. In fact, he often looked untidy because he continued to wipe brushes on his clothes while painting.

Unfortunately, Rembrandt was not interested in financial matters. Consequently, he

---

[1]George Rowley, *Principles of Chinese Painting*, (Princeton, N.J.: Princeton University Press, 1947), p. 55.

[2]*Ibid.*, p. 17.

spent beyond his means and soon found himself deeply in debt. Therefore, in 1658, all his possessions, including his house, were auctioned away in an effort to settle his financial affairs, and he died 11 years later without enough money to pay for his own burial.

Although Rembrandt was penniless when he died, he was never poor in spirit or in creativity. Dutch painters, as a group, were experts in making landscapes and portraits, but Rembrandt was much more versatile. Biblical stories, portraits, animals, landscapes, and everyday events all served as subjects for his art, and he occasionally used his wife Saskia or another member of the household as a model. The figure in Plate 7-2 is thought to be Hendrickje Stoffels, the young girl who took care of Rembrandt's son after the death of his wife.

Although Rembrandt was an excellent painter, he was equally good as a printmaker and draftsman. Early in his career, he established a pattern that he followed for the rest of his life. Once he had decided upon a theme, he drew it, etched it, and painted it. Sometimes the order was reversed, but habitually he explored all three modes of expression in dealing with each of his subjects. It is also interesting to note that although Rembrandt made a practice of signing and dating his paintings and etchings, only two dozen of the two thousand drawings attributed to him bear his signature. Some people believe that the drawings were meant for his own personal use, and for that reason they did not need a signature. They were carefully arranged in portfolios according to subject matter and stored in the artist's studio. Art historians believe that these particular drawings were not all made as preparatory studies for future paintings or etchings, but were made to satisfy an insatiable urge to record what he saw. At times, the urge to record caused Rembrandt to make drawings on any material at hand, including bills, funeral announcements, and printed pages. But the majority of his drawings were done on a grainy white paper which he occasionally tinted with a grayish or brownish wash. Probably the brush was his

Plate 7-2.   Rembrandt van Rijn. A *Girl Sleeping*. 1655. Brush and sepia, 9" x 8". Courtesy of The British Museum.

favorite drawing instrument during the later years of his life.

Many characteristics of Rembrandt's mature style can be found in the small drawing of Hendrickje (Plate 7-2), which was done around 1655. It was rapidly sketched, like all his drawings, and it was made with a minimum of line and little or no detail. This indicates that he concentrated largely on the essential aspects of form after 1640, and he did so without a loss of warmth or intimacy. Without a doubt, part of his success can be attributed to the sensitivity with which he handled linear elements. In A *Girl Sleeping*, for example, he varied his lines from thick to thin and from heavy to soft. The heavy lines were made with a brush that had been loaded with bistre, while the soft, open-textured lines were probably made with a dry brush.

It has also been said that Rembrandt often created shadows by rubbing his finger over the ink while it was still wet.[3] Perhaps this was done in the upper left-hand corner of the exemplar. At any rate, the darkness in that area helps to produce the atmospheric effect frequently found in Rembrandt's work. Apparently, the artist as a young man had been influenced by the elaborate contrasts of light and dark in Baroque paintings by Caravaggio. But the lighting in such paintings fell on the major figure in much the same way as a spotlight falls on the main character in a theatrical production. Rembrandt did not want that effect. He wanted a light and dark pattern that would produce an atmosphere more common to the real world, and he achieved that effect in *A Girl Sleeping*. The girl does not appear to be on stage but in the privacy of her home, and she looks that way because the artist created a minimum of darkness in the upper left-hand corner while allowing large amounts of white, unpainted paper to give the effect of light. The small amount of darkness, the empty space, and the open-textured lines combine to make a soft, dreamy, mysterious atmosphere.

FERNAND LÉGER (Lay-zhay'), 1881–1955

Léger, a Frenchman, was five feet seven inches tall with reddish hair, broad shoulders, and a stocky appearance. He was raised on a cattle farm, and as a young boy was not especially interested in art. But, at the age of 16, he made his first sculpture, and three years later he enrolled as an art student. From that time until his death, he was committed to art. He entered his red-floored studio each day at 6:30 A.M. and worked at least until noon. He did not believe that one should sit and wait for inspiration to strike, but he felt that it should come through working hard.

Although there are parallels between the training of Mu Ch'i, Rembrandt, and Léger, the

similarities between the last two are more pronounced. Both Rembrandt and Léger studied with a master painter interested in architecture as subject matter. And between 1914 and 1917, while working as a stretcher bearer in World War I, Léger became fascinated by the mechanical forms of military equipment. This fascination, plus his previous background in architectural delineation, culminated in several early drawings of magnified machine parts. As a result, Léger is said to be the first painter to interpret industrial civilization.

A second similarity between Léger and Rembrandt is the manner in which they worked. Both would select a theme and proceed to make many drawings and paintings of the topic. But Léger did not work on as many themes or subjects, despite the fact that he lived to be eleven years older than the Dutch artist. He did, however, express himself in more media than Rembrandt. He made drawings, paintings, murals, mosaics, and films as well as illustrations for books, sets for plays, costumes for the ballet, and stained glass for architectural settings.

In all of Léger's work, there are certain characteristics that clearly serve as the stamp of the artist. These unique qualities are simplicity, shallow space, and magnification. His architectural training can account for the first and second characteristics while magnification is probably a result of his interest in the techniques of motion pictures. Each of the characteristics can be found in the drawing entitled *Face and Hands* (Plate 7-3). At first glance, one might dismiss the work as being quickly and easily done. But rejections should not be based upon the amount of real or apparent effort involved. They should be determined by the quality or the worthiness of the art, and surely the Léger drawing is low neither in quality nor value. It is a beautiful, bold, and powerfully delineated piece, because the head and hands were made with simple, heavy, black lines which vary subtly from thick to thin. In addition, there is no shading, no texture, and no unnecessary detail which might detract from the fundamentals of the image. After

[3]Otto Benesch, *Rembrandt, Selected Drawings* (London: Phaidon Press, Ltd., 1947), p. 13.

Plate 7-3.   Fernand Léger. *Face and Hands*. 1952. Brush and ink, 26" x 19¾". Collection, The Museum of Modern Art, New York (Mrs. Wendell T. Bush Fund).

carefully divided with lines to form shapes that fit together like pieces in a jig-saw puzzle. Although certain shapes were repeated to unify the composition of the drawing, no two forms are exactly the same size. The circular shapes in the necklace, for example, were repeated on a smaller scale in the eye, the fingernails, and the bracelet. The shape of the upper eyelid was repeated in the lower lip. And certain linear qualities were also reproduced again and again with sufficient variation. The wavyness of the hair was repeated in the bracelets, the nose, and the lip, and again in the line extending upward from the hand on the left. The semicircular arch of the eyebrow was also reproduced in the eye, the mouth, and the outer curve of the left hand.

Among the three exemplars of brush drawing, *Face and Hands* is the largest. It measures 26 x 19¾ inches, which means that the face and hands have been magnified to almost twice their normal size. The drawing by Rembrandt, on the other hand, is very small; the sleeping girl is much tinier than she was in reality. Clearly, her size has a lot to do with the total effect created by the work. Bigness suggests power, and smallness suggests weakness. What other qualities do bigness and smallness convey?

all, Léger and Rembrandt were both interested in the essential or basic aspects of visual form. Consequently, they eliminated whatever was superfluous.

Unlike Rembrandt, Léger placed his forms in a relatively shallow space which he called an "animated landscape."[4] The shallow space was

---

[4]Robert L. Herbert, "Léger," *Encyclopedia of World Art*, 1946, IX, p. 198.

ADDITIONAL EXEMPLARS

To expose youngsters to other brush drawings, try showing them the work of Stuart Davis, Jean Fragonard, Anthony Van Dyck, Eugéne Delacroix, Théodore Géricault, Francisco Goya, Edouard Manet, and Honoré Daumier.

BRUSH ACTIVITIES FOR THE PRIMARY GRADES (AGES 6 THROUGH 8)

Unfortunately, brush drawing is rarely seen in the elementary schools, but it is one of the easiest and most impressive art activities children can undertake. It makes a good introduction to painting, and it gives the primary teacher an opportunity to cover the fundamentals of working with brushes.

CONCEPTS FOR POSSIBLE DEVELOPMENT

The artistic terms or concepts listed below can be developed through the brush activities that follow:

line	strong lines	magnify	portrait
thick	powerful lines	model	self-portrait
thin	bold lines	larger than life	

SUGGESTED ACTIVITIES

Suitable activities for the primary grades are listed below:

1. Léger frequently magnified or enlarged faces, hands, bodies, machinery, and other everyday objects. After examining the Léger drawing and discussing its size with your students, have them make large, simple, powerful drawings of birds, tools, vegetables, shoes, or any other small object. They will need ¼-inch bristle brushes, black opaque tempera paint, and 18-x-24-inch sheets of paper. Perhaps it will be easiest for them to work on the floor.

2. Ask the children to imagine how activities such as hopscotch, leapfrog, roller-skating, jumping rope, and batting a ball would look if they were drawn larger than usual. Use the Léger drawing to illustrate how things look different when they are made larger than normal, and have the children make big brush drawings of one of the above topics on a piece of colored Kraft paper (36 x 48 inches). Instead of using black tempera, the children may enjoy drawing with opaque white tempera and a ½-inch bristle brush. Be sure to select colored paper that will contrast with the white tempera paint.

3. Another activity that can evolve from a discussion of *Face and Hands* by Léger is that of using a large sheet of white paper (18 x 24 inches), a ½-inch or a ¼-inch bristle brush, and opaque black tempera to make a large, bold self-portrait including at least one hand. In a discussion of the drawing by Léger, have the children talk about facial features and details. The shape and placement of those features is especially important to point out, and a small cosmetic mirror for each child will permit the youngsters to visualize themselves more easily. See Figure 7-1.

Figure 7-1.   *Self-Portrait.*

4. A highly enjoyable and amusing activity is to make large brush drawings of all the teachers in the school. Arrange to have your students visit the teachers before and after school to make small pencil sketches. Then give them some 18-x-24-inch white paper, some ¼-inch bristle brushes, and some black tempera and let them transform their sketches into big brush drawings. When finished, hang them in the hallway with the names of the teachers attached to them.

5. Show your students the Rembrandt drawing; emphasize the title of the work; and talk with the children about beds, bedrooms, and sleeping. Discuss the appearance of different bedrooms, the width and height of different beds, the number of blankets ordinarily used, the warmth or coldness of the beds, and the varieties of other furniture normally found in the room. Then have the children use ¼-inch bristle brushes, brown tempera, and 12-x-18-inch sheets of paper to make pictures about sleeping in a favorite place.

6. Show your students all three of the exemplars and ask them which one seems to whisper; which seems to shout; and which appears to speak in an ordinary tone of voice. Then give them some black tempera, brushes, and 12-x-18-inch paper, and ask them to make three drawings of a kitten. One should whisper; one should shout; and one should speak in an ordinary voice. But talk about kittens beforehand; look at photographs of kittens; or bring one to school for observation.

BRUSH ACTIVITIES FOR THE INTERMEDIATE GRADES (AGES 9 THROUGH 11)

By the time a youngster reaches the intermediate grades he has acquired some skill in manipulating the brush, and he is interested in learning new and different ways of using such tools. Consequently, it is important to give him new experiences and new instruction.

CONCEPTS FOR POSSIBLE DEVELOPMENT

The artistic terms or concepts listed here can be developed through the brush activities explained below:

dry-brush	sketches	value
intermediate shades	still life	wet on dry
linear	technique	wet on wet
mural	texture	floating lines
repetition	unity	

SUGGESTED ACTIVITIES

Brush-drawing activities that work nicely with children are outlined in the paragraphs that follow:

1. Show the three exemplars to your students and ask them to describe the kinds of lines used by each of the artists. Explain that the heavy, bold, crisp lines in the Léger were created by drawing with a wet brush on dry paper; the speckled or open-textured lines in the Rembrandt were made with a relatively dry brush on dry paper; and the blurred line on top of the second

persimmon from the left in the Mu Ch'i was produced with a wet brush on wet paper.

Give each student a bottle of India ink, some white paper, and brushes of different sizes and types. Show them how to produce the dry-brush effect by dipping a brush in the ink, wiping it on the side of the bottle, wiping it still more on a damp sponge or paper towel, and dragging it across the paper. Then demonstrate the wet on wet technique by wetting the paper with clear water and a sponge before drawing on it with a wet brush. Although the paper should be wet for this exercise, no pools of water should be allowed on the paper. If any exist, soak them up with a facial tissue or a clean, dry brush.

Encourage your students to experiment in producing all the lines that have been described. When finished, let them experiment further by drawing with India ink and match sticks, twigs, slivers of wood, cotton swabs, and bamboo brushes.

2. While studying the Léger drawing, point out the fact that: 1) no texture appears in the drawing; 2) the ink was applied in a flat, even tone; 3) the lines vary slightly in their thickness; and 4) some areas have been painted a solid black. The lines are simple, bold, strong, hard, and powerful.

After discussing the drawing, students can use black tempera paint, a ½-inch or a ¼-inch flat bristle brush, and 18-x-24-inch white paper to make a big, bold, simple, line drawing of hands, coffee pots, pencil sharpeners, flowers, movie projectors, overhead projectors, typewriters, tape recorders, electric fans, animals, bicycles, buildings, faucets, doorknobs, light sockets, posed models, or objects arranged in a still life. And, if it would help, let them draw their objects with chalk or pencil before painting over the lines with tempera. See Figure 7-2 at the beginning of the chapter.

Recommend that the students work on the composition of their drawings by doing the following things:

a) Make some lines thicker than others (see Activity 1 under pencil drawing).

b) Vary the thickness within lines.

c) Place objects on the paper in such a way that they divide it unevenly.

d) Avoid floating lines or lines that do not attach themselves to anything. Such lines make the drawing look spotty, busy, and chaotic.

e) Make part of the drawing solid black. This will produce variety and make the linear elements more effective.

f) Do not allow forms to barely touch each other or the side of the paper. If they do, the drawing will look crowded. Instead, let them clearly overlap; let them go off the paper; or keep them clearly separated and away from the edge of the paper.

g) Make the drawing balance asymmetrically.

h) Part of the object might extend off the paper, but if you draw the whole object, keep it slightly out of the center.

3. Try the foregoing activity on 3-x-4- or 3-x-5-foot pieces of Kraft paper, and paint with brushes that are one or two inches in width.

4. To vary Activities 2 and 3, have the students paint a color or paste colored tissue onto the backgrounds of their drawings. See Figure 7-3.

Figure 7-3.   *Self-Portrait with Painted Orange Background.*

5. Glue two 3-x-10-foot pieces of Kraft paper together making a sheet 6 x 10 feet in size. Then talk to your students about the size and simplicity of the Léger drawing. Ask them to make a big brush drawing of small things in their environment (insects, flowers, weeds, grass, birds, toys, and small animals). To do so each child might make several small pencil sketches of small objects. One drawing from each child might then be transferred to the 6-x-10-foot paper using chalk. If the tallest object is a flower, for example, it should be made six feet tall, and the other objects should be drawn in proportion. This will require that the 6-x-10-foot paper be placed on the floor where the drawing will occur. When the chalk drawings are finished, students can go over them with brushes at least one inch wide. The result should be a huge mural. Use only one color. Then discuss the effect of the finished product. What adjectives could be used to describe the mural? Would soft and weak be appropriate?

6. A field trip to the furnace room, an automobile repair shop, a bridge, a construction site, or a parking lot might offer excellent subject matter for bold brush and ink drawings done in either the Léger or the Rembrandt manner. Manila or white paper (12 x 18 inches), a size 5 or 6 hair brush, a drawing board, and a small bottle of India ink are the recommended materials for this activity. The paper and brush can be taped to the drawing board with masking tape. And each child can carry paper toweling, a small damp sponge, and a bottle of ink in a plastic container. The container should have a lid, and it might be similar to those used for cottage cheese, gelatin, ice cream, or refrigerator storage. On arrival at the drawing site, the ink and sponge can be removed from the container and replaced with a small amount of water for rinsing brushes. At the end of the lesson, the water may be discarded or returned to the wide-mouth plastic bottle used to carry it.

Before leaving the classroom, discuss the Léger and Rembrandt techniques, placing special emphasis on the wet and dry brush. Urge youngsters to use one of the two methods in making their drawings.

7. Sometimes it is difficult to distinguish between brush drawings and paintings. The exemplar by Mu Ch'i, for example, is not as linear as the drawings by Léger and Rembrandt. Consequently, it might be called a painting rather than a drawing, but we shall consider it a drawing because the background is not painted.

While looking at the Mu Ch'i, discuss the amount of detail, the brush techniques, the number of shapes given to the persimmons, the different shades of ink, and the placement of each of the fruits. In short, explain the theory behind Chinese art. Then have the children make drawings of six apples, pears, tomatoes, lemons, or peppers. Ask them to try the Mu Ch'i methods and to make their drawings whisper.

To encourage the use of several shades of India ink or black tempera paint, have them put some of the drawing liquid into the compartments of a muffin tin or egg carton, and show them how to add differing amounts of water to the compartments to produce light and intermediate shades.

Have the students work with a ¼-inch bristle brush, a number 12 hair brush, and a number 7 hair brush. The drawing may be made on a 12-x-18- or 18-x-24-inch piece of white paper.

When finished, discuss the pleasing compositions that are produced as a result of variations in the color and size of the fruit, variations in the size of intervals between the fruit, and variations in the placement of the fruit. You might also call attention to the placement of the fruit on the page. It will look better if it is placed slightly away from the center.

8. On another occasion, the drawing might be allowed to dry, and the students could be asked to add linear details with a small hair brush or pen and ink.

9. Try Activity 2, but have the students paint dried weeds, grasses, seed pods, or flowers. Make sure the children know that the stems can extend off the page. See Figure 7-4.

Figure 7-4.   *Flowers.*

10. Display the Rembrandt drawing, and point out that although it was sketched quickly, the drawing looks unified. This is because certain linear elements have been repeated and placed close together in a small, compact area. There are solid, open-textured, thick, and thin lines, and each distinctive line is repeated throughout the composition. After your talk, give the children some 12-x-18-inch colored paper, a ¼-inch bristle brush, and tempera paint to make brush drawings of the quick poses assumed by a student selected as a model. Activities such as brushing or combing hair, reaching high to catch a ball, and

swinging a baseball bat can be acted out by the model. Or children on the gym floor or the playground can offer a wealth of spontaneous poses for quick sketches. When making these sketches, the children can repeat different types of lines in an effort to make their drawings look unified; they can try to capture the basic form of the pose without using a large amount of detail; and they can try to create a little darkness behind the figure as Rembrandt did. By placing the dark color properly they may give the impression that light is falling gently on the figure.

11. Because children of this age enjoy working with their peers, give them the responsibility for making several murals or large drawings of topics such as a city street, an assembly line, a parade, or a supermarket. The children might make simple line drawings, similar to the Léger exemplar, on 3-x-8-foot sheets of brown Kraft paper. Other materials for the activity are ½-inch or ¾-inch flat bristle brushes and black tempera paint.

PART 3

Easel Painting and Collage

Painting is the process of creating an image by applying pigments to a surface. The products of such work may be divided into two basic types: wall paintings (or murals) and easel paintings. Wall paintings are the older of the two; they originated with the caveman. Later on, color was also applied in water-soluble mixtures to the walls of architectural structures all over the world. This type of painting was very popular until the Renaissance, at which time the number of wall paintings of all kinds tended to decline. It was not until the depression of the 1930s that such paintings returned to favor in the United States and Mexico. American artists were commissioned by the government to paint murals in public buildings as part of a concerted effort to improve the buildings and help artists at the same time. The Mexican muralists, meanwhile, produced some of the finest wall paintings of modern times to be used as a form of social commentary.

Easel paintings grew in stature during the Renaissance because of the invention of oil paint. This medium has continued to be popular, but many artists now also choose the quicker drying acrylic paint.

In the 1900s, an extension of the easel painting was created by a group of artists living in Paris. This new art form, called collage, consisted of pasting and gluing papers and other objects to a ground.

Although mural paintings can be made by children in the elementary school, they are rarely made directly on walls. They are usually produced on large, moveable sheets of paper which can be put up and taken down with ease. Hence, mural painting in the elementary school is not unlike making an easel painting or a collage. We have chosen, therefore, to concentrate on the appreciation and creation of easel paintings and collages.

CHAPTER 8

EASEL PAINTING

Figure 8-7. Tempera painting by a sixth-grader.

Easel paintings are images created most often on moveable wooden panels, stretched canvas, cardboard, or paper. They are called easel paintings because a stand called an easel is frequently employed to hold them while they are being produced. Moveable paintings have been made since ancient times, but they grew in popularity and in stature during the Renaissance largely because of humanistic interests, the growing power of merchants, and the invention of oil paint. Wealthy merchants began to buy art, and they began to ask for portraits, landscapes, and other works that could be placed in the home. Oil paint allowed the artist to apply pigment in numerous ways to a variety of surfaces, and it permitted him to create a wide range of effects on either a small or a large scale.

Easel paintings can also be made with watercolor, tempera, casein, gouache, encaustics, and polymer acrylics. All paintings are made with colored pigments suspended in a binding vehicle or medium of some kind. The vehicle not only permits the dispensing of the color, but it binds the pigment to the surface. Application is made most often with a brush, but some paints can be applied with other devices such as cotton, cloth, sticks, sponges, or palette knives.

EXEMPLARS OF EASEL PAINTING

It is obviously difficult to select six exemplars of easel painting for discussion in these pages when thousands of works have been produced all over the world. We have tried to select artists whose work represents a variety of styles.

HENRI ROUSSEAU (Roo-so'), 1844–1910

Henri Rousseau was born poor and remained poor all his life. He began his artistic career at the age of 40 after working as a lawyer's clerk and as a minor inspector in a toll station.[1] When he retired from the position of inspector in 1855, he did so in hope of becoming a professional artist. He soon realized that his pension was not enough to support his family, so he frequently accepted odd jobs. He taught drawing classes in a local school, although he had no formal training in art.

Rousseau's paintings are said to be naive, amateurish, or primitive. They are described that

way because they possess characteristics found in the work of untrained artists. They show a lack of knowledge about the structure of human and animal figures; they contain certain exaggerations or distortions characteristic of child art; the relative sizes of things are different from the way they appear in visual reality; and many of the paintings are comparatively shallow in depth. All these features can be seen in *The Waterfall* in Plate 8-1. Individual blades of grass, leaves on the trees, and plants are much larger than they are in reality; the human and animal figures are anatomically incorrect; and there is practically no background in the picture.

Rousseau had an intuitive sense of design. He painted the shapes of leaves and grass again and again, and he painted them with sharpness and clarity. Repetition produces a visual rhythm or pattern that is lush and exotic. The luxuriance and appealing strangeness is also caused by the closeness of forms and the richness of color.

Rousseau's paintings are so full of pattern that portions free from pattern stand out clearly and attract our attention. That is the case with the human figures and animals which appear in his jungle paintings. They become the focal point of the work.

---

[1]Although Rousseau said that he had served in the army in Mexico, there is strong belief that he never left France.

Plate 8-1.   Henri Rousseau. *The Waterfall.* 1910. Oil on canvas, 45½" x 59".
Courtesy of The Art Institute of Chicago (Helen Birch Bartlett Memorial Collection).

He began painting tropical jungle scenes in 1891. Although several historians suggest that these topics were inspired by a trip to Mexico, it is more likely that he developed his ideas as a result of visits to the zoo and botanical gardens in Paris.

It also appears that Rousseau did not make preliminary sketches for his paintings. He simply began each of the canvases at the top and proceeded to paint step by step towards the bottom. He was slow and deliberate. Because most of his works were as large as *The Waterfall* (45½ x 59 inches), a single painting might take as long as two or three months to complete.

HENRI de TOULOUSE-LAUTREC (Too-looz-Low-trek), 1864–1901

Rather than slow, deliberate, static works of art, Toulouse-Lautrec created simple yet expressive linear summaries of what he saw. This artist, born 20 years after the birth of Rousseau, lived to be only 37 years of age. Unlike Rousseau, Toulouse-Lautrec came from a wealthy family which provided him with money whenever it was needed.

As a child, Lautrec drew landscapes as well as horses and other animals. Because of this great interest, he decided at an early age to pursue a career in painting. No doubt the decision became especially important when, at the age of 13, he fell and broke his left hip. Fifteen months later, while walking with his mother, he fell and fractured the other hip. While recuperating from these accidents, he spent much of his time drawing. The time and care given to his convalescence, however, did not cause a happy ending. His torso developed normally, but his legs did not, resulting in an unusual appearance that caused him considerable unhappiness.

Lautrec first studied art with Réné Princeteau, and at the age of 18, he went to Paris to continue his art education with Leon Bonnat. During the 15 months he studied there, Lautrec made sketches of models in a style similar to that of Ingres (see page 42). He also studied at the studio of Fernand Cormon where he met Emile Bernard and Vincent van Gogh (see pages 96 and 78). Like van Gogh, Lautrec dedicated himself to

his work. It is said that he worked so hard and enjoyed life so much that by the age of 30 he was mentally and physically exhausted. Toward the end of his life there were periods when he did little, if any, artwork.

The work that he did accomplish during his productive years, however, gives us a glimpse of Parisian life during the last two decades of the nineteenth century. It reveals the nature of the entertainment world because Lautrec was attracted to dance halls, cafés, theaters, and to the people who worked and relaxed there. One example is entitled *Moulin de la Galette* (Plate 8-2). It was one of Lautrec's first large works devoted to dancing and dance halls, and it shows ordinary people enjoying themselves on a Sunday afternoon. Sundays and holidays were the times when artists, students, and working people came to the hall to meet old friends and make new ones. The meeting place had originally been a

Plate 8-2.   Henri de Toulouse-Lautrec. *Moulin de la Galette.* 1889. Oil on canvas, 35" x 39⅞". Courtesy of The Art Institute of Chicago (Mr. and Mrs. Lewis L. Coburn Memorial Collection).

windmill, but in 1830, the millers converted the structure into a dance hall, part of which was in the open air.

Before beginning his painting, Lautrec usually made numerous preliminary sketches on the spot. He then returned to his studio where he developed the sketches into permanent configurations in oil on canvas. The actual application of the paint frequently began with violet, red, or brown outlines which remain visible in many of the finished products. It is possible to see them because the artist diluted much of his paint with turpentine to make the medium thin and transparent. The transparency of the paint, the obviousness of the brush strokes, and the highly linear quality peculiar to all his work can be seen in Plate 8-2. The painting indicates, moreover, that Lautrec often created a challenge for himself by cutting off one of the corners of the composition with a strong diagonal line. This in effect divided the canvas into two separate areas which were difficult to combine into one unified painting.

When looking at *Moulin de la Galette* for the first time, the observer probably is attracted to the middle figure in the group of three in the right foreground. From there the eyes move to the left until they reach the area over the head of the woman in the left foreground. Then they move downward to the strong diagonal of the railing, and they follow the railing upward and to the right until they reach the man in the right foreground. The area within this triangle constitutes the center of interest in this painting, and the faces in that area stand out against the background because they are light and opaque in color while the background is darker, more linear, and more transparent. It was common for Lautrec to use such devices to center attention upon certain figures in his paintings.

---

[2]For more information about expressionism, see Ludwig Kirchner (page 216), Rolf Nesch (page 197), and Oscar Kokoschka (page 58).

EMIL NOLDE (Nol'-day), 1867–1956

The life of Emil Nolde was in many ways similar to that of Henri Rousseau. Both were poor; they began professional painting after the age of 30; and they endured considerable criticism aimed at their work.

Born in the town of Nolde in northern Germany near the Danish border, Nolde was christened Emil Hansen. Although he traveled and met many people, he always felt more comfortable with the residents of his own home town. As a result, he changed his surname to Nolde, and he lived in and around the town of Nolde for most of his life.

As a youngster, Nolde enjoyed the drawing that he did in school, but he did not embark immediately on an artistic career. Instead, he studied art off and on; he spent a number of years as an apprentice wood carver in a furniture factory before accepting a position as a teacher of commercial drawing. Then, after making a considerable amount of money selling postcards printed with his designs, he left his teaching position to study art and to produce it with professional seriousness.

By 1906, Nolde had made enough of a name for himself to be recognized by a number of younger German artists who invited him to join a new expressionist group called Die Brücke.[2] He accepted the invitation, but his quiet, introverted personality made it difficult for him to make friends, so he associated with the group for only a year and a half. Furthermore, he soon came to realize that he could not solve artistic problems satisfactorily in a group situation.

By the 1930s, Nolde had achieved widespread recognition as a highly innovative painter; he had published the first of his memoirs; and he had been elected to the Prussian Academy of Fine Arts. Yet his achievements meant nothing to the Nazi regime, because his work was revolutionary in the sense that it was different from the accepted art of the day. It was highly personal and expressionistic; it was the kind of unusual art that comes from the mind of a creative person who values the ideas and feelings of the individual above the traditional views of society and the collective political views of the state. Consequently, Nolde might have looked like a potential troublemaker for Hitler and his followers, in spite of the fact that the artist was a loyal German citizen who did not oppose the Nazi movement. For whatever reasons, Nolde's works were labeled "degenerate," and they were removed from museums and sold. In 1937, over a thousand pieces of his art were confiscated, and in 1941, he was forbidden by the Nazis to buy materials and to make art. Supplies were smuggled to him, however, and he continued in secret to create approximately 1300 small watercolor paintings which he called "unpainted pictures." He chose watercolor as a medium because there was no telltale scent to the paint, and it dried much faster than oil. In addition, the paintings were small (approximately 6 x 8 inches) and easy to

hide. They were called "unpainted pictures" because they were not premeditated.

Plate 8-3, entitled *Marsh Landscape*, is a watercolor painting, but it does not belong to the "unpainted" series. This larger work, measuring 14 x 18 inches, is typical of the watercolor paintings of Nolde. The soft, feathery edges of color show that the paint was applied to a wet surface. Nolde liked to work that way, and he often controlled his colors with a bit of cotton rather than a brush. His paintings were made spontaneously, without preliminary sketches, and he allowed the glowing color to set the mood as it does in *Marsh Landscape*. The warm, bright yellows with touches of orange on the horizon give the feeling of a peaceful sunrise or sunset in the marshy region of northern Germany or southern Denmark. After these large color areas were in place, the artist defined them more clearly by outlining them with black.

Because of the strong emphasis that Nolde gave to the spontaneity of the creative process, watercolor was an ideal medium for him. It can-

Plate 8-3.   Emil Nolde. *Marsh Landscape.*
n.d. Watercolor, 14" x 18".
Copyright: Stiftung Seebüll Ada
und Emil Nolde.

not be changed and reworked like oil paint. The idea has to be set down quickly and correctly, because there is no time or opportunity for prolonged translation from the beginning concept to the finished product.

JOHN SLOAN, 1871–1951

During the nineteenth century, the American people did not value American art. Instead, they preferred historical pictures and allegories that were painted according to standards established by the French Academy of Painting and Sculpture, an official government agency that fostered sterile mediocrity by discouraging new ideas and methods.[3] During the next half-century, however, an enormous change took place in American taste—the people began to appreciate their own art. This change was helped immensely by John Sloan and his friends.

Sloan was born in Lock Haven, Pennsylvania, in 1871, but at the age of six, he moved to Philadelphia where he lived for the next 26 years. As a youngster, he loved reading; he spent large amounts of time in the library; he worked in a bookstore; he taught himself how to make prints; and he obtained work decorating Christmas cards, matchboxes, and bookmarks. These early literary and artistic interests continued to grow, and eventually they led to employment as an illustrator for the Philadelphia newspapers. Among his colleagues in the city's newspaper business were George Luks, William Glackens, and Everett Shinn, all of whom were to become

well-known American painters. The newspapers needed such artists to illustrate the news because the technique for printing photographs had not yet been invented. When the process did become known, however, the illustrators shifted to other occupations.

Sloan, like his colleagues before him, moved to New York where he made a living by illustrating books. He also worked for magazines such as *Colliers, The Century,* and *Harper's Weekly,* and he began to devote more of his time to painting and printmaking. As a former newspaper artist, he had accumulated years of experience in drawing scenes from everyday life, and he continued to produce such scenes in his paintings and prints. He thought it was important to deal with life in the streets because it allowed him to be true to himself.

The painting by John Sloan in Plate 8-4 contains the kind of subject matter associated with the "ash can school" of art.[4] It depicts people hurrying along a city street on a windy day. The dust storm has interrupted their Sunday outing, and they are hurrying for shelter. Some must hold onto their hats to keep them from blowing away in the wind; others must brace themselves to avoid being blown over. To show this kind of action, Sloan painted the arms, legs, and bodies of the people in positions of movement. There isn't a single person in the whole painting who is standing perfectly straight with arms and legs in a vertical position. Sloan probably painted the scene from memory, because that is the way he worked at that time.

The finished painting looks as if Sloan were interested in capturing a familiar event on canvas. To represent this event he did not fuss with detail or with precise delineation of form. But the figures in the foreground are more clearly defined than those in the background, which are merely suggested by spots of color. The spots look as if they were made freely, easily, and quickly, instead of slowly and painstakingly. A thin coat of light brown was painted in the background to show the air filled with dust particles.

[3] Allegorical art is art that presents concepts indirectly through the use of symbolism. A mythological figure, for example, might be used to represent love, thus avoiding any direct presentation of love as it manifests itself in everyday life.

[4] In the 1930s, the first American School of art became known as the "ash can school" because the paintings presented images of the streets, the slums, and the backyards of New York.

Plate 8-4. John Sloan. *Dust Storm, Fifth Avenue.* 1906. Oil on canvas, 22" x 27". The Metropolitan Museum of Art (George A. Hearn Fund, 1921).

A blue-black cloud hangs overhead threatening to open up and drop rain on the people.

GEORGIA O'KEEFFE, 1887–

Georgia O'Keeffe was born on a farm in Sun Prairie, Wisconsin, and at the age of seventeen she enrolled at the Chicago Art Institute. After further preparation at the Art Student's League in New York and subsequent work as a commercial artist, O'Keeffe became a supervisor of art in the public schools of Amarillo, Texas. Following this, she returned to New York City to attend Teachers College at Columbia University. Some of the classes were taught by Arthur Wesley Dow, who played a prominent role in art educa-

tion during the early 1900s. Dow was different from the usual academicians because he rejected realism and based his instruction on the principles of design that he had gleaned from a careful analysis of Japanese and Chinese art. In essence, he stressed flat patterning, simplification, and visual harmony; he also emphasized the importance of intervals between forms (see Mu Ch'i, page 122). Careful attention to such things is evident in the work of Georgia O'Keeffe, and she readily admits that Dow had a strong effect upon her.

Subsequent to her study at Columbia University, O'Keeffe taught at Columbia College in South Carolina, and she served as head of the art department at West Texas State Normal College. While she was in South Carolina, she sent some of her sketches to a friend in New York. The friend showed them to Alfred Stieglitz who was one of the world's great pioneer photographers as well as a benefactor of young experimental artists. Stieglitz liked the drawings and exhibited them in the 291 Gallery which he had established as a place where promising artists could show their work. Shortly thereafter, at the age of 31, Georgia O'Keeffe abandoned her teaching career to become one of a group of young artists sponsored by Stieglitz.

O'Keeffe's early work was nonrepresentational, but in 1920, she began to paint natural objects such as flowers, barns, clouds, leaves, hills, and bleached bones from the southwestern desert. She often painted them again and again, creating, in time, a series of paintings on each subject. As she proceeded through each series, the rendering of the subject frequently became more and more abstract without losing the essential qualities which made the subject recognizable. In the *Yellow Cactus Flower* (Plate 8-5), for example, the artist has reduced the detailed shapes, textures, and colorations of the flower to its basic essentials. These elements have an especially powerful effect upon the observer because they are magnified. The canvas upon which the cactus flower has been painted is 41½ x 29¾ inches in size, making the flower much larger than it is in real life. O'Keeffe's treatment of subject matter is not unlike the work of Fernand Léger (see Plate 7-3). Both artists magnified and simplified their subject matter; both produced numerous drawings and paintings that are relatively shallow in depth; and they both placed a heavy emphasis on formal structure or composition. The ultimate effect of their work, however, is different. Léger's creations seem mechanical and bold, while O'Keeffe's paintings seem organic and gentle.

Plate 8-5. Georgia O'Keeffe. *Yellow Cactus Flower.* 1929. Oil on canvas, 41½" x 29¾". Collection of The Fort Worth Art Museum (gift of the William E. Scott Foundation).

JACOB LAWRENCE, 1917–

It is said that Jacob Lawrence is an artist who is very sensitive to life around him and who can express his feelings in a direct manner.[5] Perhaps this is due to Lawrence's early experiences and the fact that he has used art materials since his youth.

As a youngster growing up in Harlem, he attended arts and crafts classes after school hours. When he was 15 years old, he attended the

[5]Milton Brown, *Jacob Lawrence* (New York: Whitney Museum of Art, 1974), p. 9.

Harlem Art Workshop, where Charles Alston was his teacher. Five years later he was fortunate enough to be given a scholarship to attend the American Artists School in New York. At the age of 18, he joined the WPA Federal Arts Project and worked with the easel painters' section for a time. The government support of the arts helped many artists through a difficult financial period. It was also important because it helped bring the work of Lawrence and other artists to the attention of the art world.

For Lawrence, it was not long before his work was recognized. In 1940, he received the first of three fellowships from the Rosenwald Fund, which allowed him to begin work on a series of paintings depicting the migration of the Black people from the small, rural communities of the South to the large, urban centers of the North. Before Lawrence's time, there were no paintings telling the history of the Black migration. The works are an important social commentary and record of historical events.

The painting in Plate 8-6 is from the *Migration* series. All of these works are the same size, of the same palette, and are done in the same medium. In this piece, Lawrence is trying to show that education is important for all children. The size is 12 x 18 inches and he has used the three primary colors as well as brown, black, and white. The tempera colors have been applied thinly over a gessoed ground which allows some of the white gesso to appear through the paint and reveals the brush strokes of the artist. As with the Rousseau work, Lawrence keeps the viewer's eyes on the foreground. The observer sees three girls reaching up to print a number on the blackboard. The border around the painting, the horizontal rectangle at the bottom, and the

Plate 8-6. Jacob Lawrence. *The Migration of the Negro (#58).* c. 1940–41. Tempera on composition board, 12" x 18". Collection, The Museum of Modern Art, New York (gift of Mrs. David M. Levy).

vertical rectangle on the right-hand side, which are brown in color, contrast with the angular gestures of the three figures. Each dress has been painted in a bright shade: red, yellow, or blue. Their poses, which are angular and stiff, contrast with the background of horizontals and verticals. The shapes of clothes, hair, arms, legs, faces, and socks are simple with no detail.

The *Migration* series was one of six series that Lawrence portrayed in his paintings. Other series were painted about John Brown, Harlem, war, and struggle.

Lawrence, presently a Professor of Art at the University of Washington, has influenced many younger artists. Part of the reason is due to the fact that he is the first Black artist to be recognized so greatly by the art world. Other reasons for his being regarded so highly are his consistency of style and his serious commitment to reveal a true statement of Black life.

ADDITIONAL EXEMPLARS

To show more examples of paintings, try using the work of Pierre August Renoir, Edgar Degas, Mary Cassatt, Rembrandt van Rijn, Arthur Dove, Edward Hopper, Paul Cezanne, Edvard Munch, Georges Rouault, Marc Chagall, Vincent van Gogh, Claude Monet, Henri Matisse, Charles Scheeler, and Andrew Wyeth.

EASEL-PAINTING ACTIVITIES FOR THE PRIMARY GRADES (AGES 6 THROUGH 8)

Children enjoy painting, but they are sometimes denied the opportunity because their teachers feel that painting is too messy. It need not be if attention is given to the selection and distribution of tools and materials as well as to the organization of the classroom.

Liquid tempera is preferred over the powdered variety; it has a creamy consistency that is difficult to match when mixing powdered paint. When kept in its original container or in another that is tightly sealed, it can be preserved for a long time. Solutions made from powdered tempera tend to dry or spoil more quickly.

Children can pour the paint they need into pie tins, muffin tins, or styrofoam egg cartons, and then proceed to paint. These containers do not tip over, and they facilitate the mixing of color. If this arrangement is not possible, we suggest that prepared or powdered paint be given to children in flat-bottomed, plastic refrigerator jars with tight-fitting lids. Cardboard milk cartons, baby food jars, or juice cans are also suitable. A set of colors can be provided for each group of four youngsters.

It is most convenient if youngsters have the nine basic colors at their disposal (red, yellow, blue, orange, green, violet, brown, white, and black). However, it is possible to have a good program with nothing more than red, yellow, blue, black, and white. Red, yellow, and blue are called the primary colors because all other colors can be made by mixing them, one with another. Red and yellow make orange; yellow and blue make green; and blue and red make violet. Orange, green, and violet are called secondary colors. Black will make all colors darker and white makes them lighter. When we make colors lighter or darker we say that we have changed their value. And when we alter the brightness of a certain hue, we say that we have changed its chroma or intensity.

Manila, colored construction, gray bogus, and Kraft papers are excellent supports for tempera paint. All are absorbent, sturdy, and readily available.

Long-handled easel brushes made of bristles are most appropriate for the primary grades if purchased in ¼-, ½-, ¾-, and 1-inch sizes. Before using the brushes, children should be shown how to wipe excess paint into the paint container before applying a brush to paper. To change colors, they must clean the brush in water before dipping the tool into a new color. To keep the paint at a creamy consistency, the excess water should be removed from the brush by wiping it on a sponge or paper towel before dipping it into a fresh color. When the paintings are finished, the brushes should be washed with soap in warm water and allowed to dry with the bristles up.

Before painting, arrange a flat drying space for the finished works. Various types of drying racks are available for purchase, but table and desk tops as well as floor space in classrooms and hallways are the areas most likely to be used.

Finally, tell the children that tempera paint is an opaque medium. That means that it will cover paper and other tempera paint. Before one color may be placed on top of another, the first layer of paint must be dry. If it is not, the two colors will mix together. When placing one color next to another, check to see that the first color is dry or the newly applied hue will blend with the first.

CONCEPTS FOR POSSIBLE DEVELOPMENT

The concepts listed below should be introduced when talking about the painting exemplars:

dark	light	pattern	subject matter
details	linear	rhythm	transparent
expressive	magnify	simplified shapes	value
landscape	outline	space	watercolor

SUGGESTED ACTIVITIES

Before introducing the painting experiences, spend some time preparing the necessary materials and working spaces. Sheets of newspaper can cover desks, tables, or the floor. Painting stations where four or five children can work comfortably may be set up on the floor of the classroom or hallway.

1. Show your students the exemplars by Toulouse-Lautrec and John Sloan and offer a little information about the artists. Stress the fact that both of them painted pictures about ordinary people doing ordinary things, and both painted the whole surface of the canvas. Then stimulate your class by discussing one of the subjects listed below, and ask your students to make a painting that shows what it would be like to engage in that activity.

Camping in the forest   Digging a deep hole in my yard
Building a fire   Enjoying soup with a friend
My arms are wings, and I fly

Use 18-x-24-inch colored construction paper, bristle brushes, and tempera paint. See Figure 8-1.

Figure 8-1.   Tempera applied with brush and
sponges by first-grade student.

2. Provide your students with colored construction paper and all the other tools and materials necessary for painting in tempera. Then examine the exemplar by Lawrence. Discuss the part of the classroom the artist showed in the painting. Ask the students to name different parts of their classroom. Go on to discuss the different rooms found in their school and list them on the chalkboard. Explain that the class will be making their school containing all those rooms and each child will be responsible for making the room of his choice. Try to make sure that there is at least one volunteer for each room.

When all the rooms have been painted, fasten the paintings to a large wall with loops of masking tape. Arrange them in the shape of the school, and leave about two inches between the rooms. Then make an outline around the outside of the building with a black, crepe-paper streamer, and have the children make details to be added to the top and sides of the building.

3. Try the foregoing activity, but use one of the following themes in place of the school:

A hospital   A department store
A hotel   An ocean liner

4. Georgia O'Keeffe enlarged her subject matter to fill the entire surface of the canvas when she painted the *Yellow Cactus Flower*. Thus, she and Léger (see p. 126) have a characteristic in common, but their final products are very different. The brush drawing by Léger (Plate 7-3) is composed of black lines while the O'Keeffe painting is composed of shapes of color. Look at both exemplars and talk about the way each artist filled the space on his or her canvas. Discuss the fact that the person and flowers look unusual because they were made larger than normal. Then ask the children if the colors in each work have an effect upon how it looks. If Léger had used pale yellows, blues, and pinks, would the drawing still look bold, strong, and powerful? Would the flowers look soft and gentle if they had been done in black?

    At the conclusion of your discussion, give each child an 18-x-24-inch sheet of manila paper, colored construction paper, or bogus paper. In addition, give the children bristle brushes and tempera paints. Then ask them to make large self-portraits. As they paint, have them use small cosmetic mirrors to look at their faces. Ask them to notice the shapes and placement of their features. After they complete the self-portrait encourage them to finish the painting by filling in the background. See Figure 8-2.

5. After discussing the O'Keeffe and Léger exemplars, have the children make large paintings of flowers. If possible, bring a number of different flowers to class, and have the children examine them to see the shapes and details. Have them use large paper and ask them to fill the space with flowers which look real or imaginary. See Figure 8-3 on page 153.

6. Colorful imaginative tempera paintings of jungle scenes can result from a discussion of *The Waterfall* by Henri Rousseau. Like O'Keeffe and Léger, Rousseau magnified his subject matter, but he preferred to include more objects in his paintings than did O'Keeffe who often focused on one item.

    Call attention to the grasslike and leaflike forms in the foliage of the Rousseau painting. Give the students grass and leaves to examine more carefully. Then show that those forms in the painting are so close together that

Figure 8-2. *Self-Portrait in Tempera,* by a third-grader.

they make you think of a dense jungle. Give the children some sheets of colored construction paper, tempera paint, and brushes, and ask them to show you what they think it would be like to walk through the thickest jungle in Africa or South America. Encourage them to use their imaginations, and to show the jungle at night, in the heat of the day, or in a rainstorm.

7. Show your students a film such as *Autumn Pastorale,* a filmstrip such as *The Sea,* or a concept loop film such as *The Sky* or *The Desert.*[6] Use the film to stimulate discussion about different kinds of landscapes, and relate the discussion to the Nolde exemplar. Then have the children use tempera paints to make pictures about one of the following topics:

---

[6] *Autumn Pastorale* is produced by William Murray and distributed by Portafilms; *The Sea, Parts 1 and 2, Perception,* produced by Educational Dimensions Corporation, P. O. Box 488, Great Neck, New York; *The Sky* and *The Desert,* part of the *Awareness* Series, produced by Hester and Associates, 111422 Hines Boulevard, Dallas, Texas.

Figure 8-3.   Large flowers painted by a
second-grade student.

My yard	A place I once visited
The park	A storm at sea
A rainy day at the beach	

A second-grader's painting of a storm at sea is illustrated in Figure 8-4.

8. The Sloan painting (Plate 8-4) can be used in a discussion about various kinds of storms. As the children examine the painting, have them describe the things that express the idea of a dust storm. Perhaps they will talk about the colors Sloan used and how some parts of the painting are blurred while others are not. Following this, involve the children in a discussion about their experiences in storms (rain, snow, sleet, ice, wind, sand, hurricane, tornado, blizzard). If these were frightening experiences, encourage them to talk about them further. Was it the color of the storms that made them frightening? What were the colors? Ask if the sky was clear, cloudy, dark, or light. Following the discussion, have the children make a painting about a storm. Have them select gray or manila paper, bristle brushes, and tempera colors including black and white. After the paintings are dry, the students may write stories about the storm.

Figure 8-4. Tempera painting by a seven-
year-old.

9. While looking at the painting by Toulouse-Lautrec (Plate 8-2) share some information about the artist. Lautrec's style of painting was quite different from
most of the other painters described in this chapter. Instead of using oil paint
in an opaque manner, he preferred to dilute the medium with turpentine to
make a transparent solution. He then painted the thin mixture over previously
painted areas. Sometimes the solution was added in the form of thin linear
strokes, and at other times it was brushed on as an area of color. As he
repeated the quick, sketchy strokes he created a rhythmical pattern. This
quality helped express the subject matter that Lautrec was most interested in
painting.

Continue the discussion by asking the children about the things they enjoy
doing in their leisure time and have them illustrate this in a painting. After the
paintings dry, details may be added with colored felt-tip markers or oil pastels.

EASEL-PAINTING ACTIVITIES FOR THE INTERMEDIATE GRADES
(AGES 9 THROUGH 11)

The materials recommended for the preceding experiences are appropriate for
youngsters in grades four through six. Most of the procedures at the intermediate
level involve the use of thick tempera paint, but a few of the experiences require
a transparent medium. If watercolors are not available, opaque tempera may be
diluted with water. A few procedures involve a technique called tempera batik.

The process includes a number of steps requiring time for the paintings to dry. It also calls for the use of waterproof black India ink. If such ink is not available, the activities may end in the making of tempera paintings.

Materials for the tempera batik are soft chalk, tempera paint, sturdy paper (light colored construction paper or gray bogus), waterproof black India ink, bristle and hair brushes, water, sponges, and newspaper or paper toweling.

The procedure begins by using chalk to make a linear drawing on the paper. The lines should not be covered when the picture is painted. Any space that is to be black in the finished work should not be filled with tempera. It will become black when the ink is brushed over the surface. When the painting is complete, all works should be set aside to dry. When dry, the process is continued by brushing a coat of black India ink over the entire painting. Demonstrate that step for your students by using a wide bristle brush to stroke the ink across the width of the paper. Start at the top of the picture and move toward the bottom. When the painting is fully covered with ink, allow the work to dry for two or three minutes. Place the painting on a piece of Masonite and rinse off some of the India ink by allowing water to run over it. Be sure not to use too much water on one spot or you may wash too much paint off. When the desired amount of ink has been removed, place some paper towels on the painting to soak up excess water. After drying, the colors may be enhanced with a coat of polymer acrylic medium, liquid wax, or white shellac.

Youngsters in the intermediate grades can use a full range of tempera colors, and they are capable of mixing light and dark hues as well as bright and dull ones. Encourage them to do so, and show them that colors can be made dull or less bright by adding a little of their complements. Red and green, for example, are complementary colors; consequently either of them can be dulled by adding a little of the other. The same kind of intensity reduction can be achieved with other complementary colors such as yellow and violet, and blue and orange. It may also be interesting for children to learn that complementary colors when used next to each other in a painting do not produce dullness; they do exactly the opposite. They tend to stimulate each other in the observer's eye because they are strongly contrasting colors, and the effect is a high level of visual excitement.

Although long-handled bristle brushes continue to be useful for painting large areas, it is important to give youngsters in the intermediate grades a selection of hair brushes in sizes 3, 5, 6, 7, 8, and 12. Hair brushes permit the painting of details, and they are the best tools to use with transparent solutions such as watercolor and thin tempera.

At this age, children should be given responsibility for caring for tools and materials and for cleaning up. They should help to get out all the items necessary for painting; they should cover working and drying spaces with newspaper; they should wash all mixing pans and brushes; they should store the brushes carefully with the bristles up; and they should return all tools and materials to the proper storage area.

CONCEPTS FOR POSSIBLE DEVELOPMENT

background	foreground	movement	tempera batik
bright colors	gestures	opaque	transparent
dry brush	hard-edge shape	preliminary sketch	watercolor
dull colors	highlight	shadow	wet on dry
focal point	linear	simplified shapes	wet on wet

SUGGESTED ACTIVITIES

The easel painting procedures suggested in Activities 4, 5, 8, and 9 at the primary level may be used with youngsters in this age group.

1. While examining the painting in Plate 8-1 share some information about Henri Rousseau. Explain why he was often called a naive painter, and tell the children that he got the inspiration for his jungle pictures from the zoo and the botanical gardens. Have the children go outdoors to pick up interesting leaves, grasses, and flowers. On their return to the classroom, ask them to examine the forms carefully. Have the children create a fantastic jungle scene by magnifying the objects and turning them into gigantic trees and plants. Remind them that Rousseau repeated leaf shapes throughout his work, and urge them to do the same when organizing their composition. Ask them to add people and animals to their jungle scenes as a way of creating a relief from the pattern of the foliage. Encourage them to make their jungle seem dense by placing the foliage close together in the foreground. An example is illustrated in Figure 8-5.

    If India ink is available, have the children do the project in tempera batik. Work on large surfaces of colored or bogus paper. This experience can be followed by Activity 1 in the section on *Collage Activities for the Intermediate Grades* (page 172).

2. Georgia O'Keeffe's style is often compared with that of artists who painted machines and industrial forms in a sharp and precise way. She is compared with them because she painted flowers with the same clear color and the same crisp, hard edges. Display the exemplar by O'Keeffe (Plate 8-5) and call attention to these edges. Point to other edges which are blurred and show how one color fades into another color. Have the children notice the use of bright and dull colors; show them how parts of the flower appear to be in the shadow while other areas seem to be highlighted; and ask the children to explain how the artist created this effect. Do bright and dull colors play a part? Following your discussion, the children can use tempera paints, bristle brushes, and 18-x-24-inch papers to make big paintings of flowers or machines. Try to have

Figure 8-5. Tempera painting of a jungle by a fifth-grader.

flowers or machines available for the students to examine. Remind them to use bright and dull colors to show highlights and shadows. Encourage them to use hard edges on some shapes. If it will help them to draw with chalk before they begin painting, let them do so.

3. A mural can be made by starting with two pieces of Kraft paper about 3 x 20 feet in size. Glue the two pieces together along their longest sides, producing a sheet that is approximately 6 x 20 feet. Lay the sheet on the floor and have one or two children use chalk to draw the outline of a large school bus that fills the paper. Cut the bus out and fasten it to the wall of the classroom with thumbtacks or loops of masking tape.

Have the class make believe they are looking at a cross-section of the bus. In other words, one side of the vehicle has been cut away, revealing the inside. Then ask a few children to paint windows in the vehicle while other youngsters are making side views of the seats out of paper. Don't forget the one for the driver. Fasten the finished seats to the bus with loops of masking tape.

Examine the figures in the painting by Lawrence (Plate 8-6). Talk about the body gestures and how the artist showed the girls were reaching up to write on the board. Discuss the simplified shapes. Then give each student the job of making one passenger. The people can be painted and cut out and the finished products can be attached to the bus with loops of masking tape. The standing passengers will have to be fastened in front of the seated figures, and extra ones may be fastened to the wall outside the bus.

When all the figures and seats have been satisfactorily placed, they can be glued permanently to the bus, and your students can add finishing touches where they are needed. Try the same activity, but change the subject to an airplane, a yacht, or an elevator. See Figure 8-6.

Figure 8-6.　Painting done in an art methods
class.

4. The landscape by Emil Nolde was done in watercolor. Because the medium is transparent the paper can be seen through the paint. Be sure the youngsters understand the difference between opaque tempera and transparent watercolor. Review the dry brush, wet on dry, and wet on wet techniques introduced on page 130. Following this, examine the watercolor painting by Nolde (Plate 8-3) and the brush drawing by Mu Ch'i (Plate 7-1). Find places where each artist used the various techniques. Then have the children use watercolor or thinned-down tempera colors and different sizes and types of brushes to create a landscape using the three techniques of dry brush, wet on dry, and wet on wet. Use white paper as a background. After the paintings dry, encourage the children to add details with pens or felt-tipped markers.

5. Activity 7 in the section on Brush Drawing suggests an activity which may be done with watercolor or thin tempera on white paper (see page 133). Use both the Mu Ch'i exemplar (Plate 7-1) and the one by Georgia O'Keeffe (Plate 8-5).

6. Show your class the painting by Lawrence (Plate 8-6). Call attention to the way the artist contrasted transparent and opaque paint. The chalkboard and walls, brushed in with thinned-down paint, show many strokes, while the figures are done in a thick paint. The brush strokes are not as visible in these figures. Examine the use of shapes and lines. The shapes are simple and Lawrence has used a few lines for emphasis and clarification. Continue by discussing the various activities the children are involved in during the school day. Have them use tempera colors and different-sized brushes to make a painting of one of the school activities. Perhaps it might be an activity related to physical education, music, or art. Encourage them to contrast some opaque areas in their painting with some that are transparent. Suggest that their compositions show some areas where brush strokes are visible.

7. Display the paintings by Sloan and Toulouse-Lautrec. Explain that each artist was attempting to show people involved in everyday experiences. Call attention to the sketchy, transparent quality of the Toulouse-Lautrec work. Compare it with the more controlled and opaque look of the painting by Sloan. Things that are closer to the viewer are larger and brighter in color, while the people and objects in the background are smaller and duller in color. Both exemplars depict some kind of movement. Ask the children to identify and discuss the types of movement in one of the following activities:

Running	Playing football	Jumping
A traffic jam	The dance	The race

As a few children take turns assuming quick poses which show the action discussed previously, have the rest of the class use chalk to make a number of quick sketches on paper. After the students have made six to eight preliminary sketches, have them organize all or some of the figures in a composition on a single sheet of colored construction paper. Ask them to place some figures in the foreground and some in the background. Some may overlap others. Continue the experience using the tempera batik technique. Encourage students to use brighter colors for things in the foreground and duller colors for objects in the background.

8. A variation of the foregoing activity is to arrange the sketches in a larger composition and to paint in areas with tempera paint. Set the paintings aside to dry; look at the exemplar by Toulouse-Lautrec, and discuss his painting style. Encourage the children to use paint, chalk, oil pastels, or felt-tipped markers to repeat expressive short lines over areas in their paintings. The idea is to create linear qualities similar to those used by the artist.

9. When looking at the painting in Plate 8-2, our eyes are drawn to the faces and heads of the four people in the bottom half of the picture. Toulouse-Lautrec made this area the focal point of the painting by using the bright red-orange color for the hair of the lady. He also directed the viewer's eyes to that area by painting a diagonal that slants from the lower left-hand corner up to the seated man. Another device was to use highlights and shadows on the heads of these four people. It looks as if a spotlight is shining on them. The people in the foreground are more clearly delineated than those in the background. He has also created some interesting shapes around these figures. The bare dance floor separates the figures in the foreground from those in the background.

After the preceding discussion, continue by talking about the topics below:

Modeling a hat	At the bank
Watching television	Sitting around the dinner table
Being on stage	In the movies

Have three or four students assume poses suitable to the topic discussed. If a spotlight is available, shine it on the posed figures and assist the children in seeing the highlight and shadow areas. Using tempera paints, bristle and hair brushes, and large sheets of paper, the children may then arrange their compositions with one or more figures in the foreground. Ask them to try creating a focal point in their composition by using some of the techniques Lautrec used in his work. Suggest that they place their figures in an imaginary environment. See Figure 8-7 at the beginning of the chapter.

CHAPTER 9

COLLAGE

Figure 9-4.   Paper collage of legs and loafers
done by a student in an art
methods class.

Before 1900, people made representations of
flowers and trees with human and horse hair.
They also made cutout valentines and covered
bottles, boxes, and other three-dimensional objects with pieces of cut paper or cloth.[1] These
products were not considered examples of fine

---

[1]The art of decorating surfaces with applied paper cutouts is
called papier découpage.

art, but rather a folk art. History indicates that they were forerunners of a highly regarded art form known as the collage.

→ A collage is a picture or a design produced by gluing paper, cloth, or other materials to a supporting surface. These materials are often combined with drawing or painting. The first serious art of this kind was created by Georges Braque or Pablo Picasso shortly after the turn of the century. It is not certain which of the men made the first collage, because both were working with the idea at the same time. It is known

that Picasso pasted a piece of patterned oil cloth to one of his canvases around 1912, and it is generally acknowledged that Braque made the first paper collage (papier collé) at about the same time. Since then collages have come to include materials such as sand, cloth, sawdust, cardboard, window screening, photographs, wood, metal, and found objects of all kinds. Recent works of art have included paint cans, rubber tires, and blankets. When they do include such things, however, it is difficult to tell the difference between a collage and a piece of sculpture.

EXEMPLARS OF COLLAGE

Georges Braque, Kurt Schwitters, and Henri Matisse pioneered the medium of collage, and also produced some of its finest results. Braque created highly sophisticated compositions that were both limited and subtle in their coloration; Schwitters used a larger selection of found materials than anyone up to his time; and Matisse constructed some of the most colorful collages of the modern era.

GEORGES BRAQUE (Brahk), 1882–1963

Braque was born in the small town of Argenteuil near Paris, but he spent the greater part of his youth at Le Havre where he became an apprentice house painter and a student of drawing. It was understandable that he should become a house painter and an interior decorator because his father and his grandfather had both been house painters. Braque's interest in fine art also reflected his father's participation in painting pictures in the manner of Corot.

Eventually, Braque moved to Paris where he continued as an apprentice house painter, but he soon decided to become a full-time artist. He enrolled at the École des Beaux Arts and at the

Académie Humbert where he studied for two years before embarking on an artistic career.

Braque's early paintings were done in the fauve style, which means that they were done with bright, wild colors and heavy outlines (see page 253). The young painter soon came under the influence of Cézanne whose work displayed a deep and abiding interest in clear, solid form. At the same time, Braque met Pablo Picasso, and they became close friends. Picasso had been influenced by African sculpture as well as by the work of Cézanne. Hence, the two young artists shared an interest in form and composition.

Within two years of their first meeting, Braque and Picasso were sharing so many ideas about art and artistic experimentation that their products began to look alike. The artists themselves occasionally had difficulty in identifying their own work. Both men tried to show multiple views of a given object in a single picture; they tried to unite objects with each other and with the surrounding space; they distorted the shapes of objects to achieve the foregoing aims; they restricted themselves to somber tones of green, brown, and gray; they often used an imitation of wood grain in their paintings; they both employed lettering in their work; and they tried to reveal the fundamental or essential form of

Plate 9-1.   Georges Braque. *Clarinet*. 1913.
Pastel papers, charcoal, chalk, and
oil on canvas; 37¼″ x 47⅜″.
Collection, The Museum of
Modern Art, New York (Nelson A.
Rockefeller Bequest).

the objects they painted. As a result, they were called cubists.[2,3]

Apparently, the first paper collage developed as a result of Braque's discovery of some printed wallpaper which resembled the grain of oak wood. He pasted the paper to another paper surface and added a charcoal drawing of a dish, some grapes, and a goblet. Many of his early collages were similar combinations of charcoal drawing and pasted paper, but his later collages included corregated cardboard, paint, sand, sawdust, tobacco, ashes, and a greater variety in the color and texture of the pasted paper.

In 1914, Braque entered the army. He was seriously wounded during the following year, and it was many months before he resumed his art work. The war ended his association with Picasso, and it interrupted the development of the style he and Picasso had created. But Braque gradually built his earlier cubist technique into a style that is characterized by a high degree of subtlety and refinement in color and composition. Everything fits together with the precision of a picture puzzle.

Although some people may not consider Braque's collages to be as innovative in the use of materials as those produced by Picasso and Gris, his works are often more simply presented with fewer elements to confuse the eye. For example, in *The Clarinet* (Plate 9-1), Braque organized a few thin, delicate shapes so they appear to float in front and to the center of a white canvas. He also pasted to the canvas a piece of newspaper containing the word *L'Echo*, and he drew a musical

---

[2]Braque learned the technique of imitating wood grain during his apprenticeship as an interior decorator. Apparently, middle-class clients wanted to have their homes look like the homes of the rich, who could afford real marble and richly grained wood in their living quarters.

[3]For more information about cubism, see pages 43 and 44.

instrument on top of the paper. One end of the instrument contains a curve which is repeated again and again throughout the picture. In addition to the newspaper, he used charcoal, chalk, and oil paint; the oil paint was used to create an imitation of wood grain on the large orange rectangle in the middle of the picture. The work is an example of mixed media.

KURT SCHWITTERS (Shwitt'erz), 1887–1948

The collage flourished in the hands of Kurt Schwitters, a German painter, sculptor, and poet.

Schwitters created his collages with ordinary materials. He is said to have carried a suitcase for storing and transporting the objects that he collected from wastebaskets, sidewalks, and elsewhere. The suitcase also contained wire, brushes, and glue for fastening the found objects to cardboard or to canvas backgrounds. Schwitters called these products *Merz*, which is a meaningless term that he used in one of his early collages.

Considering the nonrepresentational nature of Schwitters' most important work, it is interesting that his training was altogether different. He studied art at the Dresden Academy in Germany,

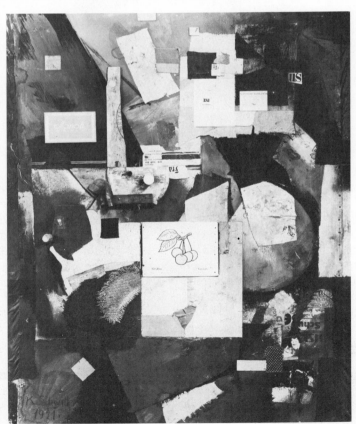

Plate 9-2.   Kurt Schwitters. *Cherry Picture.* 1921. Collage and gouache on cardboard, 36⅛" x 27¾". Collection, The Museum of Modern Art, New York (Mr. and Mrs. A. Atwater Kent, Jr. Fund).

where he received a highly academic form of instruction. To make a living, he painted portraits in an academic manner nearly all his life. Making a living, however, was all that he was able to achieve with his portraits. It was the collages that made him famous. He produced the first in 1919, and like most of his early work it was large and a mixture of oil paint and discarded materials. The *Cherry Picture* in Plate 9-2 is an example of his early work. It measures 27¾ x 36⅛ inches and it is composed of oil paint, cut paper, cloth, nails, photographs, pieces of wood, and a pipe bowl. Red and green colors are repeated throughout the design and so are the shapes of the cherries, the leaves, and the rectangular paper upon which the cherries were printed. Most of the rectangular shapes have been arranged in vertical or horizontal positions so their edges are parallel with the edges of the collage. The repetitiveness of the vertical and horizontal movements tends to give the collage unity and stability. If the rectangles had been tipped, the resulting diagonals would produce rapid eye movement and attract a lot of attention. This could be appealing if the composition were carefully organized, but if it were not, the diagonals could cause excessive visual busyness; they could lead the eye completely out of the design; or they could attract attention to areas that possess little visual interest.

One of the important contributions that Schwitters made to art was that he demonstrated the beauty in ordinary, discarded materials and in designs composed of those materials. His work was so appealing in its visual structure that it demanded the observer's attention.

HENRI MATISSE
1869–1954

Matisse was one of the great artists of modern times. He excelled in drawing, painting, printmaking, and sculpture, as well as in collage (see pages 81 to 83). He began using cut and pasted paper in the 1930s when he found it helpful in planning the design for a mural at the Barnes Foundation in Merion, Pennsylvania. Then, near the end of the same decade, he used it again in composing the cover for *Verve* magazine and in designing the costumes and scenery for the ballet *Rouge et Noir*, performed by the Ballet Russe de Monte Carlo.

The papier collé, or paper collage, became even more important in the life of Matisse when, following a series of operations in 1941, he was confined to his bed as an invalid. He could not paint very easily, but he could make cutouts from colored paper. Some of those cutouts culminated in a book entitled *Jazz*, which contained 150 reproductions of the paper collages. A different set of cutouts was employed in the design of the Rosary Chapel for the convent of the Dominican nuns at Vence. Matisse cut the shapes for the chapel from paper and had them arranged on the wall of his bedroom by one of his assistants. When the arrangement suited him, it was transformed into stained glass windows for the convent.

Matisse considered the collage technique to be the simplest and most direct way to express himself, but he was not satisfied with the color

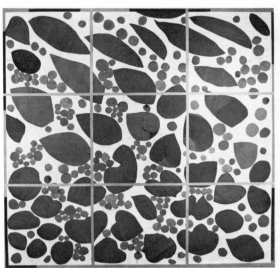

Plate 9-3. Henri Matisse. *Ivy in Flower.* 1953. Collage, 9'4" x 9'4". Dallas Museum of Fine Arts (Foundation for the Arts Collection, Gift of the Albert and Mary Lasker Foundation, New York City). Photo credit: Bill J. Strehorn, Dallas.

of prepared papers. Therefore, he arranged to have his paper painted with hues that appealed to him. The colors were usually bright and gay like the colors from his paintings.

The paper collage entitled *Ivy in Flower* (Plate 9-3) was completed in 1953 when Matisse was 84 years old. It is a finished work of art; it is not a model to be executed in another medium. The big green and blue leaf shapes contrast sharply with the yellow ochre background, and the red ivy blossoms are interspersed among the leaves. In front of the ivy are some vertical and horizontal stripes which suggest the framework of a window. Since the stripes are in front of the leaves it appears that the observer is looking out the window, through the ivy, and into the yellow ochre sunlight.

It is obvious from looking at *Ivy in Flower* that an artist does not need to use a high degree of detail, linear perspective, exuberant brush strokes, shading, or a lot of other artistic devices to present a concept. All he needs is color, shape, and a sensitivity to visual organization. Matisse repeated his shapes and colors often enough to give his work unity or coherence, and he placed them sufficiently close to each other to make sure that they were perceived as one integrated whole. At the same time, he altered, or varied, some of the shapes enough to give the work a satisfying appearance.

ADDITIONAL EXEMPLARS

For additional exemplars of collage, you might choose works of Pablo Picasso, Juan Gris, Jean DuBuffet, Jasper Johns, and Robert Rauschenberg.

COLLAGE ACTIVITIES FOR THE PRIMARY GRADES (AGES 6 THROUGH 8)

To make collages in grades one, two, and three, it will be helpful to have scissors, white glue, paper, cloth, lightweight cardboard, and a variety of other materials such as lace, ribbon, rickrack, feathers, leaves, and scraps of all kinds. Scissors can be obtained with round, pointed, or clipped ends, but we suggest the latter, because they can be pushed through cloth or paper more easily than the rounded type, and they are less dangerous than pointed ones. The teacher will always need to give instructions about cutting, however, no matter which instrument is given to the children. It is also important to demonstrate techniques for conserving paper by indicating that small shapes can be cut from scrap, and showing how shapes of any kind can be cut near the edge of the paper instead of the middle.

If cloth is used it should be thin and easy to cut, and the same can be said for paper and cardboard. All the paper normally found in schools is suitable for use in collages, but poster paper is especially good because it comes in a wide variety of colors, it cuts easily, and it costs about half as much as construction paper. It is best to give students paper that is 9 x 12, or 12 x 18 inches in size so they can handle it easily. Usable scrap can be stored in a large box and used in place of new paper whenever it is possible.

The base or background upon which collage materials are fastened need not be anything more than the art papers normally found in an elementary school if students are constructing a simple paper collage. A much stronger base is needed if cloth, cardboard, wood, and heavy items are to be glued to it. In that case we recommend chipboard, corrugated cardboard, or railroad board.

After arranging the cut or torn materials on a background, fasten them securely in place. A few drops of liquid white glue will fasten almost anything permanently in place.

CONCEPTS FOR POSSIBLE DEVELOPMENT

The concepts or terms listed below are a few that can be developed through the activities that follow. We expect that the ideas will come up in a discussion of the exemplars, the procedures, or the relationship of one to the other.

bright colors	dull colors	overlapping	transparent
collage	lines	papier collé	unity
cool colors	mixed media	pattern	variety
details	opaque	repetition	warm colors

SUGGESTED ACTIVITIES

The exemplars by Braque, Schwitters, and Matisse should be shown to the children when introducing the following procedures:

1. Display the exemplar by Kurt Schwitters, and explain that artists like Schwitters often put bits of magazine, newspaper, cloth, and other objects into their collages simply because they are the right color for a certain spot. Artists also use such materials because they know that works of art can be made from ordinary objects as well as from special art materials. Give the children some printed newspapers, magazines, glue, scissors, and tempera paint, and ask them to make large collages of animals or people.

    To begin, show the class how to glue two big pieces of newspaper together along the edges. Using a piece of colored chalk, draw a big animal or person on the paper, and paint over the lines with a big bristle brush and tempera paint. Cut the shape out, and glue it to a big piece of Kraft paper (colored, if possible). Then cut it out once again, leaving a border of Kraft paper about half an inch wide. The next step is to cut colorful shapes from magazines and paste them on the animal or person. They might be used for eyes, ears, feathers, scales, hair, whiskers, teeth, or clothing. Shapes can be repeated to make polka dots or stripes. In no case should the children cut eyes, mouths, and other such things out of the magazines for use as eyes and mouths in their collages. They should use the magazines simply for color. When the animals or people are complete, place them around the room and in the school halls.

2. While looking at Plate 9-3, introduce the words "collage" and "papier collé." Explain that the second term is French and is used to describe an artwork made of cut and pasted paper. Call attention to the irregular pattern created by the berry and leaf shapes in the Matisse work. The sizes of both motifs are varied and the blue and green leaves differ in shape. Both of these devices help to make the work interesting to the viewer. Because of the arrangement of the cut paper stripes, the viewer may get the idea he is looking out of a window at a large ivy plant. Ask the children to indicate if they have seen similar things through windows at school or at home. Then, with colored construction paper, scissors, and glue, have the children make a papier collé of what they have seen through a window. Suggest that they select a background paper that resembles the shape of the opening they are going to represent. Their windows may show the frame and individual panes, or curtains, shades, and draperies. Encourage the repetition of shapes in the process.

3. Repetition, pattern, and unity can be discussed when looking at the work by Matisse. These concepts may then be used by children when making torn-paper collages. Before they begin working with the art materials, have them examine the exemplar to see where shapes have been repeated to form a pattern. Assist them in seeing that the repetition of shapes and the use of a limited number of hues have unified the composition. Continue the discussion by talking about the different kinds of leaf and flower shapes that might be used in a collage. Show the youngsters some real flowers and leaves and point out the various parts of these objects that could be used in a design. Then give the children some glue and colored paper, and ask them to make a torn collage of flowers and plant forms. Encourage them to select a few colors which will contrast with the color of the background they have chosen. Also, remind them to repeat shapes in their collages. An example of a torn-paper collage of trees in the woods is illustrated in Figure 9-1.

Figure 9-1. Torn-paper collage of trees in the woods.

4. As the children look at the collage in Plate 9-2, share some information about Kurt Schwitters. Explain that he used many different materials in his collages, and ask the youngsters to point out the various things they see in the *Cherry Picture*. In the event they do not mention that paint was used, call their attention to it. Tell them that in some places a thinned-down paint has been brushed over materials, creating a transparent effect. In other places the materials and paint are opaque and do not allow the viewer to see what is beneath them. Schwitters overlapped many of the elements in his collages, and he probably spent a great deal of time arranging them. More than likely he arranged and rearranged the composition before adhering anything to the background.

After discussing the concepts of overlapping, transparent, and opaque, select one of the following themes and talk about it:

Real or imaginary birds (flying, nesting, eating)
Real or imaginary animals (running, drinking, sleeping)

Give special emphasis to the different kinds of birds or animals that might be made into a collage and see if your students can name the identifying characteristics of the creatures. As you do so, let the children see and feel the paper, cloth, and other materials available for their collages, and have them suggest uses for those materials. Try to use items that are transparent, opaque, smooth, rough, hairy, and so on. As your students fasten things to the backgrounds, encourage them to overlap and move things around before gluing them down. See Figure 9-2.

Figure 9-2.   A *Bird with Large Ears.* Cloth collage by second-grader.

5. A variation on the above procedure is to encourage the students to use overlapping in a collage made entirely of cloth. The texture of the cloth can give the feeling of the animal being represented. It will help to discuss the following creatures and how it would feel to touch them. Would they feel hard, soft, brittle, prickly, rough, smooth, wet, or slippery?

Snail	Pig	Horse
Porcupine	Cat	Turtle
Dog	Fish	Elephant

After each child chooses an animal, have him cut a 12-x-18 inch piece of oak tag into the shape of the animal or of the creature's head. Then have him select textures for his animal and glue the fabric to the oak tag shape. After gluing, the cloth can be trimmed with scissors to conform to the shape of the animal's body or head.

6. In the collage in Plate 9-3, the artist worked with three warm colors (red, yellow, and orange) and two cool ones (blue and green). Most of the colors are bright, but a few are dull. After discussing the brightness of the colors with the children, point out the square format used by the artist. Tell them that an artist usually works on a background which is square, rectangular, or circular. Then give the class some colored construction paper in the shape of 12-inch or 18-inch circles, 8-x-12-inch rectangles, or 9-x-24-inch rectangles. Make sure you provide an assortment of warm, cool, bright, and dull colors. Have them select colored poster and construction papers to make a papier collé for one of the following.

For those youngsters who select round paper, suggest one of the following topics and talk about it with your students:

Riding the merry-go-round	Playing in a swimming pool
The circus ring	Riding a Ferris wheel

If youngsters select long, thin rectangles for their background paper, recommend one of the themes listed below, and discuss the subject with them:

Climbing the stairs	Flying a kite
In a skyscraper	Netting butterflies

7. The mixed-media collage in Plate 9-1 was made with charcoal, oil paint, chalk, and pasted paper. The pasted shapes include pieces of colored paper and newspaper, over which Braque drew lines with charcoal and chalk. A number of the lines were used to create the clarinet, and several circular lines were repeated throughout the work. Lines were also used to form the simulated wood texture on the large orange rectangle, and other rectangular forms occur again and again in the picture.

When the children look at Plate 9-1, introduce the term "mixed media." Ask them to point out the different materials used, and to talk about the linear quality. After discussing one of the following topics, give the children some colored construction paper and poster paper, and have them show you what they think about the topic.

Roller skating	A snowy day
Self-portrait	Favorite animals
Walking in the rain	

After they have arranged and pasted the shapes to the background, have them use crayons or felt-tipped markers to add lines to their collages.

8. The first procedure in the *Stitchery and Appliqué* chapter can be done as a collage experience (see page 340). In place of the Krevitsky exemplar, introduce the concepts of overlapping shapes when looking at the collage by Kurt Schwitters (Plate 9-2).

COLLAGE ACTIVITIES FOR THE INTERMEDIATE GRADES (AGES 9 THROUGH 11)

One of the benefits derived from making collages in grades four through six is that children are less critical of their collages than they are of their drawings and paintings. They seem to accept the fact that paper, cloth, and scrap materials cannot be easily transformed into detailed and highly naturalistic configurations.

Along with the materials recommended for the primary grades, collages can be made with colored tissue paper. The best adhesive for such paper is liquid starch or diluted white glue (half water and half glue).[4] Simply brush the starch or glue on the area where the tissue is to be fastened and lay the tissue on top of the wet adhesive. As one color overlaps another, the students will immediately perceive that a third color is produced. This offers the opportunity for learning about color and the results that can be obtained from different combinations.

In addition, it is possible to draw on top of a damp or a dry tissue-paper collage by using a pen or a felt-tipped marker. If the paper is damp, the drawing will appear blurred or fuzzy, but if the paper is dry, the lines will be crisp and clean.

CONCEPTS FOR POSSIBLE DEVELOPMENT

artistic elements	found objects	motifs	repetition -
composition -	ground	negative space	shading
distortion	intervals	overlapping -	simplified shapes
dominance -	limited color	patterns	stylized
figure	linear	placement	transparent
focal point -	Merz	positive space	unity -

---

[4]If you use white glue, do not let it dry in the brushes, and make sure that the brushes are washed thoroughly with soap and warm water before they are stored.

SUGGESTED ACTIVITIES

All the collage activities recommended for the primary grades can be repeated at this level with variations. It would be advantageous to complete at least one of the following activities before making collagraph prints due to the fact that they are made from collages.

1. In the section devoted to easel-painting activities for the intermediate grades it is recommended that the following activity be used as a follow-up procedure for Activity 1 on page 156. Begin this activity with an examination of the exemplars by Rousseau and Matisse and point out that both artists were interested in leaves and plants. Rousseau studied the shapes of foliage and reproduced them in great detail. Matisse, however, simplified the foliage in his collages.

When looking at the collage by Matisse, have your students note the repetition of berry and leaf motifs throughout the work. This helps to give the collage unity because similar shapes tend to be seen as a coherent group rather than as separate entities. Endless repetition of size, shape, and color produces boredom, but repeated shapes that vary in size and color, repeated colors that vary in shape and size, and repeated sizes that change color and shape are compositional devices which create interest.

As Matisse worked on his collage, he gave further attention to figure and ground. The ground or the negative space is the base against which the figures or the positive areas seem to be placed. Artists pay attention to the relationships between positive and negative space because it is possible to create shapes or figures and then destroy their beauty by organizing them in a way that makes the negative space around them appear dull or disturbing. For example, Matisse could have arranged the shapes of his leaves and berries so the intervals between them were all the same size or shape, but this would have made the composition extremely dull.

Having called the foregoing compositional techniques to the attention of your class give them glue, scissors, large sheets of colored construction paper, and an assortment of colored scrap paper. Then discuss one or more of the following topics with them, and ask them to produce a collage involving one of these topics:

Seeds and seed pods (put a variety on display)
Small office supplies (paper clips, tacks, ink erasers, rubber bands, pen points, and so on)
Candy and gum (wrapped bubble gum, sticks of gum, gum drops, lollipops, licorice sticks, fudge, peppermints, and the like)

See Figure 9-3.

2. Try essentially the same project described in the preceding activity but direct the student's attention to both the exemplar by Matisse and the one by

Figure 9-3.   Office supplies collage done by a
student in an art methods class.

Schwitters. Stress the fact that both collages would have been chaotic if the
artists had used too many different shapes and colors. Matisse restricted himself
to two or three fundamental shapes and about five colors, and he allowed blue
and yellow to dominate the others. Schwitters also used a limited range of colors and shapes, and he permitted rectangular shapes to dominate. By limiting
one's palette (number of colors) and one's shapes, and by making one color or
shape dominate, the artist can create unity in a composition. Urge your students to do these things.

3. Display the exemplar by Matisse and point out the fact that it has no shading
and it is very two-dimensional. Because collages do not have to be made that
way, have your students try to produce shading in a collage that is more three-
dimensional than the Matisse.

To begin, give them some 18-x-24-inch sheets of newsprint, and arrange to
have them work in pairs. Ask them to make a large line drawing in pencil
showing their partner's legs and feet from the knees downward. Urge them to
omit tiny details while retaining shoelaces, heels, and soles on the shoes. Encourage them to pose with their legs and feet in different positions, and ask
them to draw the folds in trousers and the wrinkles in shoes. Ask them also to
let the legs go off the paper.

When the drawings are finished, the students should cut them apart along
the pencil lines. Place the cutout pieces on colored construction paper; trace
around them with a pencil, cut them out, and arrange them on a sheet of
18-x-24-inch colored construction paper. When all the pieces are in place, glue
them down.

As the students begin to cut their drawings apart, help them to see that
they can create the effect of shading by making depressed parts of the trousers
and shoes dark while making the high parts light; that they can also create
shading by making one side of a leg darker than the other side. Remind them

to make their areas of color merge into cohesive units of color. See Figure 9-4 at the beginning of the chapter.

4. Read the portion of this text that deals with Juan Gris, Pablo Picasso, and Georges Braque. Display the exemplars by those men, and explain what they, as cubists, were trying to do. Stress the emphasis that they placed on the composition. They repeated artistic elements (color, shape, pattern, texture, etc.), but they also arranged shapes or objects so the observer's eye would follow a certain path in, around, and through the work of art. Concentrate on those two compositional devices and have your students use them in making a collage of a still life.

    Create at least three small still-life arrangements. In one of them you might have a musical instrument, a dinner plate, some knives and forks, napkins, a rectangular piece of plywood, an empty egg shell, and some rectangular pieces of colored construction paper. A second still life might include a piece of torn corrugated cardboard, a meat grinder, some printed newspapers, a bunch of celery, some nuts, and a tall glass. The third still life might contain some small cardboard boxes, a golf ball, a soft ball, a frying pan, some small posters, scraps of cloth, a small can containing pencils, and a tall container of dried weeds.

    Give your students scissors, glue, large sheets of colored construction paper, newspapers, scrap cloth, and crayons. Explain that they do not need to put all the still-life objects in their collages and that parts of those objects can go off the edges of the paper. Urge them to make things life-size or slightly smaller, and let them draw on top of the collages with their crayons if they wish. The crayons might be used in the same manner as Braque used charcoal.

5. Instead of making a collage of the above still-life arrangements, have a student in the class pose with a musical instrument. Precede the activity with the discussion in Activity 4. Then have background paper of 18 x 24 inches, or 24 x 36 inches for mixed media collages. Encourage the students to cut the paper shapes large enough to fill the ground. Remind them to add details with crayons, oil pastels, or colored felt-tipped markers.

6. A variation on Activity 4 could be made by emphasizing distortion as a compositional device. The cubists often distorted the shapes of objects in an effort to show more than one view of those objects, and also in an effort to repeat shapes. Ask your students to distort some of the objects in their collages for the same reasons. They can show both the top and side views of a glass, for instance, and they can do it all within the outline of one glass. The same can be done with the boxes, cans, musical instruments, vases, and other objects recommended for the still lifes in Activity 4.

    A less complicated still life, than the previous one, can contain a bottle and glass, a trumpet, a violin, or a cup and saucer with a spoon. Let them work on paper large enough to permit the creation of life-size objects. Omit the drawing of details as suggested in the previous activity.

7. Show your students the exemplars by Kurt Schwitters and Jean Arp (page 272). Tell them that Schwitters and Arp both produced collages that were non-representational, and both saw beauty in ordinary things. Ask your pupils to identify the commonplace materials that Schwitters used in the *Cherry Picture*. Then have the children act as Schwitters did when they go home—ask them to search their environment for discarded materials which they can bring to school for a collage.

When the collections of scrap materials are sufficiently large, give the youngsters scissors, glue, and colored construction paper.[5] Briefly discuss overlapping, the repetition of shape and color, and the placement of rectangular forms in the *Cherry Picture*. Then urge your students to employ some of the same compositional techniques as they fasten their materials to the paper. Indicate that Schwitters probably moved his objects around before he glued them in place, and encourage your students to follow the same procedure.

Merz was the name that Schwitters gave to his collages. Have your pupils think of a name for theirs. Try to develop an appreciation for their collages and the materials they used to make them. See Figure 9-5.

Figure 9-5.   Collage of found objects by a fourth-grade student.

8. Show your class the *Clarinet* by Braque (Plate 9-1). Call special attention to the way the artist used chalk, charcoal, and paint to draw on top of his collage. In

---

[5]If the children bring heavy discarded materials to class, give them some oak tag or chipboard in place of the construction paper. Cardboard from empty cereal boxes will also work.

places, he created single lines; elsewhere, as in the big central rectangle, he simulated the grain of wood by making his lines close together; and, in the clarinet as well as in the table at the bottom of the picture, he did some shading. Notice also that the clarinet was drawn in such a way that the letters on the paper show through it; the clarinet looks transparent.

Give your students some scrap construction paper, newspapers, glue, 18-x-24-inch white drawing paper and scissors, and ask them to arrange some rectangular pieces of newspaper and scrap on the white drawing paper. Suggest that they do it in a manner similar to Braque. Then give them some black wax crayons, and urge them to add single lines, patterns of line, and shading to the top of their collages. Once again, ask the students to do it in the manner of Braque and to create the effect of transparency in some of their objects. They might draw glasses, books, eye glasses, pipes, potted plants, and bowls of fruit. Remind them to repeat their linear elements and patterns often enough to produce a unified, coherent picture.

9. Using scrap paper and pencils, have your students make line drawings of mechanical objects in their classroom and throughout the school. Faucets, light switches, pencil sharpeners, door locks, vises, hinges, fire extinguishers, door handles, light sockets, and other similar objects would be excellent. Then have each child cut a small rectangular window in a piece of paper, and have him move the window around on top of his drawing until he finds a segment of the drawing that has a focal point or a center of interest, shows balance, and contains shapes of differing widths and heights, and linear elements with some variety in their angles, curves, and widths.

Before continuing, display the exemplars by Braque and Schwitters. Find areas in each work that look transparent. Discuss the different ways in which each artist accomplished this effect.

The next step is to enlarge the drawing inside the paper window while transferring it to a 12-x-18-inch (or an 18-x-24-inch) sheet of white drawing paper. Then give the class a selection of colored tissue papers, newspapers, scissors, brushes, and cold liquid starch. Show the students how to place the tissue on top of their drawings so they can trace around the different shapes they want to cover with colored paper. Cut the shapes out with scissors, and brush liquid starch onto the drawing wherever the tissue paper is to be placed. Lay the cutout paper into the wet starch and brush over it with starch.

If two pieces of colored tissue overlap, another color will be formed. If the overlapping is done with thoughtfulness, it can result in interesting patterns. Urge your students to do this. Also encourage them to use small amounts of printed newspaper in their collages.

As the collages dry, they will warp, but this can be corrected by stacking the dry works in a pile and placing a heavy weight on top. When they are flat, return them to the students to go over their original pencil lines with a black, felt-tipped marker, a black crayon, or a brush dipped in India ink.

PART 4

Printmaking

A print is an image that has been transferred from one surface to another by pressing one against the other. The fact that multiple impressions are frequently made from a single printing surface does not change their status as original works of art, but it does mean that prints are usually less expensive than other art objects.

Prints were first made in China, but how or when is not known with certainty. We do know, however, that block prints bearing Chinese characters were created as early as the sixth to eighth centuries. Printing in the Western world, on the other hand, did not occur until the fifteenth century, and it developed independent of Oriental influence. The earliest prints, made from wooden blocks, were designs on playing cards and images of religious figures on small devotional papers. Before long, wood-block illustrations, along with movable type, were used in early religious books. Since that time, fine prints have continued to appear in illustrated books, but they have also become valuable as art objects apart from books. Prints have been created as posters, as illustrations and advertisements in newspapers, and as artistic expressions similar to paintings. Prints have served both religious and secular interests throughout their history.

By examining the reproductions in almost any book on printmaking, it becomes obvious that prints differ considerably in their appearance. This is caused in part by the fact that there are four fundamental methods of making prints: relief, intaglio, planographic, and stencil. The relief method is one in which the areas that are not to be printed are cut from the printing plate causing the printable image to project from the background. This raised or relief image is then inked and pressed against paper to make a print. Woodcuts and linocuts are examples of relief prints.

The intaglio method is the opposite of the relief technique because the low, cut-out portions of the plate do the printing instead of the raised areas. The method requires that lines be etched with acid, cut with engraving tools, or scratched with drypoint needles into a metal plate, usually copper. The plate is then heated, and printing ink is rubbed into the incised lines. Any excess ink remaining on the surface of the plate is wiped off with tarlatan. The plate is placed face up on the bed of the printing press; damp paper is placed over the plate; a blotter is laid on the paper; and two or three felt blankets are placed on top. As the plate and its covering layers are run between the steel rollers of the press, pressure forces the soft, damp paper into the incised lines where it receives the ink.

Next to the relief process, the intaglio system is the oldest method of creating prints; the earliest of the printmakers to use the intaglio method were often goldsmiths or armorers who were skilled at cutting lines in metal. Gradually, they learned that lines and larger areas could be removed from the printing plate in a variety of ways. This made possible a broad range of effects, and it made the intaglio method the most versatile of all printing techniques. Because of this versatility, we have intaglio prints known as etchings, engravings, drypoints, mezzotints, aquatints, and combinations of one with another.

Unlike the relief and intaglio methods of printmaking, the planographic process involves printing from a *flat* surface. A lithograph, for example, is a planographic print made from a flat piece of stone, zinc, or aluminum. The printing surface, which is usually limestone, is carefully ground until it is even and smooth. An image is then made on the stone with a greasy lithographic crayon or a greasy liquid called tusche. After the drawing is finished, the surface of the stone is treated with a solution of gum arabic and dilute nitric acid. The drawing is then removed from the stone with turpentine and water, but the area underneath remains impregnated with grease from the drawing. Since the area is greasy, it resists water and accepts ink. Consequently, when an artist wets the stone and applies ink with a roller, the ink adheres only to the area that had been covered by the drawing. Printing paper is then placed over the inked stone, and the two are run through a special lithographic printing press. Except for the fact that it is a reverse image, the result looks almost exactly like the original drawing. For that reason, it is often said that the planographic process is most suitable for the printmaker who likes to work directly, rapidly, and spontaneously.

The stencil method of making prints is the only method that does not result in a reverse image. The desired figure is cut from a thin but strong piece of sheet metal, paper, tag board, or other material, and the product is called a stencil. The stencil is placed upon the surface that is to receive the print, and ink or paint is applied through the openings with a stiff brush. The process has been used in the Orient for hundreds of years, but a new variation on the stencil method became popular with American artists in the 1930s. It is called the silk-screen process or serigraphy, and it requires the use of a silk screen. The screen is made by stretching silk across a frame and fastening it. The image to be printed is then painted on the screen with tusche, a water-resistant liquid. When the tusche is dry, the rest of the screen is coated with water-soluble glue which fills the holes in the silk. Then the tusche is removed with turpentine, leaving the glue in the form of a stencil. The screen is then placed on the paper that is to receive the print; pigment is placed inside the screen; and a rubber-edged squeegee is pulled across the stencil to force the pigment through the openings where the tusche had been. By following this procedure, hundreds of prints can be made in a relatively short time.

In addition to tusche and glue, many other materials can be used to create the stencil inside the silk screen. These materials allow the artist to produce a large number of effects ranging from hard, clear-cut edges to soft, fuzzy edges and from abstraction to photographic naturalism. And, since all the materials can be removed from the screen, several different stencils can be made using the same screen, and one color can be printed on top of another, producing multicolored prints.

Obviously, some of the foregoing printing procedures are too difficult for children in the elementary school. But a few basic methods are definitely suitable, and several variations on these procedures have become popular with children. Let us turn our attention to those methods and to the artists who use them.

CHAPTER 10

MONOPRINTS

Figure 10-4. *Owl.*

Monoprints are produced by using the plano-graphic method of printmaking.[1] The invention of this enjoyable kind of printing is usually attributed to Giovanni Benedetto Castiglione (1616-1670), an Italian painter, who created his

---

[1]*Mono* comes from the Greek word *monos*, which means "one." Hence, monoprint means one print. Only one print of a kind can be made using this method of printmaking.

first monoprint in Rome in 1635. Apparently, he used three different methods of making his prints, and the same methods are still used today. One of them involves painting an image on a flat, metal plate and pressing a piece of paper against the paint to make a print. A second method requires that the plate be coated with printing ink; a picture is scratched in the ink with a stick; and paper is pressed against the ink to reproduce the image. The third technique includes: 1) painting an image on a flat surface; 2) wiping away parts of the painting with brushes, sticks, or cloths; and 3) pressing paper against the paint to make the print.

After Castiglione's death, almost nothing was done with monoprints until the last half of the nineteenth century. At that time, a number of artists began to make monoprints and, among that group, Edgar Degas was probably the most serious. It is said, in fact, that he produced more than five hundred monoprints. The reason that other artists have been less interested in making them as serious works of art is not clear. Perhaps the technique is not sufficiently versatile, or it may not produce enough prints to justify the effort involved. Or it may be that artists have avoided the method because monoprints have been accepted neither as prints nor as paintings in most exhibitions and competitions. Unfortunately, this lack of acceptance has occurred because monoprints seem to fall into the never-never land between painting and printing.

EXEMPLARS OF MONOPRINTING

A monoprint is an image that has been transferred from a wet drawing or a wet painting to another surface. As a consequence, observers often wonder why it would not be more sensible to save the original drawing or painting thereby avoiding what seems to be the unnecessary task of transferring an image to another surface. But these observers fail to realize that effects can be obtained through the transfer of images that cannot be achieved through direct painting or drawing.

PAUL GAUGUIN, 1848–1903

Elsewhere we have discussed some of Gauguin's distinctive ideas about art (pages 96 to 97), but it is important to add that he was firm in believing that visual nourishment exists in the primitive arts. His preference for primitive qualities can be seen in all his work, but it is especially evident in his prints. They possess little or no shading and no detail or other refinements. Instead, they contain numerous flat, simplified shapes and plenty of bold contrasts. This makes them look crudely executed, which is the effect Gauguin hoped to create. He believed that details were unnecessary, and he felt that the freshness of a visual impression was not sufficiently durable to survive prolonged refinement.

As one might expect, Gauguin's ideas and graphic productions were not accepted by the people of his own time. Popular taste favored prints that were more naturalistic and technically more refined. Eventually, however, Gauguin's accomplishments led to a revolution in the graphic arts. They helped people to see that primitive configurations have their own unique charm, honesty, directness, power, and beauty. The distinctive nature of primitive images permits them to convey information which cannot be communicated through works of a more polished type. Consequently, artists such as the German expressionists began to experiment with primitive methods in an effort to give more emotional impact to their work. Gauguin had made it easier for them to break away from traditional content and accepted techniques (see page 216).

During the last years of his life, Gauguin lived in the Marquesas Islands, where he found the inhabitants to be good subjects for his drawings and paintings. The monoprint in Plate 10-1, for example, is an image of two Marquesans; it illustrates some of the primitive characteristics already mentioned. It appears to be crudely executed; it lacks detail; it contains coarse shading or modeling; and it possesses almost no visual depth. The apparent crudeness in the execution is caused in part by the spontaneous quality of the lines and by the smudgy-looking ink spots in places where they do not seem to belong. The smudges are a direct result of the technique Gauguin used in making the print. He coated a flat surface with printing ink and placed a piece of paper on top of the ink. After drawing on the paper, he removed it from the plate. The ink ad-

hered to the under side of the paper beneath each of his marks, and it also adhered elsewhere in lesser amounts, causing the smudgy spots.

By comparing the Gauguin with the prints by Degas and Prendergast you can see that different techniques were used to produce them. Apparently, Degas and Prendergast did not draw on their paper while it was on the ink plate, but they did apply pressure to the whole piece either with their hands or with a press.

EDGAR DEGAS, 1834–1917

In Chapter 2, we indicated that Edgar Degas was one of the most accomplished advocates of the pastel medium in the history of art, and we described his method of drawing. But we did not mention the relatively unknown fact that at least a quarter of his pastels were produced on a monoprint base. Apparently, the monoprint gave Degas a preliminary compositional foundation upon which to add pastels and to gradually build a finished work of art.

The printing techniques that Degas used are the same as those used by Castiglione two hundred years earlier. Sometimes the desired image was painted directly on a metal plate, and paper was pressed against the image to create the monoprint. Eugenia Janis, an authority on Degas' graphic work, calls this method the light-field technique because it produces a print with a light background.[2] The dark-field technique, on the other hand, begins with a metal plate coated with printing ink. The artist creates an image on the plate by removing some of the ink with rags and pointed instruments. By pressing paper against this image the artist obtains a monoprint with a dark background. And it is also possible to combine this method with the light-field technique to produce interesting results.

The monoprint in Plate 10-2 is a dark-field product without the addition of pastels. The costumes on the dancers and the diagonal striations on the floor were created by wiping ink from the

Plate 10-1.　Paul Gaugin. *Two Marquesans.* 1902. Monotype, 14⅝" x 12½". Philadelphia Museum of Art (purchased with funds from Frank and Alice Osborn Fund).

[2]Eugenia Janis, *Degas Monotypes* (Cambridge: Fogg Museum, 1968), pg. XVII.

Plate 10-2. Edgar Degas. *Three Ballet Dancers.* c. 1878–1887. Monotype, 7⅞" x 16⅞".
Sterling and Francine Clark Art Institute, Williamstown, Massachusetts.

printing plate with a rag. Highlights on the fingers and faces were created with a pointed instrument, and so were selected contours on the legs and arms. Degas obviously was skilled at doing this because he removed the ink in a way that makes the light look as if it is coming from below or from the footlights.

Janis says that the dark-field technique is especially advantageous in the creation of theatrical effects because the dark background serves beautifully as unlighted stage space.[3] The technique would probably work equally well in any instance that calls for a vague, mysterious, or ethereal background.

Finally, it seems worthwhile to call attention to a simple compositional feature evident in Plate 10-2. Instead of separating the dancers into three visual units, Degas placed them in units of one and two, and he overlapped the figures in the unit of two. This divides the picture space unequally and it makes the composition more interesting.

[3] *Ibid.*

MAURICE PRENDERGAST, 1859-1924

Like the creations of numerous artists before and since, the works of Maurice Prendergast attracted only three or four patrons during his life. This meant that Prendergast found it necessary to carve frames and design show cards in an effort to earn his livelihood. He was a good-natured fellow, however, who did not require a high standard of living to be happy. His primary necessity was the opportunity to create art, and he managed to satisfy that requirement.

Born in Newfoundland, Prendergast moved to Boston with his family at the age of two, and despite numerous trips to Europe and a period of residence in New York City, Boston was the place where he spent most of his life. He enjoyed the New England coast from Maine to New York, and much of it became the subject of his paintings. Scenes from France, Italy, and New York City were also among his favorite artistic concerns, but regardless of the subject, his work was always fresh, bright, and cheerful. His watercolors were especially lively, and he painted more of them than of oils, because they were less expensive to produce.

Prendergast was one of the artists who later became known as "The Eight" (Robert Henri, George Luks, Everett Shinn, William Glackens, Ernest Lawson, Arthur Davies, John Sloan, and Prendergast). This was the group that attempted to call attention to European and American art simultaneously by creating and participating in the famous Armory Show of 1913. It was also the group that formed the nucleus of a larger assortment of artists ultimately referred to as the Ash Can School of American art. The Ash Can School received that name because the artists drew and painted life in the streets, alleys, and backyards of America. This was different from the favored art of the early twentieth century, which was much more restricted in its subject matter.

Prendergast painted many watercolors outdoors, and he made numerous sketches which were later taken indoors where they were developed into finished paintings and prints. He preferred working from sketches and from prints because, unlike most of his friends, he was not interested in making faithful reproductions of nature. He used nature merely as a point of departure. He was more concerned with structural organization and about the qualities that make art appealing as an entity in itself, apart from nature. Hence, he tended to apply visual organization and pattern to his work instead of allowing it to be determined by nature. His point of view, therefore, was not unlike the philosophy of Paul Gauguin (page 96), and it helped to make him the first American to anticipate the direction of art in the twentieth century.

In addition to his paintings, Prendergast produced approximately two hundred monoprints, a number which makes him one of the most prolific artists to work in that medium. His technique, according to Hedley Rhys, was to paint with oils on a copper plate.[4] He then placed Japanese paper on top of the paint and rubbed the back of the paper with a spoon, or he placed the plate and paper in a printing press to apply pressure. Sometimes, he pulled more than one print from a given painting because he liked the softer effects obtained subsequent to the first impression. The result can be seen in *Bareback Rider* (Plate 10-3), which also exemplifies the circus theme that Prendergast used only in his monoprints. The print has a sparkle similar to that which characterizes his watercolors, and it is caused by the fresh color and the white or light areas which have been left unpainted. Some of these light areas were also created by removing paint from the printing plate with a rag, a stick, or a pointed instrument of some kind. This can be seen in the horse, the clown, the rider, and the whip. Notice also how clearly the brush strokes can be seen, a feature characteristic of monoprints.

In making a monoprint like the Prendergast or the Degas, it is possible to create a wide range of effects by altering the consistency of the paint or ink. If the medium is thin or runny, it is impossible to scratch it away with a pointed instrument because the marks immediately fill and disappear. But a thin medium will create interesting effects, and it can be combined with thick ink or paint on the same plate. Degas and Prendergast were both experts at manipulating the consistency of their medium to extend its expressive capabilities.

ADDITIONAL EXEMPLARS

In addition to the exemplars by Gauguin, Degas, and Prendergast, try to find and show some monoprints by Toulouse-Lautrec, Corot, Forain, Pissarro, Renoir, Valadon, Cassatt, Matisse, Picasso, Ernst, Rouault, Chagall, Hunt, and Sloan. Reproductions of works by the last four will probably be the easiest to obtain.

---

[4]Hedley Howell Rhys, *Maurice Prendergast* (Cambridge, Mass.: Harvard University Press, 1960), p. 34.

Plate 10-3. Maurice Prendergast. *Bareback Rider.* n.d. Monotype, 11⅕″ x 9⅕″. The Cleveland Museum of Art (Purchase, Dudley P. Allen Collection).

MONOPRINTING ACTIVITIES FOR THE PRIMARY GRADES (AGES 6 THROUGH 8)

Children enjoy printmaking, yet they rarely engage in it because teachers feel that it is too messy or too troublesome. Making prints need not be dirty or inconvenient, however, if appropriate tools and materials are used and if the classroom is properly prepared. In organizing the room for monoprinting, it is advisable to create five or six inking stations on a large table or counter. The working area can be covered with Kraft paper, and each station can be equipped with a 12-x-18-inch piece of safety glass or plexiglass,[5] a small rubber brayer,[6] a supply of printing ink or paint,[7] a rag, and a small can of mineral spirits or turpentine (if oil-based inks are to be used).

To increase efficiency and reduce accidents and congestion, it also helps to prepare a place for drying the finished prints. A wire strung across a room will serve nicely as a place to hang wet products, and it will work most satisfactorily if the children can reach it and if the wire is threaded through holes drilled in the handles of pinch clothespins. This arrangement permits each print to be suspended by one of its corners, and it allows the prints to hang close to one another without damaging them.

White drawing paper, construction paper, gray manila paper, poster paper, and newsprint are suitable for monoprinting, and an ample amount should be located conveniently in the classroom. Aprons or old shirts should also be available because printing ink can produce permanent stains in clothing.

CONCEPTS FOR POSSIBLE DEVELOPMENT

The following terms or concepts can be taught successfully in connection with the activities recommended in succeeding paragraphs:

print	oil-based ink	Vaseline	the Degas technique
monoprint	reverse image	brayer	the Gauguin technique
transfer	fingerpaint	detergent	the Prendergast technique

SUGGESTED ACTIVITIES

Monoprinting is ideal for the public school because it is a simple process, and it does not require a lot of time. We recommend it as one of the first printing processes to be introduced to children.

1. Get five or six quarts of prepared·fingerpaint in black, blue, red, green, orange, and violet colors. Place a tongue depressor in each jar, and put one jar by each

---

[5]Safety glass or plexiglass is recommended because of its versatility, but a piece of tempered Masonite makes a good substitute.

[6]A brayer is not always needed, but when it is, it can make the difference between success and failure. Consequently, it is important to use a soft rubber brayer rather than a hard one, and the roller should turn easily.

[7]Several different inks and paints can be used in monoprinting, but water-soluble printing ink dries too quickly to produce good results.

of the inking stations. Then explain what a monoprint is; show the class the exemplars by Gauguin, Degas, and Prendergast, and discuss the differences in their appearance. The Degas and the Prendergast look like paintings, but the Gauguin resembles a drawing. It appears that Gauguin printed dark lines on light paper, while Degas printed the areas around white spaces. Prendergast, however, did both. See if the children can find the lines in the Prendergast that look as if they were made the same way as the lines by Degas. Then ask the youngsters which artists might have used a rag in making their prints. Both Degas and Prendergast used rags.

To introduce the Degas technique, explain and demonstrate the system he used. But instead of using oil-based ink, spread some fingerpaint evenly across a piece of Masonite by rolling the paint with a rubber brayer. If Masonite is not available, use a desk that has a Formica top. Cleanliness will be aided by keeping the fingerpaint inside a rectangle formed by four pieces of masking tape attached to the table, or Masonite. The rectangle should be smaller than the printing paper.

After rolling out the fingerpaint, draw in it with a rag, with one of your fingers, or with a wide-pointed stick such as a broken tongue depressor. Then place a piece of white or colored paper on top of the drawing, and rub the back of the paper gently with one hand. When the paper is removed, the print is finished and ready for drying on a wire "clothesline."

Since everything must be done at the inking stations, only five or six children can work on the project at one time. This means that it is good to introduce the activity when most of the youngsters are able to keep busy with other work. Then they can take turns at the monoprinting. They might use the theme of kings and queens, dancing clowns, or some other subject. When the prints are finished, call attention to the similarities between the piece by Degas and the work by the children. See if the children can detect the use of a rag or stick in any of the prints.

2. Instead of using fingerpaint in the foregoing project use a mixture of black powdered tempera paint and Vaseline. To do this, remove half of the contents of a one-pound jar of Vaseline (petroleum jelly), and place it in another container. Next, add (little by little) 1½ cups of powdered tempera to the remaining half-pound of Vaseline, and stir the mixture with a strong stick. Then roll out the ink; make the print; and place the finished product, face up, on a flat surface. Put a clean piece of white paper on top of the wet print, and rub the back of the paper gently with your hand. When the paper is removed, it will show a reverse image of the original print. This means that it has removed some of the Vaseline from the original. This process shortens to about one day the time required for drying. If the prints require more than three days to dry, add more powdered tempera to the Vaseline, or add as much as a third of a cup of powdered clay and mix thoroughly.

To clean the brayers, roll them over a piece of clean paper. Then remove the rest of the Vaseline with a rag. To clean the Vaseline from the inking plates, scrape it off with a spatula and wipe the plates with crumpled newspaper until they are almost clean. Then finish the job with a rag.

3. To use the Gauguin monoprinting technique, prepare some Vaseline printing ink according to the directions given in the preceding activity, and place the mixture at the inking stations. One half-pound is enough for thirty students.

Begin with the discussion in Activity 1, but ask the children which print looks as if a pencil could have been used in making it. Then explain how the exemplar by Gauguin was produced and how a pencil was involved, but indicate that Vaseline will be used instead of oil-based ink because Vaseline is less expensive. Demonstrate how to spread the ink evenly across the inking plate with a brayer, and show how a pencil drawing is placed, face up, on top of the Vaseline. Without touching the paper with your fingers, go over the lines of the pencil drawing with a ballpoint pen. Then remove the print from the inking plate, and lay it on a table with the Vaseline side facing up. Place a clean sheet of paper on top of the print, and rub the back of the paper thoroughly. When the paper is removed, it will have a reverse image of the original print. A third print can then be obtained by placing a piece of paper on top of the inking plate and rubbing the back of the paper. All three prints will look different.

After your demonstration, give the children some pencils, white paper, and small mirrors. Ask them to draw a self-portrait, smaller than the inking plate and free of tiny details. Little drawings and small details do not come out well when this printing method is employed.

As the children finish their drawings, they can take turns making their prints. The teacher may wish to stay at the inking areas to offer help, especially if the youngsters have not engaged in this activity before. With a little experience, however, they should be able to complete the whole procedure without assistance. When the prints are dry, trim and mount them on black construction paper. See Figure 10-1.

4. A variation of Lesson 3 is to print with white Vaseline on black or colored paper. Simply color the Vaseline with white powdered tempera instead of black.

5. To make monoprints in the Prendergast manner, create five or six inking stations, each containing a glass plate, an aluminum pie pan, some ready-mixed tempera paint,[8] a bottle of liquid detergent, a can of water, and a number 12 watercolor brush. Then begin your lesson with a discussion similar to the one described in Activity 1, but ask the children which print looks most like a painting. It is likely to be the Prendergast because it is the only one that was actually printed from a painting.

To demonstrate a procedure similar to the one used by Prendergast, place a drawing of an animal or some other object under one of the glass plates. Put about a tablespoon of paint in the pie pan, and mix a little liquid detergent

---

[8]Thick, powdered tempera will work, but the prepared variety will work better.

Figure 10-1. The original pencil drawing is on the reverse side of the print.

Figure 10-2. Teddy Bear.

with the paint to make it adhere evenly to the glass. Then paint a line drawing on the glass using the sketch underneath as a guide. When finished, place a sheet of white paper on top, and rub its back gently. Then remove the finished print, and hang it on a "clothesline" to dry. Wash the brush and plate at the sink; dry the plate with a paper towel; and return the brush and plate to the inking station. See Figure 10-2.

As the children begin their drawings based on a predetermined theme (animals, insects, birds, weeds, flowers, faces, and the like), urge them to avoid details and lines that are close together, because features of that kind will merge when the back of the paper is rubbed, and the desired image will be lost.

MONOPRINTING ACTIVITIES FOR THE INTERMEDIATE GRADES (AGES 9 THROUGH 11)

Although it is acceptable to repeat monoprinting activities covered in the primary grades, it is assumed that teachers will offer additional information about: 1) the history of printmaking; 2) the four basic types of printmaking; 3) the history of monoprinting; 4) the ideas and techniques of artists who have engaged in monoprinting; and 5) the characteristics of work produced by those artists.

CONCEPTS FOR POSSIBLE DEVELOPMENT

To carry out the foregoing suggestions, it is recommended that the following terms or concepts be taught. We also suggest the continued use of concepts covered in the primary grades.

relief printing	primitive qualities	whimsical lines
intaglio printing	refinements	cubism
planographic printing	dark-field technique	surrealism
stencil printing	light-field technique	smudges
lithograph	fanciful colors	consistency of paint

SUGGESTED ACTIVITIES

Although mature and professional-looking prints can be made in the intermediate grades, we believe that the materials and equipment required for such prints are too expensive to be justified in schools. Consequently, we emphasize activities that feature inexpensive materials and equipment.

1. Before beginning the monoprinting projects, it would be good to devote one lesson to the history and basic techniques of printmaking. Perhaps the discussion could conclude with comments about planographic printing because monoprinting falls into that category. The exemplars from Chapters 10 through 13 should be helpful in illustrating the basic techniques, and the whole effort should offer an opportunity to introduce, for the first time, some of the concepts listed above.

2. Review Activity 3 for the primary grades before involving your class in the creation of multicolored prints of the Gauguin type. We recommend that students deal with subjects such as shoes, light fixtures, tools, angry couples, weeds against the sky, or a head-on collision. But first, place a different color of Vaseline at each of several printing stations. Then display the monoprint in Plate 10-1; describe Gauguin's life; and repeat his ideas about primitive qualities in art. This introduction will offer the opportunity to indicate that monoprinting lends itself to producing primitive qualities. It does so because it does not permit the making of details, and it produces accidental smudges which make the prints look crude or technically unrefined.

After pencil drawings have been made of the theme, take the youngsters to the printing stations, and show them how to trace over part of a drawing on one color before moving it to another color to trace a different part. This can continue until they have three or four colors in their prints. To make shading or solid areas of color, simply scribble inside the portion of the drawing that you want to be colored. Then discuss the finished prints, and relate the primitive qualities to those appearing in the Gauguin. See Figure 10-3.

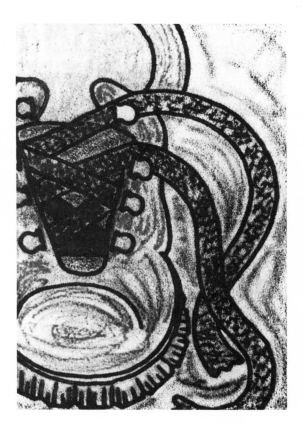

Figure 10-3.   *Shoe.*

3. Discuss the Degas dark-field technique described on page 184 and in Activities 1 and 2 on page 189. Then have students produce their own dark-field prints using oil-based ink. This will require that they rub the back of the paper with a baren while the paper is on the printing plate. If barens cannot be purchased from a school supply house, they can be made by placing three four-inch discs of corregated cardboard on top of each other and covering the stack with a piece of nylon. The loose edge of the cloth can be gathered and fastened tightly on top of the stack with a string or with a wire from a bread wrapper.

The subject for these prints might be flowers, dried weeds, branches of trees, performers in the spotlight, early morning, or a big batch of fish ready to be cleaned. When the prints are dry, you might have the students use their monoprints as a foundation for pastel drawings. Simply display the pastel exemplar by Degas, and explain how he used the hatching technique as he drew on top of his monoprints. To preserve these drawings they must be sprayed with a fixing solution.

If your printing plate is glass and if it is placed on white paper, the monoprinting will be easier because the white paper helps you to see what you are doing more clearly.

4. To make multicolored monoprints of the Prendergast type, proceed in the way described in Activity 5 on page 190. But, instead of using one color of tempera, give the youngsters a set of the eight basic colors. Then, using a little masking tape, fasten a drawing of the proposed print to a counter or table. Place a glass printing plate over the drawing; lay a large piece of white paper on top of the glass; and tape the most distant edge of the paper to the table with two or three small pieces of masking tape. These will act as hinges, and they will help to position the paper over the printing plate each time a new color is printed.

After the paper has been fastened, lift the closest edge, and swing the paper out of the way. Then place one tablespoon of color in a pie tin; add a little detergent; and mix it into the color. Begin painting on the glass by using the drawing underneath as a guide, but stay about one-fourth of an inch away from the pencil lines. When the first color has been applied, swing the hinged paper over the painted glass, and rub the back of the paper gently. Then lift the closest edge of the paper, and swing the print out of the way to dry. Mix the second color; paint it on the glass, and proceed until all the desired colors have been printed. Then prepare some black; paint it over the lines in the drawing, and print it as you did the other colors. See Figure 10-4 at the beginning of the chapter.

Prendergast used oil paint in creating his prints, and he printed all the colors in one operation. But oil paint is too expensive for most elementary schools, and tempera colors will merge if they are placed on the printing plate at the same time. That is why it is necessary to print one color at a time in this project. On the other hand, children often enjoy experimenting. So, they might like to try more than one color at a time on the printing plate. Also, they might enjoy working with a variety of colored papers. Printing on black construction paper, for example, will produce results different from those obtained on white paper.

Problems can be caused by watery paint, by painting large areas too slowly, and by making drawings with too many small details. If anything does go wrong, however, it is a simple matter to wash and dry the printing plate before trying again.

If this project is being done for the first time, it is important not to select topics that present special technical problems. Consequently, it helps to avoid landscapes or other topics that involve complicated backgrounds. It is better to begin with single items such as animals, birds, and insects, and it helps to have photographs of those things to show the children.

Finally, the beauty of these prints will be enhanced if you urge the children to be whimsical or fanciful with their colors and lines. If they feel compelled to use naturalistic colors, the results will be brown, gray, black, and dull. To avoid such results, show the children the print by Prendergast, and stress the fact that he made relatively colorless objects very colorful, which helped to make his work appear happy and cheerful.

CHAPTER 11

COLLAGRAPHS, EMBOSSMENTS, AND CARDBOARD PRINTS

Figure 11-5.   Truck, by a sixth-grader.

A collagraph is a print made from a collage, and a collage is an image created by fastening materials to a supporting surface of some kind. Naturally, the materials rise above the supporting surface, and when they are inked with a brayer, the ink is deposited on top, or on the raised portion, of the collage. Because the raised parts do the printing, it is justifiable to call the collagraph a relief print.

On the other hand, a collage can also be inked and printed like an intaglio. In other words, ink can be applied to the depressed parts of the collage as well as to the raised areas, and the piece can then be wiped and printed. The wiping removes the ink from the raised surfaces, leaving the ink in the depressed places to do the printing.

To make things a little more complicated, it is also possible to ink and wipe the collage as an intaglio and then ink it again with another color as if it were a relief. This means that intaglio and relief effects can both be produced in one print.

Sometimes the raised portions of a collage are not much higher than the surface that supports them. In that case, the supporting surface and the raised areas both receive ink from the brayer, and they both print. The result is similar to a planographic print because the impression is made from a surface that is almost flat. This indicates that a wide variety of effects can be achieved with collagraph prints, and it suggests that they are exciting to make and to observe. Some of these unique and exciting features can be seen in the work of Rolf Nesch and Clare Romano.

The characteristics of a cardboard print, on the other hand, can be found in the work of Edmond Casarella. A cardboard print by Casarella is not a true collagraph, but it is similar to one, and for that reason it is mentioned here. The Casarella method will be explained in a moment. But first it seems appropriate to point out that an embossment or an embossing can be made both from collages and from cardboard printing plates. An embossment is a figure made by raising the surface of something into bosses or protuberances. Raised images or swellings of this kind can be made in metal, leather, textiles, or paper, but making them in paper is easy and inexpensive. Consequently, it is a good activity for the elementary school.

EXEMPLARS OF COLLAGRAPH AND CARDBOARD PRINTING AND EMBOSSING

Nesch, Romano, and Casarella live in Europe and North America, respectively. This indicates that the inventive use of materials in printmaking is not confined to one country or to one region. Imaginative printing techniques can be found all over the world, and they often demonstrate that good prints do not necessarily require expensive equipment and supplies. This can be seen very clearly in the exemplars that follow.

ROLF NESCH (Nesh), 1893–

Rolf Nesch makes his home in Norway, but he was born in Germany, and he received his early training at the Dresden Academy of Art which he entered in 1913. Dresden had been one of the centers of German expressionism for at least a decade prior to that time.[1] Consequently, it is understandable that Nesch was influenced by the expressionist movement (see pages 58 and 216). The expressionists attempted to build a bridge between the solid artistic foundation of the past and the spirit of their own time. They tried to find graphic equivalents for emotion

---

[1]The expressionist group centered in Dresden was called The Bridge (Die Brücke), and its leader was Ernst Kirchner. Another group, located in Munich, was called the Blue Rider (Der Blaue Reiter), and its leader was Wassily Kandinsky.

because they considered the emotional impact of their work to be more important than technical polish and subject matter. Hence it was not unusual for them to distort or exaggerate color and form to achieve intensity in their visual statements. It is interesting to note, however, that the emotion they conveyed was seldom cheerful.

In 1924, Nesch spent considerable time with Ernst Kirchner in Switzerland, and the experience was clearly influential. Kirchner was unlike the other printmakers of his day because he did all his own printing; he did not employ professional printers to make finished prints from his plates. Apparently, Nesch followed Kirchner's example, which led him to discoveries and innovations that otherwise might not have occurred. In 1925, for example, he made the mistake of leaving a metal printing plate too long in the etching solution. The acid ate a hole through the metal, and when he printed with the plate, he found that a new effect had been created by the hole. This led him to deliberately cut and bore holes in his plates, and it prompted him to ink the cut-out pieces and put them back in the plate. By doing so, Nesch was able to print more than one color in a single printing.

By 1958, Nesch had produced 270 collagraphs from metal collages. One of them appears in Plate 11-1, and it shows that he created a variety of patterns by using different kinds of metal in the printing plate. Notice also that a narrow, white area surrounds each of the flower parts. This indicates that the print was made on white paper. The large number of colors suggests that the printing plate was not one that had all the parts soldered to a single piece of flat metal. If all the parts had been soldered together, it would have been impossible to ink the separate pieces with different colors; it would have been necessary to ink everything with the same color. Apparently Nesch created this particular metal collage with loose parts that could be changed in subsequent prints. He probably began by inking a flat metal plate with light purple ink. Then he undoubtedly inked each of the flower parts sep-

arately and placed them carefully onto the purple plate. Some of the parts were probably placed on top of others, and the whole thing was covered with a piece of moist paper and a thick layer of felt. Then it was run through a press that forced the paper tightly against the ink and down into the low spots. The areas around the flower parts remained white because the paper could not be forced into the ink that was below and immediately adjacent to the edges of the raised pieces of metal.

Plate 11-1.   Rolf Nesch. *Yellow Flower*. 1953. Metal print, 22" x 19½". Philadelphia Museum of Art (Purchased: Seeler Fund).

The print in Plate 11-1 has the flavor of German expressionism because it is bold in shape and color. It is abstract and possesses certain primitive qualities that were regarded highly by the expressionists. It also has an emotional power generated by the foregoing characteristics. Perhaps the collagraph lends itself to such expressionistic statements because it produces strong, crude shapes and does not permit highly detailed refinements.

CLARE ROMANO, 1922–

For many years Clare Romano has been one of the most distinguished printmakers in America. Her stature as an artist can be deduced in part from the fact that her work is included in numerous private and public collections, including the Museum of Modern Art, the Whitney Museum, the Metropolitan Museum of Art, and the Library of Congress. In addition, she has won acclaim as both a teacher and a writer. Especially noteworthy in this respect is a book entitled *The Complete Printmaker* which she wrote together with John Ross.[2] The book grew out of work that the two artists had been doing with cardboard prints and collagraphs in the 1950s and '60s. During that time they served as "artists in residence" with the U.S.I.A. exhibition (Graphic Arts U.S.A.) in Yugoslavia and Romania, and they discovered an enormous interest in the new techniques they had developed.[3] Apparently, no information on the new methods had been published, and people were eager to have it.

In their book, as well as in their teaching, Romano and Ross place an emphasis upon the workshop approach to printmaking because they believe that people learn best by doing. They also believe that tightly structured sequences of academically oriented problems are not as effective as flexible approaches which give the student more freedom to work out her own ideas and methods at her own pace.

Since collagraphs can be made from a wide assortment of exciting materials, Romano and Ross also caution the printmaker against letting himself become dominated or overly fascinated by these materials. They feel that an artist can become so intrigued by such things that he neglects the personal statement which should receive the bulk of his attention.

The collagraph in Plate 11-2 is an example of the kind of print that became popular in the 1960s. The printing plate, or collage, was made from cardboard or chipboard, which was cut into several segments. Each segment was inked separately and reassembled with the other parts before printing. To get the linear effects evident throughout the print, the plate was inked in both

---

[2]John Ross and Clare Romano, *The Complete Printmaker* (New York: The Free Press, 1972).

[3]The U.S.I.A. is the United States Information Agency.

Plate 11-2.   Clare Romano. *On the Grass.* 1971. Color collagraph; comp.: 10⅛" x 30¹³⁄₁₆", sheet: 20⁹⁄₁₆" x 37⁵⁄₁₆". Collection, The Museum of Modern Art, New York (John B. Turner Fund).

intaglio and relief. The whole body, for example, was inked with purple and wiped, leaving the purple close to the edges of the raised pieces. Then the dress and the hat were inked in relief with red and blue respectively. The grass and the stripes on the hat were inked separately and re-assembled with the body before printing.

The construction of the collage or printing plate is also interesting and important. Pieces of cardboard were glued to the supporting surface with gesso, which was also used to coat the whole collage after the pieces had been fastened. Finally, a layer of plastic was probably sprayed over the dry gesso to make the plate easier to wipe.

As a pioneer of the collagraph technique, Clare Romano has pointed imaginative artists in a new direction. She has helped them to see a whole new world of visual effects that can be obtained with uncomplicated methods and inexpensive equipment. The implications for art in the public school are especially significant.

EDMOND CASARELLA, 1920–

Edmond Casarella is an American who has produced a number of cardboard prints of considerable beauty. According to Gabor Peterdi, Casarella makes his printing plate by cutting heavy, laminated cardboard with a sharp tool and by peeling away the areas that are not to print.[4] Then he probably sprays the plate with plastic to keep the cardboard from absorbing the oil in the printing ink. The ink is then rolled onto the raised areas with a brayer, and paper is pressed against the plate to make a relief print. Evidently, Casarella uses more than one card-

board plate because the print in Plate 11-3 shows that certain colors are printed on top of others, and that cannot be done with only one plate.

From the foregoing description of Casarella's technique it is easy to see why his prints are not collagraphs. They are simply not made from collages, but instead, they are made from cardboard plates that have had certain areas cut out and peeled away. The remaining raised surfaces do the printing.

Like a collagraph, the cardboard print is often strong and bold in appearance. This is because the procedure of making such prints does not allow for many details or refinements. It lends itself more satisfactorily to the creation of simple, harsh, flat shapes with power and emotional impact. In the Casarella print, for example, the shapes are all extremely simple in outline; they possess no gradations of color; and their edges are firm and sharp. This makes them ideal as a means of projecting massiveness, brutishness, solidity, weight, power, and other similar qualities.

Casarella obviously uses the medium of cardboard printing to its best advantage because he selects subject matter in keeping with the qualities projected naturally by the medium. He makes prints about rocks, moments of panic, and other such topics which can be handled effectively with simple, raw shapes, and with no gradations in color. If he should try to communicate the gentleness of a kitten through the use of cardboard prints, he would be attempting something not nearly as appropriate for cardboard printing. He might succeed, of course, but the task would be more difficult.

Plate 11-3 is entitled *Rock Cross*, and there does seem to be a vague, crosslike area in the central portion of the print. The area is filled with more small shapes than any other part of the artwork, and it also contains more contrast between light and dark. *Rock Cross* is, therefore, a good illustration of how an artist can make a figure visible in a work of art. He simply makes it different in some way from its surroundings.

---

[4]Gabor Peterdi, *Printmaking* (New York: Macmillan, 1959), p. 261.

Plate 11-3. Edmond Casarella. *Rock Cross*. 1955.
Cardboard print, 24" x 22½".
Collection, Krannert Art Museum,
University of Illinois, Champaign.

ADDITIONAL EXEMPLARS

If possible, show your students some collagraphs, embossings, and cardboard prints by artists other than those discussed in this book. It would be good to show and display the work of Omar Rayo, Boris Margo, John Ross, Donald Stoltenberg, and Antonio Berni.

COLLAGRAPH- AND CARDBOARD-PRINTING AND EMBOSSING ACTIVITIES FOR THE PRIMARY GRADES (AGES 6 THROUGH 8)

Cardboard printing is not recommended for the primary grades because it is time-consuming and involves the use of sharp tools which cannot be handled safely by young children. It is possible, on the other hand, to do collagraph printing as early as the first grade, but it requires a considerable amount of assistance from the teacher. The children are able to make the printing plate without difficulty, but they have trouble when it comes to inking and printing. Consequently, collagraph printing is recommended most enthusiastically for the intermediate level. If it is attempted in the primary grades, the printing plates should be simple to construct; the ink should be restricted to one color; and a helping hand from another teacher or from a parent should be requested. Simply pick the first of the activities suggested for the intermediate grades, and try them with the younger children.

Embossing is definitely possible at the primary level, but the children must be able to cut heavy twine and glue it to paper. When they can do that, we recommend Activity 7 on page 208.

COLLAGRAPH- AND CARDBOARD-PRINTING AND EMBOSSING ACTIVITIES FOR THE INTERMEDIATE GRADES (AGES 9 THROUGH 11)

The secret to successful printmaking in the elementary school is partly in the selection of tools and materials and in the organization of the classroom. We have found the arrangement described in Chapter 10, page 187, to be both efficient and convenient. Collagraph and cardboard prints will be most successful, however, if oil-based ink is used instead of the Vaseline mixture discussed on page 189. But if oil-based ink is not available the Vaseline makes a satisfactory, albeit imperfect, substitute.

It also helps to have a printing area close to the inking stations. The area might be a large open space on a sturdy table or the floor, but it should be smooth and as clean as possible, and it should contain five or six barens. Barens take the place of a printing press which is seldom available in the elementary school. They can be purchased from school supply companies, or substitutes can be made by covering three circular-shaped layers of corrugated cardboard with a piece of heavy nylon. The barens are used, of course, to apply pressure to the back of the printing paper after the paper has been placed on the printing plate.

CONCEPTS FOR POSSIBLE DEVELOPMENT

The concepts or terms that might be taught in connection with collagraph and cardboard printing and embossing are listed below:

relief print	gesso	brayer
planographic print	printing plate	bosses
collage	inking station	embossing
collagraph	oak tag	embossment
metal print	chipboard	inkless embossing
intaglio	baren	cardboard print
crude shapes	patina	German expressionism

SUGGESTED ACTIVITIES

Monoprints may be less difficult to create than collagraphs. Hence, it may be wise to make monoprints before undertaking the projects in this chapter. When ready, however, we recommend a sequential progression from the first to the last project because the lessons have been ordered according to their difficulty. The exceptions are Activities 7 and 8, which are relatively easy embossing projects.

1. If you have not done so, give your students a brief history of printmaking; explain the four basic methods of printmaking; and conclude with information about collagraphs. Since a collagraph is made from a collage, one might assume that it should be classified as a relief print, but that is not necessarily correct. Some collages have raised areas not much higher than the surface upon which they were glued. This means that the base of the collage receives as much ink as the raised portion, and it also prints. Because the resulting image has been made from a plate so flat that the base of the collage also prints, we may not be remiss in calling the image a planographic print. Make these points while displaying the collage exemplars by Schwitters and Matisse as well as the collagraph exemplar by Romano. Explain that the collage from which Romano produced her print was not significantly thicker than the collages by Schwitters and Matisse.

   To make a print from a collage thinner than Romano's, give each of your students a piece of 9-x-12-inch oak tag, a pair of scissors, and a small bottle of Elmer's glue.[5] Then select a theme such as imaginative beasts, monsters, or birds, and demonstrate how to draw one of the creatures as large as possible on the oak tag. When finished, cut the figure out, and use the leftover scraps to make eyes, wings, scales, feathers, horns, or other body parts. Glue the parts onto the creature and let them dry.

   Take the finished printing plate to an inking station. Place some oil-based printing ink or some of the Vaseline mixture described on page 189 on a sheet of glass. Roll out the ink until it is evenly distributed on the brayer.[6] Roll the brayer across the printing plate several times, making certain that the whole surface has received an even coat of ink. Then take the plate to the printing area, and place it, face up, on a smooth surface. After covering the plate with a sheet of newsprint, rub the back of the paper thoroughly with a baren, a wooden drawer pull, a spoon, or some other smooth object.[7] Peel the paper away, and hang the finished collagraph on a "clothesline" to dry. See Figure 11-1.

---

[5] Oak tag is the material from which manila folders are made; hence, it is readily available.
[6] In the beginning, it is usually best to print with only one color. Black is used most often, but excellent prints can be made with light-colored inks on dark paper.
[7] Experimentation will indicate the merits of each tool.

Figure 11-1.   *Bird.*

As the children build and ink their own printing plates, they will need assistance at the inking and printing stations, and they will need encouragement. The first print frequently is unsuccessful because of inexperience or because the new oak tag absorbs too much ink. But subsequent prints should turn out well. If not, the following things could be sources of trouble:

a) Not enough ink on the inking plate (light image).

b) Printing plate insufficiently inked (light, incomplete image).

c) Back of newsprint not rubbed hard enough or completely enough (light, incomplete image).

d) Too much ink on the inking plate and, consequently, too much ink on the printing plate (dark, thick image; interior form lost).

e) Brayer too hard. Ink not deposited on parts of the printing plate, especially if pieces of oak tag were glued close together (incomplete image).

f) Paper slipped while being rubbed (blurred image).

When the prints are finished, the oil-based ink must be cleaned from plates and brayers with rags and turpentine. If you have used colored vaseline, however, simply clean up with crumpled newspaper and rags.

2. Display the exemplar by Rolf Nesch, and explain how he made his prints. Emphasize that he followed the unusual practice of cutting or boring holes in his printing plates. Then ask students to make collagraph prints of fancy clocks, watches, and chronometers. Have the youngsters draw their images on pieces of 12-x-18-inch oak tag and print on 18-x-24-inch white drawing paper. But instead of having the students add the parts, as they did in Activity 1, have them cut out some of the parts with an X-Acto knife or a single-edged razor

blade. Make sure that the cutting is done on a piece of cardboard, and give the class instructions about the use of sharp tools.

As the printing proceeds, see if the effect of shading can be produced by rubbing the back of the paper harder in some places than in others. Then mount the finished prints on black construction paper, and discuss the effect of the cut-out parts with your pupils.

3. Show your students some of their own previous prints as well as the exemplar by Romano. Discuss the technique that was used to create the lines or shapes in the exemplar. Then advise the children about how to make those lines and shapes in a slightly different way. Give each of them a manila folder torn in half, making two 8-x-11-inch pieces of oak tag. Have them draw the front or side of an automobile or truck on one piece of oak tag. Perhaps they could go outside to draw real vehicles, or they could use photographs from magazines as their visual resources. When the drawings are complete, cut the vehicles out of the oak tag, and show the class how to cut them apart along all the pencil lines. Then demonstrate how to glue the parts on another piece of oak tag, leaving about one-eighth of an inch between the pieces.

The next step is to cut the vehicle out once again by cutting around its outline. Ink the result, and print with white ink on dark paper; then clean the plate with a rag, and print with black ink on light paper. When finished, have the class compare their new prints with older ones and with the exemplars. Are there differences among the lines? See Figure 11-2.

Figure 11-2.   *Truck.*

4. Activities 1 through 3 can be done several times to develop skill, and the repetition can be made interesting by changing the size of the printing plate, the color of the printing ink, the color of the paper you print on, and the subject matter. Try making prints of imaginative plants, buildings, household appliances, and photographic equipment.

Further variation can be achieved by gluing the printing plates from Activities 1 through 3 to rectangular pieces of mat board. Then the plate and the background of mat board can be inked and printed. The bumpy surface of the mat board will produce a patterned background which provides an effective contrast to the plainness of the printed object. How would the background of the Romano exemplar look if it had been printed with a mat board instead of a smooth-surfaced material?

Another interest-producing variation on the foregoing projects can be achieved by having each student make five prints of beasts, vehicles, or whatever the theme happens to be. Four of those prints can be exchanged for prints produced by other students. The five different images can then be placed inside a folder made of colored construction paper; the booklet can be stapled along its folded edge; a suitable title can be printed on the outside; and the product will be ready to take home.

5. Ask your class to look at the exemplars by Nesch and Romano, and see if they can determine how the artists managed to put several colors into their prints without running the printing plate through the press more than once. If the youngsters cannot figure it out, explain the process to them. They could use the same process to produce their own multicolored prints, of course, but there is an easier, neater system for them to use. To illustrate, let's assume that you want to print a human torso. Make separate printing plates for the shirt, the neck and face, the hair, the lips, the eyes, and any other parts that you wish. Ink each part a different color, and print one at a time. You might begin with the neck and face and print the other things on top of them. If you print one color on top of another, however, you will get the best results by letting the first color dry before you apply the second. Use oil-based ink.

To get more objects as well as colors into a print, you can urge youngsters to make landscapes, cityscapes, seascapes, and other configurations that contain figurative backgrounds. You might select vehicles as a theme, for example, and the students might provide a setting or background for the vehicles they create. This will lead them to print hills and fields, water, a sun, clouds, or buildings before they print a vehicle on top. See Figure 11-3.

From this project children can learn that the most prominent visual element in a print is the part that contrasts most strongly with its surroundings. This means that a black vehicle will attract more attention than a yellow vehicle if it is printed on white paper, and the black image will seem to be closer than the yellow image if both appear on the same light background. Which flower seems to be closest in the print by Nesch?

6. Compare the collagraph by Rolf Nesch with the one by Clare Romano. The Nesch was clearly produced from a collage made of many materials while the

Figure 11-3.   *Riding a Unicycle,* by a sixth-grader.

Romano was not. Romano feels that the artist has to be careful not to let his interest in materials interfere with the statement he is trying to make. By using a variety of materials, however, the artist is able to produce a wider selection of lines, patterns, tones, and shapes, which gives him greater potential for expression. As an expressionist, Nesch was deeply interested in the communication of ideas and emotion, so he did not let his materials consume all of his attention. He carefully used them to his advantage.

After discussing such things with your students, let them experiment by seeing what kinds of printed effects they can obtain from items such as paper doilies, thread, string, yarn, crumpled paper, and textured cloth (corduroy, rickrack, cheesecloth, toweling, lace, curtain, and the like). Make sure that the materials are firmly glued to the base of the collage and that they are not too thick. Materials that rise more than a dime's thickness above the base will not work satisfactorily unless something other than a baren is used to apply pressure to the back of the printing paper. Systems for printing from slightly thicker materials are explained in Activities 7 and 8.

Following the experimentation, have your students make some expressionistic prints of the Nesch type. Perhaps they could work on some of the following or similar topics: Baron Steinkopf (stone head), Lady Agatha Frillyfront, Horace Horsingaround, Mary Mistake, flowers, a window with curtains, or a howling dog on a dark night.

7. When advancing to the use of thicker printing plates or collages, it is inevitable that embossings will be produced. Thus, a good introductory project is the making of a simple inkless embossing. But first, explain what an embossing is, and demonstrate how to create one on aluminum foil. Then have your students follow the same procedure by making pencil drawings on pieces of 12-x-18-inch paper. Perhaps they could draw chickens, groves of maple trees, a man in a diving suit, a woman in a flowery hat, or two tired mosquitoes. Heavy twine is then glued to the pencil lines with Elmer's glue and allowed to dry. The next step is to place a piece of 12-x-18-inch heavy-duty foil on top of the twine; cover the foil with four layers of felt (1 yard, folded); hold all the layers steady with one hand; and slap the sandwich hard with the other hand.[8] When the whole piece has been thoroughly slapped, remove the foil. It will be nicely embossed. Such work can be done by children in the first grade.

Youngsters in the intermediate grades can give an embossing a nice patina or an aged appearance by: 1) fastening it to a table with four small pieces of masking tape; 2) painting the embossing with black tempera mixed with liquid detergent; and 3) wiping the tempera gently off the foil with a soft rag. The wiping will not destroy the embossing, but a thin film of black will be deposited on the foil. See Figure 11-4.

8. Inkless and inked embossings and collagraphs can be made from thick printing plates that are more complicated than the one used in Activity 7. But first, show your students the exemplar by Nesch and describe his ideas and techniques. His prints were usually called metal prints rather than collagraphs, but the latter designation is not inappropriate because he printed from a metal collage. The collage was relatively thick, producing embossed prints, and it occasionally contained parts that were not fastened down.

Using one-ply chipboard, cardboard from shoe boxes, hard twine, rickrack, thin buttons, washers, plastic doilies, sand, tongue depressors, popsicle sticks, twigs, and other hard materials, have each of your students construct an expressive collage of a person who wears a distinctive hat, headpiece, or coiffeur.[9] Try welders, cooks, firemen, policemen, construction workers, princesses, exotic dancers, or masked tribesmen.

---

[8]Thirty-seven square feet of heavy duty foil 18 inches wide will produce 22 pieces about one foot long. To avoid wasting the foil, tear it into pieces before giving it to students.

[9]None of the materials should be thicker than a dime, or they will cause the printing paper to tear.

Figure 11-4.   *Queen.* Aluminum foil embossing with patina.

The first step is to draw the torso on a piece of 12-x-18-inch chipboard. Cut the figure out, and cut the hat from the face, the face from the neck, the neck from the shoulders, and the arms from the body. Then glue all these pieces to a 12-x-18-inch sheet of drawing paper or oak tag, but leave about one-eighth of an inch between the parts. Twine, buttons, rickrack, and other items can be added, along with chipboard noses, lips, and other elements, and the torso can be cut out around its outline.

While the collage is drying, soak some white drawing paper in a sink full of water. When ready to print, remove the paper and put it between two blotters to remove excess water. Place the collage on a clean surface with the moist paper on top. Cover the paper with four to six layers of felt (1 yard, folded), and pound the whole thing vigorously with a rubber mallet.[10] Hang the finished embossing on a "clothesline" to dry.

---

[10]Pounding with a rubber mallet has been suggested as a way of applying pressure to paper because printing presses are rarely available in the elementary schools. If the mallet causes the paper to tear, remove the felt and go over the moist paper with a clean, soft, rubber brayer. You can also press the paper with your hand as long as you do not rub with it.

An embossing on aluminum foil can also be made from this printing plate. Simply follow the directions given in Activity 7.

To make an inked embossing from this collage, shellac the printing plate after the glue dries (or spray it with plastic). This will keep the collage from absorbing too much moisture from the printing ink. Then ink the plate with a brayer and oil-based ink; place moist paper and felt on top of the collage; pound the whole thing firmly with a rubber mallet; and hang the finished print to dry.

9. When students are mature enough to stay with a relatively difficult and time-consuming task, and when they are old enough to handle sharp tools without cutting themselves, they are capable of making the kind of cardboard prints produced by Edmond Casarella. To get them started, exhibit the exemplar by Casarella and describe the technique that he employed. See if the students can articulate the difference between a cardboard print and a collage, and call attention to the fact that cardboard printing does not lend itself to making details or highly naturalistic images. It seems better suited to the creation of bold, primitive configurations. Consequently, it might be good for the students to use warriors, buildings, trucks, machines, rock formations, weeds, thorny bushes, and other strong, massive, violent, or crude things as topics to deal with in their prints.

To introduce the procedure, arrange the usual inking and printing stations as well as a place where youngsters can shellac their printing plates. Then give each person an X-Acto knife, a pencil, and a piece of $\frac{1}{8}$-x-9-x-12-inch three-ply chipboard. Having already prepared a drawing on a duplicate piece of cardboard, show your students how to cut around an area that is not meant to print, and peel it away. Cut and peel until you have removed about $\frac{1}{16}$ of an inch of cardboard in all the places that are not going to print. Do not cut a hole through the cardboard. Then take the printing plate to the shellacing area, and give it several coats of shellac.[11]

When the shellac is dry, show the class how to apply ink with a brayer. Try to keep the ink from getting into areas that you have cut away, but if it does, wipe it out with a rag. Then take the plate to the printing area and cover it with a piece of dry newsprint, Kraft paper, or drawing paper, and rub the back of the paper with a baren. The finished print is likely to have qualities similar to those in Figure 11-5 at the beginning of this chapter.

10. Display the exemplar of linoleum printing by Picasso and the exemplar of cardboard printing by Casarella. Indicate that the Casarella was made with more than one printing plate while the Picasso was made with only one. Then explain the Picasso reduction technique (page 218), and indi-

---

[11] If shellac is not available, use polymer acrylic emulsion, gesso, or diluted Elmer's glue (half water and half glue). Use an inexpensive 2-inch brush.

cate that the same procedure can be used with three-ply chipboard. Let the students try it after giving them some 9-x-12-inch pieces of chipboard that have been given two or three coats of shellac. Simply cut the cardboard with an X-Acto knife, and peel away the areas you do not want to print.

After each color is printed, press some newsprint against the wet ink and rub the back of the paper with your hand. This will remove excess ink, and it will make subsequent layers of ink easier to apply.

Compare the finished prints with the work of Casarella, and see if students can think of any artistic benefits that might be derived from the Casarella method of using more than one printing plate.

CHAPTER 12

WOODCUTS, LINOCUTS, AND OTHER SIMPLE RELIEF PRINTS

Figure 12-6. Woodcut in three colors, by a fifth-grader.

A woodcut is a relief print made from a wooden block, but if the design is cut from the end grain of the block, the resultant print is called a wood engraving instead of a woodcut. Wood engravings are characterized by their relatively small size and by the presence of thin, white lines and details on a dark background. The fine lines are achieved by cutting the block with a graver. A woodcut, however, is made by cutting the side grain of the block or plank, and the cuts are made with gouges, veiners, and knives. The result usually looks more harsh than a wood engraving, and it also is more likely to show the mark of the grain.

A linocut is a relief print made from a linoleum printing plate. Linoleum was invented about 1860 by an Englishman named Frederick Walton. It is the first smooth-surfaced floor covering to be used extensively in homes, factories, and public buildings, and it is composed of oxidized linseed oil, rosin, whiting, and pulverized cork or dried wood.

Although linoleum was developed more than a hundred years ago, it has not enjoyed widespread use by professional printmakers. Apparently, most of them have rejected it in favor of wood because the texture of linoleum is rather dull and uninteresting. It is equally possible, of course, that they have avoided it because of its association with children and amateur artists. But, whatever the reasons for its neglect, it is too bad that linoleum has not enjoyed greater popularity with printmakers. It is relatively inexpensive; it cuts easily; the tools employed in working it are not costly or difficult to obtain; and the effects that it can produce have not been fully explored. Furthermore, an ordinary material in the hands of a gifted artist can be made to do extraordinary things. Matisse, for example, used linoleum successfully as early as 1906, and the quality of the remarkable linocuts produced by Picasso can hardly be denied.

A plaster print is a relief print made from a plaster printing plate. The plate is cut in the same way as a woodcut or linocut, but the prints are usually made without a press. It is less expen-

sive than wood or linoleum, which makes it attractive for use in the public schools. Professional artists rarely print with plaster, however, so the exemplars that follow are prints made from wood or linoleum blocks.

There are several kinds of plastic prints; one type is a relief print made with sheets of polystyrene foam. The foam is not used extensively by professionals, although a Gauguin, Picasso, or Matisse could probably make it do remarkable things. It is easy to impress and cut, so it is especially suitable for children in the primary grades.

Vegetable and scrap prints are made with the materials that their names imply. Professionals usually do not make such prints because the results tend to be monoprints and require too much time. The technique also has been associated with children for many years, which may cause adult artists to avoid it. It is, however, one of the best methods for introducing fundamental printmaking concepts to children.

EXEMPLARS OF WOODCUT AND LINOCUT PRINTING

Woodcuts and linocuts can be made by children, but wood engravings are too difficult. For that reason, a wood engraving is not included among the following exemplars. We begin, instead, with a print by William Johnson, one of the great Black artists of the twentieth century.

WILLIAM H. JOHNSON, 1901–1970

Born in the small town of Florence, South Carolina, at the beginning of the twentieth century, William Johnson found life for a young Black to be confined largely to church activities and to work on the surrounding plantations. Yet, he did manage to obtain considerable enjoyment from learning to draw by copying cartoons from the local newspapers. The experience convinced him that he wanted to be an artist, and it motivated him to save enough money to reach New York City, the foremost center of art in America. He arrived at the age of 17 and immediately began a struggle for existence which involved work as a stevedore, a cook, and a hotel porter. After three years of such labor, Johnson had accumulated enough funds to enroll in a five-year program at The National Academy of Design. Shortly after his graduation in 1926, one of his teachers gathered the resources that would send Johnson to Paris for further development.

In Paris, Johnson soon came under the influence of Chaim Soutine, a powerful expressionist painter. Some of the emotional excitement of Soutine's work carried over to Johnson's painting which sparkled with color and spontaneous brush-work. These characteristics continued to dominate his canvases as he traveled outside Paris. On one of those excursions, he met and fell in love with Holcha Krake, a Danish artist who was 15 years his senior. Before marrying her, however, he returned to America, rented a loft in Harlem, and produced several paintings, one of which captured an award for "Distinguished Achievement among Negroes." One of the jurors who picked the winner of that award was George Luks, a former friend and teacher, who called Johnson "one of our coming great painters."

On returning to Denmark, Johnson married Holcha Krake and settled down in Kerteminde as a practicing artist. By 1932, he and his wife needed more stimulation than a small town could provide, so they traveled to Tunisia and later to Norway. In Norway, Johnson began to make his own woodcuts. Unfortunately, his work did not sell despite the fact that the Harmon Foundation in New York City tried to arrange exhibitions of his work in museums and commercial galleries. The Harmon Foundation was for many years the only organization sympathetic to the plight of Black artists who found it almost impossible to exhibit their work.

Although Johnson felt happier and less oppressed in Europe than he did in America, he missed his own people. So, in 1938, he returned once again to New York, where he found employment with the Works Progress Administra-

tion. It was during this time that he produced his finest work, including the linocut in Plate 12-1. Much of it was religious, and the rest dealt with the day-to-day life of Blacks in America. Johnson was not a social crusader, so his work was not created in behalf of a cause. But, like everyone else, it was most natural for him to deal with subjects that he knew best and meant the most to him.

Perhaps Johnson's work did not sell because he remained true to himself all his life. He did not attempt to satisfy the popular taste of his

Plate 12-1.   William H. Johnson. *Farm Couple at Well.* c. 1940–41. Woodcut, hand-colored, 17⅞" x 14⅛". National Collection of Fine Arts, Smithsonian Institute.

time, and he did not try to imitate the artistic pioneers of his era. The quality of his work was dependent upon a plain but lyrical sense of visual poetry and vitality rather than innovation.

Unlike most artists with a background of professional training and experience, Johnson liked to think of himself as a primitive. He assumed a style similar to the style of untrained artists, but he did so intentionally. He believed that a simple, flat, rustic manner of working was most suitable for depicting the life-style of the poor people of the South as he knew them. This primitive-appearing style can be seen in Plate 12-1. The woodcut was made with black ink and hand-colored. It reveals Johnson's strong sense of composition, his lively color, his use of pattern, and his linear power.

ERNST LUDWIG KIRCHNER (Keerkh'-ner), 1880–1938

Near the beginning of the twentieth century there was, among artists, a broad reaction against the highly academic and naturalistic representation of scenes from everyday life, and there was also a reaction against impressionism. The feeling was that academic art was sterile and uninspired and that the impressionists were giving too much attention to the changing effects of light on the appearance of objects while form, composition, and emotion were being neglected. This led the postimpressionists such as Cézanne, Toulouse-Lautrec, van Gogh, Gauguin, and others to stress the missing factors. The same point of view also led to the development of cubism and fauvism in France and to expressionism in Germany.[1] Although there were strong similarities among the three movements, the cubists stressed composi-

tion, the fauves emphasized the liberation of color and texture, and the expressionists advocated the presentation of subjective emotions.

The first manifestation of an expressionist *movement* occurred in 1905 when Ernst Kirchner, Erich Heckel, Karl Schmidt-Rottluff, and Fritz Bleyel formed an organization known as The Bridge (Die Brücke).[2] The group advocated the expression of emotion undistorted by restraints, and several authors have suggested that this kind of art suits the northern temperament. They have argued that there is a Nordic tendency toward introspection which accounts for the German discovery of psychoanalysis as well as the Norwegian and German creation of expressionism. Certainly it would not be unreasonable to describe Ernst Kirchner as introspective.

Kirchner has been said to be egocentric, intense, hard-working, articulate, well-read, and prolific. He was the leading spirit of The Bridge, and he was also the first in the group to be influenced by van Gogh, African sculpture, and the sculpture of the Pacific islands. Some of the primitive vigor of these sources can be seen in his paintings and prints. The woodcut in Plate 12-2, for example, possesses considerable rugged power and vitality. It also is nervous or restless in its appearance because the composition is broken into many small areas of black and white. An artist must be careful about breaking the picture plane (the plane of the paper) this way because it can make a work of art busy and hard to perceive; it can make the figures difficult to separate from the background.

The Kirchner print exemplifies German expressionism because the design or composition seems to have evolved spontaneously without the constraint that comes from a concentration on visual organization (as in cubism) or simplification (as in classical or neoclassical drawing). Expressionist prints also have a monumentality that earlier prints did not have, because they are larger and more primitive than earlier works. Fifteenth- and sixteenth-century prints, for example, were made small to fit on the printed page.

---

[1] For a discussion of postimpressionism, see page 96. For a discussion of cubism, see pages 43 to 45, and for fauvism see pages 253 to 254.

[2] Once The Bridge was formed, other artists joined, and the organization lasted until 1913, when the members went their separate ways.

Plate 12-2. Ludwig Kirchner. *Swiss Peasant—The Blacksmith.* 1917. Woodcut, 19¾" x 15½". Courtesy of The Art Institute of Chicago (gift of the Print and Drawing Club).

PABLO PICASSO, 1881–1972

Pablo Picasso lived to be more than 90 years old, and he worked at printmaking for more than 60 of those years. He probably made the most monumental contribution to the art of the print in the twentieth century, and he did so while making equally grand achievements in painting, drawing, sculpture, and ceramics. He made monumental contributions to printmaking not only because he used a variety of printing techniques with authority but because he added to the development of those techniques.

At first, Picasso experimented with etching and drypoint; later, he devoted considerable time to lithography; and he produced a large number of linoleum prints between 1958 and 1963. During each of those printmaking periods, he managed to vary the style of his work, and he succeeded in doing things that had not been done before.[3] In linoleum printing, for example, he produced works that might be called cubist, expressionist, or classical in style, and he demonstrated that multicolored prints could be made with one printing plate instead of several. He also proved that linoleum prints could be made visually dynamic through the use of rich colors, inventive patterns, and hard work.

Picasso's stylistic and technical inventiveness are clear indications of his mental independence. They show that he was tied neither to past concepts and mannerisms of his own nor to bygone ideas of others. Instead, he lived in the present and drew his inspiration from the current environment. And because of the importance of his immediate environment, he did not like to have anything in his workshop moved. He may have been studying it carefully in preparation for a new work of art.[4]

Picasso's acknowledgment of inspiration from his environment is an indication that he found it necessary to have an idea before he began work. But it has been said that he did not need more than a *vague* idea. Apparently, he developed and clarified the concept as he proceeded to give it shape.

When an artist gets an idea that excites him, he frequently likes to work without interference until he is finished. Picasso was like that. When he began a print, he preferred to continue, uninterrupted, until the work was done. That is one reason why he employed expert printers who could print his material and return it quickly for further refinement. If he happened to be living near his printer, as in Paris, for example, the system worked well. But, while living in Vallauris, the lengthy interruption occasioned by sending printing plates to Paris and back was not to his liking, so Picasso turned to linoleum. He chose linoleum because a young printer who lived in Vallauris was an expert at printing linoleum plates. Together, they produced printed posters for local festivals, and they made multicolor prints by using a separate linoleum plate for each of several colors. Before long, however, Picasso developed a technique that allowed him to print a number of colors from one piece of linoleum. He used this technique in making the print in Plate 12-3. He probably drew the intended image on the linoleum with permanent ink and cut away the parts he wanted to remain white. Then he undoubtedly inked the plate with yellow, and printed on sheets of white paper.[5] After cleaning the plate, he probably cut away everything he wanted to remain yellow, inked the plate with red, and printed on top of the yellow. Then he cut out the parts he wanted red, inked the plate with green, and printed on top of the red. He probably proceeded to cut away everything he wanted green, inked the plate with black, and finished by printing the black on top of the green. By following such a procedure, he gradually destroyed the printing plate. This system is called the reduction technique.

The flat areas of color in Plate 12-3 are characteristic of linoleum prints, but Picasso managed to introduce exciting linear patterns within those areas, creating more visual variety. He added to this variety by using several colors, by making the left side of the print different from the right, by varying the sizes of circular forms, and by using straight as well as curved lines.

At the same time, Picasso created a unified or coherent image. He did so by repeating colors, linear patterns, and shapes, and by creating linear movements that lead the eye from one portion of the print to another. These instances of linear continuity are diagrammed in Figure 12-1. They are probably carry-overs from cubism because the cubists frequently extended the planes of an ob-

---

[3]Style in art is the distinctive or characteristic manner of expression used by an artist or by a group of artists. It typically reveals the individualistic spirit of the artist.

[4]David Douglas Duncan, *The Private World of Pablo Picasso* (New York: Harper and Brothers, 1946), p. 27.

[5]It is possible, of course, to begin with dark colors, and it is possible to make numerous prints in a given series. Picasso often made as many as fifty prints in a series (or fifty prints of a kind).

Plate 12-3.   Pablo Picasso. *Still Life Under the Lamp.* 1962. Linoleum cut, printed in color; comp.: 20⅞" x 25³⁄₁₆", sheet: 24½" x 29⅝". Collection, The Museum of Modern Art, New York (gift of Mrs. Donald B. Straus).

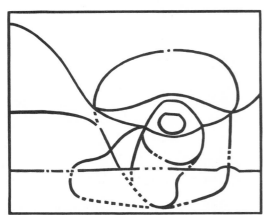

Figure 12-1.   Lines continue from one object to another through the print. The effect is a unified composition.

ject into the surrounding space to create a tightly organized work of art.

Notice that the print in Plate 12-3 contains a plain background; there is no overlapping, no variation in color within a given color area, and no major difference in the brightness or intensity of colors. The result is an image that is extremely shallow. It is a condition that many artists try to achieve in two-dimensional works of art because they think it is consistent with the flatness of the surface upon which they are working. They feel that illusions of depth tend to destroy the natural flatness of the picture plane and are therefore out of harmony with it.

Finally, we need not call attention to the fact that forms in the Picasso print are not highly naturalistic. They are recognizable, but they do not look a lot like the fruits, lamps, and glasses we experience in visual reality. We mention this only to point out that Picasso did not believe in the existence of naturalistic art. He believed that art and nature were two different things, and for that reason, he argued that forms in art were neither concrete (natural) nor abstract; they were more or less lies. And, in a sense, he is right. But writers and critics use words like natural and abstract to indicate that there are differences in the visual appearance of forms. They do not mean to imply that a real or natural tree could be constructed on a two-dimensional piece of paper.

ADDITIONAL EXEMPLARS

If possible, show your students some woodcuts and linocuts by artists other than those discussed in the book. Try showing woodcuts by Antonio Frasconi, Leonard Baskin, Leopoldo Mendez, and Edvard Munch. Linocuts by Matisse would also be good to see.

RELIEF-PRINTING ACTIVITIES FOR THE PRIMARY GRADES (AGES 6 THROUGH 8)

Wood, linoleum, and plaster are clearly inappropriate for making prints in the primary grades. They require strength that little children do not have, and they involve sharp tools. Consequently, printing with polystyrene foam, vegetables, and scrap objects is much more reasonable.

CONCEPTS FOR POSSIBLE DEVELOPMENT

Simple relief prints are probably the first prints that should be attempted with youngsters in the primary grades. They are easy to make, and they can be used as vehicles for teaching the following concepts:

pattern	relief print	scrap print
raised areas	open form	vegetable print
depressed areas	solid form	plastic print

SUGGESTED ACTIVITIES

It is recommended that the following activities be introduced in the sequence in which they are presented:

1. In nursery school, kindergarten, or the first grade, it is advisable to begin print-making by explaining that a print is made by inking or painting an object and pressing it against another surface such as paper or cloth. Then, having collected a large number of small scrap objects, show the children how to paint a piece of scrap and press it against some newsprint. Let them try it, and then show them that a pattern can be made by repeating the same printed shape again and again. Encourage the children to make several different kinds of patterns.

2. Have your students paint large full-figure portraits of themselves or a teacher. When the paint is dry, ask the youngsters to make patterns on the shirts, blouses, pants, or dresses by printing in those areas with scrap objects. Explain that patterns often help to make drawings and paintings more interesting to see. See Figure 12-2.

Figure 12-2.   *Self-Portrait with Printed Pattern,* by a kindergarten child.

3. Show your class that many diffent kinds of patterns can be made by alternating the printed shapes in a variety of ways and by printing shapes on top of each other. See if they can think of other ways of creating unusual patterns. Then show them that some forms seem to be open (like a print from the end of a tin can) while others seems to be solid (like a print from the end of a spool). Too many open forms can make a busy pattern that is not very appealing. Thus it would be advisable to use a mixture of open and solid forms.

Make a pattern with the repeated units far apart; then make one with the units close together. Ask the children which looks the best. Usually it is the one with parts close together. Then urge the class to experiment in making several patterns. When they get one they like, they might reproduce it on colored construction paper and make the paper into a folder. Or, they could cut a fish out of the paper and fasten the patterned fish all over the room.

4. Ask the children to bring a number of small cardboard boxes to class. Demonstrate how to paint one side of the boxes before pressing them on paper to make a funny human figure or animal. Use other scrap objects, if necessary, and use paper that is no larger than 12 x 18 inches. Furthermore, it would be wise to avoid printing backgrounds in these early efforts because the figures tend to become lost in their backgrounds. See Figure 12-3.

5. Bring some cabbage, peppers, large onions, carrots, potatoes, oranges, lemons, apples, and pears to class. Cut some of them in half, and cut others in quarters. Call attention to the beautiful patterns inside the fruits and vegetables. Then paint a few pieces with tempera paint and press them onto some newsprint. Many of the interesting patterns should appear in the prints. Try to create attractive patterns and figures by combining the printed shapes in different ways. Let the children do the same; let them try some of the previous activities while using fruits and vegetables instead of scrap.

Figure 12-3. Print made by a teacher in training.

6. Several days before starting this project, ask your students to bring from home some of the plastic foam trays in which their meat is purchased. Select the trays that have flat bottoms, and cut the sides off with scissors. Then draw on a piece of foam with a ball-point pen to show the children how the pen makes a depression in the plastic. Ink the finished drawing with a brayer and oil-based ink (or the Vaseline mixture on page 189); place a piece of newsprint or poster paper on top of the ink; and rub the back of the paper with a baren. Hang the print on a "clothesline" to dry.

After the demonstration, indicate that the raised portion of the plastic did the printing while the areas depressed by the pen did not. The result is a relief print. The children should know that all the prints they have been making are relief prints, and they should begin to recognize relief prints made by others. Show them the exemplars by Johnson and Kirchner; explain how they were made; and compare them to the print you have just completed. The light areas were cut away in the exemplars, and they were depressed in the plastic print.

Before turning everyone loose to make their own prints, pick a theme for them to deal with, and discuss it. You might try themes such as bowling, eating a banana, fishing from a rowboat, the bird that landed on my head, or my idea of a dead fly.

RELIEF-PRINTING ACTIVITIES FOR THE INTERMEDIATE GRADES (AGES 9 THROUGH 11)

The making of linocuts, woodcuts, and plaster prints can be aided substantially through the use of bench hooks. A bench hook is a device that holds the printing plate while the plate is being cut. It fits over the edge of a table or desk, and it helps to prevent accidental cutting of the hands from sharp tools. To make a bench hook, fasten a ¾-x-1-x-12-inch piece of wood to one end of a 12-x-12-inch piece of ¼-inch Masonite. Use two ¾-inch screws to do the fastening; and countersink them. Then attach an identical strip of wood to the opposite side and the opposite end of the Masonite. Place the completed hook on the edge of your working surface and put your printing plate on top of the hook so that the plate fits tightly against the raised wooden strip. In this position the plate is ready for cutting, but it is still essential to caution students against cutting toward their fingers.

CONCEPTS FOR POSSIBLE DEVELOPMENT

Linocuts, woodcuts, and plaster prints are made in essentially the same way, but there are minor differences in the preparation of the printing plate. We shall describe these differences in a moment, but first we wish to recommend several concepts that can be taught in conjunction with relief printing. They are listed below:

fauvism	graver	flat color areas
cubism	gouge	visual variety
expressionism	veiner	naturalistic
linoleum	sateen	abstract
linocut	unbleached muslin	a unified image
woodcut	scratchboard	repetition
wood engraving	two-dimensional	linear continuity
wood grain	contrast	brightness
bench hook	style	intensity
Printmaker's Plate	a reduction print	picture plane

SUGGESTED ACTIVITIES

Although the following activities need not be done in sequence, we have tried to present them in the order of their difficulty. This will allow teachers to make better judgments about which activity to offer first.

1. Show your class the exemplars by Johnson, Kirchner, and Picasso, and discuss briefly the history of woodcuts and linocuts. Then focus on the work of Johnson, and emphasize that he chose a simple, flat, rustic style because he believed it to be most compatible with his subject matter. Indicate further that woodcuts and linocuts lend themselves to a rustic style because the wood offers resistance to cutting and to the creation of detail, and both materials produce flat areas of color.

    Give each student a 6-x-9-inch piece of ⅛-inch linoleum, a black wax crayon, and a set of linoleum-cutting tools or at least a gouge and veiner. The cutting edge of a gouge is shaped like a "U" while the sharp end of a veiner looks like a "V." The former is used to remove large, wide spaces, and the latter is meant for cutting lines or small areas.

    About six inking stations should be sufficient if equipped with glass or Masonite plates, tubes of oil-based ink, soft brayers, and newspapers. Nearby, a printing area containing several barens and a supply of printing paper would be helpful. The most sensible papers to use are newsprint (plain or colored), poster paper, construction paper, or Kraft paper.

    Show the students how to draw on the linoleum with a wax crayon and how to cut away the lines with the gouge and veiner. Roll out the ink on glass or Masonite until the ink is evenly distributed on the brayer; then roll the brayer over the linoleum until the ink is deposited on all parts of the raised surface. Take the inked linoleum to the printing station; cover it with paper; rub the back of the paper with a baren; remove the paper; and hang it up to dry. Clean the ink from the plate and brayer with a rag dipped in turpentine or mineral spirits.

Be sure to indicate that the cut-out portion of the plate did not print. Then discuss with your students a theme they can use in their prints. Remind them that bold, heavy, hard, strong, or mechanical topics are especially good because the medium lends itself to such themes. The following topics would be excellent:

Circus people (strong man, fat lady, acrobat)	The bride and groom
Spiders, scorpions, bats, mosquitoes	The coal miner and his wife
Farm workers and truck drivers	Cornstalks and sunflowers

As the children begin cutting their linoleum, remind them to use their bench hooks and to cut away from their hands. When the prints are dry, trim them with a paper cutter, and mount them on white or gray drawing paper. Then display the woodcuts by Johnson and Kirchner, and ask the children if they can identify the similarities and differences between their work and the exemplars.

2. Show and discuss the woodcut by Kirchner giving any information about the artist and his work that would be interesting to your students. Suggest that the print might have been made by drawing on the wood and cutting away almost everything but the lines. Urge your students to try that technique by drawing on their linoleum blocks with wax crayons, which produce highly desirable wide lines. Then have them cut away almost everything but the lines. Other than this, the activity might proceed in the same way as Activity 1.

Notice that some areas in the Kirchner print are left uncut (the hair and the beard). This gives the print visual variety, and it helps to reduce the busyness that comes from an excess of black and white lines. Recommend that your students leave some areas uncut. See Figure 12-4.

3. A technique devised by Natalie Cole produces excellent results in linoleum printing.[6] Let us assume that you have discussed a topic such as brides and grooms, and the pupils have drawn such figures on their linoleum blocks with crayons. Have them use their largest veiners to cut a ditch around the outside of their figures. The cutter should barely touch the outside edge of the crayon line. When finished, have the children cut a ditch around the inside edge of the crayon lines, and urge them to follow that by cutting away areas of the figures they would like to be white. These might be faces, hands, shirts, or wedding gowns. The linoleum should then be inked and printed in the manner suggested in Activity 1. See Figure 12-5.

In all these activities, the children should be told that there are many ways to cut a linoleum block and they will learn the different techniques as time goes by.

---

[6]Natalie Robinson Cole, *Children's Art From Deep Down Inside* (New York: John Day Co., 1966).

Figure 12-4. *Tiger,* by a sixth-grader.

Figure 12-5. *Dancing with Joy,* by a sixth-grader.
Printed on sateen.

4. To introduce a group project, display the exemplars by Johnson and Picasso, and discuss the way patterns have contributed to the beauty of those prints. Ask students to suggest ways in which Johnson might have created patterns in the clothing of the farmer and his wife. Then tell the students that they will have a chance to try their ideas in a print about children who are jumping with joy and excitement. Talk about how the parts of the body move when people are acting that way. Then ask the youngsters to draw a dancing figure on their linoleum blocks with crayon, and remind them to draw patterns in some of the clothing. If considerable open space seems to be left on the linoleum, suggest that smaller figures be drawn in those areas. Then begin cutting the plate using the Cole technique described in the foregoing activity.

While the students are cutting, place on the floor an old blanket with a large piece of sateen (shiny side up) on top. Determine how to place the children's prints side by side on the sateen to produce a collection of prints centered on the fabric. Then as the children finish cutting, have each of them ink his linoleum with oil-based ink; place it on the fabric; have him stand on it and stamp; stand on it yourself; and remove the linoleum. Let the next piece of linoleum overlap the first print slightly and continue using the same color of ink until each student has printed. The result may be used as a curtain or as a wall hanging. But first, have the class appraise the patterns in their work. Did the patterns help to enrich the beauty of the prints? See Figure 12-5.

5. Everything done with linoleum can be done with a new material called Printmaker's Plate, which can be obtained from a school supply house. The significant difference is that Printmaker's Plate is thinner, and it can be cut with scissors. To take advantage of these features, give students some mirrors and pencils, and have them draw self-portraits on 9-x-12-inch pieces of white paper. Place each drawing, face down, on a 9-x-12-inch piece of Printmaker's Plate, and rub the back of the paper. The drawing will transfer to the Plate. Then go over the lines on the Plate with a number 7 brush and some India ink containing a little liquid detergent. Paint some areas solid black, and make sure the lines are heavy and bold.

When the ink is dry, cut the black parts out with scissors. Remove the paper backing on the lines, and fasten them to a 9-x-12-inch piece of drawing paper or oak tag. The black portions of the portrait will now be raised above the surface of the paper or tag board. Simply ink this raised surface and print in the manner described in previous activities. This project can be done with lightweight cardboard from cereal boxes in place of Printmaker's Plate, but cardboard is more difficult to cut.

6. Display the exemplar of collagraph printing by Romano and discuss her way of making prints in more than one color. Remember that she cut the cardboard into pieces, inked the parts separately, and reassembled them before printing. This saves time and money, and it works exceptionally well for relief printing with linoleum.

To begin, show the class some photographs of interesting animals and talk about the distinctive parts of those animals. Then ask the students to make crayon drawings of animals on their blocks of linoleum or Printmaker's Plate. Recommend that they put both the sky and ground in their drawings and urge them to cut their blocks into two or three pieces (like Romano) after their designs have been cut away. The sky, for example, might be cut away from the rest of the printing plate, and the two pieces could be inked and reassembled before printing. Consider that this technique becomes more difficult as the line along which the parts are cut apart becomes complicated and irregular. Try to keep that line as simple as possible.

7. While showing the print by Picasso, explain the reduction technique that allowed him to print numerous colors with one piece of linoleum. It is the easiest system for children to use in making multicolored relief prints, and the Picasso compositional techniques are also relatively easy for them to employ. Consequently, it pays to take enough time to discuss these things thoroughly with your students. Then have them begin a reduction print by making a drawing on the linoleum with a felt-tip marker and permanent ink (pencil may also be used). If you are doing the project with twenty or more students, however, restrict them to printing with only three colors (such as yellow, orange, and green). And, as they print, show them how to place the linoleum on the printing paper, how to pull the paper and linoleum to the edge of the table where the two can be grasped, how to turn them over without slippage, and how to rub the back of the paper with a baren. Remember that the oil-based ink must be cleaned from the linoleum with turpentine and a rag after printing with each color. See Figure 12-6 at the beginning of the chapter.

8. Woodcuts can be introduced in the fifth grade. If you give your students some 7-x-10-inch pieces of clear pine and some wood-cutting tools, you will find that they can make three-color woodcuts in about five hours. But, the work is difficult, and their hands will get tired. Have them proceed in the same way as they did in making the linocuts already described, but the wood blocks have to be specially prepared. Give the blocks two coats of white shellac and let them dry before drawing and cutting. The shellac keeps the wood from absorbing the oil in the ink. Sometimes youngsters will also get better results if they make a ¼- to ½-inch crayon line around the border of the block. They should then try *not* to cut the border away as their printing proceeds. See Figure 12-6.

To begin the project, show students the exemplar by Johnson and discuss his life. Explain that he often printed with black ink and then colored the print with watercolor after the ink was dry. Urge your students to do the same. When finished, have them compare their work with Johnson's to see if they have produced any of the same primitive characteristics. Try having the students work on themes such as: the fighter, the mad dog, the old soldier, or chrysanthemums, zinnias, and daisies.

9. Plaster prints can be made in the same way as linocuts and woodcuts, but the printing plate must be prepared differently. Using strips of wood that are 1 x 2 x 7 inches and 1 x 2 x 12 inches in size, make about three frames having interior dimensions of 7 x 10 inches. Place the frames on a smooth surface such as a desk top or a piece of Masonite. Then pour one two-pound coffee can full of water into a large plastic bowl, and add two two-pound coffee cans of moulding plaster by sifting the plaster through your fingers. The plaster should eventually remain on the surface of the water and begin to develop little cracks. When it does so, put your hand in the bowl and smash any lumps that you can feel. Keeping your hand under the surface, stir the plaster vigorously, and continue to do so until a mark on the surface will not disappear. This indicates that the plaster is ready to pour into the three frames. Pour it quickly, and pat it so it goes into the corners. If you have divided it evenly, the plaster should be almost three-fourths of an inch deep in each frame.

The quick-drying plaster will get warm as it dries (something that fascinates children), and it should be sufficiently dry in minutes to remove the frames. To take them off, tap them with a hammer to knock the sides outward.

Reassemble the frames and continue making plaster blocks until you have enough for the whole class. When the blocks are thoroughly dry, paint the smooth sides with two coats of shellac. They should then be ready to cut in the same manner as linoleum or wood. We recommend that you use old linoleum-cutting tools for the job.

Although it is work to prepare the blocks, plaster is much less expensive than linoleum or wood. Its only drawback is that it can be dirty if the teacher does not do something to keep it from getting on the floor. We recommend the use of many cardboard boxes as waste containers for the plaster cut from the blocks.

CHAPTER 13

STENCILS

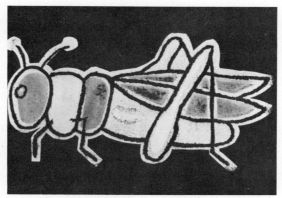

Figure 13-7.   *Grasshopper.* A three-color print on black paper.

The exact origin of the stencil is not known. Probably, it had its beginning in more than one place. We do know, however, that the teachings of Buddha were disseminated by means of stenciled images, and we know that the Japanese used stencils for centuries in decorating robes, screens, and other objects. They cut their designs from two layers of waterproof paper and held them in position by pasting thin strands of raw silk across the designs and between the two layers of paper.

In the Western Hemisphere, stencils were used along with woodcuts to create the playing cards and religious devotional papers that were so popular during the Middle Ages, and by the end of the seventeenth century, stencils were widely employed in the making of wallpaper.[1] Flocked wallpaper was especially fashionable in England at the time, and it required that an adhesive be applied to the paper through a stencil. Finely chopped woolen fibers known as flock were then sprinkled over the sticky print producing a raised design having the appearance of velvet or brocade.

Stencils were used to decorate walls as early as the Middle Ages; they were used for the same purpose in colonial America; and they continue to be used in that way today. But the New England settlers used stencils to decorate their household goods as well as their walls. The practice was so widespread that artists traveled from village to village decorating furniture and walls in return for room and board.

The idea of using silk fabric as a support for the stencil became known in 1907 when Samuel Simon, an Englishman, obtained a patent for the process. Once discovered, it did not take long for sign makers and display designers to use the process because it made their work easier and more profitable, and manufacturers were eager to use it because it simplified the decoration of furniture, clothing, rugs, book jackets, textiles, and other things too numerous to mention. The only professional image makers who did not exploit the silk screen were the fine artists. But in 1938, after thirty years of neglect, fine artists started to explore its possibilities with the financial support of the Works Progress Administration.[2] The result is that silk screening has become one of the four major methods of producing artistic prints.

---

[1]One of the best and most famous wallpaper designers of the eighteenth century was Jean Papillon, a Frenchman. He is often called the father of wallpaper.

[2]During the depression of the 1930s, the WPA made work available to artists. As a result, we have art in federal buildings that otherwise would not have been there (i.e., murals in post offices).

EXEMPLARS OF STENCILING (SILK SCREENING)

The silk screen has made it possible for the average man to own a work of art by a master artist, and it has given the artist freedom to make large as well as small prints without investing large sums of money in equipment and supplies. The silk screen has also made possible certain visual effects that did not exist before, and it may produce even more of those effects in the future because its potential has not yet been fully realized.

BEN SHAHN, 1898–1969

Born in Lithuania, Ben Shahn came to America in 1906, and by 1932, he had achieved worldwide prominence as a painter and printmaker. One reason that he received favorable attention was the content of his art. He was sensitive to social events, especially political events, and he depicted them in his work. Perhaps one could say that he engaged in the kind of humanitarian protest which has almost always elicited strong reactions of one kind or another. In this case, the reaction was positive, and so was the response to his style. It was highly distinctive, like handwriting, because it was highly linear, harsh, full of sureness, and free of superfluous elements. In some ways it was similar to the technique of George Grosz who also used art for social commentary (see pages 80 to 81).

Ben Shahn was a noted speaker and a gifted writer, and his statements about art, artists, and education will probably be studied for years to come. Many of his comments may be found in a book entitled *The Shape of Content.*[3] There Shahn emphasizes the importance of content and explains its relationship to the form or shape of art. Some artists believe that the epitome of art is form devoid of content or form without meaning, but Shahn argues that it is impossible to produce form that has no content. The content may be minimal, but there is always content, even in a painting of a white square on a white background. The content or meaning in that case is simply "white square on white background." According to Shahn, form is the shape of content, and content is what the artist thinks, feels, and imagines. Consequently, the form of art is an indication of the artist's mental powers and mental limitations. If a person wants to be certain that

her art does not misrepresent her ideas and feelings, she has to be alert to what she really thinks and honestly feels, and she has to pay careful attention to the shape of the image she creates.

Shahn also believed that visual artistic form arises out of an effort to make concepts and emotions endure. Hence it is produced intentionally rather than accidentally. The success the artist has in giving accurate and impressive form to his ideas and feelings may depend not only upon his alertness to what he thinks and feels, but it may also depend upon the fullness of feeling with which he addresses himself to his task.

The content of art, according to Shahn's view, may be anything, and the successful shaping of that content may result in any kind of form. But one thing is certain: the form can never exceed the content that went into it. This means, for example, that the form or shape of the print in Plate 13-1 is no more comprehensive or profound than the idea that prompted it. Shahn had in mind the visual embodiment of the

---

[3]Ben Shahn, *The Shape of Content* (New York: Vintage Books, Inc., 1960).

Plate 13-1.   Ben Shahn. *Silent Music.* 1950. Serigraph, 17¼" x 35". Philadelphia Museum of Art (Thomas Skelton Harrison Fund).

idea, and it seems safe to say that he must have known about the music stands and folding chairs used by orchestras and bands. He must have known that they are highly linear objects which produce their own idiosyncratic visual rhythms when the musicians are not sitting in them. By remaining constantly alert to these fundamental ideas, he was able to give them visual form.

Shahn probably made the print by drawing on the silk screen with tusche and a brush. When the tusche was dry, he undoubtedly filled the screen with water soluble glue, and subsequently removed the tusche. With the stencil complete, he then placed some paint in the screen and forced it through the silk and onto the paper with a rubber-edged squeegee. The result certainly contains the distinctive linear qualities associated with Shahn's work. The lines are made with short, sketchy strokes instead of long, flowing movements. They are lively and bold with uneven, rough edges, and they are uniform in width and darkness. Variety is achieved through differing shapes and differing distances between the lines.

CLAYTON POND, 1941–

From the history of silk screening, one can conclude that artists who use the screen are comparatively young. Certainly this is the case with Clayton Pond, who is clearly the youngest artist represented in this book. Pond was born in Bayside, New York, shortly after artists began using the silk screen seriously as a tool for making prints. He attended Hiram College and studied art at the Carnegie Institute of Technology before accepting his first teaching position in a junior high school in 1964. He subsequently taught at the C. W. Post College of Long Island University and the School of Visual Arts in New York City, but more important by far is the fact that since 1964, Pond has become one of the most outstanding young printmakers in America.

The Stove in My Studio on Broome Street (Plate 13-2) was printed by Pond in 1969. It looks bright, cheerful, loud, and hard, because it contains numerous colors used at full strength. The shapes that are employed also contribute to the strong, loud, hard impact of the work because they are relatively large, sharp-edged, and simple in outline. They are certainly not delicate, dainty, frilly, soft, gentle, or quiet. Notice also that the print is not highly naturalistic. A stove, some bricks and pipes, a sign, assorted pots and pans, and a few other items are obviously represented, but none look exactly as we experience them in visual reality. This is because the colors are not natural;

Plate 13-2. Clayton Pond. *The Stove in My Studio on Broome Street.* 1969. Serigraph, 27¼" x 18½". Collection, Krannert Art Museum, University of Illinois, Champaign.

lines that are straight in reality are not straight in the print; sharp corners are not sharp; and all the shapes are flat, with no shading. The lack of a high degree of naturalism, however, does not in any way spoil the appearance of the print. It is delightfully appealing—perhaps beautiful. This shows that a work of art need not be naturalistic to be attractive. If the Pond print had been made in a naturalistic fashion it would not communicate the qualities we have described.

Ben Shahn used tusche and glue in preparing the silk screen employed in making his print. Tusche produces edges that are slightly fuzzy. But look at the Pond print. The edges of shapes are sharp. This indicates that tusche and glue were not used in the preparation of the screen. Instead, Pond probably made a stencil from a special kind of film that can be made to adhere to the bottom of the screen. A separate stencil was made for each color, and it was cleaned from the screen after the artist finished using it.

Prints are usually signed in pencil by the artist in the bottom margin. In addition to his signature, he usually includes the title of the work, the date it was done, and the number of the print within the sequence of duplicate prints that were produced. Thus the 17/100 in the margin of the Pond piece indicates that it was the seventeenth print in a sequence of a hundred prints.

ANDY WARHOL, 1928–

After the Second World War, an art movement known as abstract expressionism developed in New York City, and within a decade it became an international phenomenon. There were many variations within the movement, but in general it was characterized by a lack of representational imagery and by an emphasis upon the artist's intuitive response to form as it appeared on his canvas. It placed primary importance upon the presentation of personal feelings free from the distorting influence of recognized configurations. By the early 1960s, however, people began to tire of the highly introspective nature of abstract expressionism, and they looked forward to the reintroduction of representational images. In addition, many artists began to feel that art had become too precious or too far removed from the average man and from everyday life. This meant that the climate was conducive to the emergence of a new art form, and the first to appear was pop art.

Pop art was an irreverent imitation of commercial art and popular art. It rejected the introspective and often idealistic qualities of abstract expressionism in favor of the anti-individualistic, banal images and techniques used in sales promotion, cartooning, and calendar art. In other words, pop art was a simple parody of billboard advertisements, soup cans, cartoons, and common objects of all kinds.

Andy Warhol rose to fame as one of the leading figures in the pop art movement. He came to New York in the 1950s and soon obtained work creating shoe advertisements for I. Miller. The work paid well, and the advertisements were well-received by the business community because they were new and distinctive. Soon, Warhol was designing stationary for Bergdorf Goodman, Christmas cards for Tiffany's, and record jackets for Columbia Records. He also decorated store windows, wrote books, and worked for television and women's magazines. Obviously, he had talent as a commercial artist, and his success, from a financial standpoint, meant that he did not need to change the focus of his artistic efforts. Yet, that is exactly what he did, in 1960, when be began making paintings for exhibition.

Warhol's earliest pop paintings were similar to those of other pop artists (Lichtenstein, Rosenquist, Oldenburg, and others), but in 1962, a friend suggested that he paint money and soup cans. The results were an immediate success, and they were followed by paintings and prints of other common objects such as the banana in

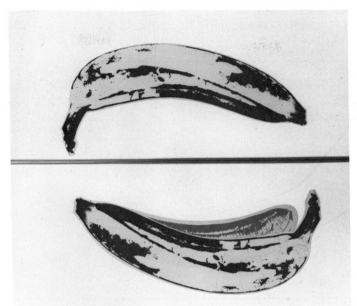

Plate 13-3.   Andy Warhol. *Banana*. 1966. Silk-
screen, ink, and collage on paper; 24" x 52"
each. Courtesy of Leo Castelli Gallery,
New York. Eric Pollitzer, photographer.

Plate 13-3. Some people incorrectly assume that Warhol was the first person to lift the common object to the level of art, although artists had been depicting ordinary objects in still-life paintings for generations. Even the use of single, bizarre objects was not new because Marcel Duchamp had used them more than fifty years earlier when he displayed a urinal as art in the famous Armory Show of 1913. Duchamp not only removed art from its lofty pedestal, but he extended the parameters of the concept of art while doing so. If Warhol differed from Duchamp and the earlier still-life painters, it was largely in the degree to which he projected himself into his work. Warhol was much less subjective. He offered no interpretation of life, no comment on it, no reaction to it, no emotion, no judgment of any kind. He simply reproduced common objects in a cold, precise, mechanical way. In fact, he eventually mass-produced much of his work by silk-screening it, and he often dis-

played multiple copies of the same image in a single show. This tended to make his work seem even less individualistic than it was before, and it emphasized his connection with commercial art.

The silk-screened banana in Plate 13-3 has all the characteristics of Warhol's Brillo boxes, his Campbell's soup cans, and his Coke bottles. The banana is highly naturalistic, common, precise, and relatively free from any indication of the artist's own ideas and feelings. It indicates that an artist can take for his subject matter a banal, trite, or commonplace object and still produce a work of art if he manages to organize the final configuration in a pleasurable way. But one wonders what Ben Shahn would say about it.

ADDITIONAL EXEMPLARS

Numerous artists have printed with the silk screen since the 1930s. But it would be good to exhibit the work of Corita Kent, Maria Termini, Victor Vasarely, Robert Gwathmey, and Robert Indiana, in addition to the exemplars already discussed.

SCREEN-PRINTING ACTIVITIES FOR THE PRIMARY GRADES (AGES 6 THROUGH 8)

Children in the primary grades are capable of making screen prints, but the activity is more appropriate for grades four, five, and six. The older youngsters are able to construct their screens with less assistance from the teacher; they are able to cut stencils from lightweight paper without difficulty; and they are able to solve problems and foresee results more easily than the younger children. On the other hand, some primary classes are more mature than others. If a group seems ready for the complications of silk-screen printing, we recommend that it begin with the first three activities suggested for the intermediate grades.

SCREEN-PRINTING ACTIVITIES FOR THE INTERMEDIATE GRADES (AGES 9 THROUGH 12)

A genuine silk-screen print is created most often with a screen made of silk, a squeegee made of wood and rubber, and an oil-based paint made especially for the purpose. But these materials are not to be found in the elementary schools because silk, squeegees, and silk-screen paint are expensive, and the latter is difficult for children to remove from the screen. Consequently, substitute materials must be employed.

There are two acceptable replacements for silk-screen paint. One is prepared fingerpaint, and the other is liquid tempera thickened to the consistency of pudding through the addition of powdered soap or Prang Media Mixer. Both materials work satisfactorily, but if they are a little too thin, they will seep under the stencil attached to the screen and enter areas where they are not wanted. If that happens, add a little more powdered soap or detergent to thicken them a bit. Too much soap, however, is likely to clog the screen. If it does, clean the fabric with a damp sponge, and thin the mixture of paint and soap by adding more paint or some colorless Prang Media Mixer.[4] The Media Mixer can be purchased by the gallon from school supply houses, and it is very useful.

---

[4]If you can obtain sufficient Media Mixer, use it in place of powdered soap. Simply add enough of it to the prepared liquid tempera to make the paint the consistency of pudding. The mixer will not clog the screen as easily as soap.

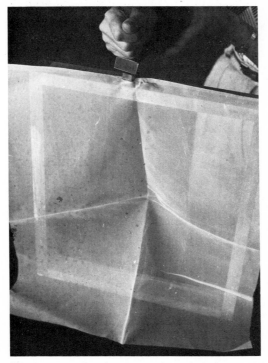

Figure 13-1.   Stapling organdy to wooden frame.

As a substitute for professional squeegees children can use pieces of stiff cardboard about 2 x 3 inches in size. Scrap pieces of mat board and illustration board serve adequately if they are given straight edges by cutting them on a paper cutter.

To avoid making new screens each year and to encourage the creation of high-quality prints, it makes sense to build a screen that has a wooden frame. Begin with two strips of wood about 1 x 2 x 16 inches, and two pieces approximately 1 x 2 x 12 inches. Arrange the strips to make a frame having interior dimensions of 12 x 14 inches, and place two nails in each corner. Stretch the screening material tightly across the frame, and fasten it on the four outer sides with thumbtacks, carpet tacks, or staples. To stretch the material without leaving wrinkles, work gradually from the middle of each side toward the corners. See Figure 13-1. Then put two strips of masking tape around the outside of the frame to cover the tacks and the loose edges of the cloth. Turning to the interior of the frame, place masking tape along each side from corner to corner, making certain that half of the tape sticks to the cloth while the other half sticks to the wooden sides. Then place another strip of masking tape along each side from corner to corner, but this time make half of the tape overlap the first layer of masking tape while the other half

Figure 13-2. Applying second strip of
masking tape to inside of screen.
Note strips already applied.

covers the screening material. See Figure 13-2. The last step is to turn the screen
over and fasten two overlapping strips of masking tape to the cloth on the bottom
margins of the frame. The inside edge of the innermost strip of tape should coincide with the inside edge of the tape fastened to the other side of the screen. See
Figure 13-3.

One yard of screening cloth will cover about six frames if the fabric is 45
inches wide. But, instead of using expensive silk cloth, use either polyester organdy
or cotton organdy.

It would be nice, of course, if each child could be furnished with a screen
with a wooden frame, but low budgets occasionally prevent such an arrangement.
When that occurs, it is still possible to print by having students take turns with

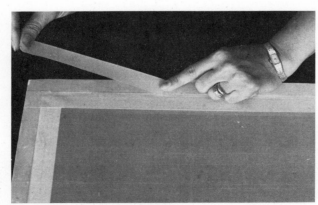

Figure 13-3. Applying masking tape to
bottom of screen.

five to ten screens. And it is also possible to construct screens from cardboard boxes approximately 2 x 10 x 12 inches in size.[5] Use a single-edge razor blade or an X-Acto knife to cut a rectangular hole in the bottom of each container, leaving one inch between the edges of the opening and the sides of the box. Stretch a piece of organdy across the outside of the box, and fasten it to the vertical sides with a stapler. Turning to the inside of the container, place a strip of masking tape along each side of the rectangular opening, making certain that half of the tape sticks to the organdy while the other half sticks to the cardboard box. Then turn the screen over and fasten two overlapping strips of masking tape to the organdy on the bottom margins of the box. The inside edge of the innermost piece of tape should coincide with the inside edge of the tape fastened to the other side of the screen. When finished, shellac the inside of the box making certain that none of the shellac touches the organdy.

CONCEPTS FOR POSSIBLE DEVELOPMENT

Once the screens are finished, the activity of printing may begin, and along with it the teacher may wish to discuss exemplars of screen printing and strive to develop an understanding of appropriate artistic terms or concepts. Some of those terms are listed below:

stencil	Works Progress Administration (WPA)	form
flocked wallpaper	abstract expressionism	tusche
silk screen	humanitarian protest	squeegee
commercial artists	social commentary	organdy
fine artists	content	pop art
linear		

SUGGESTED ACTIVITIES

If conditions permit, it is advisable for youngsters to build their own screens. It makes the art activity more educational and more fun. When they are finished, try some of the projects listed below:

1. Display the exemplars by Shahn, Pond, and Warhol, and explain briefly how each print was made. Discuss Shahn's ideas about content and ask a few questions of the following types:
   a) Do any of the exemplars appear to have no content?
   b) Which print has the most content? Which has the least? What is the content in each of the prints?

---

[5] Boxes made to hold a shirt or a blouse are ideal.

Figure 13-4.   *Jumping Rope,* by a fourth-grader.
White print on black paper.

c) Does content tell you anything about the artist? What does it tell you?

d) Ben Shahn made a totally linear print without color, shading, or other artistic elements. Why do you think he did so?

After the discussion, demonstrate how to make a print similar to the one by Shahn, and ask your students how the technique differs from the procedure used by Shahn. Begin with a pencil drawing on 9-x-12-inch paper. Place your screen on top of the drawing, and trace over the pencil markings with an oil crayon, making certain to press hard enough for the crayon to fill the holes in the organdy.[6] Then place the screen on a 12-x-18-inch piece of black construction paper; put two tablespoons of light-colored paint into the screen; and drag the paint firmly across the organdy with a cardboard squeegee. This forces the paint through the fabric everywhere except where the screen is filled with crayon. The result, when you lift the screen, will be a print that looks like a black drawing on a light background. Different effects can be obtained, of course, by using paint and paper of different colors. Urge your students to experiment. See Figure 13-4.

To clean the screen, place it on a stack of newspapers, and remove the

---

[6]An oil crayon such as Cray-pas is sometimes called an oil pastel.

paint with a damp sponge. Then dry the screen with a rag or paper towel; place it on a clean newspaper; and remove the oil crayon by rubbing it with a cloth containing turpentine.

Next, talk to the children about the topic they are to deal with in their drawings. The subject may be one that was recommended for a drawing activity in Part I, or you might use one of the ideas listed below:

My favorite sport	My shoe
Using a hair dryer	An electric fan
Talking on the telephone	Riding a unicycle
Sipping soda through a straw	Birds on a limb

Clearly, screen printing requires an organized classroom with printing stations containing paint, squeegees, paper, powdered soap, Media Mixer, containers for mixing paint, and tongue depressors. A place for cleaning the screens and a "clothesline" for drying the prints are also necessary. Then, when the prints are dry, study the exemplar by Pond. Note the way the product was titled and signed, and have students follow the same procedure in signing their own prints.

2. In the foregoing activity, as well as in Activities 3 and 4, the prints can be made next to each other on one large sheet of Kraft paper instead of on small pieces of paper. The large sheet can then be hung in the classroom or in the hallway of the school.

3. Begin with a discussion of the exemplars as indicated in Activity 1, but concentrate on the work of Clayton Pond. Call attention to the clean, hard, sharp edges on all his forms, and explain that they were obtained through the use of a stencil attached to the bottom of the silk screen.

To show youngsters how to use a simple, paper stencil in screen printing, draw the profile of an animal or a person on a piece of 12-x-14-inch waxed paper. Cut the figure out with a scissors or a single-edge razor blade, and place it on a piece of colored construction paper. Put your screen on top of the waxed paper figure; place two tablespoons of paint in the screen; and drag the paint across the organdy with a cardboard squeegee. The paint will go through the screen and onto the construction paper in all places except where the waxed paper is located. In the process, the paint will cause the waxed paper to adhere to the bottom of the screen. This will allow you to lift the screen and place it on another piece of construction paper for further printing.

Cleaning the screen is simply a matter of peeling the waxed paper from the fabric, placing the screen on a stack of newspapers, and washing the paint away with a damp sponge. You are then ready to get the students started on their own prints by talking with them about possible topics. Things that are identifiable in profile are especially good. Consequently, you might discuss one or more of the following:

Animals (elephants, giraffes, gorillas, goats)
People (funny, tough, old, beautiful, ugly)
Vehicles (cars, trucks, airplanes, ships, trains, helicopters)
Birds (turkeys, owls, doves, swans, storks, eagles)

4. A simple variation on Activity 3 can be achieved if you are careful not to cut or tear the waxed paper that is left after a head of a tough person (or some other object) has been cut out. Place the remaining paper (which now contains a hole in the shape of a head) on a piece of colored construction paper. Then put the screen on top of the waxed paper, and draw the eyes, ears, nose, mouth, and hair on the organdy screen. Keep the drawing within the outline of the head. Then put two tablespoons of paint in the screen, and print as before.

5. Perhaps the most attractive and exciting screen prints are done in several colors. Begin by discussing the exemplars, especially the Pond and the Warhol. Explain how they were made and indicate that a separate stencil is needed for each color. See if your pupils can think of adjectives to describe the exemplars. Ask them what causes the prints to look that way. Perhaps they will begin to understand that bright colors, unnaturalistic shapes and colors, sharp edges, and simplified forms help to give special meaning to works of art. Then it might be appropriate to ask your students to help you make a list of topics that they might use in their prints. A few suggestions appear below:

Parts of a bicycle

A gum ball machine

A deluxe hamburger

An ice cream sundae or soda

A bird in a cage

A plate of food

A dragonfly or other insect

Fruits and vegetables

There is more than one way to make a multicolored screen print. Consequently, you might demonstrate one or more of the methods before you allow your students to begin their own prints. Instructions for four of those methods appear in the following paragraphs:

a) Screen printing with more than one color requires that the screen be placed on the printing paper in the same position each time a new color is added. To do this, the side of the screen farthest from the operator must be hinged to the surface of the printing station. This can be done with three 7-inch strips of masking tape. Fasten one end of each piece of tape to the inside, vertical portion of the screen; run it up the inside and down the outside of the screen; and stick the remainder of the tape to the table. Then fasten a piece of tape parallel to the screen on top of the ends that are stuck to the table, and make certain that one edge of the strip is touching the side of the screen. See Figure 13-5.

Having secured the screen to the surface of the printing station, draw a

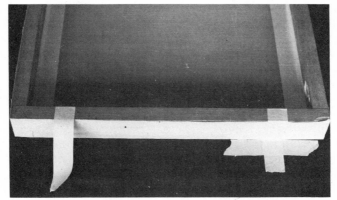

Figure 13-5.   Hinging the screen to a table
with masking tape. Finished
hinge is on right.

bee on a piece of 9-x-12-inch paper. Position the drawing under the screen so
that the whole bee can be seen through the organdy. Then tape the corners of
the drawing to the table; place a 12-x-14-inch piece of waxed paper over the
drawing; and trace the wings of the insect with a pencil. Cut the wings out of
the paper; place another 12-x-14-inch piece of waxed paper over the drawing;
trace the head and body with a pencil; and cut the head and body out of the
paper. Lay the waxed paper (with the wing-shaped hole) on top of the original
pencil drawing, and lower the screen onto the waxed paper. Using your finger,
rub a little paint through the organdy and onto the waxed paper in several
places. This will cause the paper to adhere to the bottom of the screen.

To print, lift the screen; place a piece of colored construction paper on top
of the original pencil drawing; and mark the two corners of the paper so it can
be placed in the same position later. Lower the screen onto the construction
paper and print in the manner described in Activity 1. When three or four
prints have been made, peel the waxed paper stencil from the bottom of the
organdy; place a newspaper under the fabric; and clean the screen with a
damp sponge. The body of the bee may then be printed with a different color.
When doing so, you might like to use an oil crayon to create lines in the body.
The system for doing this is described in Activity 4, and if more colors are
desired, simply cut a new stencil for each color. Remember that you can print
one color over another.

Prints completed this way will resemble the exemplar by Clayton Pond.
The colors will touch each other; the edges of the shapes will be hard and
clear; and there will be no lines in the print unless you use crayons as described in the previous paragraph.

As you examine the finished work with your students, ask them to compare their colors with those of Clayton Pond. Ask them how they might produce a richer and more varied array of colors in subsequent prints. Then discuss the possibility of printing objects in the background as Pond did. How could it be done? If possible, let the children experiment in solving some of these problems.

b) Show your students the exemplar of stenciling by Warhol as well as the exemplars of paper sculpture by Oldenburg and Saint-Phalle. Explain the purpose behind pop art, and suggest that the students make pop art prints of fruits and vegetables similar to the one by Warhol. In other words, the prints will contain some dark lines, but they will not be full of details. To make the procedure clear, a demonstration will be necessary. As you give the demonstration, explain that the attractiveness of the final print will have a lot to do with the placement of the printed image on the page. Try to place it so the image does not divide the paper into symmetrical halves.

Begin by drawing an ice cream soda with a *crayon* on a 9-x-12-inch piece of paper. Tape the corners of the drawing to the table so the drawing is properly positioned under the screen. Cover the drawing with a 12-x-14-inch piece of waxed paper, and trace with a pencil around the outside edges of the lines that outline the soda. Cut the soda out of the waxed paper, and lay the paper soda on top of the original crayon drawing. Lower the screen onto the waxed paper, and rub a little paint through the organdy onto the waxed paper in several places. This will cause the paper to adhere to the bottom of the screen.

To print, lift the screen; place a sheet of black construction paper on top of the original crayon drawing; and mark the corners of the paper so it can be placed in the same position later. Lower the screen and print as before. This will result in the printing of the background around the soda.

Clean the screen. Then cover the original crayon drawing with another 12-x-14-inch sheet of waxed paper, and trace with a pencil around the *inside* edges of the lines that outline the whipped cream on top of the soda. Cut the shape out and place the stencil containing the hole on top of the original crayon drawing, and fasten the stencil to the bottom of the screen by rubbing paint through the organdy in several places. Lift the screen; position the construction paper containing the first print; lower the screen; and print the whipped cream. Proceed in the same manner to make a stencil for the other parts of the soda and to print them. The result will be a multicolored soda outlined in black. See Figure 13-6.

c) To have your students make prints with an outline different from the one in the foregoing project, begin your demonstration by drawing a grasshopper in *crayon* on a 9-x-12-inch piece of paper. Lower your screen on top of the crayon drawing of the grasshopper. Trace over the drawing with an oil crayon, making certain that the crayon fills the holes in the organdy. Place a piece of colored construction paper under the screen; print; and clean the screen. Make a stencil for the inside of each of the body parts and print using a different color with each of the stencils.

Figure 13-6.   *Ice Cream Soda.* A four-color print
on black paper.

d) Another print containing lines can be demonstrated by drawing another
grasshopper on a 9-x-12-inch sheet of paper with a crayon. Lower your screen
on top of the crayon drawing. Trace over the drawing with an oil crayon, making certain that the crayon fills the holes in the organdy. Lift the screen, and
place a 12-x-14-inch sheet of waxed paper on top of the crayon drawing. Using
a pencil, trace around the outline of the grasshopper, but make the line about
one-fourth of an inch away from the outside edge of the crayon line. Cut the
insect out; throw it away; and place the remaining waxed paper on top of the
crayon drawing. Lower the screen and rub paint through the screen to fasten
the waxed paper. Then place some construction paper under the screen and
print.

Clean the screen; cut other stencils for the inside of the insect by tracing
about one-fourth of an inch inside the crayon lines, and print as before. See
Figure 13-7 at the beginning of the chapter.

6. Having experimented with a number of screen-printing projects, spend some
time talking with students about what they have accomplished, what went

wrong, and what could be done to improve their work. You must have discovered that many different effects can be achieved through the use of inexpensive waxed-paper stencils and oil crayons. But did you know that paper stencils can be attached to the bottom of the screen in more than one piece? Try fastening two pear shapes and several leaf shapes to the bottom of your screen; then print. How could you print a wheel with a hubcap and spokes in it? Try it. Try tearing shapes from tracing paper instead of waxed paper. Try making the colors overlap.

Without a doubt you have also discovered that positioning the screen properly for the multicolored print is sometimes difficult. Consequently, it helps to make prints that do not contain a lot of detail, and it also helps if the design is one that will not suffer too much when the positioning of the screen is less than perfect.

Probably, the consistency of the paint causes more problems than anything else. Thus, it is important for the teacher to check it constantly and to make certain that the children understand its importance. The Prang Media Mixer will help considerably to produce the proper consistency in the paint. Experiment a little; try making the paint thinner, then thicker. What happens?

PART 5

Sculpture

Sculpture is the creation of three-dimensional objects by carving, modeling, or assembling. Carving entails the subtraction or removal of unwanted material from a block of wood, stone, or some other hard substance. Modeling, on the other hand, is an additive process by means of which the sculptor produces a new form through the buildup of pliable or impressionable materials. Sometimes modeling in clay or wax precedes casting in a more permanent substance such as metal or plastic. Although assembling or constructing is also an additive process, it is different from modeling. Assembling or constructing usually does not involve impressionable materials, but it does entail the joining of prefabricated items such as metal, glass, paper, and cloth.

Frequently, a sculptor's work is described as sculpture in the round. This means that it stands by itself; a person can walk around it; and it is meant to be observed from any direction. Relief sculpture, however, is intended for viewing largely from the front, and the figures within it project from a background. In high relief, the forms protrude at least half of their natural circumference, while in low or bas-relief, the figures emerge only slightly.

Strangely enough, sculpture has not always been valued as much as the other arts. In China, for example, it has not been as highly regarded as painting and calligraphy. Although the Chinese have produced magnificent three-dimensional works, their connoisseurs have considered sculpture to be more imitative of surface qualities and less capable of revealing the essence or spirit of things. In the West, on the other hand, attitudes toward sculpture have been much less consistent. During the days of Plato and Aristotle, the Greeks believed sculpture to be superior to painting because they felt that it was more naturalistic. Then, at the time of the Renaissance, Leonardo da Vinci argued that painting was of a higher order than sculpture because it was more intellectual. His argument proceeded as follows:

> In the first place, sculpture is dependent on certain lights—namely, those from above—while a picture carries everywhere with it its own light

and shade; light and shade therefore are essential to sculpture. In this respect the sculptor is aided by the nature of the relief, which produces these of its own accord, but the painter artificially creates them by his art in places where nature would normally do the like. The sculptor cannot render the difference in the varying natures of the colors of objects; painting does not fail to do so in any particular. The lines of perspective of sculptors do not seem in any way true; those of painters may appear to extend a hundred miles beyond the work itself. The effects of aerial perspective are outside the scope of sculptors' work; they can represent neither transparent bodies, nor luminous bodies, nor angles of reflection, nor shining bodies such as mirrors and like things of glittering surface, nor mists, nor dull weather, nor an infinite number of things which I forbear to mention lest they should prove wearisome.[1]

In contrast to Leonardo, Benvenuto Cellini (another Renaissance artist) believed that sculpture was the mother of all the arts having anything to do with drawing.[2] According to his view, sculpture based on drawing is likely to be poorly made and clumsy while a drawing based on sculpture is likely to be graceful. He argued, moreover, that sculpture must be built for viewing from more than forty different directions, while drawing or painting need not be made for observation from more than one direction. Consequently, sculpture is more complicated.

Debates about the relative merits of the two arts occur today, but the intensity of the argument has declined because painting and sculpture have become more homogeneous. Before the twentieth century, sculpture served a celebrative and laudatory function, and its primary and almost exclusive theme was the human figure. It involved either carving or modeling, and the capturing of nature in sculptural material was seen as an elevating or ennobling act. With the turn of the century, however, sculpture began to change in the same direction as painting. It turned to new subjects, and began to deal with the integration of form and space. Thus, it followed in the footsteps of cubism, and, like cubism, it made use of nontraditional materials and techniques, especially those of modern technology. In other words, the age-old use of stone, clay, wood, and bronze was supplemented by the use of iron, steel, concrete, glass, paper, and wire.

Along with the new trend came a change in attitude toward art materials and a different idea about craftsmanship. Artists began to feel that the nature and integrity of their materials should be preserved rather than disguised. As a result, they gave up the habit of refining or polishing their work, choosing instead to allow the nature of the medium to show, as well as the

---

[1]from *The Notebooks of Leonardo da Vinci* (London: Jonathan Cape, Ltd., n.d.), edited and translated by Edward MacCurdy. Courtesy of the estate of Edward MacCurdy.
[2]Robert Goldwater and Marco Treves, *Artists on Art* (New York: Pantheon Books, 1945), pp. 87–90.

marks of the process. The effect was that sculpture began to look woody, metallic, stony, or wiry, and brush marks, joints, fastening devices, scratches, and tool marks were permitted to show on the finished products. This informality of technique eventually led to the use of perishable materials and the creation of impermanent or throwaway products exhibiting little or no evidence of craftsmanship. The idea of making temporary objects of visual interest was not new, of course, because primitive or folk art had included such objects for hundreds of years. The difference was that earlier examples were produced for magical, supernatural, or mimetic purposes, while the new art was created for its immediate effect. It was made in an experimental way to deal with psychological, optical, and spatial ideas. The artists were not concerned with tradition or conceptual content but with fundamental forces in life and with the immediate effects of their materials, one upon the other.

CHAPTER 14

CERAMIC SCULPTURE

Figure 14-4.   *Torso of a Man,* by a sixth-grader.

Sculpture can be made from a variety of materials, many of which are not suitable for use in the elementary school. Clay, wood, and paper are probably the most appropriate sculptural materials for children. Consequently, we shall limit our exemplars to works made from those substances.

EXEMPLARS OF CERAMIC SCULPTURE

Most artists work in more than one medium, but their products in one dimension of art do not always become as well-known as their accomplishments in another. André Derain and Honoré Daumier, for example, have become famous for their paintings, and Daumier has received considerable acclaim for his lithographs; yet neither Derain nor Daumier has obtained much recognition for sculpture. One of the reasons for this is simply that most people have not seen their work.

ANDRÉ DERAIN (Day-rahn'), 1880–1954

Derain achieved fame as one of the original fauves between 1905 and 1907. The fauves were largely young Frenchmen impressed by the bright hues in the postimpressionist work of van Gogh and Gauguin (see pages 78 and 96). Therefore, they proceeded to paint with brilliant color, thick paint, clearly evident brush strokes, heavy texture, and spontaneous composition. The paintings were a shocking departure from the accepted academic art of the early twentieth century, and because of this, the producers of such work were called fauves, or "wild beasts."

After 1918, however, it became obvious that none of the maligned artists were really wild animals. Certainly Derain did not fit that description because he had changed his manner of working to the more popular neoclassic style. The change was a disappointment to those who felt that Derain possessed immense potential as an innovator, but they did not know that he had continued his inventiveness in other directions. He had begun to produce original and amusing sculpture which he did not show to anyone outside his family. But, after his death, Madame Derain preserved the sculptures by having them cast in bronze.

Although Derain had created a few pieces of sculpture early in his career, it was not until 1938

that he produced sculpture in quantity. During that year, one of his fir trees was uprooted by the wind, and the excavation yielded some reddish ochre clay of the kind used in making bricks. Derain enjoyed washing and sifting the clay because the process offered an opportunity to make new discoveries, and when the original supply of clay was gone, the whole family looked for more. They found several different colors which the artist mixed experimentally into different combinations.

The plaque in Plate 14-1 is an example of Derain's work. It is primitive, because it looks

Plate 14-1. André Derain. *Personnage à La Gourde.* n.d. Terra cotta, 6⅜". Musée d'art Moderne de la Ville de Paris.

like the work of an untrained sculptor, but Derain was an admirer of primitive art. Without a doubt, he liked the direct and unrefined way in which untrained people did their work, so he used the same simplified techniques. He probably began with a slab of clay and added other pieces by pressing them firmly onto the slab. The legs and arms were made from little ropes of clay, and the buttons and eyes were formed from balls flattened and depressed in the center. The depressions in the hem of the skirt as well as those in the buttons and eyes were made by pushing a small object into the clay. Sometimes, Derain created fingers on some of his figures, but the hands in Plate 14-1 were simply flattened and left fingerless.

Some people might say that Derain's sculpture is so highly simplified that it lacks distinction. Yet, they must admit that details and technical polish often serve as pretentious camouflage for elementary concepts. Derain had the wisdom and courage to show that basic, unostentatious forms can be attractive and that plain, undisguised clay can be beautiful.

HONORÉ DAUMIER (Dome-yeh), 1808–1879

John Canaday says that artists are assumed to be rebels, bohemians, or persons totally unconcerned with the social problems of their time.[3] Moreover, Canaday believes that the third assumption is correct. He thinks that artists have concentrated, for the most part, on ideas and values of permanent importance while avoiding social issues of less enduring interest. If Canaday is right, then the majority of artists may have chosen topics of lasting concern because they were aware that social commentary loses much

of its artistic stature and impact when its subject is no longer current. After all, artists have enough trouble trying to gain acceptance without choosing topics that will soon cause their work to be unappreciated or misunderstood.

Artists who comment on the social scene, despite its passing interest, are probably individuals who feel a strong personal responsibility for the welfare of society. Honoré Daumier was such a man. He was the most powerful social commentator of his time and a staunch champion of civil liberties and human rights. His fame began with the revolution of 1830 and the rise of Louis-Philippe to political leadership in France. Daumier and his fellow Republicans had dreamed of a genuine republic governed by elected representatives of the people, but the dreams were not to be realized. Instead, the new king gained personal control over the government by winning the support of many irresponsible legislators. Furthermore, the members of the legislative assembly were elected by only 240,000 property owners, while 28 million French citizens did not have the right to vote. Without representation, the people were heavily taxed, and much of that money went to the king, who received wages 148 times greater than the President of the United States. Daumier reacted to these injustices by making lithographic prints critical of the king and the government. For this, he was arrested and sentenced to six months in prison.

Fortunately for the French people and for the world of art, Daumier's power as a satirical artist was not overlooked. When he emerged from prison, he was hired by Charles Philipon, the founder of two satirical newspapers, *La Caricature* (1830–1835) and *Charvari* (1832–1836). The caricatures that Daumier made for these newspapers were destined to become famous as works of art and as powerful social documents. They were the forerunners of political cartooning and the beginning of Daumier's vast artistic output which, in the end, amounted to about four thousand lithographs, hundreds of drawings, a large number of paintings, scores of engravings, and some sculpture.

[3]John Canaday, *Metropolitan Seminars in Art, Portfolio II: The Artist as a Social Critic* (New York: Metropolitan Museum of Art, 1959), p. 5.

Much of Daumier's sculpture was produced while working for Charles Philipon on *La Caricature.* Apparently, Philipon suggested that the artist make satirical clay busts of lawmen who supported King Louis-Philippe. The busts were not created for exhibition, but they were made to assist the artist in studying subjects to be handled in another medium, lithography. Since he did not intend to make the busts permanent, he did not make them hollow and he did not fire them. Hence, it is remarkable that most of the sculpture has survived to this day.

Daumier's clay caricatures have been described as "plastic slang," and the bust of Jacques Lefèbvre, the banker-assemblyman, shows why (see Plate 14-2). The artist has not flattered his subject in any way. Instead, he has exaggerated the features that identify the banker and make him look pompous and untrustworthy. The face has been pulled forward until it seems almost detached from the skull, and the incredible nose thrusts ahead like the beak of a bird. The nose is balanced, in the opposite direction, by the rear of the skull which extends a considerable distance behind the scrawny neck. A weak, receding chin and a thin mouth complete the portrait. It is a good piece of sculpture, but as John Canaday's remarks would indicate, the bust loses some of its original effectiveness for us simply because we are too far removed from Lefèbvre and the problems he symbolized. That is the trouble with social commentary as timeless art.

It is possible that Daumier made the bust of Lefèbvre by starting with a column of clay shaped like the end of a large sausage. By squeezing the clay in the region of the neck he could have established the location of the head and shoulders. Then he might have depressed the eye sockets and added clay for the nose, chin, and eyebrows. With his tools, he could have smoothed the top of the head and the face, and he could have created the nostrils, the mouth, the inside of the ears, and the lapels on the coat. Next, he might have added an irregular slab to the head to make the hair appear to stand up. And, he undoubtedly used his favorite comblike

Plate 14-2.   Honoré Daumier. *Bust of Jacques Lefèbvre.* c. 1832–35. Unfired clay, 7 $^{15}/_{16}$" high. Courtesy of Sagot-Le Garrec, Paris.

tool to give texture to the hair and clothing. When dry, the sculpture was painted to make it more lifelike.

Unfortunately, Daumier did not make much sculpture; it was not exhibited; and it was kept in the homes of two families for over a hundred years. Consequently, it did not receive much attention from scholars until recently. It is considered to be excellent work because it seems to make the characters live, perhaps by his superb use of exaggeration.

A PRE-HISPANIC ARTIST,
ca. sixth century A.D.

The art of Mexico, prior to the arrival of Cortes, is usually divided into three periods: the archaic (before 50 A.D.), the classic (50–650 A.D.), and the postclassic (650–1540 A.D.). The sculpture of the archaic period began to appear in the form of small clay figurines soon after 1500 B.C. The figurines were solid, symmetrical, two-dimensional, rigid in their pose, and meant to be seen from the front. In time, however, sculpture was created on a larger scale, and, to keep it from breaking as it was fired, the sculptors made it hollow. Although some pieces reached a height of thirty to sixty inches, the size and character of the sculpture varied considerably from one part of Mexico to another. On the Yucatan Peninsula, for example, the clay figures were small, naturalistic, stiff, cylindrical, and intended for viewing from several directions. In the central valley of Mexico, around Oaxaca (Wah-hah-ka'), the sculptural figures were clearly religious in nature. They were constructed as braziers and funerary urns, and they varied from a few inches to three or four feet in height. They were hollow, largely symmetrical, rigid in pose, and meant to be seen from the front. The sculpture of western Mexico, on the other hand, displayed considerable movement and asymmetry. The figures are hollow, moderate in size, and constructed for viewing from all angles.

The artists of ancient Mexico were highly favored people who produced large quantities of magnificent work, yet we do not know their names. The reason we are unable to identify them is that pre-Hispanic artists were members of the clergy. Their work was meant to serve religion and the community but not themselves. In fact, the idea of making art for pleasure or for personal advancement would have been completely meaningless because the prevailing philosophy of life did not assign a very important role to man. Man was created for the purpose of giving strength and adoration to the gods. The role of the artist was to interpret myths or to give visual form to mythological concepts. He did not represent objects and events in the world of sense as much as he created visual symbols of the deities and objects required for the worship of deities. It was considered important for artists to be born on certain favorable days if they were to be granted the talent necessary for their work. When they were busy creating images of the gods, they were isolated from the rest of the community and required to follow a specific ritual. They were expected to burn copal, to fast, to extract their own blood, and to abstain from sexual intercourse. They were also expected to follow the canons, rules, or standards of judgment established by the artists who preceded them, and as a result, centuries of work by different persons culminated in highly similar objects. The resemblance between works, however, is largely regional, which means that the character of ancient Mexican art differs considerably from one part of the country to another.

The standing *Maize Goddess* "2J" depicted in Plate 14-3 was made by a Zapotec artist in the valley of Oaxaca. Most Zapotec sculpture was made in the form of funerary urns and placed in tombs along with the deceased. The artist began his sculpture by making a cylindrical urn. Then, on one side of the urn, he added slabs of clay to form the figure of a deity or a priest dressed as a god. The effigies were usually made in a seated position with legs crossed and hands on the knees. They served as protector deities or companions for the deceased on his journey to the lower world where he was expected to continue his life. The *Maize Goddess* in Plate 14-3, however, is not a typical funerary urn because the figure is formed on the side of the urn in a standing position.

The headpiece was the most important feature of Zapotec sculpture because it carried the reference to a particular deity. The face was second in importance, the pectoral ornament was third, jewelry was fourth, and the arms and hands were fifth. In Plate 14-3, the vertical corn-

Plate 14-3. Pre-Hispanic artist. Funerary urn, Maize Goddess "2J." Ceramic, 13¾" high. A.D. 6th century. The Metropolitan Museum of Art (The Michael C. Rockefeller Memorial Collection of Primitive Art. Bequest of Nelson A. Rockefeller, 1979).

above the tip of the ear, the other two on either side of the ear. The Goddess of Maize typically has her hair arranged as you see in Plate 14-3, and she wears loose-fitting under- and outergarments. The latter permit free use of the arms.

Notice that the arms of the *Maize Goddess* have been kept close to the body. From an artist's standpoint, this is helpful because it makes the sculpture more compact, more sturdy, and free from the deep depressions and projections that can cause busyness and disunity in a work of art. Notice also that the legs are separated. If the figure had not been attached to an urn, the separation would be an indication of the artist's skillfulness, because it is easier to make a standing figure if the legs are kept close together.

Probably, the figure in Plate 14-3 was constructed of coils and slabs. To build with coils is to make snakelike shapes with clay and coil them round and round on top of each other producing a hollow form. The coils are then pinched together, and sometimes the surface is made smooth. Slabs and other forms can then be added to the basic hollow figure, and the artist can proceed to draw in the clay or press objects into it. All these things have been done to the *Maize Goddess.*

It was common for the Indians of early Mexico to cover the finished sculpture with slip to give it a smooth surface. Slip is a fluid mixture of clay and water, and it can be made in red, buff, cream, gray, brown, or black colors. The use of several different slips made the early Mexican sculpture very colorful, and if only one slip was used, the artists often painted the sculpture after it was fired. The firing was done in open pits, underground kilns, and brick kilns, and the sculpture was rarely glazed.

ADDITIONAL EXEMPLARS

Other pieces of ceramic sculpture which might be shown to students are the works of Elie Nadelman, Ernst Barlach, Jacob Epstein, Alek-

cob in the headdress identifies the figure as the Goddess of the Fields of Maize. The leaves or husk of the ear of maize appear as three similar units which together constitute a trefoil; one sandr Archipenko, Ivan Mestrovic, Andrea Della Robia, or Picasso. The bronze reliefs by Lorenzo Ghiberti would also be excellent because they were originally produced in clay.

CERAMIC SCULPTURE ACTIVITIES FOR THE PRIMARY GRADES (AGES 6 THROUGH 8)

Clay is often obtained in ready-mixed form. This requires less work from the teacher, but it increases the cost of the clay and it keeps children from learning to prepare the material. Consequently, we recommend that clay be purchased dry and in fifty-pound bags. Red earthenware clay is appropriate, and one fifty-pound bag is enough for about ten children. This five-pound allotment per pupil is sufficient to do from one to three of the activities described in this book.

In the primary grades it is advisable for the teacher to mix the clay several days before the children are to begin working. This gives the clay a chance to age, thereby increasing its plasticity. And, if there are thirty children in the class, it is best to do the mixing in ten strong, plastic bags. Empty three two-pound coffee cans of clay into each bag. If it is red earthenware, fill three-eighths of the coffee can with medium-size grog (40 to 60 mesh), and add that amount to each bag. The grog (tiny pieces of fired clay) makes the clay more workable, and reduces shrinkage and breakage when the clay is fired. If grog is not available, use sand Then fill seven-eighths of the coffee can with water and add it to each bag. Force the air from the bags; close them with wire fasteners; and mix the content of each container by manipulating it from the outside. After two or three days, remove the clay from each bag, and knead it on a piece of half-inch plywood (24 x 48 inches). The kneading is done in the same manner as the kneading of bread, and its purpose is threefold: 1) to remove air bubbles; 2) to mix the clay thoroughly; and 3) to allow the plywood to absorb excess moisture. If the material sticks to the hands, it is too wet and requires more kneading. If it is leathery and breaks when bent, it is too dry and needs more water worked into it. When the clay from each bag is ready, divide it into three balls and keep it in the plastic bag until sculpturing is to begin. Then give each child one ball of clay. If the clay should get impossibly hard, it can be reclaimed by soaking it in a bucket of water.

When making sculpture with clay, it is important to have enough tools. Boxwood instruments, with and without wire loops at the end, are excellent. But, if they are not available, use paper clips, tongue depressors (split lengthwise), and lengths of quarter-inch wooden dowels sharpened in a pencil sharpener. Each child should also have a small piece of sponge, a one-inch dowel about twelve inches long, a plastic garbage bag big enough to cover his sculpture when he is not working on it, and a ¼-x-12-x-12-inch piece of plywood to work on.

Unfired clay sculpture is unsatisfactory because it breaks too easily, and breakage disappoints children. After all, youngsters are proud of their work, and they like to take it home. Consequently, it is important to have a kiln in each elementary school so that sculpture can be fired and thereby preserved. Probably the most appropriate kiln is the top-loading, electric type containing a firing chamber with interior dimensions of 18 x 18 x 18 inches. It also helps if the kiln is equipped with a pyrometer and a kiln-sitting attachment (with limit timer). The pyrometer allows the operator to monitor the temperature of the kiln and the kiln sitter prevents accidental overfiring. With these attachments the operator need not maintain a constant watch over the kiln.

Problems always develop when working with clay, but experience will help to reduce the number. Here are some common problems as well as suggestions for avoiding or correcting them:

1. Low-fire, earthenware clays often break when bent because they are not very plastic. Adding grog, sand, vinegar, or ball clay will be helpful. Try one-third ball clay to two-thirds earthenware.

2. If the clay gets too dry, it will not model easily. Keep it moist by storing it in a plastic bag when you are not working with it, and avoid projects that extend over long periods of time. If the sculpture gets dry as you work, spray it with water. Try using spray bottles that once contained window cleaner.

3. Before it is fired, sculpture is easily broken. Sometimes broken pieces can be put together by wetting the surfaces to be joined with vinegar. In addition, make some slip with clay and vinegar and put the slip between the broken surfaces when they are pressed together.

4. If sculpture breaks in the kiln, it is possible that it was not thoroughly dry before firing; there may have been air pockets in the clay, especially at the joints; there may have been foreign matter in the clay, such as paper; or parts may have been added to the sculpture after it had dried too much. Sculpture may also break if it is fired or cooled too rapidly; thus it is important to allow about 24 hours to fire and cool.

5. Sculpture broken in the kiln can often be glued together, and if areas are missing, they can be filled with a vinyl-spackling compound obtained from a hardware store. The spackle can be sanded, and the breakage covered by painting the sculpture with tempera.

CONCEPTS FOR POSSIBLE DEVELOPMENT

An understanding of the following terms or concepts should be developed in the primary grades:

sculpture	slip	figurine	symbol
relief sculpture	grog	pattern	depression
low relief	slab	texture	decorative elements
high relief	clay coils	kiln	sculpture in the round

SUGGESTED ACTIVITIES

The activities in the paragraphs that follow are presented in the order of their difficulty:

1. An introductory clay activity in kindergarten or the first grade might begin with comments about how sculpture differs from drawings, paintings, and prints. Then show the exemplars of clay sculpture and explain the difference between relief sculpture and sculpture in the round. This can be followed by a demonstration of easy techniques for making a low relief. Simply use your hand to pound a fist-sized ball of clay into the form of a slab about half an inch thick. Then draw a front view of your face on the slab with the end of an open paper clip, and use the clip to cut through the slab along the outline. Remove the clay from around the head, and return it to the plastic bag. Using the paper clip and a split tongue depressor show the youngsters that hair, eyes, noses, and mouths can be drawn on the slab. Then show how the tongue depressor or the end of a dowel can be used in the manner of Derain to depress parts of the eyes, mouth, hair, and ears. When finished, give each child a ball of clay, some clay tools, and a 12-x-12-inch piece of plywood, and let him begin his own self-portrait. Caution him against doing too much drawing and hole-making in the clay. The finished portraits should be left to dry on the plywood sheets for about a week.

   When the portraits are dry, carefully place them on top of each other in the kiln. Fire the kiln at cone 05 (1915°F), and make sure that it is fired and cooled slowly over a period of 24 hours. Then, to finish the portraits, indicate through a demonstration that the heads can be painted with tempera and coated with white shellac, or polymer acrylic emulsion.

2. Show your students the sculpture by Derain. Explain that it is called low relief because the figure projects only a small distance from its background. Then demonstrate the Derain technique on a head-shaped slab of clay by showing how to add bits of clay to build up the eyes, nose, hair, and mouth. Press the pieces tightly against the slab to make sure no air pockets remain in the joints. Air bubbles will expand in the kiln causing the sculpture to explode.[4]

---

[4]Avoid the use of water and slip when young children work with clay. The tendency is to use too much, and the result is mud.

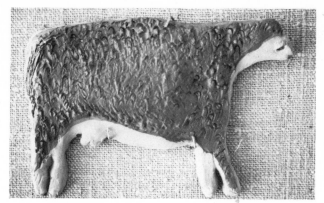

Figure 14-1.   Cow cut from slab with texture
added.

After the work has been dried, fired, painted, and coated with shellac, it can be given a nice appearance by gluing it to a piece of plywood stained with tempera or wood stain.

3. Using the technique learned in the two foregoing activities, students can cut birds, animals, human figures, buildings, or other objects out of clay slabs. But they might proceed further to add texture to their sculpture. Texture can indicate the nature of hair, feathers, scales, or clothing, and it can be used to simulate bricks, boards, stones, and other such things. Texture can be made by pressing objects into the clay, by drawing on the clay, and by adding pieces of clay. Illustrate this fact by pointing to the hair of the Daumier exemplar and the clothing of the *Maize Goddess*. See Figure 14-1.

4. Instead of cutting an object out of a clay slab, it is possible to leave the slab uncut and build the object on top of it. Show Derain's work, and explain how the various parts of the figure were produced. Demonstrate the technique. Then select a theme and discuss it with the class. Trimming the Christmas tree, running a race, picking flowers, climbing trees, or feeding animals would be good topics. As work progresses, the figures made by the children may begin to merge with the background, making the figures difficult to see. If so, show how Derain made a little corner at the point where the figure touches the background. Then demonstrate how to make that corner with a tongue depressor, or draw an outline around the figure with a pointed dowel or an open paper clip. Fire the piece as indicated earlier.

Demonstrate how to paint the sculpture with tempera or with liquid floor wax slightly colored with green or brown powdered tempera. The wax will produce an interesting patina. Remove excess wax with a rag.

Figure 14-2.   *Mother and Brother,* a high-relief sculpture from grades two and three. (From color slide set to accompany *Art, Artists, and Art Education* by Kenneth M. Lansing. Copyright 1969, McGraw-Hill. Used with the permission of McGraw-Hill Book Company.)

5. In the second or third grade it is possible to do sculpture in high relief. To demonstrate, crumple some newspapers into the shape of a softball, and place it on a 12-x-12-inch piece of plywood. Roll out a slab of clay about half an inch thick and as large as a dinner plate. Place the slab on top of the newspaper. This will cause the center of the slab to rise, suggesting a head. To make it look more like a head, press with your thumbs to create eye sockets; build up the nose and mouth; add clay pieces or ropes for hair; and use a tongue depressor to create a corner where the face meets the flat, clay background. Indicate that eyes, noses, mouths, and hair can be made in many ways; show a few of those techniques; use the exemplars to indicate other possibilities; and encourage youngsters to invent their own methods. Then turn them loose to create faces of their mothers and fathers in high relief.

After a week of drying, remove the newspaper from the back of the sculpture; fire the clay at cone 05 (1915°F); and finish it with liquid floor wax (such as Klear) that has been slightly colored with green or brown powdered tempera. After brushing the wax on with a bristle brush, wipe some of it off with a soft cloth. See Figure 14-2.

6. Children are often eager to make standing figures in the round, but it is difficult for them to do so, especially if they try to make people. It is helpful to have them begin with four-legged animals. But first, show the children that animals can be made either by pulling the neck and legs out of a lump of clay or by adding those parts to a piece representing the body. If the additive method is used, press the parts together firmly so they will not come apart in the kiln. Then demonstrate how the animal can be made to stand on a slab of clay by pressing each of the four feet tightly onto the slab. Having secured the animal, for example, a dog, make a child out of clay and fasten his feet to the slab near the dog. Then connect one of the child's hands to the dog by pressing them together with two opposing fingers. This connecting of one figure with another will help to make all of them stand more easily. And it will also help if the children are urged to make legs thicker than normal.

These pieces of sculpture must be handled carefully, and they cannot be stacked on top of each other in the kiln. Hence, it will be necessary to use kiln shelves inside the firing chamber, and it will be important to fire slowly. When the pieces are cool, paint them with tempera, and coat the painted figures with white shellac or polymer acrylic emulsion.

Good themes for this activity are: cowboys and horses, washing the dog, milking the cows, herding sheep, a boxing match, or my family. As you discuss these themes, tell about the figurines of ancient Mexico. Show the exemplar of Mexican sculpture and explain that the figurines looked somewhat the same but smaller.

CERAMIC SCULPTURE ACTIVITIES FOR THE INTERMEDIATE GRADES (AGES 9 THROUGH 11)

In the intermediate grades, children like to prepare clay. A few of them might do the job after school using the technique described on page 258, or each child could mix his own clay in class. Simply give each person a small but strong plastic bag, and have him empty a two-pound coffee can full of clay into the bag. Then add one-eighth of a can of grog or sand and 18 ounces of water. Close and fasten the bag with a wire fastener, and mix the clay by hand from the outside. Let it stay in the bag for about two days. Then remove and knead it on a sheet of plywood. When it is the proper consistency, put it back in the bag for about a week to improve the plasticity of the clay.

In all the following activities, it is important to work on composition. Consequently, the suggestions listed below should be helpful to beginners. We realize, however, that deviations can and should occur as students develop skill and sophistication.

1. Keep individual appendages from extending too far out from the main portion of the sculpture. If they stick out, they increase construction problems, and they lead the eye away from the figure. This decreases the unity of the work.

2. Create visual variety by giving different textures to different parts of the object. One part might be made rough by adding pieces of clay or by streaking with a comb, for example, while another part might be made smooth.

3. Variety can also be obtained by pressing objects into certain places to produce a pattern while other areas are left without a pattern.

4. Unity can be aided by repeating patterns or textures.

5. To make an area smooth, go over it with a damp sponge.

6. If visual movement, detail, or some other factor attracts the eye to one side of the figure, do something to the other side to counteract that attractiveness. In other words, make the figure balance.

7. Avoid undercutting or making deep holes in the figure.

8. Make a visual separation of the parts of the figure by creating a corner where the parts meet.

9. To increase visual interest, put some of the following items into your human figures: eyelids, fingernails, buckles, cuffs, short sleeves, buttons, shoelaces, nostrils, belts, ties, hair ribbons, wristwatches, handkerchiefs, ears, and folds in clothing.

CONCEPTS FOR POSSIBLE DEVELOPMENT

Make sure that concepts recommended for the primary grades are understood by the children. Then proceed to develop an understanding of the following terms or concepts:

earthenware clay	assembling	projections
terra cotta	additive process	exaggeration
stoneware	subtractive process	patina
green ware	three-dimensional	effigies
bisque ware	low-relief sculpture	braziers
pyrometer	bas-relief	funerary urns
kiln sitter	high relief	fauves
firing chamber	plastic	coil building
limit timer	pliable	armature
wedging	bust	symmetrical
kneading	torso	asymmetrical
carving	compact form	social commentary
modeling	depressions	satire

SUGGESTED ACTIVITIES

All activities recommended for the primary level can be done successfully in the intermediate grades. The difference is that older children can add more detail and texture; they can build larger figures; and they can do more with composition.

1. Do Activities 2, 3, and 4 in the section on ceramic sculpture for the primary grades, but spend more time talking about André Derain and his sculpture. Discuss the reasons why he and others have simplified their art. Perhaps it would help to show the exemplars by Gauguin, Arp, Johnson, Kollwitz, Léger, and Seurat. Talk about the strength, power, and beauty of uncomplicated forms free of detail. Talk about how easy they are to see because they are not broken by small shapes, and call attention to the fact that the proportions within and among the simplified forms are often the same as the basic and highly satisfying proportions found again and again in nature (2:3, 3:5, 5:8, 8:13, and so on). Then urge your students to make an uncomplicated relief sculpture while concentrating on proportional relationships. Try to avoid symmetrical arrangements and figures divided into segments of equal size.

2. See Activity 4 for the primary grades. Do it again, but try to have your students make the human or animal figure fit more closely the shape of the slab on which they are working. If a child is working on a square slab, for example, urge him to distort his figure slightly (if necessary) to make sure that the corners of the slab are utilized. Perhaps arms or legs can be bent to fit the space; hair or clothing can be made to fill unused areas; and the tails of animals can be made to do the same thing. This helps children to learn to design something appropriate for a given space, and it tends to give their work a strong sculptural quality.

3. Tell the story of André Derain and how he dug and mixed his own clay. Perhaps you and your students could find and dig some clay in your own neighborhood. If so, mix it in a bucket with an excess of water. Then pour the fluid mixture through a window screen to remove pebbles and other debris. Let the strained clay settle in a bucket, and pour off the water that rises to the top. Scoop the clay from the bucket and place it on a sheet of plywood where it can dry in the open air. When it reaches the workable stage (not too wet and sticky), add a little grog and knead it into the clay. If the clay breaks when bent, add some red earthenware or ball clay, and try shaping it again into small, simple forms. Allow them to dry for several days, and fire them at cone 05 or 06.

It is likely that the clay you dig yourself will not be good for sculpture and pottery. It may be difficult to shape, and it may break in firing. Nevertheless, trying to process your own clay can be a worthwhile learning experience.

4. Using the technique described in Activity 5 for the primary grades, encourage your students to make some high-relief sculptures of animals, full-length humans, light bulbs and electrical cords, automobiles, tools, boats, and other such objects. Give more instruction in the various ways of making eyes, mouths, hair, feathers, scales, patterns, and textural effects. Use the Mexican exemplar as well as the one by Daumier to illustrate some of those techniques. Then let the students begin, but make a special effort to see that the finished slabs have the same outside dimensions, such as 10 x 10 inches or 8 x 10 inches. When they are fired and finished, fasten them to uniform pieces of stained plywood, and attach the plywood to the wall of the school with long screws. The result will resemble a mural in high relief that can be removed and replaced.

5. The fourth grade is a good place to begin small, hollow sculpture in the round. To do so, display the exemplars of ceramic sculpture, and discuss the differences among them. Develop an understanding of terms such as assembling, carving, modeling, bust, compact form, depressions, projections, and satire. Then concentrate on the bust by Daumier; explain what he was trying to do; and ask your class to do the same thing by modeling small satirical busts (heads and shoulders) of the teachers in a school for scoundrels. A few comments about *Oliver Twist* by Charles Dickens might clarify the meaning of a school for scoundrels.

   The sculpture by Daumier was made of solid clay. If it had been fired, it would have broken in the kiln. Therefore, if the classes' work is to be fired, each bust must be made hollow either by constructing it with coils or by building it around a removable armature. We recommend the use of a paper armature.

   Crumple some newspapers into a column about seven inches tall and four inches wide. Roll out a slab of clay about half an inch thick, and wrap the clay around the column and over its top. Press the clay firmly, especially where it overlaps; fill in any cracks or holes; try to keep the clay uniform in thickness; and make the outside reasonably smooth. The result should be a column of clay that looks like the end of a big frankfurter (open at the bottom). With two hands, gently squeeze the frankfurter where you would like the neck to be. Do not squeeze too much, because the paper in the head will eventually have to be removed from the bottom through the neck.

   Put one hand on the front of the shoulders and the other on the back and press them together slightly. The result should begin to resemble a head with shoulders. Continue by depressing the eye sockets with your thumbs and by building the nose, eyebrows, ears, hair, and chin. Then work on collars, necklines, necklaces, ties, earrings, and other such items. The children may get ideas about these elements by studying the exemplars, but remember that hair and other parts can be made with clay ropes, balls, and slabs, or they can be made by drawing on the clay or by depressing it.

   When the busts are finished and leather hard, pull the paper carefully from

Figure 14-3. *Man with Glasses.* Note depressed design on shirt.

the inside, and let the busts dry thoroughly. Fire the figures slowly at cone 05, and finish them with liquid floor wax slightly colored with powdered tempera. See Figure 14-3.

Finally, the children should learn to stack a kiln with green ware (unfired clay pieces) and fire it. The fired pieces are called bisque ware. Since this sculpture is not glazed, the pieces can touch each other in the kiln, but be careful. Green ware breaks easily.

6. While looking at the reproduction of the *Maize Goddess,* indicate that the class will be making sculpture similar to the top half of the exemplar. Call attention to the arms which were kept tight against the body, and advise your students to make two arms in the same way. This will reduce construction problems and make the sculpture more compact and unified.

In a demonstration, do the things described in Activity 5, but start with a crumpled paper column about nine inches tall and five inches wide. Then, after starting the face, show how to begin the arms by drawing them lightly on the clay. Put your thumbs on each side of one arm, and press in on the clay. This will make the arm project slightly from the body. To increase the projection, add more clay. To distinguish the arm from the body and to make the arm serve more fully as a part of the total design of the sculpture, use a split tongue depressor to create a corner where the arm meets the body. Use the same tongue depressor to separate the fingers or to create incised lines like those on the clothing of the *Maize Goddess*.

When adding slabs, balls, or coils to make hats, hair, necklaces, and other details, put a little slip where the pieces join the basic figure, and spray the figure frequently with water. If it should get too dry, the added pieces will come off in the kiln.

Remember that sculpture in the round must be viewed from all directions. Hence, it is important to turn the sculpture as you work, and it is advisable to make the back as interesting as the front. The judicious placement of hair, arms, hats, and clothing can make a big difference, and so can the turn of a head. See Figure 14-4 at the beginning of the chapter.

7. Talk about the special attributes of sculpture and the function it has served. Stress its role in the lives of the Indians of early Mexico, and discuss the duty of the artist. The *Maize Goddess* may serve as illustrative material and as a model to emulate.

To make an eighteen-inch, full-standing figure like the *Maize Goddess* will require about twice as much clay as the mixture on page 263 produces. The best way to do it is to start with the top half, and make it according to the directions in Activity 6. Then put the top aside, and cover it with plastic to keep it from drying.

Start the bottom (from feet to waist) by crumpling a newspaper into two columns about nine to ten inches high and three to four inches wide. Put the columns together so they resemble two legs that are touching, and wrap a slab of clay around the legs. Press the clay firmly, especially where it overlaps, and make an indentation, front and back, where the legs meet.

To make shoes, put a ball of crumpled paper in front of each leg and cover the top and sides with a slab of clay. Press the clay tightly against the leg where the shoe joins the leg. When the basic form of the legs, hips, and feet have been formed, begin to add details such as belts, pockets, skirts, cuffs, buttons, and flies. Do not allow the clay to become more than an inch thick at any point.

When the bottom has dried enough to support the weight, place the upper part of the figure on top of the lower. By adding or carving away clay, make the top fit the bottom. As the figure dries in the open air, continue to adjust the top and bottom as necessary. When the clay is leather hard, remove the paper and eliminate excess clay by scraping from the inside.

After drying and firing, the piece may be finished in the ways already discussed, or paste wax may be applied with a toothbrush and buffed by hand with a shoe brush. After buffing, an antique patina can be attained by brushing

Figure 14-5.   *Janitor in Two Parts* (joined at the
waist), by a sixth-grader.

on a color glaze (such as Sherwin-Williams delft or heirloom brown). The glaze
is then partially wiped off, leaving color in the depressed areas. See Figure 14-5.

8. Do the foregoing activities again using slightly different themes. Give more information about the exemplars and the artists who produced them. Spend
more time explaining the concepts listed at the beginning of this section, and
give more attention to composition. Try finishing the sculpture by painting it
with a bristle brush dipped in turpentine and brown shoe polish. Then wipe
the piece with a rag to obtain an attractive coloration or patina.

To create still another finish, you must begin before the object is fired.
Discuss the ideas and techniques of the ancient artists who produced work like
the *Maize Goddess.* Explain that colored slip was often painted on the piece
before it was fired. Then mix some slip from Gold Art Clay (a buff-colored
clay) and paint it on a part of the sculpture you would like to appear light. Fire
the piece, and add the wax and antique glaze mentioned in Activity 7.

CHAPTER 15

WOOD SCULPTURE

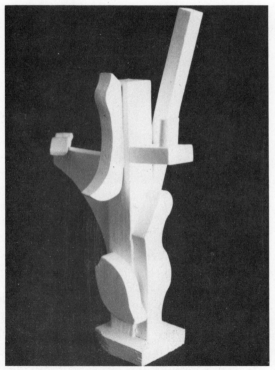

Figure 15-4.   Abstract wood sculpture in the round.

Wood has been a premier sculptural medium since ancient times. In most parts of the world it is easy to obtain; it is relatively inexpensive; and it can be cut, carved, and assembled without difficulty. Wood is also pleasantly warm in appearance and rich in the beauty of its grain. The grain can be accented or enhanced through oiling, staining, or polishing, and if necessary, it can be painted. Hence, it is easy to see that wood has great potential for the sculptor.

EXEMPLARS OF WOOD SCULPTURE

Although wood carving can be done in the fifth and sixth grades, most elementary schools cannot provide the necessary tools, equipment, and instruction. Consequently, the exemplars that follow have been selected from the works of artists who assemble their sculpture rather than carve it.

JEAN (HANS) ARP, 1887–1966

According to his own account, Arp became interested in poetry and art while still a child. As he grew older, he continued to create in both disciplines, and by 1914 he had established himself, among his fellow artists, as a person of originality and artistic significance. But he was a German citizen, and at the beginning of the first World War, he found himself in Paris where he was under considerable pressure to return to Germany. Not wishing to enter the war on either side, he moved to Switzerland where his parents had been living for several years.

Meanwhile, Hugo Ball, a German writer and producer, arrived in Zurich and founded the Cabaret Voltaire on February 1, 1916. The new nightclub was a literary cabaret specializing in poetry, music, and art. The club revolved around the activities of Hugo Ball, Emmy Hennings, Tristan Tzara, Marcel Janco, Richard Huelsenbeck, and Jean Arp. The participants were different from each other and highly individualistic, yet they had a common goal. According to Ball, the purpose was to "draw attention, across the barriers of war and nationalism, to the few independent spirits who live for other ideals."[1] Or, to put it differently, their aim was to protest against the collapse of social and moral values and against the traditions of logic and art. The protest took the form of nihilism, a negation of all standards, values, and conventions. Apparently, the persons involved felt that conditions of life had become so bad that they wanted to expose them, eliminate them, and begin again. The technique they used was to ridicule existing standards through the production of nonsense poetry, bizarre music, and highly abstract art. To give these efforts a name, the participants coined the term *dada*, which now signifies both art and antiart at the same time.[2]

An interesting aspect of the dada story has to do with troublemakers and who they are perceived to be. The performers at the Cabaret Voltaire were regarded with suspicion by Swiss authorities because of their disrespectful antics, but the three studious speechmakers who lived across the street were considered less troublesome. The three quiet men, as it turns out, were planning the Russian revolution. Their names were Radek, Zinoviev, and Lenin.[3]

[1] Hans Richter, *Dada: Art and Anti-Art* (New York: McGraw-Hill), pp. 13–14.

[2] Although the spirit of dada began at the Cabaret Voltaire in 1916, it also developed spontaneously in several other places at about the same time. It was not an organized movement, but a simultaneous reaction of kindred spirits to world events.

[3] Richter, op. cit., p. 16.

Arp, as a troublesome dadaist, objected to that which he considered unnatural in art. He disapproved of the illusionism in all naturalistic products, and he felt the same way about the overintellectualization frequently associated with cubism. In Arp's opinion, natural or genuine art does not evolve from copying or intellectualizing; it originates in nature, and it undergoes spiritualization and beautification through refinement by the person who makes it. Under what condition does the refinement take place? It occurs, according to Arp, only if the artist maintains a balance between the conscious and the unconscious. This means that he must consciously study nature because it is the source of artistic form, but he must sublimate or refine those forms and he must improve their relationship in the art object by relying on guidance from the unconscious.[4]

Arp came to realize the power of unconscious forces after discovering the law of chance. One day, after tearing a drawing and throwing it to the floor, he noticed that the pieces had formed an expressive pattern that he had previously tried in vain to achieve. From then on, he tried to arrange his compositions by chance, unconsciously, and without will. Apparently, he came to believe that chance was not accidental but based on laws that govern the cosmos.

Arp's philosophy must have exerted a powerful and never-ending influence upon his artistic behavior because the style of his work remained consistent throughout his life. The four distinguishing characteristics of the style have been identified by Herbert Read as "precision, organic vitality, grace, and humor."[5] All four qualities can be seen in Plate 15-1. Precision is evident in the clean, strong, and sharply cut shapes; organic vitality is apparent in forms derived from the natural shapes of plates, forks, and navels; and

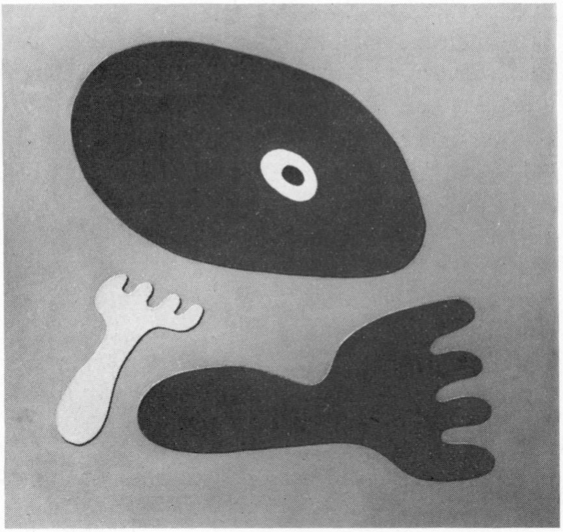

Plate 15-1. Jean Arp. *Plate, Fork and Navel.* 1923. Painted wood relief, 23¼" x 24". Courtesy Sidney Janis Gallery, New York. Geoffrey Clements, photographer.

grace is seen in the spontaneous distillation and arrangement of those natural forms. The humor, obviously, is evident in the choice of subject matter.

In conclusion, it is important to point out that Arp was one of the first artists in modern times to assemble wooden relief sculpture instead of carving it. He was the first to make a painted wooden relief, and he was also among the pioneers of highly abstract sculpture. He liked to think of such work as being concrete, however, because it was fundamental, solid, and close to the essence of things.

LOUISE NEVELSON, 1900–

Born in Kiev, Russia, Louise Nevelson came to America in 1905, settling in Rockland, Maine. After marrying in 1920, she moved to New York, where she studied music, voice, drama, poetry,

[4]Jean Arp, *On My Way: Poetry and Essays, 1912–1947* (New York: Whittenborn, Schultz, 1948), p. 77.

[5]Herbert Read, *Arp* (New York: Abrams, 1968), p. 158.

and dancing, as well as drawing and painting. She studied these subjects because she believed then, as she does now, that knowledge of all the arts contributes to the development of a well-rounded artist. Near the end of the decade, however, she began to concentrate more heavily on the visual arts by enrolling at the Art Students' League and by studying with Hans Hoffman in Munich (1931).

On her return to America, she and Ben Shahn assisted Diego Rivera in creating his murals at the New Workers School in New York City. This was the age of the Great Depression, when life was especially difficult for artists, because they could not get the public to develop an interest in their work. It was not until 1940, in fact, that Nevelson was able to obtain her first one-woman show, and it was 1955 before her work was actively sought. During that year, she began to work with wood, and before long, she was constructing wooden walls from discarded wooden objects. The pieces of scrap were arranged inside wooden boxes, and the boxes were joined to form a wall, which was then painted monochromatically with black, white, or gold. Nevelson called these constructions sculptural environments.

The work in Plate 15-2 is a column rather than a wall, and it is not made of wooden pieces arranged inside boxes. Yet it does reveal the basic characteristic of Nevelson's sculpture. Like the rest of her work, it is nonrepresentational; the pieces of wood are attached to a central column with purely formal intentions. In other words, the primary concern in assembling the parts was the relationship of their sizes, shapes, textures, shadows, and spatial configurations. To give the piece unity, the artist painted it a single color. If she had left it uncolored, the different hues and patterns in the wood would probably have caused a visual chaos or, at the least, an excess of busyness.

Notice how the circular shapes stand out against the rest of the forms which are largely rectangular. Observe also the variety in the

Plate 15-2.   Louise Nevelson. *Rain Forest Column I.* 1967. Black wood, 48" high. Pace Gallery, New York.

heights and widths of the assembled parts. The pieces have been put together in such a way that they divide all spaces into unequal and asymmetrical segments. Without a doubt, they were arranged this way on the basis of feeling rather than reason, in which case the approach to composition is similar to that of Jean Arp. And the result is an artifact that communicates feeling in spite of the fact that it does not imitate surface appearances in nature. If anything, it is a distillation or simplification of nature into elemental forms and relationships.

MARISOL ESCOBAR, 1930–

Marisol Escobar uses her given name as a means of identification. Consequently, one of the best-known practitioners of pop art is known throughout the world simply as Marisol. She was born of Venezuelan parents, but she divided her youth between Los Angeles and Paris, where she studied art in the time-honored Ecole de Beaux-Arts and the famous Académie Julian. At the age of twenty, Marisol moved to New York, and three years later, she began her work in sculpture. By 1957, she had obtained her first one-woman show, and from then on, she continued to produce the mixed-media assemblages for which she has become famous. Often these works contain drawing, painting, carving, plaster casts, and found objects all at the same time. Some of the figures are single units while others are meant to be seen in groups, but they are all unique.

The piece in Plate 15-3 is characteristic of Marisol's efforts with mixed media. It is composed of a wooden box, a long plank, a slightly carved block for the head, a real hat, a real umbrella, and a plaster cast for the hand. On the front of the wooden head-block is a drawing of a face, and on top of the box are drawings of two shoes. The suit, the shirt, and the tie are obviously painted on the plank that forms the body. Clearly, Marisol has produced something different from the work of Arp and Nevelson because her constructions are representational. Furthermore, she gives her sculpture a distinctive

Plate 15-3. Marisol Escobar. ABCDEFG&HI. c. 1961–62. Mixed media, 70" x 19" x 11½". Courtesy Sidney Janis Gallery, New York.

character by avoiding a high degree of naturalism. The effect is usually a witty, satirical comment on individuals and on society as a whole.

ADDITIONAL EXEMPLARS

Naturally, we encourage the use of as many exemplars as possible. Consequently we would recommend showing wood sculpture by various artists including the following: Pablo Picasso, Henri Laurens, Ben Nicholson, Constantin Brancusi, Leonard Baskin, Forman Onderdonk, Jack Squire, Henry Moore, and George Sugerman.

WOOD SCULPTURE ACTIVITIES FOR THE PRIMARY GRADES (AGES 6 THROUGH 8)

Like printmaking, sculpture is a favorite activity with children. The trouble is that youngsters are often denied the opportunity to engage in three-dimensional construction because teachers believe it is excessively difficult or messy. The secret to satisfactory experiences with sculpture, however, is fourfold; an efficiently organized classroom, activities appropriate for the ages of the children, sufficient time, and the proper tools, equipment, and supplies. Recommendations about classroom arrangements and time allotments are offered in Chapter 1, while wood-building projects suitable for the different grades are described on subsequent pages. First, we will recommend the tools, equipment, and supplies most useful for making wood sculpture in the elementary school. The suggested amounts are based on a class size of thirty.

Probably, the most essential tool is a hammer. Eight 7-ounce hammers and two 13-ounce hammers will offer enough variety in weight to accommodate children with different degrees of muscular development. An 8-ounce ball peen hammer will also be useful for tooling bits of metal in the fifth and sixth grades.

To drill holes, we recommend at least one hand drill with a three-jaw chuck having a ¼-inch capacity. It should be made of malleable steel with two driving gears touching the geared handwheel. In addition, a set of 10 drill points varying in size from ⅟₁₆ to ¼ of an inch is required. Less essential, but useful, is one brace and four bits numbered 6, 8, 10, and 16. The brace and the bits will permit boring holes that are ⅜, ½, ⅝, and 1 inch in diameter, respectively.

Two 12- to 14-inch backsaws are better for young children than crosscut saws because the stiff band at the top keeps the backsaws from bending. At the intermediate level, however, one 20-inch crosscut saw with 10 teeth to the inch would be useful. Three coping saws with flat spring frames and solid handles are less necessary but very desirable. About three dozen coping saw blades will be needed to replace those that are broken. The blades should be 6½ inches long with 15 teeth to the inch. And, to make all kinds of sawing easier for children it is important to have from one to four malleable iron woodworking vises that clamp onto tables or workbenches.

Two standard screwdrivers (one 6-inch and one 8-inch), three trysquares (with wooden handles and 6-inch blades), one pair of 6-inch combination pliers, two or three surform planes, and one regular tin snip with a 2½-inch cut should be sufficient to complete the list of tools.

Several pieces of equipment are desirable. A strong, heavy table or workbench with a vise clamped to each corner is ideal. If such a work surface is unavailable, we recommend that a 4-x-4-foot sheet of ¾-inch plywood be placed on top of four school desks, and we suggest that the plywood and desks be clamped together by fastening a woodworking vise to each corner of the plywood. A box for wood scraps, an anvil, a dustpan, a yardstick, a bench brush, and some plastic refrigerator dishes for nails should complete the equipment.

Supplies of the following kinds will also be useful; one box each of ½-, ¾-, and 1-inch wire brads; a one-pound box each of 4-, 6-, 8-, and 10-penny nails; a one-pound box each of 4-, 6-, 8-, and 10-penny finishing nails; one box each of ⅝-, ¾-, and 1-inch wire nails; an assortment of carpet and upholstery tacks; escutcheon pins; washers; leather scraps; white glue; tempera paint; a variety of wood stains; a variety of garnet sandpaper; and a large selection of soft scrap wood.

Although all the foregoing items are highly desirable, they are not all necessary for wood sculpture. Worthwhile activities can be undertaken with nothing more than wood and glue, but the added materials increase the number of things that can be accomplished and learned.

CONCEPTS FOR POSSIBLE DEVELOPMENT

The concepts listed below should be introduced in kindergarten and repeated in subsequent grades:

brace	coping saw	pliers	finishing nails
bit	hammer	sandpaper	carpet tacks
hand drill	vise	nails	upholstery tacks
drill point	screwdriver	wire nails	wood grain
backsaw	trysquare		

SUGGESTED ACTIVITIES

To get scrap wood for the following projects, we recommend that you go to the school shop, a construction site, a cabinetmaker, a factory that makes wooden toys, or a lumber company that does millwork.

1. Wood sculpture can begin in nursery school, kindergarten, or the first grade, but wherever it is introduced, the first step is to show children how to use tools and equipment. Then suggest a number of things to make, and let the children choose their own projects. They might fasten wood together as an experiment, or they might assemble a nonrepresentational object like the exemplar by Nevelson. Show them the exemplar and explain that the artist was not trying to make her sculpture resemble anything. She was simply attempting to make it look interesting and pleasing, and she fastened the pieces together with glue and nails. Of course, boats, automobiles, trucks, airplanes, trains, tractors, feeding stations for birds, and other such objects are also good to build. As the objects are constructed, the children may wish to attach wheels, in which case it helps to have on hand a supply of small, screw-on jar tops. When the constructions are complete, they can be painted with tempera or left unfinished.

2. The foregoing activity can be repeated several times in the primary grades, and each time the teacher can give additional help with sawing, drilling, hammering, and fastening. To reduce the noise from hammering, have the students do their pounding on the floor or outdoors.

   Because white glue does not dry rapidly, it is advantageous to have a system for holding two pieces of wood together while the glue in the joint dries. Simply use your pliers to cut the heads off several 4-penny finishing nails, and place one of the decapitated nails into a hand drill. The nail will serve as a drill point. Then show the children how to drill a hole into each of the pieces to be joined. Tap another beheaded nail halfway into one of the holes; apply glue to the surfaces to be joined; and push the two pieces of wood together. The nail, which is embedded halfway in one piece of wood and halfway in the other, will hold the units together while they dry.

3. After telling your students that they will be making wooden animals, ask them to help you list as many of the creatures as possible. The object is to help them realize that there are several animals to make. Encourage them to make a wide variety, and remind them that the animals can be walking, standing still, or lying down. When the pieces are finished, they can be painted with tempera. The results will be most appealing if you persuade the children to use imaginative rather than naturalistic colors.

4. Obtain some assorted sizes of scrap wood in the shape of cubes and rectangular boxes. Then give each child either a piece of ¼-x-8-x-12-inch plywood or a piece of ¼-x-12-x-12-inch plywood. Ask the youngsters to imagine that the plywood is a city block, and urge them to make wooden buildings that can be painted and glued to the plywood. The buildings can have flat or pointed roofs; windows and doors can be painted on the sides; and grass can be painted on the plywood. If desirable, holes can be drilled near the edges of the streets and small wooden dowels can be inserted to form telephone poles and streetlights. Wire can be used for television antennae, and string makes good telephone wires. But see if the children can figure out how to use those materials.

   If you plan beforehand, the finished pieces can be placed in a row forming several city blocks with buildings on each side and streets between them. This may lead to the integration of art with social studies or safety education. The possibilities are numerous.

5. Display the exemplar by Marisol and explain that she created many humorous pieces of sculpture by drawing and painting human figures and animals on pieces of wood she had fastened together. Challenge the children to see if they can do the same. And, if you have cotton, scrap cloth, tacks, buttons, and yarn for them to use, the children will produce charming additions to their figures.

WOOD SCULPTURE ACTIVITIES FOR THE INTERMEDIATE GRADES (AGES 9 THROUGH 11)

By the time youngsters have reached grade four, they should have acquired enough basic experience with woodworking tools to permit greater concentration on expression and on the refinement of their techniques. They should also be able to start using a coping saw, a crosscut saw, and a ball peen hammer.

CONCEPTS FOR POSSIBLE DEVELOPMENT

The following terms or concepts are suitable for development in the intermediate grades:

carving	wire brads	mixed-media assemblage
modeling	escutcheon pins	monochromatic
assembling	tin snips	proportion
dada	ball peen hammer	unity
precision	crosscut saw	variety
organic vitality	craftsmanship	metal tooling
anvil	satire	focal point

SUGGESTED ACTIVITIES

As the following activities are attempted, remember that variety in an art program is achieved in part by varying the size of the objects produced. This means that it would be good to make some things as much as four feet tall while others could be no more than five or six inches in height.

1. Display the exemplar by Jean Arp. Discuss the political background that affected his work, and explain his belief in simplifying natural forms and organizing them intuitively. For example, he might have worked in wood to reduce the shapes of clouds and raindrops to elemental but recognizable forms, and he might have arranged the forms thoughtlessly on another piece of wood wherever it felt good to place them.

   Arp's work was often humorous because he combined amusing forms such as mustaches and backbones or mustaches and navels. Humor, of course, was characteristic of dada art. Explain why. Then suggest a few amusing subjects that the children might use in their own sculpture. Try two eyes and a bow tie, two flying birds, three trees in the rain, two rocks and a baby chick, a light bulb and five flies, four falling leaves, two spoons and a dead ladybug, three sick ticks and a healthy caterpillar, or two flowers with the "blahs."

   Give each student an 8-x-12-inch piece of ¼-inch plywood, and let him select some scrap from the assortment made available. Show the students how to draw an object on the scrap and how to cut it out with a coping saw. The cutouts are then sanded, glued to the plywood, and painted with tempera. The painting can be monochromatic or multicolored, and when the paint is dry, cover the whole piece with a coat of polymer acrylic emulsion or white shellac. Try to get your students to make their forms as sharp, clear, and precise as the forms produced by Arp. See Figure 15-1.

2. While studying the exemplar by Arp, explain the nature of low-relief sculpture. Compare it with other sculptural exemplars and discuss how it differs from high relief and from sculpture in the round. Then give the children some 12-x-12-inch pieces of ¼-inch plywood, and ask them to create part of a city street in low relief on the plywood. The students can saw three 6-foot pieces of 1-x-8-inch clear pine into segments big enough for buildings, and scrap can

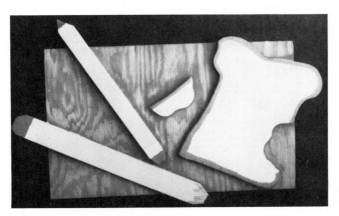

Figure 15-1.   *Two Pencils and a Piece of Bread on Plywood.* Stained with tempera.

be used for chimneys, signs, awnings, fire hydrants, telephone poles, and other such objects. Urge the children to get variety into their compositions by varying the heights and widths of buildings as well as the distances between the buildings. Still more variety can be obtained when the reliefs are painted. Windows can be made large, small, open, closed, curtained, uncurtained, light, or dark. And the buildings can be made to look like brick, wood, stone, steel, or glass.

Coat the final products with polymer acrylic emulsion or white shellac, and fasten them to a bulletin board for display. If they are placed next to each other, they will form a long relief mural that can be dismantled and taken home.

3. Discuss briefly the history of sculpture, and explain the difference between carving, modeling, and assembling. Talk about the attractive animals that can be made by combining wood and other materials in a mixed-media assemblage. Stained wood together with tooled metal, wire, tacks, and cloth, for example, can be fashioned into beautiful creatures. To make your point, show the children how to use tin snips to cut an ear or a wing from a piece of copper or aluminum. Then hold the metal on top of a small anvil and tap the whole surface of the metal with the rounded head of a ball peen hammer. This is called tooling, and it will produce tiny dents on the surface of the copper or aluminum. When finished, drill a small hole in the metal and attach it to a piece of wood with an escutcheon pin or a wire nail. See Figure 15-2.

Next, demonstrate how to brush stain onto a piece of wood, and wipe it off with a rag. Explain that this can be done after the animal is completely built, or it can be done before the parts are assembled. The latter is a better technique to use if the parts are to be stained different colors.

Before allowing the children to select their scraps and start their animals, urge them to do as little sawing as possible. Sometimes, children make the mis-

Figure 15-2. Stained wooden animals.

take of trying too hard to make their animals naturalistic. It is almost impossible to make a truly naturalistic animal even if hours are spent working with a coping saw and sandpaper. Consequently, it makes sense to give the impression of a certain animal instead of trying to reproduce it naturalistically.

Although a few artists of the modern era have eschewed craftsmanship, it is probably correct to say that success with wood sculpture depends to a large extent upon craftsmanship. Hence, it is important to emphasize sandpapering, the making of clean strong joints, and neat staining. Use the exemplar by Marisol as an example of work that is always well-crafted. The joints are neither weak nor sloppy.

4. Show the exemplar by Louise Nevelson, and explain her intention to create appealing environmental sculpture that is nonrepresentational. In other words, it is not intended to resemble anything. It is pleasing to look at because the artist has created an interesting composition. She has arranged the pieces of wood so they produce variety in spacing and shape from left to right and from top to bottom.

Give your students some 8-x-12-inch pieces of ¼-inch plywood and a quantity of scrap. Ask them to attach the scrap to the plywood in the manner of Louise Nevelson. Stress the importance of producing variety in the widths and lengths of the wood as well as variety in the degree of projection and recession. The children should feel free to let the scrap extend beyond the edges of the plywood.

When finished, paint each piece of sculpture a single color to give it more visual unity. Then fasten the completed objects to the wall to make a relief mural. In most cases, the mural will look best if all pieces are the same color, but there are exceptions. You might try several small murals of different colors. See Figure 15-3.

Figure 15-3.   Abstract, low-relief sculpture in shades of blue.

5. In the fifth or sixth grade, it is possible to create abstract sculpture in the round, and there are two techniques that work successfully. One is the system used by Nevelson in the exemplar. It requires that you begin with a wooden base and attach pieces to it. Some pieces might be vertical and others horizontal, or a sculpture might be composed entirely of vertical pieces while another might be made of horizontal or diagonal elements. The object, of course, is to produce a unified piece of sculpture which provides a moving visual experience. Furthermore, it must balance, and it must have enough visual variety to make it interesting. Use pieces of different lengths and thicknesses, and fasten them together so they do not divide each other into equal segments. The fastening technique described on page 277 will be helpful in this kind of construction, and so will the practice of looking at the sculpture from all directions. It should be attractive from all viewpoints. Use 2-x-2-x-12-inch wood as a base from which to begin.

A second approach to building this kind of sculpture requires that you show the children how to nail and glue three or four pieces of wood together to make a structure that stands on two or more legs. Once the sculpture is started, additional pieces are fastened to it in ways that have already been described. Remember that curved shapes will attract considerable attention in a structure composed largely of straight or rectilinear pieces and vice versa. Attention will also center on areas with the most pieces. Some artists believe that it is good to have at least one such focal point in each piece of sculpture.

These structures can be large or small, and they can be painted with tempera or stained with wood stain. The best results are usually obtained by making each sculpture monochromatic. Multiple colors often destroy the unity of the work. See Figure 15-4 at the beginning of the chapter.

6. If you are fortunate enough to be able to get several 6-foot lengths of 1-x-6-inch wood, have a few of your students make human figures about 2 feet tall. The rest of the class will undoubtedly have to make smaller figures with scrap.

Talk about the exemplar by Marisol, and use the word "satire" to describe it. Explain that satire is a form of criticism or ridicule; it is a way of attacking something you dislike in individuals or groups. Marisol is especially good at making fun of people because of the way she makes her sculpture. The boxy and unnaturalistic wooden forms do not conform to the shapes of the human figures she paints on them. This helps to make the depicted people seem more ridiculous than they would otherwise be, and it is especially effective in deflating those who try to appear dignified, proper, or moralistic. It also tends to make clownish people appear more amusing than they are in real life.

Encourage your students to try satire of the Marisol type. Perhaps the following topics will stimulate ideas:

Prominent socialite	Construction worker	Truck driver
Diplomat	Miss America	Little ol' lady
A jogger standing still	Schoolteacher	Beach boy
General of the army	Lady cop	Politician

After the figure has been painted on the wood, it can be given a coat of white shellac or polymer acrylic emulsion if you want a shiny, cleanable surface. And do not forget that found objects can be fastened to the finished product. See Figure 15-5.

Figure 15-5.   *Graduate.*

CHAPTER 16

PAPER
SCULPTURE

Figure 16-4.   *Fighter.*

Paper can be either modeled or assembled to create sculpture or other three-dimensional objects. Although it has been employed for these purposes for a long time, paper has not enjoyed widespread use as a medium for serious sculpture by major artists. Probably the reason for this is that paper is not as durable as clay, wood, stone, or metal, and it doesn't have the same natural beauty. It does have the virtue of being inexpensive, however, which explains why it has been used extensively in folk art and commerce.

By cutting, scoring, tearing, bending, and assembling, paper can be transformed from flat sheets into beautiful three-dimensional forms. This technique has been employed most often in window displays, in packaging, and in the public schools, where it serves the needs of children to perfection. When wet or reduced to a pulp, on the other hand, paper can be shaped into sculpture through modeling, and it can be made into numerous utilitarian objects. We call this moist, manipulative substance papier-mâché.

Papier-mâché is a French term meaning "chewed paper." The process of reducing paper to a pulp and adding glue was developed by the Chinese shortly after they invented paper late in the second century A.D. They used the mixture to construct a variety of small objects including war helmets, which were coated with lacquer to give them strength. Six hundred years later, the Arabs learned to make paper from the Chinese, and by the tenth century A.D. paper replaced papyrus as the primary surface for writing. The system for making the new material spread through Spain to France, Germany, and eventually to the rest of the continent. The manufactur-

ing process was slow and small in its productive capacity. This meant that paper was scarce and expensive, and it meant that there was a great desire to find additional uses for paper after it had served its original purpose. Converting the material into papier-mâché objects was, therefore, a natural development which reached its peak in England and France during the eighteenth and nineteenth centuries. In Paris, papier-mâché snuffboxes, trays, and other small items were made from the vast quantities of waste that accumulated when notices and posters were torn down each day to make room for more. And, in England, where the manufacturing of objects from papier-mâché became a brisk industry, the products ranged from small boxes, buttons, trays, and toys to tables, chairs, and other furniture for Victorian homes. Decorative moldings on picture frames and ceilings were made of papier-mâché and so were the walls of steamers and railway carriages. Perhaps one of the most remarkable uses for the substance was conceived by Charles Bielfeld who constructed ten prefabricated houses from waterproof papier-mâché in 1853.

By the twentieth century, materials of a more durable nature evolved, and papier-mâché diminished in popularity. It has survived to a limited extent, however, as a sculptural medium in the common schools and in folk art all over the world.

EXEMPLARS OF PAPER SCULPTURE

The technological developments of the twentieth century have made many new materials available to the artist. At the same time, the artist has freed himself from reliance upon traditional philosophies, styles, and methods of construction, and he has been willing to experiment in almost any direction. As a result, a few professional artists have been working seriously with paper. Two of the pioneers were Pablo Picasso and Aleksandr Archipenko, and among the younger experimentalists are Claes Oldenburg, Jean Dubuffet, and Niki de Saint-Phalle.

CLAES OLDENBURG, 1929–

Born in Stockholm, the son of a Swedish diplomat, Oldenburg came to the United States as an infant. In 1936, he moved with his family to Chicago, where his father served as Consul and where Claes attended the Chicago Latin School. During this period, he spent an enormous amount of time working out in his mind the history, economics, geography, sociology, and science of an imaginary country called "Neubern."[1] It is clear, especially when combined with other evidence, that Claes Oldenburg was a bright and imaginative youngster. He continued his intellectual and imaginative interests by majoring in literature and art at Yale, and in 1950 he returned to Chicago where he served for six months as a novice reporter with the city news bureau. Although he soon discovered that he did not like such work, it did provide his first extended exposure to the seamy side of city life, a segment of reality that he eventually recognized as a legitimate subject for art.

After the reporting adventure, Oldenburg took a series of odd jobs and attended the Chicago Art Institute. This was the point at which he finally began to focus his attention on the visual arts. Then, in 1956, he moved to New York to avoid the narrow or restrictive thinking that can come to a person who remains too long in one locality. His arrival in the big city occurred at about the time abstract expressionism reached its peak, and young artists with new ideas were beginning to expand the concept of art to include new forms and new directions.[2] Allan Kaprow, for example, was beginning to create "happenings" which were meant to bring environmental elements, including the spectator,

into art. This appealed to Oldenburg more than abstract expressionism because it was more theatrical and less precious. It was more akin to his interest in representational art, and it involved all aspects of the environment instead of merely the traditional and the proper. Consequently, it is fair to say that Oldenburg's natural tendencies placed him in the group that was breaking away from the influence of abstract expressionism.

Oldenburg has always been extremely broad-minded about the form, subject matter, and content appropriate for art. But in his own work he has concentrated on the ordinary, the erotic, the discarded, the distasteful, and the lowest common denominators of life, especially urban life. His subjects have been toilets, ray guns, electric fans, light switches, clothespins, pies, hamburgers, and environmental elements from the streets. Consequently, he is often described as a pop artist because he deals with the subjects found in popular art rather than the traditional subjects occurring in fine art. Like many of the other pop artists, Oldenburg is also compared to the dadaists because of his desire to overcome the dullness and lack of inspiration that he found in the accepted art of his day.

The *Street Chick* in Plate 16-1 is an example of Oldenburg's work. It was made largely of corregated cardboard, but it also consists of burlap, muslin, wood, and string, and it was painted with casein. Most of the materials were discards from the New York streets, and they were assembled in much the same way that a child would put them together. The shapes were torn, crudely fastened, and painted with a supreme lack of elegance, yet the effect is perfect. The figure suggests a poor, dirty, little waif from the garbage-strewn alleys of a big city. It is successful because the materials, the construction technique, and the painting were in keeping with each other and with the idea the artist was trying to convey. If Oldenburg had selected precious materials he would not have achieved the same results, and by the same token, he would not

[1]Barbara Rose, *Claes Oldenburg* (New York: The Museum of Modern Art, 1970), p. 19.

[2]For a brief explanation of abstract expressionism see page 234.

Plate 16-1.　　Claes Oldenburg. *Street Chick.* 1960. Burlap, muslin, cardboard, wood, string, painted with casein; 120" x 38" x 15". Collection, Museum Ludwig, Cologne, West Germany. Photograph by Nathan Rabin, New York.

have produced a satisfactory piece if he had tried to transform his junk materials into a highly naturalistic or refined figure. Instead, he wisely chose to create intentional crudeness by treating his crude materials crudely. The lesson to be learned from this is that an artist should use a medium that is conducive to the effect he is trying to convey, and he should not try to make his medium create effects that it will not create easily.

JEAN DUBUFFET (Doo-boo-fay), 1901–

In most instances, the exemplars presented in this text exemplify the works of art most closely

associated with the artists under discussion. But, in the case of Jean Dubuffet, the exemplar (Plate 16-2) is not an example of the work most intimately connected with him. Instead, it represents an earlier, formative period in Dubuffet's artistic development before he had completely formulated his ideas about the nature and purpose of art. To clarify the difference between his earlier and later works, however, we need to describe a little of the artist's life and ideas.

Dubuffet was born in Le Havre, France, in 1901, and he received a traditional French formal education before turning to painting. During those early years he continued to study languages, literature, philosophy, and other subjects in addition to painting. But in his judgment, these attempts to grow culturally and to find his way in the world were not successful. He felt that he had gained nothing and that ordinary men and women expressed more life, more humanism, and more profundity than he did after all his training. So, in 1930 he gave up the pursuit of arts and letters and went into the wholesale wine business. He painted briefly between 1933 and 1937, but he did not pick up his brushes again as a full-time painter until 1942.

Probably, Dubuffet's most influential experience occurred in 1923, during the early formative period of his life. The experience was his discovery of the art of the mentally ill through the writings of Dr. Hans Prinzhorn, who argued that the work of asylum inmates was worthy of aesthetic consideration. Dubuffet came to believe that the art of the mentally ill, like the art of children and of primitive people, was highly creative because it was free from the inhibitions imposed by culture. He considered the cultural state of existence to be in opposition to the natural state, and therefore he regarded culture as a contaminating element to be overcome.

Culture is a human creation; it is a characteristic that separates human beings from other animals and objects. Consequently, to reject culture, as Dubuffet did, is to reject the things that make human beings distinctive. This explains

Plate 16-2. Jean Dubuffet. *Three Masks.* 1935. Papier-mâché; a. 11¼" x 6⅞", b. 9⅛" x 6", c. 9¾" x 7⅛". Hirshhorn Museum and Sculpture Garden, Smithsonian Institute.

why Dubuffet has continued to reject logic and analysis in art. He sees them as manifestations of culture; hence, he feels that they place unnatural restraints upon creativity.[3]

By the same token, Dubuffet refuses to acknowledge the notions of beauty and ugliness; he finds all objects to be fascinating or illuminating. He believes that all things are relative, equal, and subject to change. As a result, he refuses to accept given values or hierarchies, and he does not acknowledge such notions as "real" and "unreal" or "true" and "false." These are ideas different from those held by most of the artists represented in this book, but they are interesting ideas and they do lead Dubuffet to produce a distinctive form of art. It is an art that emphasizes materials rather than form or composition, because the artist regards our traditional interest in form to be a manifestation of culture. Furthermore, he does not aim to achieve beauty or elaboration in his work. Instead he prefers the

ugly, the ordinary, and the banal. He believes that art is meant for the mind and not for the eyes.

Since 1942, when he first came to prominence, Dubuffet's art has not been imitative, beautiful, or three-dimensional. It has included recognizable objects such as cows and people as subject matter, but they have been made in a crude, primitive manner without shading or other devices that produce the illusion of three dimensions. Consequently, the work seen in Plate 16-2 is different from the work that has made him famous since 1942. The masks are naturalistic with strong three-dimensional qualities. If they are unusual in any way, it is only because they are made from papier-mâché, a material that most artists have not been willing to use. Dubuffet would undoubtedly reject these masks today in favor of images having less clearly perceivable form, but his willingness to experiment with unusual materials would be as strong today as it has always been.

Look at Plate 16-2, and notice the differences among the eyes of the three figures. Some appear to be squinting while the others are wide open. The irises are all partially covered by the

[3]Dubuffet's objections to culture are well-outlined by Margit Rowell in *Jean Debuffet: A Retrospective* (New York: The Solomon R. Guggenheim Foundation, 1973), pp. 15–38.

eyelids, which is normal, and the most wide-open eyes seem to be accompanied by raised eyebrows and heavily wrinkled foreheads. Notice also how the cheeks, nose, and eyebrows have been built outward from the basic frontal plane of the face. Then study the way the eyes have been painted.

NIKI de SAINT-PHALLE, 1930–

Niki de Saint-Phalle is a French sculptress and painter. She is one of the few well-known artists working in papier-mâché today, and she does so on a large scale. Many of her creations are life-size or larger; they are constructed of chicken wire and papier-mâché; and the papier-mâché is made by dipping pieces of torn paper into a paste of some kind. The figures are then painted with bright colors and patterns, and often they have other materials and objects fastened to them. The added elements might include plastic dolls of different sizes, jersey loops, clothing, plastic insects, bits of cloth, and other unusual items. Or, to be more accurate, we should say that the additions seem unusual because they often cover the whole surface of a human figure. The result in such cases is that the subject matter and content of the work seem bizarre to some people.

On other occasions, however, Saint-Phalle's sculpture is delightfully amusing. In Plate 16-3, for example, we are treated to one of her life-size Nanas called *Elizabeth*. There is something about the plumpness of the figure as well as the boldness of the pattern that brings a smile to the face of the observer. Furthermore, the exaggerated width of the shoulders and hips in relation to the smallness of the hands, head, and feet produces unexpected and interesting proportional relationships as well as humorous ones. It also gives the contour of the figure a little variety, which keeps the sculpture from being dull. And additional visual excitement or liveliness is provided by the bold, simple designs on the body.

Plate 16-3. Niki de Sainte-Phalle. *Elizabeth*. 1965. Grillage, tisou; 98" x 64" x 44". Courtesy of Brooks Jackson Gallery Iolas, New York.

Humor can be found in art from ancient to modern times, but it is not common. The reasons for this are interesting to contemplate. Does humor suggest a frivolous approach to art, which already suffers from being regarded as a frill or a waste of time? Is humor considered to be more appropriate for popular art rather than fine art, and if so, why? Is humorous work easier to produce than nonhumorous work; is it any less serious? Marisol, Claes Oldenburg, Andy Warhol, Hans Arp, and Niki de Saint-Phalle have all produced amusing sculpture. Sometimes their work has not been well-received because of its humorous qualities. Is this because people suspect that they are having their "legs pulled"? What can be said in favor of amusing art? Compare the work of Kaethe Kollwitz (page 98) with the work of Niki Saint-Phalle. Would the world be any better off if it had one without the other, or is there a need for a broad range of expression in human life? These questions and others of a similar nature can act as a basis for worthwhile discussions.

ADDITIONAL EXEMPLARS

Other paper art objects which might be studied in class are works by Aleksandr Archipenko, Pablo Picasso, Elie Nadelman, and a number of Mexican folk artists.

PAPER SCULPTURE ACTIVITIES FOR THE PRIMARY GRADES (AGES 6 THROUGH 8)

For youngsters in the primary grades, paper sculpture is probably more difficult than clay or wood sculpture. It is hard for young children to make paper stand up or project from the wall, and it is not easy for them to fasten three-dimensional units together. Consequently, it is important to introduce sculptural activities that do not present difficult construction problems. Projects of that kind are described in the following pages, and some are presented in the section devoted to crafts. In both instances, however, we recommend that assembling be introduced first and that modeling be postponed until the third grade.

CONCEPTS FOR POSSIBLE DEVELOPMENT

Some of the concepts that might be developed through paper sculpture are listed below:

facial features	bold designs	papier-mâché
tube	scoring	corregated cardboard
cylinder	assembling	wallpaper paste
project (to stick out)	joints	low-relief sculpture

SUGGESTED ACTIVITIES

The following activities have been done for many years in the elementary schools because they are effective vehicles for developing skills in sculpture:

1. Show your students a piece of 12-x-18-inch colored construction paper, and ask them how you could make it stand up. Hopefully, they will suggest bending it to form a tube, or they will recommend folding it in the shape of an open-ended box. Then demonstrate how heads can be made by adding paper in a variety of ways to the basic cylinder or box. Use rubber cement and staples to secure the seam of the cylinder, and use the same cement to add additional

paper. As you add the paper, show how it can be curled, torn, scored, punched, and folded to make hair, ears, and noses, which project outward from the basic cylinder.

Although it is possible to add materials other than paper we recommend that students be restricted to the use of paper, at least part of the time, because it makes them explore the possibilities of the medium more fully. We also recommend the creation of specific people such as firemen, cowboys, soldiers, and nurses because it causes youngsters to think about features that characterize such people, and it helps to eliminate the production of heads that lack distinction. Visual interest can also be increased with the addition of details such as freckles, moles, earrings, and eyebrows.

2. If students manage the foregoing activity without difficulty, have them try a full figure by starting with a 24-inch tube made from a sheet of 18-x-24-inch colored construction paper. They can add paper belts, tissue paper dresses, ears, noses, and arms. To separate the head, the torso, and the legs simply fasten paper of a different color around the tube in two of those areas. The addition of paper buttons, eyelashes, belt buckles, ties, polka dots, stripes, and other finishing touches will make the figures much more appealing. Display the exemplar by Saint-Phalle for the purpose of showing how bold designs can add to the visual excitement of the figure.

3. Show the exemplar by Claes Oldenburg, and explain that it was made by fastening corregated cardboard to pieces of wood reaching from the head of the figure to the feet. Using two three-foot pieces of 1-x-2-inch pine, lay them parallel to each other on the floor with about six inches of space between them. Then nail a piece of 1/4-x-4-x-10-inch plywood to the two strips of wood. Use at least four short nails, and fasten the plywood about eight inches from the ends of the two strips. Next, show the youngsters several pieces of torn cardboard, and ask them to suggest ways of arranging the cardboard on top of the wood to make a person. When it is satisfactorily placed, glue or nail it to the wooden frame. Make certain to point out that figures can be made in front or side view.

Divide the class into teams and give each team some wood, cardboard boxes, nails, and hammers, and let them proceed to make figures. When they are finished, the products can be painted with tempera paint and displayed against the walls of the classroom and hallway. As the children work, it is important to keep reminding yourself and your students that the figures need not be naturalistic; in fact, they will be better if no struggle is made to make them naturalistic. Use the Oldenburg exemplar to make your point. See Figure 16-1.

4. Bring a refrigerator box to school and lay it on its side. Let the children bring more corregated boxes. Then urge the class to make a convertible automobile out of the reclining refrigerator box. Give them a start by cutting away two-

Figure 16-1.   *Little Girl.* Cardboard, wood, and tempera.

thirds of the top side of the automobile. This will allow chairs to be placed inside for seats, and it will make clear that the remaining third of the top side is to be the hood of the convertible. Then have the children suggest auto parts to make and paint, and have them locate the placement of wheels, doors, radiators, headlights, and other parts by drawing them on the box with chalk. The teacher can cut out the doors, and the children can proceed to make and attach headlights, windshields, bumpers, and other elements. These items can be made from boxes, tin cans, and other scrap material, and the whole automobile can be painted with tempera paint containing a little liquid detergent. The detergent helps the paint to cover more satisfactorily.

5. The use of papier-mâché can begin in the third grade by making heads in low relief, like the masks by Dubuffet. Divide the class into groups of four and cover the desks with newspaper. Give each group a roll of masking tape, some white paper toweling, a stack of newspapers, and a box of newspaper that has already been torn into pieces about one inch in diameter. Each group should also have a pie tin filled with wallpaper paste mixed in the ratio of one pound of paste to ten pints of water. A five-pound bag of the powdered paste should be sufficient for 25 children.

With everything ready, display the exemplar by Dubuffet, and discuss the features in the faces. Then show the children how to crumple sheets of newspaper into the shape of a flat pancake about two inches thick. Wrap the crumpled lump with another sheet of newspaper so the loose ends can be fastened in back with a piece of masking tape. Dip pieces of torn newspaper into the paste and apply them to the front of the paper pancake. Other wet pieces of paper may be crumpled into the shape of a nose, ear, lip, or eye and placed in position on the head (see the Dubuffet). The whole head should then be covered with two more layers of papier-mâché, and a final layer of torn paper toweling (dipped in paste) should give a smooth, light-colored surface. Do not use too much paste when applying the final layer of toweling, because it produces a crackled surface when painted. Then indicate where to store the sculpture to dry, and show everyone how to fasten a piece of string to the back of their sculpture with papier-mâché. The string allows the work to be hung.

As the youngsters begin their own work, urge them to make special people with definite personalities. Suggest nasty little kids, tough guys, nice elderly ladies, beautiful actresses, sweet babies, and other such people. When finished, the sculpture should dry for at least three days before it is painted. By painting carefully and adding materials judiciously, the low-relief head can be made magnificently expressive. Hair made from cotton roving or curled strips of construction paper, for example, is excellent.

6. Another introductory project in papier-mâché is making imaginative insects or creepy, crawly creatures. In addition to the preparatory materials and arrangements described in Activity 5, give the children some one-foot lengths of precut wire. The kind made for electric fences is good (17 gauge). Then demonstrate how to crumple newspaper into the shape of a hot dog bun or hamburger bun. This will act as an armature for the body of an insect. Simply add to the body about three layers of torn newspaper dipped in paste; roll some sheets of newspaper into tightly formed tubes; and hold them in shape with two or three pieces of masking tape. Insert a piece of wire into each tube; fasten the mid-parts of the tubes to the body with papier-mâché strips; and put the insect aside to dry. Explain that when the bug is dry the tubes will be bent into the desired shapes for legs or wings and a final layer of papier-mâché will be added to the whole insect, including the legs. When dry, the students can paint the bug and glue other materials to the surface. Try adding yarn, buttons, feathers, construction paper, rickrack, old lace, fringing material, or cloth. The finished insects can be fastened to the walls of the classroom or they can be suspended from light fixtures with rubberized string or thread.

7. A simple papier-mâché puppet may be started by rolling a piece of newspaper into a tight, strong tube about one foot long. Tape the tube to make it hold its shape. Then crumple a sheet of newspaper into the form of a ball and fasten it over one end of the tube with masking tape. Add strips of papier-mâché to the crumpled head and to the tube so the two are securely joined. At this point, papier-mâché noses, ears, lips, eyebrows, and other features may be added, or they may be left off. After drying for about three days, students can paint the head and add materials to give character and polish to the puppet. The next step is to cut a hole in the bottom of a small paper bag and insert the tube in the hole. Thus, the bag becomes clothing for the puppet, and the puppet can be manipulated by holding the tube inside the bag.

8. Have students gather a quantity of small boxes. Cereal and detergent boxes, match and cigar boxes, aluminum foil and oatmeal boxes, and other containers of a similar type are ideal. Display the exemplar of wood sculpture by Marisol, and make clear that similar work can be done with boxes and papier-mâché. Indicate how to begin an animal, a vehicle, a building, or a person by filling boxes with crumpled newspaper and fastening them together with masking tape. Then cover the whole construction with pieces of papier-mâché, and turn the children loose to begin their own sculpture. Make sure that the last layer of papier-mâché is made with torn pieces of white paper towels. When dry, add color by painting or by fastening torn pieces of colored tissue paper to the figure with cold liquid starch. Simply brush the starch onto the figure; lay the paper into the starch; and brush over the top once again. As usual, finishing touches can be added by attaching any of a number of different materials.

9. The foregoing activity can be done on a bigger scale with larger cardboard boxes. When a variety is available, divide the class into teams of four, and let them suggest animals that might be constructed by joining the boxes. Then have them proceed to build their animals (or other objects) by fastening the joints temporarily with brown paper tape and later with papier-mâché. It is not necessary to cover the whole figure with papier-mâché, but it is important to see that the joints are so covered. Then the whole animal can be painted with tempera containing a little liquid detergent, and cloth, rope, yarn, and other finishing touches can be added. Such animals can range in size from three to ten feet high.

   Before the children paint their animals, show them the exemplar by Saint-Phalle and encourage them to use bright, cheerful, colors and patterns as she did. In other words, urge the children to move away from naturalism by putting colorful polka dots, stripes, flowers, and other designs on their animals.

PAPER SCULPTURE ACTIVITIES FOR THE INTERMEDIATE GRADES (AGES 9 THROUGH 11)

In our suggestions for the primary grades, emphasis was placed upon teaching the basic procedures involved in paper sculpture. In the intermediate grades, however, we expect instruction to go well beyond that point. We expect more emphasis to be placed upon the expressive use of color, gesture, and texture, and we also believe that more elaboration should be achieved through an increase in three dimensionality and in the use of detail.

CONCEPTS FOR POSSIBLE DEVELOPMENT

Some of the terms that might be taught in the upper elementary grades are listed below:

paper pulp	glossy finish	three-dimensional	contour
modeling	flat finish	elaboration	armature
assembling	scoring	texture	exaggerate
utilitarian objects	pop art	overlapping	antiquing
folk art	crudeness	banal	patina
symmetrical	elegance	esoteric	character
gesture	medium	chicken wire	

SUGGESTED ACTIVITIES

Much of the paper sculpture recommended for the primary grades can be repeated in the intermediate grades, but an attempt should be made to have the students produce greater refinements in their work. In other words, we can expect more mixing of colors, more careful painting, and better craftsmanship in joining parts. All this takes time; consequently, most of the projects that follow will require nine or more hours to complete.

1. Discuss the history of sculpture and the attitudes toward it. Explain why paper has not been used extensively by major sculptors in the past and why it is being employed more frequently today. Indicate the difference between modeled and assembled sculpture, and encourage your students to assemble a full-length human figure from paper. We recommend, however, that the earliest attempts to make such sculpture be undertaken without the difficult requirement of self-support. Simply make the figures hang rather than stand. To do so, give each student a paper bag (number 5), two feet of string, a paper clip, and a 3-x-6-inch piece of stiff cardboard. Punch a tiny hole in the center of the cardboard and in the bottom of the bag. Tie one end of the string to a paper clip, and pass the other end through the cardboard, inside the bag, and through the bottom of the bag. By pulling the string, the cardboard should move inside the bag and fit snugly against the bottom. This will allow the bag to be hung when the sculpture is finished. See Figure 16-2.

Figure 16-2. *Lady with a Tall Hat.* About four feet tall.

The next step is to add colored construction paper to the bag. Legs in the form of tubes or open-ended boxes can be glued to the inside; arms can be fastened to the outside; and heads in the shape of tubes, cones, boxes, or flat pancakes can be slipped over the end of the string and glued to the bottom of the bag. The children can then proceed to elaborate. To get the desired variety, however, urge the youngsters to do some of the following things:

a) Invent ways of making arms and legs bend.

b) Avoid making a perfectly symmetrical figure.

c) Avoid stereotyped symbols for eyes and mouths.

d) Think of a new way of creating hair from paper.

e) Make joints neat and strong through the use of tabs and slits.

f) Experiment with different ways of making noses and ears. Make them stand out from the head.

g) Avoid excessive use of dull or neutral colors like gray and brown.

h) Invent ways of making a top on an open-ended cylinder.

i) Use detail in some places but not in others. Eyes, shoes, fingers, and belts are possible locations for detail. When the sculptures are finished, hang them from the ceiling, from light fixtures, or from wires strung across the room.

j) Use a mixture of plain and patterned areas.

k) Give the figure some personality or character.

2. Instead of making a full figure, as in the foregoing project, make a hanging head. You can begin with a large or small grocery bag, and you can get interesting results by encouraging some of the children to put distinctive hats on their creations.

3. Try the first activity recommended for the primary grades, but divide the class into groups and ask each team to make heads that illustrate characters in a famous children's story. Give each group a different story to illustrate, and slip the finished heads from each group over a separate cardboard tube (obtained from a rug store). Staple the heads to the tube in such a way that the product resembles a totem pole.

To get refinement and expression into the heads, do some of the following things:

a) Show how interesting three-dimensional eyebrows, lips, noses, and other features can be made by cutting out a shape, scoring it with the point of the scissors, and folding it along the scored line. If you score lines on both sides of the paper, you can fold the paper in one direction and then the other.

b) Indicate that eyes and other elements can be made colorful and interesting by gluing one shape within another. Then glue the latter inside another shape, and continue until the form seems exciting.

c) Talk about color and how it can influence the character of the heads. Pastels suggest softness and gentleness; bright and contrasting colors produce power and vivaciousness; grays, whites, and light blues create the feeling of old age; and yellow-green suggests sickliness. Encourage the students to name other colors that might produce the effect of a hot temper, a cold face, or a sweating fighter.

4. In the fifth or sixth grade, distribute heavy drawing paper or construction paper (12 x 18 inches), and ask students to make a piece of abstract paper sculpture that can stand by itself, hang from a string, or project from the wall. The purpose is to make a three-dimensional, nonfigurative object which looks attractive from all directions. To achieve this goal, ask the class to make two or three cuts into the paper with a scissors; bend the parts into attractive positions; and hold them in place with straight pins. Then display the objects throughout the classroom.

Some suggestions for the production of a pleasing composition follow:

a) Arrange the parts so the eye will follow a path around and through the sculpture. The eye will tend to follow the edges of planes; hence, it will help if some of the edges are made to flow into each other.

b) Make the joints neat and securely fastened. Eyelets and eyelet punches are helpful.

c) Make the object balance. A visual movement in one direction should be countered by visual weight or movement in the opposite direction.

d) The object should look good from all points. If its appearance will be helped by trimming with a scissors, feel free to trim.

e) Try not to let any area get visually cluttered.

f) Do not force the paper to do anything that it will not do easily. If it looks strained, something is wrong.

5. From the third grade onward, show and discuss the exemplar by Oldenburg plus the exemplar of silk screening by Warhol. Explain what pop artists were trying to do and why they made bananas, flashlights, lipstick tubes, and other such objects. Explain further that the pop artists have made it easier for people to use almost anything as subject matter in their work. Then suggest the creation of cheerful pop art through the making of stuffed paper fruits, vegetables, animals, fish, vehicles, or human figures.

To begin, fold a sheet of 36-x-48-inch Kraft paper in half and draw the selected object on the paper. Emphasize the importance of keeping the outline of the object simple and the legs or other appendages wide. If these directions are not followed, the paper is likely to tear when stuffed.

With the drawing complete, keep the two layers of paper from slipping by using paper clips or pieces of masking tape on the edges. Then cut the figure out, and paint the two outer sides. Make plain and patterned areas and use imaginative colors. When the paint is dry, cover it with a coat of white shellac. Next, begin stapling the two layers of paper together, and stuff the figure with crumpled newspapers as you proceed. Keep the staples at least half an inch from the edge. Then, with a large-eyed needle and rug yarn, sew around the whole figure to give it an attractive finish. Hang the products throughout the school.

6. Provide information about the history of paper and papier-mâché, and explain the reason for making objects from "chewed paper" during the eighteenth century. Display the torn-paper exemplars by Dubuffet and Saint-Phalle, and discuss the differences between the torn-paper and the paper-pulp techniques. Then repeat Activity 5 in the section devoted to the primary grades, but show the children that fancy hats, collars, ears, necks, shoulders, and other elements can be added to the heads by taping pieces of lightweight cardboard to the figure. The cardboard is then covered with strips of papier-mâché and painted, or it can also be finished with tissue paper and starch. See Figure 16-3.

Interesting hair and beards, as well as other rough textural effects, can be obtained by adding papier-mâché pulp to the head after the first layers of papier-mâché strips have dried. To make papier-mâché pulp, get one or two five-gallon plastic garbage containers with covers. Fill two-thirds of each container with water, and add small pieces of torn paper until the vessel is almost full. After allowing the paper to soak for two or three days, add a cup of salt or two or three drops of oil of cloves to each container to reduce the chance of unpleasant odor and spoilage. Then stir and tamp the mixture with

Figure 16-3.   *Man with a Cap.* Made of torn
paper, lightweight chipboard,
and tempera. Instructions for
hair are in Activity 10.

a strong stick to increase the pulverization of the paper. When it is shapeable
with the fingers, remove the pulp from the container; squeeze out the water;
place the pulp in a pie tin; mix some prepared wallpaper paste into the pulp;
and add it to the crumpled paper armature. The finished work can be
painted with tempera and then coated with white shellac.

7. Display the exemplar by Niki de Saint-Phalle, and say that it was done by
applying strips of papier-mâché to an armature made of chicken wire. An
armature is needed to support wet papier-mâché. Then demonstrate how to
construct an imaginary animal using tightly rolled tubes of newspaper as
armatures. Insert a length of coat hanger wire into each tube. Bend two tubes
over a third to form a body and four legs, and tie them in place with string.
If the body tube is long enough, bend part of it to form a neck and head;
then bend the legs. If the body or the legs seem too short, tape additional
tubes to them. Then add fullness to the form by tying or taping crumpled
newspaper to the tubes, and cover the whole thing with strips of paper
dipped in wallpaper paste. Remember that exaggerations can make the figure
both distinctive and expressive.

When the first two layers of papier-mâché are dry, give the students
some heavy oak tag or lightweight cardboard. Show them that they can add
ears, wings, tongues, fins, feathers, scales, teeth, and exotic features of all
kinds by taping cardboard to the figure and covering it with papier-mâché.
Use white paper toweling for the last layer of papier-mâché, and let it dry.
Then give color to the creature by laying torn tissue paper into cold liquid
starch brushed onto the body, and add finishing touches for elaboration.

8. Collect a quantity of cardboard boxes large enough to fit over the head. Remove the flaps on the open sides and cut semicircles in the sides to accommodate the shoulders. Then show the children how they can make highly imaginative masks of birds, animals, and dragons by cutting holes in the box and by taping materials to it before covering the form with papier-mâché. The added materials can include paper cups, cardboard tubes, small boxes, and pieces of oak tag or corregated cardboard. They can be used to make beaks, antennae, teeth, flaring nostrils, jaws, fins, and other features too numerous to mention. The mask can be finished, of course, in the ways described in other activities. Remember that too many colors and added shapes can create visual busyness that destroys the fundamental form of the object.

9. Begin with a discussion of humor in art. For examples of such humor show the work of Niki de Saint-Phalle, Andy Warhol, or Marisol, and raise some of the questions mentioned in our account of Saint-Phalle. Then assign students the task of making a humorous human figure of papier-mâché. It is possible to make one as large as the one by Niki de Saint-Phalle, but it is more practical to make smaller ones on armatures made of coat hanger wire and newspaper. Have each student use a pair of pliers to dismantle two or three wire coat hangers, and have him bend those wires into the skeletal shape of a human figure. The figure is then nailed to a wooden base (about 8 x 8 inches in size), and crumpled newspaper is tied or taped to the wire to fill out the human form. This is covered with pieces of newspaper dipped in wallpaper paste, and it is finished in ways already described. See Figure 16-4 at the beginning of the chapter. To avoid stiff and unimaginative sculpture, try the following:

a) Call attention to the exaggerated proportions of the body parts in the Saint-Phalle exemplar, and explain that exaggerations can affect the meaning communicated by a piece of sculpture. A small head, for example, can give the impression of stupidity; large legs and feet can suggest a clod; wide shoulders and neck can imply strength; and big hands can indicate clumsiness.

b) Discuss ways of avoiding a rigid, symmetrical figure. Perhaps the weight of the figure could be shifted to one leg; the head could be tilted; one forearm could be placed on top of the head; one hand could be on the hip; the figure could be bending, walking, or kneeling, or it could be holding flowers, a ball, or a child.

c) Restrict the height to 18 inches.

d) The appearance of draped clothing with folds can be achieved by wetting three paper towels with wallpaper paste and putting them together in a sandwich before draping them from the figure. Strength can be added by putting a layer of cheesecloth inside the sandwich.

e) After the completed figure has been painted and given a coat of polymer acrylic emulsion, it can be antiqued by brushing it with a glaze and wiping part of the glaze away. Antique glazes can be obtained from paint stores, and they can be wiped with cheesecloth or old nylon stockings.

f) Texture can be made with papier-mâché pulp. Information about the pulp is given in Activity 6.

10. Study the exemplars by Daumier, Marisol, and Saint-Phalle. Discuss the relationship between humor and satire (which can be caustic, sarcastic, or ironical), and see if your class can determine which of the artists tends to be the most humorous without being satirical. Then assign the task of making a humorous and perhaps satirical human figure out of papier-mâché. Making the figure over armatures of glass and plastic bottles is possible in the fifth and sixth grades. Paint and glue bottles, liquor bottles, and bleach and detergent bottles are superb as armatures because they come in a variety of shapes. Use one as a basis for the neck and upper body of a human figure, and add a head of pulpy papier-mâché. Directions for making the pulp are given in Activity 6. Then begin the construction of arms by forming them with crumpled aluminum foil and attaching them to the bottle with masking tape. The next step is to cover the bottle and the arms with pieces of paper dipped in paste. Let the paper overlap the pulp at the neck, and use pulp to build up the breasts, shoulders, and other parts of the body.

After the form has dried for about three days, it is possible to sand the pulp to make it smooth. Additional smoothness can be obtained by painting the figure with five or six coats of gesso or interior latex followed by more sanding with fine sandpaper. To achieve smoothness in still another way, fill holes or depressed areas with a vinyl-spackling compound obtained from the hardware store, and sand the surface with fine sandpaper.

Elegance and sophistication can be produced by gluing twine, rickrack, lace, buttons, papier-mâché bows or belts, cardboard hats, and other details to the figure. The additions can then be painted with white gesso or latex prior to painting the whole figure with tempera. When the tempera is dry, give the object a coat of glossy polymer acrylic emulsion.

Special effects, variety, and distinction can be achieved by doing some of the following things:

a) With an antique glaze obtained from the paint store, paint over the surface of the dry polymer emulsion, and wipe part of the glaze away with cheesecloth or an old nylon stocking. Blueish or greenish glazes work nicely.

b) To make curls, wrap twine or yarn around a pencil covered with waxed paper, and dip the curl in liquid starch or paint it lightly with white glue. When dry, remove the pencil and paper.

c) Urge your students to retain the basic shape of the bottle. This will give their figures distinctive shapes.

d) Full-length figures can be made by taping tubes of cardboard or oak tag to the bottoms of the bottles before applying papier-mâché.

11. In the fifth or sixth grades, low-relief cardboard sculpture is highly recommended. As a base for such sculpture we suggest ½-x-10-x-12-inch pieces of wood, but we think that it would be most economical to use the wood beforehand for making woodcuts (see page 228). Then cover the front and back of the used boards with pieces of paper dipped in wallpaper paste. While the papier-mâché is drying, ask your pupils to draw on lightweight cardboard all or part of the front of an interesting house. They should then cut the house out of the cardboard with X-Acto knives or single-edged razor blades. The next step is to glue pieces of oak tag, cardboard, straws, toothpicks, or twine to the cut-out house to make it look a little more three-dimensional. The parts closest to the observer should be built out the farthest; of course, there may be a few youngsters who choose to build outward as much as two or three inches. Cardboard bricks can be glued on individually; pieces of wooden siding made of oak tag can be overlapped just as they are on a real house, and cardboard awnings can be placed over windows. You might also suggest oak tag shingles, clouds of twine, and window shutters made of cardboard.

When the house is fully constructed, glue it to the papier-mâché board, and paint the whole relief with gesso or white interior latex. The dry gesso may then be painted with tempera paint, and the tempera may be covered with a coat of glossy polymer acrylic medium. When the polymer is dry, paint the whole relief with an antique glaze, and wipe the excess off with cheesecloth. See Figure 16-5.

Figure 16-5. A cardboard house in low relief. Painted with white latex.

12. Do the third activity recommended for the primary grades, but spend considerable time talking about Oldenburg's *Street Chick* beforehand. Stress the perfect match that the artist achieved between the medium and the subject matter. Then urge the class to make the same match themselves. Ask them to create numerous street orphans of the sort that appear in war-torn cities. Give strong emphasis to the view that the figure should not be naturalistic. Make them about four feet tall.

PART 6

Crafts

To some, the word "craft" means an occupation or trade requiring technical and/or artistic skill. People who are employed in one of these occupations or trades are called craftspeople. To others, the word describes an object or group of objects. These objects or craft works are made by craftspeople/artists.

During the Middle Ages there were craft guilds of stone cutters, wood cutters, sculptors, painters, embroiderers, and weavers. The craftspeople worked to make objects that were pleasing to the eye as well as being functional. For example, embroiderers made tapestries to hang on the walls of castles to keep out the cold.

Today, the objects produced by craftspeople/artists are generally appreciated more for their design qualities than for their function. In other words, the craft piece is considered a work of art.

Among the crafts of our own day are mask making, puppetry, pottery, stitchery, weaving, and photography. Photography is the newest, while the others have a long history. Early masks and puppets were made to symbolize the spirits of ancestors and animals as well as the elements of nature. Pottery on the other hand, was created for both religious and secular purposes. This was also true of weaving and stitchery. Some of the woven pieces were worn by the common man, while other articles were created as the ceremonial dress of the leaders and priests of societies. The ceremonial dress was embellished and decorated with stitches of colored threads. Photography involves the creation of an image on a light-sensitive paper. These images on paper may be made with or without the aid of a camera. Because the tools and materials for the crafts mentioned above differ greatly, information concerning them will be found in the chapter devoted to each craft.

CHAPTER 17

MASKS
AND
PUPPETS

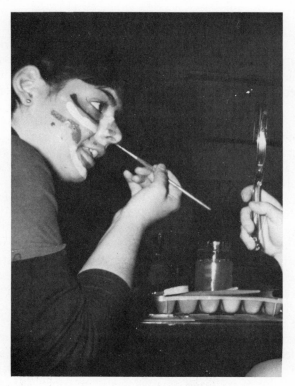

Figure 17-3. Two art methods students
working on face painting, using
a mixture of tempera, baby
lotion, and liquid soap in place
of makeup.

The mask is one of man's early creations. Representations of masked men have been found in paleolithic art and indicators suggest that masks have been used in nearly every culture since prehistoric times.

Reasons for using masks have been numerous. Because primitive man believed that masks were instruments of magical power, he wore them at festivals and rituals so he could assume the roles of gods and devils. In Egypt, Mesopotamia, Mycenae, Phoenicia, and Syria, as well as in Mexico and Peru, masks were fastened to the body of a dead person for protection. In North America, Kachina masks were buried with male members of the Hopi and Zuni Indian tribes to insure admittance to the sacred dwelling place. Besides being a protective agent, masks were worn by actors in tragic and comic productions, and they were a fashionable accessory of dress in court society in Europe. Today, masks may be worn as part of a costume disguise for such holidays as Halloween or Mardi Gras; or for protective purposes as in ski masks or fencing masks. Deep sea divers wear a form of mask in order to see and breathe underwater.

In some cultures, masks were used or made by specially designated members of a society. Besides the mask wearer being a particular member of the group, the maker of masks also held an honored position. The maker was often a trained craftsperson, as were members of his family. The tradition was handed down from father to son. In other parts of the world the distinction of mask maker was given to those members of the society who were believed to possess occult powers.

Masks have been made from and decorated with a variety of materials. Each society used materials which were easily accessible. Some of those materials were: fired clay, wood, shells, paper, leather, fur, bones, vegetable fibers, bronze, copper, tin, gold, tortoiseshell, animal teeth, ivory, cornhusks, feathers, cloth, and a variety of stones.

Puppets, like masks, originated long ago. One of the earliest references to puppets places them at Thebes, where a high priest manipulated a puppet as he proclaimed the words of the Egyptian god Amon. It is interesting that the first puppets of Greece were used in rituals, but as these ceremonies became more complex, they were replaced by live actors. During the medieval time in Europe, priests taught the scriptures through puppets. Later, in Italy, puppets were used to act out religious dramas and, because of interest in these performances, the puppeteers traveled about the countryside performing plays. As the plays became more popular and widely known, other countries adopted the idea of puppet plays as a form of entertainment.

There are four types of puppets: hand, rod, string, and finger. A hand puppet fits over the hand and is manipulated by the fingers. The index and middle fingers work the head while the thumb and little finger act as the puppet's arms. Worked from below the stage like the hand puppet, the rod puppet consists of cut-out figures with metal or wooden poles attached to moveable body parts. Shadow puppets of Java are this type. String puppets or marionettes are the most difficult to make and manipulate. The figure is made of a number of parts which are controlled by strings or wires attached to a wooden harness, and the figure is manipulated from above the stage. A finger puppet is a small figure worn on one finger of the hand.

Puppets can be small, like the finger variety, or they can be large. They can be made with any type of materials. Some of the most ancient puppets were made with ivory, wood, and animal skins, while contemporary types can be made with styrofoam, cardboard, paper, clay, and cloth.

EXEMPLARS OF MASKS AND PUPPETS

Although numerous masks and puppets from the past have been lost through neglect or destruction, there are many in museums and private collections. Three are included in this chapter. One mask was used by a tribe in Africa; another was worn by an Eskimo. The third exemplar is a hand puppet created by Paul Klee.

A BOZO ARTIST,
no date

African masks are found largely in a strip of land across the center of the continent. In the western section of this area lives the Bozo tribe, once a member of the powerful Mali empire. The descendents of the tribe live between the banks of the Niger and Bani rivers. The male members of the tribe hunt, fish, and tend livestock, clear the land and plant crops, as well as conduct foreign trade. Cultivating crops, caring for poultry, and participating in local market trading are the duties of the female members of the Bozo tribe.

Masks are used in this tribe, as in many others in Africa, to disguise the wearer and to represent another being in a ceremony. When worn, the mask in Plate 17-1 disguised the tribe member as an antelope.

Mask makers spent many years learning how to use their materials and tools. In addition, they had to develop an understanding of the rituals and ceremonies for which their work was designed. Even the selection of and the cutting down of the tree for the raw material from which the mask was to be made was a ritual. Wood from the bombax tree as well as wood similar to ebony and mahogany were used. After

Plate 17-1. Bozo ritual mask. n.d. Wood, repoussé, metal; 31⅕'' high. Musée de L'Homme, Paris, France.

shaping the wood with an adze, the mask was smoothed by rubbing the surface with splinters of stone or leaves with an abrasive surface. Many masks were painted and embellished with bits of cloth, hair, leaf fibers, string, pearls, shells, pieces of metal, and material made from bark.

Red, symbolizing energy, joy, and vitality, is the predominant color of the mask in Plate 17-1. The stripe across the nose, the dark spot halfway up the head, and the circle around the antelope's eyes are painted dark blue. The wooden base of the mask is painted red and decorated with thin sheets of tin.

The tin was cut into circular and rectangular shapes. Many of the metal pieces have designs hammered along the edges.[1] The designs on the thin bands along the antelope's horns were also made by this process, called repoussé.

---

[1]Repoussé is a process in which patterns in relief are made by hammering or pressing on the reverse side of the metal.

When worn, this mask was placed on top of the head while a costume of printed fabric covered the wearer's body. During the ceremony, the light from the sun, moon, or fire probably reflected off the metal pieces giving the feeling of swiftness or vitality to the animal.

AN ESKIMO ARTIST, no date

Between 1750 and 1900, the Eskimos of Alaska made masks of extremely high quality. The practice was frowned upon by missionaries as witchcraft and, eventually, the majority of masks were destroyed.

The Eskimos depended upon hunting for their survival. Consequently, they had many rituals and festivals honoring spirits of animals or birds which were important as food. The purpose of masks was to influence these spirits in order to insure a good hunt. The shaman who had a powerful position in Eskimo societies dictated the type of mask to be made for rituals. He or she could carve the masks, or appoint a skillful carver to create the design.

There is an endless variety of shapes used for the facial features on Eskimo masks. The shapes for eyes are round, crescent, oval, tear-drop, half-moon, and almond. In depicting the noses of spirits or mythological beings, a carver used one of the following: 1) a human-shaped nose; 2) a bulbous nose; 3) a cut-out nose in the shape of a comma or a triangle, crescent, circle, or other geometric shape; or 4) a raised ridge or mound in the middle of the face. For the mouth, such shapes as downward or upward curves, circles, or ovals were used. If teeth were present they were made of wood, bone, or ivory.

Once carved, the mask was decorated with paints or natural materials such as feathers, porcupine quills, animal hair, grass, bark, rawhide strips, shells, wood, and animal teeth. Other found materials such as string, pieces of crockery, beads, and metals were also used. The basic col-

Plate 17-2.   Eskimo *Spirit of Driftwood* mask.
n.d. Wood and seagull feathers,
9⅖" high. Lowie Museum of
Anthropology, University of
California at Berkeley.

ors of paint were red, blue-green, black, and white. The paint was applied with a rag or the hand, and dots were made with a fingertip. When decorating with feathers, the mask maker would place from two to nine feathers equidistant from each other. Upon completion, the mask was hidden until it was needed for a ceremony.

The mask, *Spirit of Driftwood*, is made of wood with feathers, rawhide strips, and bits of animal hair used as decoration. Because it represented a spirit, the mask maker suggested a nose by creating a mound down the center of the face. The forehead, protruding over the rest of the face, was painted blue-green, and white circles were repeated on it. Upon close examination, the observer may note that the white circles were applied with a finger or thumb. Along the topmost edge of the head are seven feathers thought to be from seagulls. Each whitish-gray feather was placed in a hole in the wooden shape and had a strip of rawhide tied around the bottom edge to keep it in an upright position. Rawhide strips with balls of animal fur tied to the ends were slipped through the circular mouth.

PAUL KLEE (Klay), 1879–1940

Paul Klee was born in Muchenbuchsee, Switzerland, where his father was a schoolmaster. In addition to an interest in music, Paul liked to draw, and his school notebooks were full of sketches of insects, animals, and plants. At the age of 19, he went to Munich, Germany, to study painting. While a student, he met his future wife, who was a young pianist. Eight years after their meeting they were married, and in November 1907 their only child, Felix, was born. At that time, Klee was making a meager living by playing the violin in the town orchestra and giving drawing lessons. His wife added funds for household expenses by giving music lessons. In talking about his father, Felix said:

> . . . in the same kitchen he made me wonderful toys with great skill . . . toy trains, a cardboard railway station and a puppet theatre. The heads were clay, the costumes cut and sewn by himself, the scenery pasted and painted.[2]

Klee's interest in puppets lasted beyond Felix's childhood as is evident by the example in Plate 17-3. He used the topics of puppets or puppet shows as well as ideas connected with dance, music, and the theater for subject matter for many of his paintings and drawings.

It was while Klee was teaching at the Bauhaus in Weimar, Germany, that the puppet in Plate 17-3 was made. In Weimar, as in Munich, puppet plays were performed in the Klee home. The plays were written by Paul and his son, and Paul made and decorated the hand puppets from a variety of found materials such as paper, cloth, buttons, string, and feathers. He often applied paint directly to the cloth, while facial features may have been painted on or created from found objects. The puppet in Plate 17-3 is a very

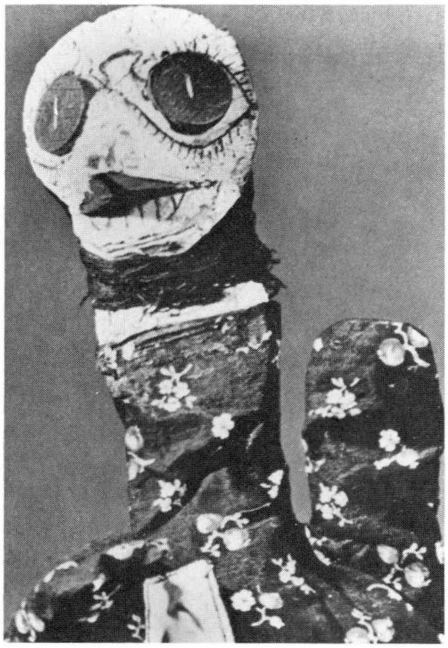

Plate 17-3.   Paul Klee. Handpuppet. n.d. Clay and cloth. © ADAGP, Paris 1981.

imaginative creature with huge eyes. Klee used paint to create the almond eye shapes and eyelashes. Large dark buttons were used as the pupils or the eyeglasses. The inverted U-shape above the eyes seems to suggest glasses of the pince-nez type. Beneath two black nostrils is an orange shape which protrudes somewhat like a beak. A row of handsome teeth show beneath the beak. Some brown silky thread was wrapped around the puppet's neck and the body was formed from a flower-patterned cloth.

Unlike the mask makers of Africa and Alaska, Klee did not have specific rituals directing the creation of his puppets. It is said that his curiosity was aroused by experimenting with different textures and materials and he had a great interest in what made things work.

ADDITIONAL EXEMPLARS

For additional exemplars of masks, refer to those made by other tribes in Africa and North and

[2]Gualtieri Di San Lazzaro, Klee, trans. by Stuart Hood (New York: Praeger, 1957), p. 46.

South America. Japanese Nō masks might present a good contrast to those referred to in the text. The Eskimos made finger masks which were used like puppets, and the shadow puppets of Java would be of interest to children.

MASK AND PUPPET ACTIVITIES FOR THE PRIMARY GRADES (AGES 6 THROUGH 8)

Young children like to dress up and pretend they are someone else. Few, if any, props or fancy costumes are needed to become a cowboy, an Indian, a ballerina, or a mother. The art of play-acting and make-believe often stops, however, when children enter school. Often their lively imaginations are not motivated and are gradually dulled. This need not be the case if children are encouraged to let their imaginations soar when engaged in mask and puppet experiences.

Although imaginations will be put to work during the mask and puppet-making processes, they will be challenged and expanded further through the actual use of the puppet or mask. A simple puppet stage may be made by draping a sheet over a table. The children can hold their puppets above the table surface while they themselves are hidden behind the sheet. The masks may be worn by the youngsters during a supervised activity such as those indicated in the following activities.

Masks and puppets can be made from materials such as: colored construction, metallic, and glossy papers; lightweight cardboard; paper plates; newspapers; sticks or dowel rods; and cloth. In addition, strings and yarns; bottle caps; paper clips; paint; crayons and colored felt-tipped markers; and natural materials such as feathers, leaves, sticks, and shells may be used to give texture and color to the creations.

CONCEPTS FOR POSSIBLE DEVELOPMENT

Each activity was designed around the exemplars illustrated in this chapter. When introducing the activities try to develop an understanding of the following concepts:

Bozo	disguise	pattern
ceremony	facial features	repetition
decoration	hand puppet	rod puppet

SUGGESTED ACTIVITIES

Methods for making masks and puppets are relatively simple. Soon after the puppets and masks are completed, plan to use them in some type of presentation.

1. Begin with a discussion of the mask in Plate 17-1. Tell your students that it represents an antelope; that it was carved from wood; painted with red and blue colors; and decorated with shapes of a silver-colored metal. Examine the number of times shapes such as the circle and rectangle were used. Also, notice where repeated shapes form a pattern. Continue the discussion by asking if they know any other animals that have patterns. Pictures of a zebra, a giraffe, a leopard, or a tiger may be shown. Compare the heads of these animals with the mask. Talk about the differences. For example, help children discover that although all animals have eyes the eyes may be very different in size and shape.

Following this discussion, have the children select a paper plate or a piece of oak tag for a mask base. Have them cut the plate or oak tag in whatever shape they desire. If eyes are to be cut from the mask, have the children help one another. Ask them to hold the plate in front of their faces with one hand while pointing out the eye placement with the other hand. As one child does this, another youngster can take a blunt crayon (*not* a sharp pencil or a scissors) and mark the placement of eyes. Removing the mask base from the face, the eye shapes may be cut out. Colored construction paper, crayons, and felt-tipped markers may be used to decorate the animals. Encourage the children to repeat shapes and to create patterns. Remind them about the various parts of the head. And do not insist that the animals be realistic. In order to wear these animal creations it will be necessary to punch a hole on either side of the mask about eye level. Then a piece of elastic can be tied to each hole. If possible, have a mirror available for the children to see themselves in their animal disguises. When all masks are finished have a zoo or circus parade.

2. Using the materials for Activity 1, talk about using masks to act out a story. The exemplars in Plates 17-1 and 17-2 were used in ceremonies where masked individuals acted or danced out stories. For younger children, a fairy tale or familiar story may be chosen before the masks are made. Perhaps third graders could make the masks before creating their own stories.

3. Looking at the work of art in Plate 17-2 explain that it was worn to hide a person's identity. Ask the children to pretend they are invited to a costume party. Then explain that they are to wear a mask to hide their identity. The base for the mask will be made from a plain brown paper bag which is large enough to fit over a child's head. Have the children work in pairs and as one child slips the bag over his head the other may mark the location of the facial features with a blunt crayon. It may be necessary to cut the sides of the bag away to make it fit comfortably over the shoulders. Colored construction paper, colored felt-tipped markers, and objects such as yarn, lace, beads, buttons, feathers, and ribbons may be used to finish the disguises.

4. Life-sized rod puppets can be made from two paper plates or two pieces of oak tag. One plate or piece of oak tag can be decorated as the face of the puppet, while the remaining piece can become the back of the head. Each piece can be decorated with tempera paint, felt-tipped markers, colored paper, fabric pieces, yarn, buttons, laces, and other materials. About five pieces of newspaper may be tightly rolled to form a rod or handle for the puppet. Fasten it to the inside of the front or back piece of oak tag with strips of masking tape. The two pieces of oak tag may be stapled together starting at the bottom edge and working toward the top. Before closing the two shapes, stuff a few pieces of newspaper into the puppet head. When it is stapled shut, the puppet will have a three-dimensional quality.

Before beginning this activity call attention to the facial features found on the Eskimo mask. Perhaps the children have experienced one of the drawing activities in which they looked in a mirror and drew a self-portrait. Have the children talk about the shapes and placement of their own features. Also include information about the variety of shapes used by the Eskimo mask maker (see page 309). In addition, discuss features such as beards, eyeglasses, mustaches, and hats. Talk with the students about special characteristics which an old man or woman, a beauty queen, a princess, a soldier, a fireman, a cowboy, or an actor would have. Urge them to use a variety of shapes. At the conclusion of this lesson the children can improvise a puppet play or act out a story.

5. When looking at the puppet in Plate 17-3, explain that it was made by Paul Klee. In addition, tell them that although the artist was a well-known painter, he enjoyed experimenting with materials to create puppets. This type of puppet is a hand puppet. Another type, a rod puppet, can be made from two tongue depressors and a piece of oak tag or thin cardboard. The puppet base is cut from the oak tag, while the tongue depressors are used as the legs for the puppet. A hole is drilled into one end of each depressor. The wooden rods are then attached to the puppet base with paper fasteners. The fasteners allow the legs and puppet base to move.

Before the children begin making their puppets you might talk briefly about body parts (head, neck, torso, limbs, feet, and hands). Discuss types of clothing the puppet can wear. Pants, shirts, blouses, dresses, and sweaters as well as details such as buttons, stripes, and buckles can be pointed out in the children's clothing. At this time have the children begin making their puppets by cutting a body shape from the oak tag and attaching the legs. Have a variety of colored paper, felt-tipped markers, and objects such as yarn, lace, feathers, ribbon, and pipe cleaners for the children to use when decorating their puppets. Suggest that the puppets become story book characters, TV personalities, or any of the people mentioned in Activity 4. Upon completion of the puppet people, allow some time for manipulating them in an improvised or planned performance.

6. As an alternative to the above activity, suggest that the children make animal puppets. See Figure 17-1.

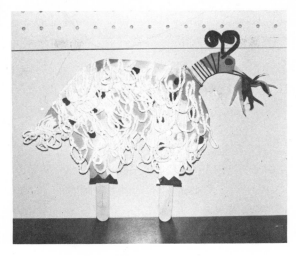

Figure 17-1. Puppet made with a variety of
materials by a student in an art
methods class.

7. Children in the second and third grades can make hand puppets using paper
bags. First, stuff the bag with a few sheets of newspaper which have been cut
in half and crumpled. When the puppet head is rounded, insert a cardboard
tube from toilet tissue or a tube made from oak tag into the open bag. Tie a
string around the tube and bag to hold the stuffing in place. Have one child
hold the puppet while a second one ties the string around the neck. To cut
holes, insert the index and third fingers in the tube and, with a crayon, mark
the position of the thumb and little finger on either side of the bag. The holes
should be large enough for the thumb and finger to slip through the paper.

Before the children use materials such as colored papers, glue, yarn and
string, scrap fabrics, crayons and felt-tipped markers, and an assortment of
feathers, beads, sequins, ribbons and laces, show them the puppet made by
Paul Klee. Notice the features of this creature. Discuss characters found on
television, in cartoons, or in children's stories.

Following the puppet making, plays may be improvised. Other students
and parents may be invited.

MASK AND PUPPET ACTIVITIES FOR THE INTERMEDIATE GRADES (AGES 9 THROUGH 11)

Periods of imagination-pushing and dreaming are more helpful to children of the
intermediate grades if they are channeled through meaningful learning experiences
such as mask making and puppetry.

Many of the art materials suggested earlier are used in the following activities. In addition, these experiences call for more challenging techniques and suggest other materials that can be handled.

CONCEPTS FOR POSSIBLE DEVELOPMENT

Many of the concepts covered in the primary grades can and should be reviewed to make certain that the children understand them. When introducing the following activities try to develop an understanding of these concepts:

armature	contour	papier-mâché	repoussé
balance	expression	protection	symmetry
Bauhaus	face mask		

SUGGESTED ACTIVITIES

Because the interest span of the youngsters is longer and they are more skillful, many of the following activities can take place over a period of hours. When planning the activities try to schedule time during successive days, or it may be advisable to set aside a whole afternoon for an activity.[3]

1. Exhibit the Eskimo mask in Plate 17-2 and tell the students it is called the *Spirit of Driftwood*. Explain that the mask was carved from a piece of wood and decorated with paint, feathers, and rawhide strips. Its overall shape is simple; the decorations are sparse; yet it has a quiet, almost elegant quality. This is probably due to the symmetry of the piece. Encourage children to create a symmetrical mask with few decorations.

   Using 9-x-12-inch pieces of colored construction paper have the children hold a piece of paper in front of their faces. Tell them to indicate the placement of eyes, nose, and mouth with a blunt crayon. Placing the paper on a flat surface, they may draw shapes for those features. The features may be cut out and the rectangular shape of the paper may be changed. Then, colored scraps can be glued on or patterns may be made with crayons, oil pastels, or colored felt-tipped markers. To wear the mask, place a piece of double gummed tape or a piece of rolled tape on the wrong side of the mask at the bridge of the nose and press it gently against the face. See Figure 17-2.

   Ask the students to title their mask and write a short story about it. Making the mask might lead to the study of the Eskimo and his art.

---

[3]Activities 6 and 7 cannot be completed in one day.

Figure 17-2. Construction paper mask decorated with crayons and feathers.

2. Show the antelope mask and explain that this animal is indigenous to the part of Africa where the Bozo tribe lives; this mask was made for and used in some type of ceremony; and the red color symbolized energy and joy. The long slender head and the thin horns give the mask a feeling of vitality, and the shiny metal pieces which reflect light add to this.

Follow this with a discussion of the characteristics of animals. Make a list of animals and words that describe them. For example, the elephant might be described as large, slow, and deliberate. Ask the students to make a mask of one of the listed animals. Remind them to use the most suitable materials to create the animal's character. Shapes and patterns can also be used expressively. A 9-x-12-inch piece of oak tag or railroad board may be used for the head of the animal. This shape can be made to fit the wearer's face by cutting 2-inch slits into the edge at the chin and temple areas. When overlapping the sides adjacent to each slit and stapling them, a three-dimensional form is produced. The eyes, nose, and mouth may be marked and later cut out with scissors. Colored papers, oil pastels, crayons, colored felt-tipped markers, and paints may be used to decorate the mask. When the masks are complete the students may wish to have a parade; use the mask to act out a story about animals; or do some research on their animal and share the information with the class. The students would enjoy watching the story and the masks in the film *The Loon's Necklace.*

3. The masks in Plates 17-1 and 17-2 were used to protect the wearers from evil spirits. The African and Eskimo artists organized and designed them so the evil spirits would not be offended. With the idea of protection in mind, have your students pretend they are going to visit another planet or galaxy in space and they need to design a mask that will protect them from the atmosphere. Perhaps a discussion of science fiction stories about outer space, the movie *Star Wars*, or the television series *Battlestar Galactica* and *Buck Rogers in the Twenty-Fifth Century* might stimulate ideas. After the discussion use the materials listed for Activity 1 along with pieces of fabric scraps; metallic and glossy papers; ribbons, laces, and strings; and a variety of found objects. Upon completion, allow the students to take their journey into space by visiting another class. Or a few members of the class may act out roles of the planet's inhabitants while others are the visitors.

4. The masks suggested in Activity 3 in the Primary Section are appropriate for the inhabitants of a planet or galaxy.

5. Certain Africans, as well as North American Indians, created disguises by applying paint directly to their faces. Mime Marcel Marceau and clowns in a circus conceal their identity by using theatrical makeup rather than the earthy mixtures employed by the Africans and Indians. Theatrical makeup is relatively inexpensive and will last through many applications. Clown white, wet rouge in shades of red, and color liners offer a wide variety of color for face painting. Other necessary materials include paint shirts, ¼-inch bristle brushes, cold cream, facial tissues or paper toweling, cosmetic mirrors, and a bar of hand soap.

    A few precautions should be taken before beginning this activity. 1) Have the children wear paint shirts and brush their hair back from their foreheads. 2) Instruct them to apply a thin layer of makeup. 3) Tell them to avoid the sensitive skin around their eyes. See Figure 17-3 at the beginning of the chapter.

    Perhaps they would enjoy presenting a clown parade, a pantomime show, or an Indian dance. Or this activity might be used along with Activities 3 and 4. In cleaning up, the children should remove the makeup with facial tissues or paper toweling and cold cream. Then they should wash their faces with warm water and soap. The makeup may be removed from the brushes by washing them in warm water and soap.

6. Papier-mâché is a substance used for both mask making and puppets. One of the drawbacks to using this material is that a mask or puppet may require a number of periods before the projects are successful. Before introducing this mask activity: 1) ask each student to bring a large grocery bag; 2) tear a stack of newspapers into half sheets; 3) gather some paper towels; 4) give each child a 6-inch piece of masking tape or a piece of string and 3 or 4 full sheets of newspaper; and 5) have containers of water and wheat paste ready for use. Be sure to demonstrate the papier-mâché process. The following procedure might be presented:

Begin making the armature of the mask by taking crumpled sheets of newspaper and stuffing them into the bag. Gather together the open end of the bag and seal it with tape or string. Once sealed, the overall shape of the mask may be changed by squeezing and pushing the bag.

Insert some paper toweling in the container of water. Cover one side of the stuffed bag with wet paper toweling to insure the easy removal of the mask from the armature. Have a stack of half sheets of newspaper, a few paper towels, and a small container with wheat paste ready. Taking one piece of newspaper, spread wheat paste over its surface with the hand. Tear the pasted sheet into strips approximately 1 to 1½ inches wide. Begin applying the strips to the wet toweling on the paper bag, and make sure the ends of the paper strips overlap each other. Cover the top and sides of the bag with paper strips. Spread wheat paste over a flat paper towel. Tear the pasted towel into strips of the same size as the newspaper. Cover all the newspaper strips with paper toweling.

Features may be added by modeling a nose, some eyes, a mouth, some cheeks, a chin, and some eyebrows from pasted paper. These shapes may be held to the mask with pasted paper strips.

After the application of one more layer of newspaper, end with one layer of paper toweling. All edges should be glued down tightly for a smooth surface. Then set the mask aside to dry. After it begins to harden, remove the stuffed bag as the mask will dry quicker without the armature.

Before the children begin, have them examine the work of art in Plate 17-1. Ask what they feel the mask maker was trying to express about the antelope. What words might be used to describe the animal? Ask if the shapes or the decorations help convey the feeling. If the children's masks are to be animals use the discussion on page 317. If the masks are to represent people you can have a similar discussion about human characteristics. For example, it is possible for the masks to represent circus people, including a strong man, a thin man, a clown, or a tatooed lady.

When the masks are dry, the children may paint them with tempera paint. After the paint dries the masks may be covered with white shellac. Finally, decorative objects such as papers, feathers, egg cartons, fabric scraps, yarn, beads, and laces may be glued to the mask. See Figure 17-4.

7. While looking at the puppet in Plate 17-3, explain that the artist loved to experiment with materials. Share some information about Klee and puppets. Explain that the exemplar is a hand puppet and is called this because it covers the hand and is manipulated with the fingers.

Before the children begin to make their papier-mâché puppet (similar to the one in Figure 17-5), have them discuss various stories that can be acted out. Perhaps you can discuss parts of a story or play, and they can work in groups of three to five to create their own story plot. As the characters are identified, the children may begin work on their puppet heads.

The following describes the various steps in the process. Before introducing the project: 1) tear newspaper into half sheets; 2) give each child three 3-foot

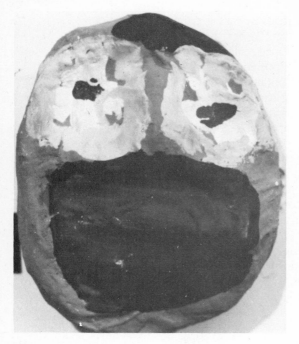

Figure 17-4. A papier-mâché mask by a fourth-grader.

Figure 17-5. A papier-mâché puppet made in an art methods class.

pieces of masking tape; 3) gather paper towels; 4) pass out two full sheets of newspaper and a cardboard tube; and 5) have containers of wheat paste ready for use. Tell the children to crumple the newspaper into a head shape. Wrap the crumpled newspaper with a piece of tape. Place the newspaper on one end of the tube. To hold the shape in place, run a piece of tape up the side, over the top of the newspaper shape, and down the other side of the tube. Put another long piece of tape at right angles to the first, crossing at the top of the puppet head. Now pasted paper may be put over all sides of the puppet head and tube (see Activity 6). Be sure to alternate layers of paper and toweling and to end with a layer of paper toweling. Features may be added after the second layer. When all four layers have been applied to the armature and the final coat has been smoothed out, the puppet head may be set on an empty pop bottle to dry. Make sure the form is completely dry before continuing.

Puppet heads may be painted with liquid tempera paint. Bristle brushes can be used to apply the face and hair colors while smaller hair brushes will be needed for details. When the tempera is dry, the heads may be coated with white shellac. After the shellac dries, buttons, yarns, sequins, beads, seashells, fur, feathers, and any number of found materials may be attached.

A pattern for a puppet costume can be started by placing one hand on a piece of paper. Spread the fingers apart. Using the middle finger as an apex, draw a line from this finger to the thumb. Upon reaching the thumb continue the straight line in the same direction until even with the wrist. Going back to the middle finger draw a straight line to the little finger. Continue this line until it is even with the wrist. Join the two lines together. See Figure 17-6. Cut the tip off the top of the triangular shape so it will fit the tube neck of the puppet. Cut the paper pattern out and lay it onto two pieces of cloth. With straight pins attach the pattern to both pieces of cloth. Cut the cloth into the pattern shape. Putting right sides of cloth together, sew up the sides with the running stitch (see page 342) and then turn the costume right side out. Decorate it and attach it to the puppet neck with a small amount of glue.

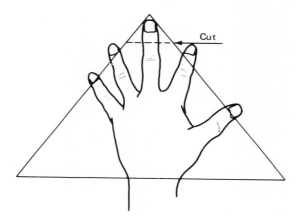

Figure 17-6.   Making a pattern for a puppet costume.

CHAPTER 18

POTTERY

Figure 18-2.   A group of pinch pots made by fifth-graders.

Pottery, or the making of clay pots, is one of the oldest crafts. It has been called the "alphabet of archaeology" because on investigating ancient pots archaeologists have found clues to the life of primitive man.[1] Before the discovery of pot-

---

[1]David Green, *Pottery: Materials and Techniques* (New York: Praeger, 1967), p. 47.

tery, man probably used hollowed stones or shells for storing his food. At some time rush baskets, which were also made for storage purposes, were taken to a river bank where they became covered with clay. Apparently these baskets were placed too close to a fire and when the rushes were burned the clay basket shapes with a decorative wicker pattern remained.

Before the potter's wheel was discovered, the coil, slab, and pinch methods of forming clay were used in making pottery. The coil process was one of the earliest methods. In this method, a pot was formed by building the sides of the container with coils of clay and then smoothing over the joints. The second method, slab, involved flat slabs of clay from which pieces of a desired size and shape were cut. These pieces were joined together with slip or liquid clay. In the pinch method the potter pushed a hole in the center of a ball of clay with his thumb. As he supported the clay in the palm of one hand he enlarged the hole by squeezing the clay wall with his fingers.

Although the potter's wheel was thought to have been invented by the Egyptians in 3500 B.C., it was used in many parts of the world. The earliest potter's wheel was made of stone. It consisted of a circular piece measuring about three feet in diameter which turned on a pivot and was hand spun.

The earliest surface decorations on clay pots were those created by the woven rushes. When primitive man realized he could control the surface he used his fingers as tools; later he used sticks and other objects. As glazes were discovered, the surfaces of the pots became more decorative.

EXEMPLARS OF POTTERY

The three pieces of pottery illustrated in this section were made by people of different cultures. The exemplar of a Greek pot was made sixteen centuries before the example from the Mayan civilization. Two contemporary European artists collaborated in making the third.

A GREEK ARTIST, Eighth century B.C.

The large forms known as the Dipylon vases are considered the most important examples of pottery from the Geometric Period (ninth to eighth century B.C.). The pottery received its name from an important gate in the city wall of Athens, Greece. Most of the artists lived, worked, and sold their pottery in the section around the Dipylon Gate. Many travelers to and from Eleusis and Piraeus passed through this gate. In addition, funeral processions on the way to the chief cemetery of the city had to pass through this gate.

These ceramic forms were an important part of the cemetery. Instead of the tombstone that is used today, the Greeks placed pottery of this type on tombs to serve as a monument to the dead. In decorating the forms the potter included a scene of the *prothesis* or lying-in-state of the dead and the funeral procession. In Plate 18-1, the *prothesis* scene is found on the upper third of the vase. The body is lying on a table and is surrounded by the family. On either side of this focal point are groups of women beating their heads. Depicted on the horizontal band below the *prothesis* is the funeral procession with warriors and horse-drawn chariots.

The human figure and animal representations on this vase are typical of those found on pottery of the Geometric Period. Represented in silhouette, the human and animal bodies have been reduced to stylized forms. For example, the human body is represented in a frontal view but

Plate 18-1.   Greek Dipylon vase. 8th century B.C., Attic. Clay, 40½" high. The Metropolitan Museum of Art, Rogers Fund, 1914.

the head is shown in a profile view much like the stylized human forms found in Egyptian art. The profile is in outline with a dot representing the eye. There is no distinction of sex as each body is composed of an inverted triangle for the upper torso, a narrow waist, wide hips, and tapering limbs. A number of the warriors' bodies have been hidden behind their shields.

The human and animal forms, along with geometric patterns, are painted on the vase shape in horizontal bands which are precise and orderly, yet show rhythmical arrangements of

form. Patterns are formed by the repetition of squares, triangles, hatched lines, and dots. By use of the simple dot of varying size, the potter has created a visual rhythm. The triangle is found in some form throughout the painted surface of the vase.

Although some Greek pottery prior to the eighth century B.C. was built using the coil and pinch methods, this example was a product of the potter's wheel. This pot shape, a krater, was thrown on the wheel in two sections and then connected with slip. After the pot was sun-dried, it was lightly baked in a simple oven which was heated with charcoal or wood. The red clay body was then covered with yellow slip on which the designs were brushed in a lustrous black color.

A MAYAN ARTIST, Early classic period, 300–600 A.D.

Just after the Dipylon vases were made, another civilization flourished in areas of Mexico, Guatemala, British Honduras, Western Honduras, and El Salvador. This culture, Mayan (seventh century B.C. to 1541 A.D.), was famous for its pottery as well as architecture, sculpture, painting, featherwork, wood carving, mosaic, goldwork, and jade carving. All of these artistic endeavors were used to create products for religious rituals. The Mayans, like the Bozo tribe and the Eskimo, needed to appease the gods who controlled the weather.

It is known that the Mayan craftsman had certain rules or traditions to which he was bound when creating his work. Unlike his Greek counterpart, the Mayan potter shaped his clay by hand. In addition, the Mayan potter treated the surface of his pot by painting, incising, carving, modeling, and appliquéing.[2]

One of the greatest centers of the Mayan civilization in the Early Classic period was Tikal. It is located in the northern part of Guatemala, in the heart of the Petén jungle. Some of the pottery that came from this center is called Teo-

---

[2]The term *appliqué*, as related to pottery, is the process of building up the surface with coils or small nodules of clay.

tihuacán type tripods. An example which was found in the painted tomb at Tikal is seen in Plate 18-2. Made of thin black clay, this tripod bowl was incised with many designs, one of which is a bird. The bird motif is repeated on top of the conical-shaped lid. The bird has been modeled from clay and attached to the lid with slip. Lines drawn into the bird shape suggest

Plate 18-2. Incised tripod vase, early Mayan period. A.D. 300–600. Black ware. The Tikal Project, University Museum, University of Pennsylvania.

---

[3] Other painters who collaborated with a professional potter were: Gauguin, Rouault, Redon, Vuillard, Bonnard, Denis, van Dongen, Derain, Vlaminck, and Braque.

wings and an eye. The lid is also decorated with incised motifs.

On the sides of the pottery form, the Mayan artist has divided the surface into different sections. A single line incised at the top is repeated by a line at the base. About one-fourth of the way up the pot, there are two lines encircling the form. These marks divide the larger, more decorative section from the smaller portion at the bottom. In the larger section, the artist has again divided the pottery surface vertically. The section on the left has been incised with lines to form a bird. The next panel has numerous smaller motifs, followed by another with a bird design.

The smaller portion around the base of the pot has been decorated with a hieroglyph composed of a circular line and three vertical lines. This motif is enclosed in two scalloped lines which form triangular shapes.

The pottery form stands on three legs. Each leg has some open areas as well as an inverted triangle. Three circles with a dot in the center have been incised into the uppermost part of the leg.

JOSÉ LLORENS ARTIGAS, 1892–, and JOAN MIRÓ (hwan me-ro), 1893–

The stoneware vase in Plate 18-3 is the result of the collaboration of two artists, Artigas and Miró. José Llorens Artigas is known for his ceramic work and for his writings. When he was an art student at the Academy of Francisco Gali, he met fellow student and painter Joan Miró. In 1919, Artigas went to Paris, and in the 1920s and 1930s he began to work with two French painters, Dufy and Marquet. Because these painters were unfamiliar with the work of the potter, they enlisted a professional to work with them. The potter would create the clay forms; the painters would decorate the forms.[3] In 1941, Artigas returned to his native city of Barcelona and taught ceramics. Three years later, he and Miró began working together.

Joan Miró is a well-known painter, graphic artist, scenic designer, and ceramist. At the age of 14, he began studying at the School of Fine Arts in Barcelona. Three years later, his parents withdrew him from school. Miró, however, continued his studies at the Academy of Gali, and in 1915 began working on his own. In 1919, he went to Paris, where he stayed for a year. Although the paintings he made during this time were realistic, they also exhibited a sense of fantasy. When in the 1920s the surrealist movement gained momentum, Miró became a staunch supporter.

When Miró became interested in ceramics, he went to his friend, Artigas, and asked to be instructed in the craft. With his friend's guidance, Miró produced many decorative plaques. He also painted or decorated various pottery forms that Artigas made. The stoneware vase (Plate 18-3) is one of these pots. It measures 11⅜ inches high, is bulbous in shape, and has a small opening on the top. On this shape Miró has painted a whimsical character with a four-sided head and free-form shaped body. The undulating line near the bottom and to the left of the figure continues around the pottery form and ends with the round shapes to the right of the figure.

Although this vase was painted many centuries after the Dipylon vase, the figures are quite similar. Miró also reduced the human figure to simple forms and used lines and dots to decorate the pottery. But, the total effect of this pot is quite different from that of the Dipylon vase.

Plate 18-3. Joan Miró. José Artigas vase. 1941. Clay, 11⅜" high. Musée d'art Moderne de la Ville de Paris.

ADDITIONAL EXEMPLARS

Additional exemplars of pottery can include the work of the ancient Chinese and the North American Indians.

POTTERY ACTIVITIES FOR THE PRIMARY GRADES (AGES 6 THROUGH 8)

The materials and tools necessary for the following activities are the same as those discussed on pages 258 to 259. There are many ways of decorating and finishing pottery. If a kiln is available the pots can be fired.[4] Because glazes may be too expensive for a school system, the fired pieces may be finished with shoe polish, wood stains, oil pastels, tempera paints, or Rub 'n Buff. Acrylic polymer medium and liquid wax may be used as a protective coating.

CONCEPTS FOR POSSIBLE DEVELOPMENT

The artistic terms or concepts to develop with pottery are listed below. Some of these terms will be found again in the section devoted to activities for the intermediate grades.

coil	pinch pot	score	slip
incise	repetition	slab	texture
pattern			

SUGGESTED ACTIVITIES

Young children enjoy working with clay and should be given many opportunities to do so. Although there are only two basic methods described below for making pottery, there are many ways in which the pots can be decorated.

1. The first experience is an exploratory one which allows the children to discover the "feel" of clay. It should be kept short, yet allow enough time to roll, push, poke, pinch, and squeeze the clay into various forms. Very young children may pound the clay into a flat piece. Urge them to try other things so they realize the clay may take on a three-dimensional form.[5] Before you introduce this experience, prepare a ball of clay for each child in your class. It would be good to have a few extra pieces ready for those who may wish more clay. The size of the ball should be no larger than what can comfortably be held in the child's hands. As their interest wanes, ask them to tell you what they discovered about clay. Then go on to the next experience, which is also exploratory in nature.

2. Show the children the reproduction of the Dipylon vase (Plate 18-1). Notice the many shapes the artist repeated to make a pattern. Ask them to point out other patterns in the classroom. Ask if they could make patterns in the clay.

---

[4]See page 260 for information on firing.
[5]For information on children's work in clay, refer to Eleese V. Brown, "Developmental Characteristics of Clay Figures Made by Children From Age Three Through Age Eleven," *Studies in Art Education*, 1975, XVI (3), pp. 45–53.

Encourage them to tell you how they might do this. Demonstrate by taking a ball of clay and pound it into the form of a slab about half an inch thick. Trim the edges of the slab with the open end of a paper clip. Then, taking a pointed dowel rod, a spoon handle, a popsicle stick, a tongue depressor, or a finger, begin imprinting a pattern into the clay slab. This process will create a textured surface and when hard will be interesting to touch. A hole may be punched through the clay for hanging purposes and the slabs may be fired. When left to dry they should never be left on a porous surface such as paper towels or cardboard. See Figure 18-1.

Figure 18-1.　　Slab with a variety of texture imprints done by a second-grader.

3. Gather the students close to you and demonstrate the pinch method of forming a pot. Take a ball of clay in one hand. With the thumb of the other hand push halfway down into the center of the clay. Begin squeezing or pinching the clay walls. As you work, rotate the clay in your hand and the clay walls will become smoother and more even. Do not make the walls too thin or they will collapse. Following the demonstration look at Plate 18-1. Explain that an artist decorated the clay pot by painting on the surface. Ask the children to close their eyes and imagine the pot without any decoration. Have them tell you which is more interesting and why. Try to help them understand that the images or textures found on pottery make the objects interesting to our eyes and to our touch. At the conclusion of this discussion have the children get

balls of clay and begin work. Upon completion encourage the children to enhance the forms with repeated patterns made with the clay tools suggested for Activity 2. Incised or drawn-in lines can also be made with the pointed end of the dowel stick. Carefully dry the pieces before firing them and finishing them by one of the methods suggested on page 327. See Figure 18-2 at the beginning of the chapter.

4. Before this activity, ask the children to bring a cylindrical jar, glass, or can. Then examine the exemplar of the Mayan pot. Explain that the technique used in building a pot similar to this is called the slab method. Remind them of the slab that they pressed textures into in Activity 2. Ask them to point out any patterns they see on the pot. Tell them to imagine they are touching the pot with their hands. Have them tell you about the rough and smooth areas. At the end of this discussion, demonstrate rolling out a slab of clay about ½ inch thick. If you flatten the clay on the fabric side of a piece of oilcloth, it can easily be removed. Next, lay a jar, glass, or can on the loosened slab and measure the length of clay to cover the sides of the object. Cut the slab slightly longer than the measurement. Loosely wrap the clay around the container which is standing in an upright position. Pinch the ends together to seal the cylinder. Following this, make a base by rolling another slab of clay to the same thickness. With the container still inside the clay cylinder, stand it on this slab. With a blunt tool trace around the cylinder bottom. Cut the base larger than the cylinder. Turn the clay cylinder upside down on the table. With a pointed dowel or popsicle stick score or draw lines in the bottom edge of the clay wall. Next, score the outside edge of the flat side on the base. Apply slip to the scored edges of both pieces.[6] The slip acts like glue and will bind the clay pieces together. Place the cylinder and base together. Erase the seam line by applying pressure with a finger. Then the pot is ready to be decorated. As children work on their pots encourage them to decorate them by drawing designs into the clay. Keep the supporting container inside until the clay begins to dry, and then gently remove it; it will not come out once the clay completely hardens. If this activity takes longer than a period keep the pots moist by sealing them in plastic. After the pots have dried and been fired they may be finished in one of the ways suggested on page 327.

5. This activity may be divided into two sections; the first, building a slab pot (Activity 4); the second, decorating the pot. For the second part, show the Artigas–Miró exemplar (Plate 18-3). Look at the figure and other symbols. Have the children make up a story about the picture they see on the pot. After a number of interpretations select one of the topics below for discussion:

Blowing bubbles	Visiting the zoo
Going for a walk	Playing ball
My pet	Road machines and workers

---

[6]Slip is made by mixing a small amount of clay with water.

Have the children use tools to draw their story onto the clay pot. Urge them to imprint objects to create some textured areas. After the pots have been fired, stain them with one of the suggested media on page 327. Because of the textured areas it might be necessary to dilute the medium before applying it. A rag or cotton swab may be dipped into the solution and applied to the pot. A protective coat (see p. 327) may be brushed onto the surface.

6. As an alternate activity, make a slab pot and use coils and pieces of clay to illustrate a story on the sides. Remind the children to score and add slip to any large coils that are added. After the pots have dried and been fired, they may be painted with tempera paint. If acrylic polymer medium is available it can be added to the paint. A gloss medium will leave a shiny surface much like a glaze. When using the polymer emulsion the brushes must be kept moist during their use and washed thoroughly at the conclusion of the activity. If this solution is not available the pieces may be brushed with liquid wax or shellac. The liquid floor wax may be washed out of the brush with cool water and soap, while the shellac must be removed with denatured alcohol. When the brush is free of shellac, it should be washed with water and soap. See Figure 18-3.

Figure 18-3. Cylindrical pots with floral decorations; one with decorations incised into the clay, the other with coils added to the surface.

POTTERY ACTIVITIES FOR THE INTERMEDIATE GRADES (AGES 9 THROUGH 11)

Before beginning the procedures in this section, review the information found on pages 258 and 259. The basic methods of pinch and slab construction will be referred to in the following activities. Refer to Activities 3 and 4 in the previous section.

CONCEPTS FOR POSSIBLE DEVELOPMENT

When your students look at the pottery exemplars try to help them develop an understanding of the artistic terms and concepts listed below:

armature	krater	pinch pot	slab
ceramic	Mayan	plasticity	slip
coil	modeled	repetition	stylized
incise	pattern	score	texture

SUGGESTED ACTIVITIES

In grades four, five, and six children should have many opportunities to make textures in clay and to build three-dimensional forms.

1. Intermediate grade children will enjoy making texture slabs like those described in Activity 2 in the primary section. In addition to the tools mentioned in that procedure, encourage the children to find objects such as buttons, bottle caps, screws, nails, paper clips, seed pods, stones, and seashells for creating textured patterns in the clay surface. Because the slabs may warp when drying, it is necessary to turn them over frequently. After being fired they may be stained or covered with wax. See Figure 18-1.

2. When looking at Plate 18-1, give some information about the exemplar. Explain the story represented on this vase. Following the discussion have the children make slab pots (see Activity 4, page 329). Upon completion of the pots, ask the children to decorate their forms with a scene depicting one of the following topics:

The marching band	Trucks, cars, and motorcycles
A football game	A parade
Window shopping	My favorite sport

Encourage the students to use the clay tools either to draw into the clay or to imprint textures in the pot surface. They may wish to arrange their scene in a band or bands surrounded by texture patterns. After the pieces have dried and been fired, any of the stains suggested on page 327 may be used. Perhaps a diluted solution of stain may be applied with a rag or a cotton swab to areas of delicate texture. Then the pieces may be coated with floor wax or acrylic polymer medium.

3. The krater in Plate 18-1 was made by joining two clay forms. In this activity two pinch pots will be put together to form a larger pottery piece. If your students are unfamiliar with the pinch method, demonstrate the process. Then proceed by making one pinch pot to be used as the base. Before turning it up-side down on a 12-x-12-inch piece of tempered Masonite, stuff the pot with newspaper for support. Score a section on the bottom of the base pinch pot. After making a second pot gently hold it in the palm of one hand and score the bottom of this piece. Apply slip to the scored areas on both pots. Then place the slipped areas of the two pots together. Roll a coil and wrap it around the joint where the two pots meet. Press the coil with a finger to blend the clay pieces together. When the two pinch pots have been joined, the students may use tools and found objects to create textured areas. Store the finished pots for drying; fire when dry; and finish with liquid floor wax that has been slightly colored with powdered tempera paint.

4. Try the fourth procedure for the primary grades. Following a discussion about Plate 18-2 have the students decorate the sides of a slab pot with incised lines to form real or imaginary animal shapes. After the pieces have dried thoroughly and been fired, they may be finished in any of the ways suggested on page 327.

5. An alternative to the last activity: Have the children construct a slab pot to which they add small pinch pot shapes to form an animal body and head. Other parts of the body may be made from coils added to the side of the pot. Remind them to score edges and to apply slip. A small coil may be wrapped around the joint and the edges blended together with the finger or a tool. Encourage them to incise lines into areas to create different textures. Finish the pot as suggested in Procedure 3.

6. The shape of the stoneware pottery in Plate 18-3 is more rounded and bulbous in shape than the other two exemplars. Although Artigas formed this shape on a potter's wheel, it is possible to make a similar shape in the following manner. Take some newspaper and wad it into a ball which will form the armature for the clay. Set it aside and roll out a slab of clay to an even thickness of approximately half an inch. Loosen the clay slab from the oilcloth and begin wrapping it around the paper armature. It may be necessary to roll another slab in order to completely cover the paper with clay. Be sure to blend the clay pieces together when adding the second slab to the one already wrapped

around the paper. When the newspaper has been covered with clay, the shape may be changed by pounding it lightly with a piece of wood. The plastic quality of the clay, supported by the newspaper, allows for any change in shape. After the shape is formed, an opening or openings may be cut into the clay with a blunt tool. Then the rough edges of the opening may be smoothed with the index finger. At this point let the pot dry thoroughly. The paper inside the pot will burn when the piece is fired. After the pots are fired the shapes may be enhanced with applied decoration. Look at the decoration on the pot in Plate 18-3. When talking about this exemplar, point out the whimsical, free-flowing, fluid shapes and lines that Joan Miró painted. Because the piece of pottery was not titled, the figure and other designs are more decorative than informative. A story might be imagined about the portrayed symbols and in fact, your students may suggest many titles. Continue the discussion by selecting one of the topics below:

Cities in outer space   A flower garden
Insects   Undersea creatures
Birds

Figure 18-4.   Ceramic pot made by a fourth-grader.

Ask them to consider the shape of their pot before they begin painting a story with liquid tempera paint or tempera mixed with acrylic polymer medium. Remind them to look at all sides of their pottery while painting. If tempera paint is used without the polymer solution, coat the pots with white shellac or liquid wax after the paint has dried. See Figure 18-4.

7. In presenting this activity, share the exemplar and discuss the applied decoration by Miró (Plate 18-3). Also discuss one of the topics suggested in the preceding activity. Instead of allowing the pots in the previous activity to dry, the shapes may be decorated by adding small pinch pots or clay coils. Textured areas may be created by incising lines or imprinting shapes. See Figure 18-5. The pinch pot forms and coils appliquéd to the pot, as well as textured areas, may take on shapes likes flowers, birds, insects, undersea creatures, and beings from outer space. After the clay pots have dried and been fired they may be decorated using any of the methods suggested on page 327.

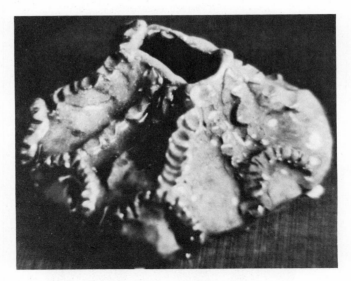

Figure 18-5.   Coils applied to the surface of this pot were pinched to form a textured pattern.

CHAPTER 19

STITCHERY AND APPLIQUÉ

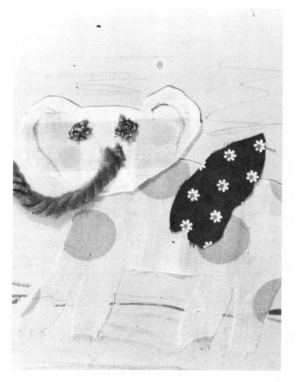

Figure 19-5. Scrap cloth elephant by a third-grader.

The needle arts are ancient crafts known throughout the world. In Neolithic times, prehistoric man stitched together skins with strips of sinew. As man domesticated animals and began growing crops, he discovered the art of spinning threads.

In the medieval world, men and women who were specialists in stitchery worked at various monasteries producing sumptuous banners and cloths used in religious ceremonies. In the sixteenth century needlework became more secular and samplers began to be a popular form. From that time to the present, the arts of the needle have changed little in the processes used and the tools needed for making stitchery.

Originally this art form was called *embroidery*, but recently has been renamed *stitchery* in order to include many types of needlework. There are about three hundred different stitches which are placed into the following categories: flat, chain and loop, and knotted. They may cover an entire cloth or only a portion of it. Sometimes other pieces of fabric are cut into interesting shapes and stitched to a background material. This type is called appliqué.

One of the tools used in making a stitchery is the needle. The earliest needles were thought to be made from thorns and fish bones. Some ancient ones were carved from wood, bone, ivory, and shell. Needles made of steel originated in China and some examples were taken to Damascus and later into Spain by the Moors. This route was also used to pass along the paper-making process (see page 122). The earliest needle-making industry was founded in Nuremberg, Germany, in the year 1370. Until the eighteenth century, needles were handmade by craftsmen.

The basic element of the arts of the needle is the stitch formed by manipulating the needle and a flexible thread. In early works, threads of linen or wool were used, as were threads made of silver and gold. The embroiderer was careful in selecting his threads and often used natural dyes to color the thread. The brilliant hues found in ancient works is said to have lasted because of the natural dyes.

Some other tools which are used for stitchery are pins, thimbles, hoops, and yardsticks. Pins, like needles, were first formed from thorns, fish bones, wood, bone, or ivory and eventually were made of bronze. These early metal pins were forged by hand. Bronze thimbles have been found at Pompeii and Herculaneum. The word thimble comes from the Old English word *thymel* which means thumb stall. The stitchery or embroidery hoop used today to stretch the background cloth is derived from a wooden frame. The cloth was stretched on these frames in order to assist the embroiderer in making straight vertical stitches. In order to correctly measure cloth, a measuring stick or meteyard was used. Today we call these measuring devices yardsticks.

EXEMPLARS OF STITCHERY AND APPLIQUÉ

Although stitchery is an ancient craft, it has recently gained recognition as an artistic medium. Craftsmen who work in the needle arts, like contemporary painters, sculptors, or printmakers, are using fiber and cloth to express their thoughts and ideas.

ENGLISH CRAFTSWOMEN,
ca. eleventh or twelfth century A.D.

The Bayeux Tapestry, a stitched hanging, derived its name from a French city where it is exhibited in the bishop's palace.[1] It is an important work of art because the hanging is a record of the events of the Norman conquest of England; the work depicts an accurate representation of eleventh-century dress and military weapons;

---

[1]A tapestry is a heavy handwoven textile used as a hanging or curtain.

and the embroidery work is significantly different from others done during the same period.

Scholars, who have studied the work, disagree about the reason why it was made. For many years it was believed that the tapestry had been made for the Cathedral at Bayeux; however, it has also been said that it was destined for a castle.[2] Regardless of its intended place, the work was commissioned by Bishop Odo, a half-brother of William the Conqueror, soon after the year 1066, and it took about two years to complete. There is further disagreement as to whether the stitchery was made in England or in Normandy. Nevertheless, the manner in which the inscription, fables, and certain individual figures have been executed suggest that it was embroidered by English craftswomen.

The story, stitched on the background cloth measuring approximately 231 feet long by 20 inches wide, covers a period of two years and includes three main sequences. The opening sequence, dating about 1064, depicts Harold's voyage to France where he is made a prisoner of Guy de Ponthieu. Depicted in the second main section is William the Conqueror's expedition against Conan of Brittany, while the third se-

---

[2]Charles Harvard Gibbs-Smith, *The Bayeux Tapestry* (London: The Phaidon Press, Ltd., 1973), p. 4.

Plate 19-1. English craftswomen. Detail of Bayeaux Tapestry. c. 1073–88. Stitchery on linen; height 1'8", entire length 231'. Courtesy of the French Government Tourist Office.

quence shows William's invasion of England including the battle with King Harold.

Stitched along the length of the work are 626 human figures, along with 202 horses and mules, 55 dogs, 505 other animals, 37 buildings, 41 ships and boats, and 49 trees. The most important figures represented are William and Harold and they are easy to recognize because of their clothing and size. The various ways the craftswomen used to indicate high-ranking members of the story were to show the figures in long capes fastened at the shoulders with a circular or square brooch, to put green garters with hangings on their legs, or to dress them in long robes.

The basic garment worn by the men in the tapestry was the tunic, belted at the waist. Beneath this, the men wore breeches and shirts made of linen. Their battle dress consisted of a suit of mail and they carried various instruments of war such as shields, swords, axes, maces, spears, lances, and bows and arrows.

The entire tapestry, originally made in about six pieces, sewn together, is divided into 72 scenes separated by trees or buildings. Running along the top and bottom of the tapestry were borders containing a variety of real and imaginary animals and birds along with fables of Aesop and Phaedrus. Plate 19-1 shows the Norman Army setting out to do battle with Harold.

On a background of bleached linen, the embroiderers have used various colors of woolen threads to create the images. Five principal colors used were terra-cotta red, blue-green, sage green, buff, and blue. Dark green, yellow, and a very dark blue were used in lesser amounts throughout. When using the colored threads, the craftswomen stitched the story with three basic stitches: 1) the stem; 2) the outline; and 3) laid and couched work. The latter is an effective way of covering large areas with color. In Plate 19-1 this stitch can be seen in the filled-in areas of horses, shields, and border animals and creatures. The outline and stem stitches have been used to create the ground, the suits of mail, and to outline the figures and objects in the work. For a further description of the processes for making the stitches, see pages 344 to 348.

The work is interesting because of the action of the story and the way in which the colors and stitches have been used. By varying the color and design of the tunics and the positions of the lances, the tapestry designer has made the visual images interesting to look at. For example, on the left side of Plate 19-1 are soldiers with lances in an upright position. Each soldier is dressed in mail with different designs, and rides a different-colored horse. Even the manes on the horses are unique. As the eye travels across the work, the lances are tilted to the right. This visual device helps to speed up the movement of the composition. Note that there are ten men depicted in this section, but only eight horses are shown.

NIK KREVITSKY
no date

Nik Krevitsky is the Director of Art of the Tucson Public Schools. Before settling in Arizona, Krevitsky taught in the Chicago Public Schools; at the University of California, Los Angeles; and at San Francisco State College. As a doctoral student at Columbia University, Krevitsky taught courses in the textile arts. His involvement with these art forms led him to write two books. In one of these, *Stitchery: Art and Craft*, he describes stitchery as a serious art medium for creative expression.

The stitcheries of Nik Krevitsky have a distinctive style which reflects his surrounding environment. These works are not naturalistic; that is, he does not stitch trees, cacti, flowers, and grasses that we can distinguish. Instead, he uses shapes of opaque and transparent cloth along with stitches to create the feeling of these objects. It might be the prickly, sharp, piercing, spiny, and barbed quality of a cactus that is expressed with the stitches and cloth. On the other hand, the fragile look of a leaf may be shown through the stitches and transparent fabric.

Krevitsky approaches his work in a very direct manner. Apparently his ideas grow and unfold as he works with materials.

Although strong color is not a striking factor in the stitchery and appliqué in Plate 19-2, it is nonetheless important in describing the landscape of the moon. In *Moonscape*, made in 1968, the artist has used a red silk background upon which he has appliquéd transparent and opaque cloth, capiz shells, and cloth-covered buttons. He has also used a variety of flat, chained, and knotted stitches. The stitchery, twenty-two inches in diameter, has been permanently framed in a large embroidery hoop. Throughout the circular piece, Krevitsky has repeated circles with cloth and stitches. In the lower left-hand corner of the work the artist has placed the white transparent circle over a green opaque circle and some stitches. What effect does this have on the stitches and cloth which have been covered? How does this compare with the portion of the green cloth and stitches which has not been covered? Compare this area with the smaller transparent white circle at the top of the stitchery. The circular shapes in the work range from the very tiny French knots to the overall shape of the stitchery.[3] The covered buttons and seashells which project from the surface create shadows in the work as it hangs on the wall.

In this work the background cloth becomes an important part of the whole stitchery. When comparing this stitchery with the Bayeux Tapestry, it is clear that the linen cloth of the earlier

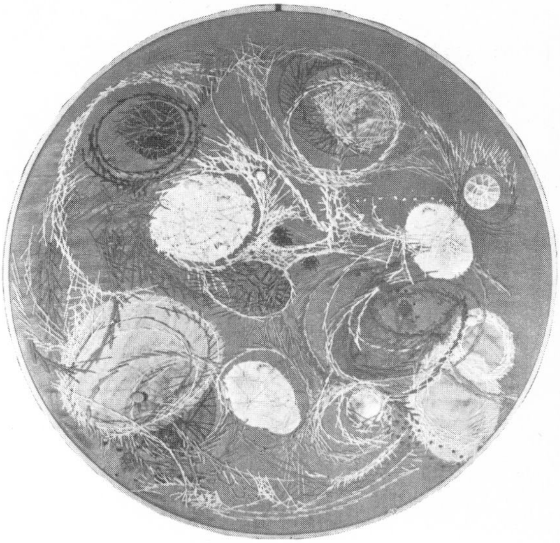

Plate 19-2. Nik Krevitsky. *Moonscape*. 1968. Appliqué wall hanging in silk, capiz shells, cloth-covered buttons, and various threads; 22" in diameter. From *Art and the Creative Teacher* by Kelly Fearing, Evelyn Beard, Nik Krevitsky, and Clyde Martin. © 1971 by W. S. Benson and Company, Inc., Austin, Texas.

work acts as a vehicle for the characters in the story. The vacant spaces or negative areas in the Bayeux Tapestry are less interesting than those in the Krevitsky work.

ADDITIONAL EXEMPLARS

To show the many ways of working with needle and thread, use the work of Marilyn Pappas, Sarita Rainey, Nancy Belfer, and Marie Tuicillo Kelly. The Mola cloths made by the Indians of San Blas, Panama are an unusual form of appliqué.

---

[3]See page 349 for a description of the French knot.

STITCHERY AND APPLIQUÉ ACTIVITIES FOR THE PRIMARY GRADES (AGES 6 THROUGH 8)

The making of stitchery and appliqué requires frequent repetition in order for children to develop skills and techniques in handling the tools and materials. In the early grades, tools and materials can be minimal with a gradual addition of others as the youngsters advance. For example, an early introduction to appliqué requires nothing more than scraps of cloth, scissors, glue, and a piece of paper or oak tag for a background. An early experience in stitchery requires a piece of open weave fabric and a piece of yarn.

As the children advance, the following tools may be introduced: tapestry needles with blunt ends and large eyes, darning needles with pointed ends, crewel needles for fine work, thimbles, and embroidery hoops. A variety of threads including string, embroidery floss, Pearl cotton, rug yarn, knitting yarn, metallic thread, raffia, and jute may be collected. In addition, an assortment of opaque and transparent fabrics may be used as background material for stitchery and appliqué work. Opaque materials might include burlap, linen, cotton, felt, wool, knit fabrics, upholstery material, fur, and leather. Transparent fabrics such as net, interfacing, chiffon, tarlatan, onion sacking, and lace can be used. Finally, feathers, rickrack, ribbon, buttons, beads, and found objects such as shells, twigs, seed pods, and grasses can be used as decorative accents.

CONCEPTS FOR POSSIBLE DEVELOPMENT

Introduce the following concepts when using the stitchery exemplars with the suggested procedures:

appliqué	opaque	running stitch	straight stitch
chain stitch	repetition	smooth	texture
couching	rough	stitchery	transparent
flat stitch			

SUGGESTED ACTIVITIES

These activities will assist in making children more aware of texture:

1. Young children need to explore and become acquainted with the qualities of various fabrics. Cloth can be gathered and separated into the following groups: rough, smooth, transparent, and opaque. The fabrics can be cut into a variety of sizes and shapes. Children in the second and third grades can generally cut

fabric without too much assistance. Even so, the pieces of fabric should be of a manageable size for children to handle. The fabric can be placed in separate containers (plastic shoe or sweater box) and labeled. The texture words, rough and smooth, and the concepts of transparent and opaque can be introduced when looking at the stitchery by Krevitsky (Plate 19-2). After discussing the terms, ask the children to select some fabric pieces to arrange and glue on a piece of oak tag or cardboard. Show the children how to use a small amount of glue when fastening the fabrics to the background. This experience is an introduction to the technique known as appliqué. See Figure 19-1.

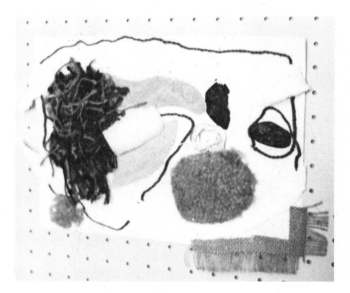

Figure 19-1.   A textured collage made in an
art methods class.

2. Yarn pictures resembling the laid and couched work in the Bayeux Tapestry can be made by gluing short lengths of rug yarn (of medium and wide widths) to a cardboard surface. The cardboard may be covered with construction paper if a colored background is desired. White or Elmer's glue can be squeezed onto the cardboard surface in a linear fashion. The yarns can then be placed on the lines of glue and pressed gently. It is important to show how much glue to use and to put the glue on the cardboard and not on the yarn.

When talking about the work of art in Plate 19-1, explain that it is a stitchery made of various threads sewn to a background. Point out the areas of solid color formed by the threads being placed close together. In addition, discuss the direction of the threads and any open areas in the work.

3. After handling the yarns and threads, the children can learn the running stitch, one of the easiest in the category of flat stitches. When making this stitch, weave the needle in and out of the fabric. The resulting stitches may be even or uneven, long or short. See Figure 19-2. A piece of yarn which has been stiffened on one end with glue, may be used as a substitute for a needle. It is important that the piece of yarn not exceed the length of the child's arm. For

Figure 19-2. The running stitch.

young children, the size of the background material should allow for easy handling. It is sometimes easier for children to handle the fabric after it has been starched or if it has been stapled to a piece of construction paper. To prevent the material from raveling, stitch around the edges with a sewing machine. An alternate solution is to run a line of glue around the edges of the fabric. Onion sacking or potato bags may be used as background cloth when using yarn without a needle. If tapestry needles are available, burlap or loosely woven fabrics may be used. See Figure 19-3.

4. Looking at the Krevitsky stitchery, notice the artist's use of straight stitches to create the design. Examine the size and direction of the stitches. Ask the children to find long and short ones. Have the students point to places where one stitch overlaps another. Talk about the way the artist repeated stitches. Demonstrate how to make a straight stitch. See Figure 19-4. Using burlap or a loosely woven fabric for background and a variety of scrap materials, have the children arrange and glue shapes to the material. The children may then stitch around or through the fabric pieces to make their design. Encourage the repetition of long and short stitches. As the children are finishing they might select objects to add to their appliqués.

5. As an alternative to the above activity, have each student select a piece of scrap cloth from a box. Have them look at the scrap to see if it resembles a living creature of some kind (animal, bird, fish, and the like). They may cut the cloth shape to make it look more like the creature. Have the children select a 9-x-12-inch or 10-x-14-inch cloth background. The creature can be glued or stitched to the surface of the cloth and an environment may be created with a variety of running stitches. Encourage the children to use the running stitch in

Figure 19-3.   Appliqué by a third-grader.

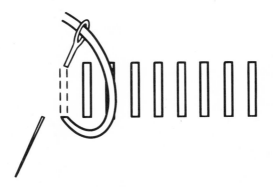

Figure 19-4.   The straight stitch.

any of the following ways: 1) even stitches with even spaces; 2) long stitches with short spaces; 3) short stitches with long spaces; or 4) alternate rows of stitches. See Figure 19-5 at the beginning of the chapter.

6. Looking at the Bayeux Tapestry, explain that it was designed to tell a story. It was told by stitching threads on cloth. One of the techniques used is called laid and couched work and a simple form of couching may be done by young children. Couching is actually the appliqueing of yarn to a fabric surface. The yarn is placed on the background and a thread is stitched over it at regular intervals. See Figure 19-6.

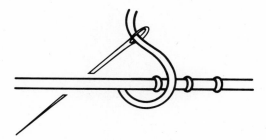

Figure 19-6. The couching stitch.

After examining the exemplar and demonstrating the technique, talk with your students about one of the topics suggested for Activity 4 under Crayon Drawing (see page 63). For this activity have pieces of bleached or unbleached muslin taped to cardboard or Masonite. The sizes and shapes of the muslin may differ to add variety. After the children select a background they can begin drawing their story of the topic on the cloth with crayons or colored felt-tipped markers. When the drawings are complete, they may remove the cloth from the cardboard. Selecting yarns and threads, they may then add stitches. Encourage them to use the couching technique. Try to supply a wide selection of yarns.

7. With third graders look at both stitchery exemplars and discuss the ways in which the artists used the fabric or threads to create images. In addition, point out that the Bayeux Tapestry has been made with stitches (stitchery) while the Krevitsky work has been made with fabric and stitches (applique). Using the same materials as in the previous activity, take the children outdoors to draw such things as the school, a house, car, truck, gas station, or tree. Urge them to add detail, but the drawings do not need to be complete. When the children have their ideas down on the muslin, return to the classroom. Have them remove the fabric from the board and then turn their drawing into a stitchery or an appliqué. This procedure may be divided into two periods: the drawings made at one time, and the stitchery or appliqué made at another.

8. At the time you introduce the above activity you may demonstrate a new stitch to your students. The simple chain stitch fills the fabric quickly and may be used in combination with the other stitches. It is a looped stitch which is similar to a crochet chain. To make the chain stitch, the needle is inserted into the fabric next to the place where the thread came out. A stitch is taken while keeping the thread under the needle. As the needle is brought through the fabric, a loop or chain is formed. See Figure 19-7.

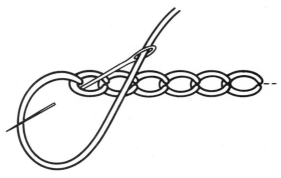

Figure 19-7. The chain stitch.

STITCHERY AND APPLIQUÉ ACTIVITIES FOR THE INTERMEDIATE GRADES (AGES 9 THROUGH 11)

Although there are about three hundred different stitches which can be used in making needlework, it is only necessary for an artist to know one stitch. He can vary the length and direction of the stitch and select yarns and threads of different textures and thicknesses to make it look different.

In this section a few more stitches will be introduced. Encourage the students to use the running, chain, and straight stitches as well as the couching technique illustrated in the primary grade activities.

The materials and tools suggested for the primary experiences may also be used for these activities. Because the children are developing skills in handling tools, darning and crewel needles will be more satisfactory. Straight pins will be helpful in holding the fabric pieces to be appliquéd. Children can assist in collecting interesting kinds of threads, yarns, and natural objects to be worked into stitcheries and appliqués.

CONCEPTS FOR POSSIBLE DEVELOPMENT

In the procedures listed below the stitchery exemplars are used to help develop these concepts:

Bayeux Tapestry	linear	naturalistic
French knot	not naturalistic	stem stitch
knotted stitch	outline stitch	unity
laid and couched	overlapping	abstract

SUGGESTED ACTIVITIES

The activities listed under the primary grades may be used with students in grades four through six. It is also possible to use topics suggested for other activities when making stitchery or applique.

1. This activity consists of three steps and may be accomplished over a number of periods or days. It is important to follow the sequence as outlined.

Figure 19-8. The chain stitch and running stitch are used in this sampler by a fifth-grader.

a) Have each child select a piece of background fabric (6-x-6-inch piece of muslin, bedsheet, or burlap), a needle, some threads, and yarns. Urge the children to use the stitches they know, and encourage them to add to these stitches or combine them to create their own. After an exploratory period, have the students share their work. See Figure 19-8.

b) After the children have made a sampler, have them try the kinds of stitches found in the Bayeux Tapestry and *Moonscape.* Three basic stitches used in making the medieval work are 1) the stem stitch; 2) the outline stitch; and 3) laid and couched work. The contemporary artist used a variety of flat, chained, and knotted stitches. Demonstrate the stitches in any order. If you feel one or more of the stitches are too difficult for your students to master at this time, introduce them when you feel they are ready.

The outline stitch is used in the Bayeux Tapestry to outline the images portrayed. Working from left to right, take a back stitch and bring the needle out where the last one went into the fabric. It is necessary to keep the thread on the same side of the needle for each stitch. See Figure 19-9.

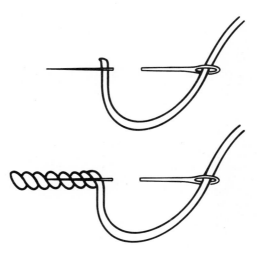

Figure 19-9.   The outline stitch.

The stem stitch is used for filling up spaces quickly. It is made in two steps. First, some running stitches are made. Then, working from right to left, the thread is brought around each running stitch. This type of stitch can be used to create any shape. See Figure 19-10.

Large areas of color in the Bayeux Tapestry are made with the laid and couched technique. The needle is brought through the fabric and a series of straight stitches are made parallel to each other. In order to have them lie flat, leave a space between each stitch. Fill in these spaces later with another series of stitches. When the area is covered with flat stitches another thread may be

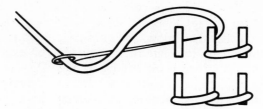

Figure 19-10. **The stem stitch.**

sewn over it. The thread is stitched at a right angle to the covered area. Fasten the second set with the couching method. See Figure 19-11.

In making the French knot, the needle and thread are brought through the fabric from the back. Thread is wrapped over the needle two or more times. Then insert the needle close to the place where the thread came out of the cloth. Holding the thread with one hand, slowly pull the needle through the fabric. A knot will form on the surface. See Figure 19-12.

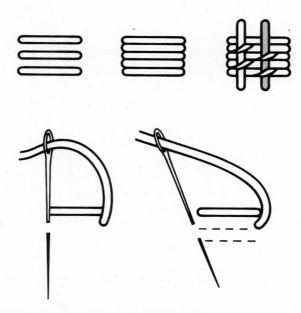

Figure 19-11. **The laid and couching technique.**

c) Using any of the new stitches learned above, the stitches the students created, or some they had learned previously, ask the children to make a stitchery of insects, flowers, or machines. Have background cloth of varying sizes and shapes from which they may choose.

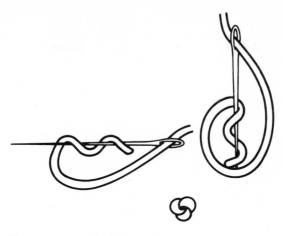

Figure 19-12.   The French knot.

2. Using the running and straight stitches and the couching technique children can create a linear type of composition similar to a drawing. Show them the linear quality of *Moonscape.* In addition, point out the color families used by the artist. This work appears unified because of the limited colors and the repetition of shapes and stitches. Using background cloth of 10 x 14 inches or larger have the children make a stitchery about one of the following:

A crowded elevator	The stores on main street
Eating my favorite food	Looking out a window
My house	The football game

Some youngsters may prefer to outline objects rather than fill them in with color, while others may prefer to fill in areas. Encourage them to use at least two different stitches, varying the size and color.

3. When looking at the appliqué in Plate 19-2, explain that this is the artist's idea of the moon. Compare the word "moonscape" to the word "landscape." Look at the landscape by Burchfield (Plate 2-3). Point out that the appliqué work is abstract while the Burchfield drawing is naturalistic. Discuss the differences between the two. Ask them to describe scenes from one of the following:

Planetscape	Starscape	Sunscape
Meteoroidscape	Cometscape	

Using background material of varying sizes and shapes, different yarns, and found objects, have the children make an appliqué about the topic.

4. With the appliqué materials from the previous lesson, the children may make an abstract or a naturalistic landscape. Before they begin, discuss various parts of the country they have visited. Ask them to describe any of these scenes. You might also have the youngsters discuss various landscapes in your own community.

5. One of the reasons the Bayeux Tapestry is important is that it records the Norman Conquest of England. The story of William the Conqueror is not only interesting as an historical event, it is also an exciting tale of adventure. Discuss the importance of recording historical events. Perhaps the students can talk about other historical events and how the events were recorded. These might be recent happenings as well as ones which occurred in the past. Some of the following might be used for a discussion:

July 4, 1776   Landing of the first man on the moon
Landing at Plymouth Rock   The Boston Tea Party
Contemporary political events

The children may wish to work on individual fabrics which are later stitched together to form a larger piece, or they may wish to work in small groups to design and make an appliqué and stitchery hanging. For individual pieces which will be stitched together at a later time, cut the pieces of fabric the same size. If the children work in groups of three or four, cut the background fabric larger. Obviously this procedure will take longer than the others suggested in this section. When finished, the work may be suspended from a rod of wood or metal.

6. Banners can also be made using the techniques of appliqué and stitchery. For this activity look at the exemplar in Plate 19-2. Ask the children to point out areas of transparent and opaque materials. Talk about the way Krevitsky overlapped cloth and stitches to make his composition interesting. Tell the children that they will be using transparent and opaque materials for this lesson. Emphasize the overlapping of cloth and stitches. Be sure to have a variety of materials available for their use. A piece of background fabric (12 x 18 inches or 18 x 24 inches) will be needed by each child along with scissors, pins, needles, and a variety of yarns and threads. When the banner is finished, the top edge may be folded over a dowel rod and glued or stitched.

CHAPTER 20

WEAVING

Figure 20-3.   Yellow and purple rug yarn
with yellow feathers form a
weaving by a kindergarten child.

Weaving is the process of interlacing a group of threads called *warp* with a second group of threads called *weft*. There are many different ways to interlace these two groups to create different weaves.

When primitive man interlaced fibers of some kind with strands of roots that were stretched between two trees, he made the first weaving. Soon man discovered that a continuous thread could be made by twisting fibers. After this, woven fabrics were used for clothing.

The earliest weavers used cotton, linen, or wool in making their weavings. Linen, which comes from the flax plant, was used at a very early period of time. Another plant, cotton, was and is the source of the cotton fiber. Wool, which was the principal fiber in the pre-Christian era in Palestine, Syria, Babylon, Greece, and Italy, came from a variety of animals. It was greatly appreciated by the ancient weavers because it was warm; it produced interesting textures; and it was easy to dye.

Fibers of cotton, linen, or wool were woven into fabric on a loom. The ancient Egyptians had two types of looms. A horizontal type of loom was used by women, and has, in a modified form, survived to the present time in the desert areas of Egypt. Because this loom required a great deal of space, a vertical loom was devised about 1500 B.C. Apparently men used this type of loom. In early Greece and Rome, a vertical loom was constructed with two posts fixed in the ground supporting an upper beam. One end of each warp thread was attached to the upper bar while a weight was attached to the opposite end of each thread. Consequently, this weaving device was called a warp-weighted loom. When using it, the weaver had to move back and forth in a standing position. This type of loom was replaced in the second century B.C. by a vertical two-bar loom. In ancient Peru, a backstrap loom was used to create extraordinary fabrics. This loom, still in use in some remote areas of Central and South America, has an upper bar which is attached to a stationary object and a lower bar attached to a belt which straps around the waist of the weaver. As the weaver leans forward and backward, the warp threads are loosened and tightened. Other people made woven pieces using the finger-weaving technique which required no loom.

EXEMPLARS OF WEAVING

The three examples of weaving have been made at different times using different techniques. One example is a Peruvian weaving; the second is a finger weaving executed by a North American Indian; and the third exemplar is a weaving made by an American artist well-known for her textile work.

A PERUVIAN ARTIST, ca. 1200–1450

Although the ancient Peruvian people lacked a form of true writing, their cultural level was extremely high, and their weaving was extraordinary. They spun the finest yarn in the world; they skillfully dyed their yarn in a wide range of colors; and they used almost every technique known to modern weavers in creating their fabrics.

Before the weaver could make his fabrics he had to prepare the fibers. To make them from cotton, he removed the lint and seeds, cleaned and carded the fiber, and with a distaff and spindle twisted the fibers into thread.[1] The Peruvian weaver also used wool for his fabrics. In fact, he used llama wool (which was coarse), alpaca wool (which was finer), or vicuna wool (which was very soft). Both the cotton and the wool were spun into threads of amazing fineness.

The cotton ranged in natural color from light tan to reddish-brown and gray, and the

---

[1]The distaff is a staff used for holding the cotton while spinning. A spindle is a round stick with tapered ends used to twist the yarn while spinning.

wools varied from white to yellow, brown, and black. The Peruvians used a variety of excellent dyes to extend the range of color. As many as 190 hues have been distinguished in their weavings. The numerous dyes were produced from three basic colors: red, yellow, and blue. Blue was obtained from the indigo plant; yellow came from the bark of the false pepper tree; and the principal source of red was the cochineal insect.

The example in Plate 20-1 is a woven doll of the Chancay style. The people of this culture were known for their magnificent textiles which exhibited a wide range of techniques and colors. Hand-dyed fibers were interlaced into stylized designs of sea birds, felines, and fish.

The doll in Plate 20-1 is thought to have come from a child's grave. It was common practice to bury the dead with their possessions. The doll represents a human figure. Rushes wound with yarn form a body shape over which clothing was fixed. The clothing was made from a piece of tapestry weave with a border along two ends. To make the fabric fit the doll shape better the weaver stitched the shoulder area. Another

Plate 20-1. Anonymous Peruvian artist. Woven Chancay doll. c. 1200-1450. Weaving, 11" high. Museum of Ethnology, Vienna, Austria. Collection Eckhardt, 1882.

piece of patterned fabric was stitched to the lower edge of the doll. A plaited cord was tied around the waist.

The fabric for the doll's head is also an example of the tapestry weave. Another technique, called slit tapestry, was used for weaving the eyes and mouth. When using this technique, the weaver did not interlock the weft threads in the lower face area with the weft threads of the mouth shape. Because the threads were not interlocked, a slit or opening was left. Weavers used this technique in small areas where they wanted to clearly define shapes. If used in larger areas, this method would tend to weaken the structure of the fabric. Instead of weaving the nose of the doll the artist used some embroidery stitches. Long strands of fiber used as hair were stitched to the top of the head.

A MENOMINEE INDIAN ARTIST, no date

The North American Indians, like those in South America, wove fabrics for blankets and articles of clothing. One of the Central Algonquin tribes belonging to the Woodland culture were the Menominees, who in precolonial days lived in a number of villages near the Menominee River in an area now called Wisconsin. The descendents of these early people still live in the northern part of that state.

The life of the early Menominee centered around fishing, gathering rice, and hunting. The male members of the village did the hunting and fishing. In addition, they made their weapons and traps for hunting, and the canoes and nets for fishing. While the men were involved in these tasks, the women gathered firewood; cooked the food; reared the children; planted and cared for the crops; and wove sashes, bags, and baskets.

The colors and designs of the Indian weavings changed over the years. Originally the women prepared their yarn and thread from vegetable fibers. The fibers were then colored with dyes made from vegetable and mineral sources. Apparently in the 1800s the Indians began to accept wool, ribbons, beads, and new color pigments from white traders. Along with the new materials, the older geometric designs of the weavings were replaced by floral designs.

Plate 20-2 is an example of an Indian belt or sash made with commercially prepared yarns.

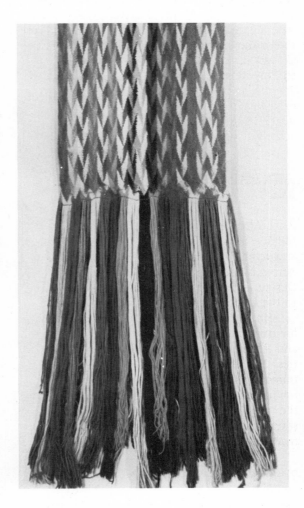

Plate 20-2. Anonymous. Menominee finger-woven yarn belt. n.d. Yarn, 100" x 16". © American Museum of Natural History, slide no. 2290.

This type of belt was worn around the waist by the Menominee women. The men of the tribe also wore sashes around the waist for decorative purposes or to keep their buckskin jackets closed. Occasionally the men wore the woven sashes over one shoulder or wound around their heads in a turban fashion.

The belts were woven by the women of the tribe using the finger braiding- or finger weaving-technique. No loom was required for this type of weaving; instead, the warp threads were fastened together at one end or were tied to a stick in parallel rows. In this technique the warp threads were taken in turn and used as the weft. For this colorful belt the weaver selected yarns of yellow, red, green, pink, brown, blue, orange, white, black, and purple to make the precise and orderly design.

ANNI ALBERS, 1899–

Anni Albers was born in Berlin, Germany. Her training began at an art school in Berlin in 1916, and later she attended the School of Applied Arts in Hamburg and the Bauhaus in Weimar and Dessau. In 1933, she and her husband Josef came to the United States.[2]

Since that time she has become well known for her textile work. She has presented lectures and seminars at various museums and universities. Her textile work has been exhibited in numerous museums. Furthermore, she is known for her books on the craft of weaving. In 1961, she received the gold medal of the American Institute of Architecture in the division of craftsmanship.

Plate 20-3, entitled Under Way, is an example of a weaving she describes as pictorial. Three col-

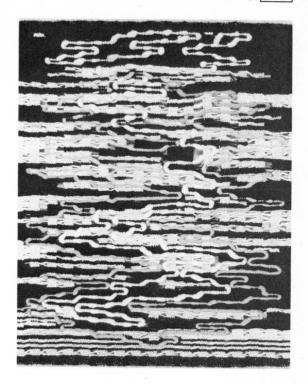

Plate 20-3. Anni Albers. Under Way. 1963. Weaving in black, white, and red; 21" x 17". Permission of Anni Albers (courtesy of The Joseph H. Hirshhorn Collection).

ors, off-white, red-orange, and black, are used to create the design. Thick and thin yarns of white and red-orange are contrasted with the fine black yarn. In warping the loom for this weaving, Albers used 17 groups of eight warp threads. Each group of eight has a space between it and the next group of warp threads. When placing the weft through the warp, an open weave was created. In contrast with the finger weaving (Plate 20-2), this weaving could be described as spontaneous, flowing, relaxed, and open. Red-orange and white strands of heavy yarn meander back and forth across the width of the work. The thinner weft threads of white and black also create a meandering pattern. In most areas of the work, the weft threads do not go completely across the weaving. Instead, some of the threads

---

[2]Josef Albers came to the United States to teach at Black Mountain College in North Carolina. He is a well-known artist who has spent many years studying the interaction of color.

are woven in sections which go a third of the way across and back. Other weft threads are woven back and forth across half the width of the weaving. The repetition of the irregular shapes creates a fluid, rhythmical pattern.

ADDITIONAL EXEMPLARS

Some artists who have designed cartoons for weaving are Arp, Braque, and Picasso.

WEAVING ACTIVITIES FOR THE PRIMARY GRADES (AGES 6 THROUGH 8)

As in the stitchery and appliqué procedures in the previous chapter, weaving activities give youngsters the opportunity to work with yarns and threads of varying colors and thicknesses. Through such activities children can develop a greater sensitivity to texture.

The activities do not need sophisticated equipment. Looms may be made of onion sacking, scrim, cardboard, soda straws, and paper. Looms may be warped with household string or carpet warp, while wool, cotton, and acrylic yarns and threads may be used for the weft. The ends of the weft threads may be stiffened with glue for weaving into the onion sacking or scrim.

Initial experiences with weaving should be simple enough so the children do not become frustrated with the process. Once the simple in and out process has been mastered the children can do some interesting things with the technique. They can also go on to master more difficult types of weaves.

CONCEPTS FOR POSSIBLE DEVELOPMENT

In the following procedures the weaving exemplars are used to help the children learn the following concepts:

cardboard loom	interlace	plain weave	texture
fibers	loom	repetition	warp
finger weaving	Menominee Indians	tabby weave	weft
hanging	Peruvian weaver		

SUGGESTED ACTIVITIES

Stitchery and weaving involve the in and out process: in stitchery and appliqué the threads are pulled in and out of a background fabric leaving designs on the cloth surface; in weaving the weft threads are pulled in and out of the warp threads to create a decorative piece of fabric.

1. Look at the Albers weaving (Plate 20-3) and talk about the different kinds of threads or fibers used by the artist. Explain that it was designed to hang on a wall. Tell the children that the Albers weaving was made on a loom. The loom she used was different from the ones they will be using. They will use looms of starched onion sacking or scrim. Fibers of varying thicknesses will be woven into the warp threads. A glue-impregnated end of a piece of yarn will assist in moving the thread in and out of the scrim or mesh. Or tapestry needles may be used. The yarns may be used to create an animal shape or a design similar to the Albers weaving. Parts of the fabric loom may be left open to create spaces like those found in the exemplar.

2. Show the exemplar illustrated in Plate 20-1 and talk about the simple animal shapes woven into the fabric dress of the Peruvian doll. Continue by discussing the patterns found on animals such as the zebra, giraffe, leopard, and tiger. Give the children some 12-x-18-inch paper and have them cut out an animal shape. The animals may be imaginary or realistic. When they have cut the shape out, have them take a marker and draw a margin of half an inch on the top edge of the paper. Fold the animal shape in half and cut strips into the folded edge stopping at the drawn margin. The cut strips become the warp threads of the loom. Various colored paper weft strips of differing widths may be woven into the animal shape. Have the children create a tabby weave by alternating weft strips. See Figure 20-1.

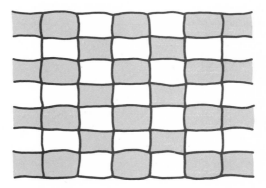

Figure 20-1.   Tabby weave.

3. When looking at the weaving entitled *Under Way*, explain that it is a nonrepresentational work of art. Albers used differing thicknesses and textures of yarn to make interesting shapes and colors in her weaving. Look at the various shapes that are repeated in the work. Point out the shapes made by the heavy yarn; show how these shapes repeat others in the work. Consider the textures used in the weaving.

For this experience, have the students construct a simple cardboard loom, which may be used for other weaving activities. Cut a piece of heavy cardboard a little larger than the size and shape desired for the completed weaving. Measure and draw a line across the top and bottom of the cardboard about half an inch from the edge. Cut an uneven number of slits from the edge to the line at intervals of approximately half an inch. With household string or carpet warp begin warping the loom by pulling one end of the string through the first slit on the top of the loom. Tape the end of the string to the back side of the loom. Continue warping by pulling the remaining string down the front side to the first slit at the bottom of the loom. Carry the thread behind the tab formed by the first and second slits. Then bring the thread to the front side of the loom through the second slit. Pull the thread up to the second slit at the top. Take the thread through the slit; around the back of the tab; and out to the front of the loom through the next slit. See Figure 20-2. Do not pull the warp thread too tightly or the cardboard will bend. Continue working in this manner until the warp has been threaded through the remaining slits. The end of the thread should be pulled through the last slit and taped to the back of the loom. Leave a fairly long end of string so that upon completion of the weaving and removal from the loom, the two ends of warp may be woven into the weaving. The loom is now ready for weaving.

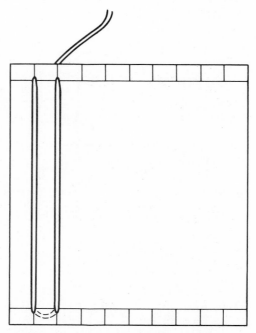

Figure 20-2.   Warping a cardboard loom.

When young children first experience the weaving process, the weft threads can be precut to approximately 2 inches wider than the loom. The precut threads may be arranged on the working surface in repeated rows of different colors. It is wise to have beginning weavers arrange alternate rows of two colors so all the threads of one color are woven into the warp in one way while all the weft threads of the second color are woven in another manner. The weft threads will form a fringe on either side of the woven piece and they may be stitched on the sewing machine if desired. See Figure 20-3 at the beginning of the chapter.

To begin weaving, demonstrate the following: 1) in the central portion of the loom pull a weft thread loosely under and over the warp threads; 2) use a comb or the fingers as a beater and push the thread to the top or bottom of the loom; 3) insert the next weft thread being sure to alternate it with the first; 4) beat this thread up to the first weft inserted in the loom; and 5) continue in this manner until the weaving is complete. To remove the weaving from the loom, loosen the threads taped to the back of the cardboard and slip the looped warp threads from around each tab.

4. After the children have mastered the plain or tabby weave, show them the Albers work (Plate 20-3) and talk about the use of different kinds of yarn to make interesting textural areas. Also talk about the ways a weaver can change the texture and pattern by making the weft threads go over and under differing numbers of warp threads. Using precut weft and the cardboard loom described in Activity 3, encourage the children to try different weaves such as the following: over one and under two, over two and under one, or over three and under two. The finished weaving may be used as a mat or slipped onto a wooden dowel rod for hanging.

5. Instead of using lengths of weft thread slightly longer than the loom width, longer strands of fiber may be used once the children have mastered the basic weave. See Figure 20-4. Using a cardboard loom, demonstrate the following. Insert the weft thread in the central portion of the loom. Be sure the end of the weft extends beyond the loom for about two inches. This end will be woven back into the weaving at a later time. Beat the weft thread up to the top or bottom edge of the loom. Make sure that the weft thread is loosely woven into the warp. Continue by weaving the weft thread in the opposite direction. If the first row ended by going *under* the last warp, the second row must begin with the weft thread going *over* the warp. By this procedure the weft is wrapped around the end warp thread. As the weaving continues, leave the weft fairly loose so the edges remain even. When ending one weft and adding a new one or another color weft, leave a short end of both yarn pieces at the edge. These ends are woven back into the warp and beat into the weaving. If

Figure 20-4.   Weaving with purple, yellow, and red yarn done by a fourth-grader.

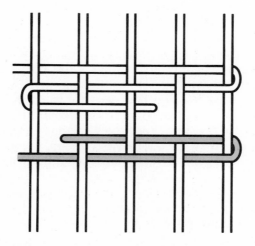

Figure 20-5.   Adding a new color.

a new color is to be added in the central portion of the weaving, overlap the two color threads for approximately 1½ inches. Then push the threads together. See Figure 20-5.

After the demonstration, show the children the Peruvian weaving in Plate 20-1. The weaver repeated cat shapes in the border to create a pattern. Give children pieces of manila paper the size of the cardboard loom and crayons or magic markers to draw simple shapes for their weaving. Geometric shapes, animals, houses, trees, flowers, or vehicles are but a few of the shapes that can be used. When ready, have them slip the paper beneath the warp threads of the loom so it may be used as a guide. If some children find this procedure too restrictive, allow them to change their ideas and experiment as they work with various colors and textures of yarn. Upon completion of the weaving, remove it from the loom. It may be hung by sliding a dowel rod through the upper row of warp loops. To add fringe, cut yarn or threads to twice the length desired. Fold the yarn in half and loop the pieces one by one over the warp loops. Pull the free ends of yarn through the loop to fasten it against the warp loop. See Figure 20-6.

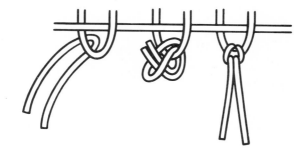

Figure 20-6. Adding fringe.

6. The belt in Plate 20-2 is a finger weaving. The process involved in making this belt required no loom; the weaver used the warp threads and interlaced them to form narrow bands. In place of the finger-weaving process, third graders can use drinking straws as a base for their weavings. Select three to six wide drinking straws. Cut a warp thread for each straw. Push the thread through each straw. After all the straws are threaded, tie one end of the warp threads in a knot. Push the straws up toward the knot. With a weft thread, weave over and under the straws. When they are almost completely covered with weaving, push the woven section up and off. To add new weft threads begin by leaving a tail of the weft on one side of the weaving and at a later time interlace the end back into the piece. When the desired length is reached, slip the straws off the warp. Then tie the warp threads together to finish the woven piece. As the children begin their straw weaving encourage them to repeat colors to make a patterned belt, band, or hanging.

WEAVING ACTIVITIES FOR THE INTERMEDIATE GRADES (AGES 9 THROUGH 11)

Many of the weaving experiences suggested for the primary grades are suitable for children in grades four through six. The materials needed for the activities do not differ greatly from those suggested earlier. Looms can be made of cardboard and wood while carpet warp or household string is needed for the warp threads. A variety of cotton, wool, or acrylic yarns can be used for the weft threads. Encourage the students to bring yarn scraps and threads from home. Yarn mills often sell spool ends to schools at a relatively inexpensive price. Other materials such as ribbon, laces, cutup plastic cleaning bags, straw, raffia, and natural objects such as dried grasses, seed pods, seashells, and branches may become the weft. These objects offer colors that are not found in commercially dyed yarns and threads.

Perhaps children in the fifth or sixth grade would be interested in dyeing their own yarns for weaving.[3] Dandelions, maple bark, onionskins, and black walnuts are only a few of the natural dyestuffs which offer interesting colors.

CONCEPTS FOR POSSIBLE DEVELOPMENT

Along with the concepts mentioned in the primary procedures, the ideas listed below should be developed in the following lessons:

back-strap loom	cartoon	open weave	shuttle
beater	Chancay	pattern	slit tapestry
blocking	dovetail	rhythm	stylized
box loom	interlock	shed	tapestry

SUGGESTED ACTIVITIES

The following procedures offer further explorations with texture and are written with the assumption that your students understand the weaving process. If they have had few or no experiences with the weaving art, it will be important to introduce some procedures suggested for the primary grades before going on to the following activities. Activity 1 is an appropriate lesson for an introduction to weaving.

---

[3] Information on dyeing yarns can be found on pages 24 to 31 in *Step-by-Step Weaving* by Nell Znemierowski or pages 268 to 289 in *Weaving: A Handbook for Fiber Craftsmen* by Shirley Held.

1. Examine the woven fabric in Plate 20-1. The technique used in this fabric is called the tapestry weave and was made on a back-strap loom. When weaving, an artist can make a patterned area first and then put in a background color. Later, colored areas can be woven together by interlocking or dovetailing weft threads. In the first method, weft threads interlock each other between two warp threads. See Figure 20-7.

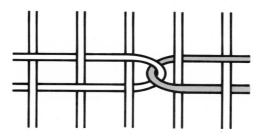

Figure 20-7.   Interlocking.

In the second method, the weft threads are carried around the same warp thread and then reversed. At the point where the threads are joined, a slight ridge will be formed. See Figure 20-8.

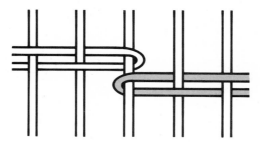

Figure 20-8.   Dovetailing.

For this activity have the children use a cardboard loom like the one suggested on page 358. Make sure they warp the loom with strong string or carpet warp. After discussing the Peruvian weaving and demonstrating the interlocking and dovetailing techniques ask the children to select paper slightly smaller than the size of their cardboard loom in order to work out a cartoon for their tapestry weaving.[4] While the children work on their cartoons remind them to

---

[4]A cartoon is a preliminary drawing used as a guide when weaving. It can be slipped beneath the warp threads of the cardboard loom.

repeat shapes which may form a band or border on one or both ends of their weaving. When the cartoons are ready, the children may begin their weaving. Upon completion, the weavings may be removed from the loom and fringe may be added. Then the piece can be transferred onto a dowel rod for hanging. If the weaving does not lay flat, it may be blocked by pinning it to a flat surface. The pins should be approximately two inches apart. Moisten the piece with warm water and let it dry slowly, keeping it away from sunlight and excess heat.

2. To make a more permanent loom, use four pieces of 1¾-x-¾-inch soft pine. Two pieces of equal length become the top and bottom of the loom and the remaining pieces of equal length become the sides. The side pieces may be longer, shorter, or of the same length as the loom top and bottom. The desired size of the weaving determines the length of the wood strips. Part of the wooden loom may be seen in Figure 20-9.

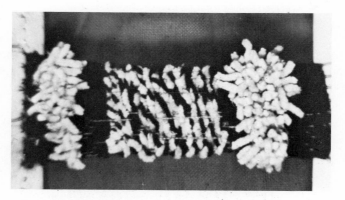

Figure 20-9. Wooden loom and weaving made by an intermediate grade student.

Lay the two side strips flat on a table surface or the floor. Place the wooden strip for the top of the loom over the side strips and hammer two nails in each corner. Do the same with the wood for the bottom of the loom. Then nail small brads into the top and bottom strips at equal intervals. See Figure 20-10, but do not use nails with heads as shown in the figure.

Warp the loom by tying the end of the thread to the first nail; bring the warp thread to the opposite end and carry it around the first two nails. The warp thread then goes back and forth across the length of the loom. It is wound around two nails each time and is finally tied to the last nail.

Once the warp is stretched on the loom, examine Plate 20-1. Have the children look at the woven head of the doll. Explain that the Peruvian weaver

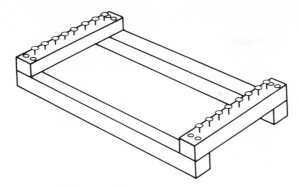

Figure 20-10.   Box loom.

used the slit tapestry technique to delineate the eye and mouth shapes. This technique allows for small openings which leave clean-cut edges between color shapes. The slits are created when the colored yarns used to weave adjoining areas do not interlock with each other, nor do they go around a common warp thread. See Figure 20-11.

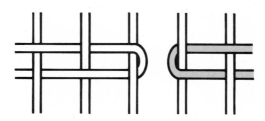

Figure 20-11.   Slit tapestry.

Demonstrate this technique. Then talk about one of the topics below:

A landscape   A self-portrait
Fish and fowl   My friend

Remind them to keep shapes fairly simple when weaving. Encourage the children to use the techniques of slit tapestry, dovetailing, and interlocking. A woven landscape can be seen in Figure 20-12.

If students are going to weave large areas of one color, they may make a cardboard shuttle to hold the yarn. The long piece of fiber is wrapped around the shuttle and then is inserted under and over the warp threads. Remind them to weave the weft threads loosely through the warp, and to use a comb or their fingers as a beater to push the weft threads together.

Figure 20-12. Landscape done in an art methods class.

3. An open weave similar to that found in the Albers work can be made by placing the brads or notches for the warp threads in an arrangement which is unevenly spaced. When showing the exemplar, point out the open areas in the weaving. Talk about the limited color scheme the artist used and point out areas where warp and weft threads of different colors form a new hue. Ask the children to use a limited color scheme (three colors) to make a woven hanging. Suggest that they warp their looms in an interesting and unusual arrangement. Ask the children to begin and end their weaving with a few rows of the tabby weave (see page 357). Rather than using a cartoon, encourage them to work out their designs as the weavings progress. Upon completion, remove the weavings from the looms; finish the edges; weave in ends; and place on dowel rods or sticks. If necessary, block the pieces before hanging.

4. An alternate to the above activity is to have children insert various nature objects such as those mentioned on page 362. See Figure 20-13.

5. A pillow, purse, or bag may be made from a fabric piece woven on a cardboard loom. This loom differs from the one described earlier in that the weft threads are woven completely around the piece of cardboard; the cardboard is removed when the weaving is completed. To make this loom, select heavy

Figure 20-13.   Weaving with feathers, brown
weeds, and grasses, along with
natural color threads.

cardboard the size and shape desired for the finished piece. Tape one edge of
the cardboard with masking tape. Insert heavy pins into this edge at equal intervals of ¼ inch or more. Allow the pins to project about ½ inch above the
cardboard edge. Tie an end of the warp thread to the first pin on one end.
Pull the thread down and around the bottom of the loom. Take the thread up
the back side and encircle the pin around which the warp thread is tied. Bring
the thread back around the bottom of the loom. Carry the thread up and
around the second pin. See Figure 20-14. Continue until all the remaining pins
have two loops over them. When reaching the last pin, carry the warp thread
down to the bottom of the loom and tie it to the end warp thread. There will
be warp threads on both sides of the cardboard. Begin weaving at the bottom
and carry the weft thread around the loom. This will create a woven piece
that is enclosed on the sides and the bottom. When finished, pull out the pins
and remove the cardboard. A pillow may be suffed with old stockings or foam
rubber scraps and the opening stitched with the chain or running stitch (see
pages 345 and 342). Or one of the woven bands described in the following procedures may form the handle for a purse or bag.

   Before the children begin their woven shapes ask them to examine the
Albers weaving (Plate 20-3) and the one made by the Chancay weaver (Plate
20-1). Point out the patterns made by the repetition of shapes and colors. En-

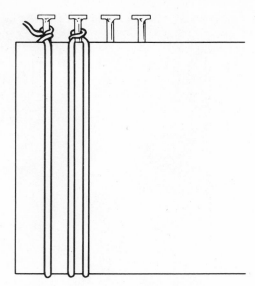

Figure 20-14. Threading the loom.

courage the students to repeat shapes and colors in their work. Remind them that the slit tapestry technique may not be the best method for this activity.

6. The process of weaving on straws (Activity 6 on page 361) can be used for making belts or handles for bags or purses. When weaving a handle for a bag or purse use warp threads of carpet warp or heavy wrapping string. Do not use a yarn fiber that will stretch or break.

7. Finger weaving is the process of interlacing warp threads together to form bands of varying designs. The North American Indians used this technique in creating belts and bands which were worn as part of their everyday dress. When looking at Plate 20-2 notice the pattern created by the repetition of one geometric shape.

For this experience have the children use two contrasting colors of a heavyweight yarn. For a short band cut 5 lengths of approximately 18 to 20 inches of each color. Arrange the warp threads on a flat surface by alternating the two colors; gathering together one end of the threads tie a knot close to the ends and attach the knot to the desk surface with a piece of masking tape. Because finger weaving is precise, the warp threads must be kept in the same order throughout the process.

To form the shed or the space between the upper and lower warp, take each thread of color A in order and hold it between the thumb and fingers of one hand. These threads form the upper warp while the threads of color B form the lower warp. Take the outside thread of color A on the right-hand side and pull it through the shed. Drop the color A threads and change the shed by picking up all the threads of color B between the thumb and finger of one hand. See Figure 20-15. Be sure to pick up the threads in order. The warp thread, which has just been woven through the shed, now takes its place as the last thread in the lower warp. Pick up the upper warp thread on the right and pull it through the shed. The weaving is continued in this manner. The woven band will have repeated stripes in a diagonal pattern.[5] This band may be stitched to the bag or purse in Activity 5.

Figure 20-15.   Changing a shed.

8. Once the finger-weaving process is mastered, the students can make longer bands or belts. The length of yarns needed for a belt is approximately 2½ yards. Wider belts or bands may be made by stitching two or more completed bands to ether using the running or chain stitch (see pages 342 and 345). Bands or belts can also be made of a solid color.

---

[5]If the weaving moves from left to right, the diagonal stripe will slant in the opposite direction.

CHAPTER 21

PHOTOGRAPHY

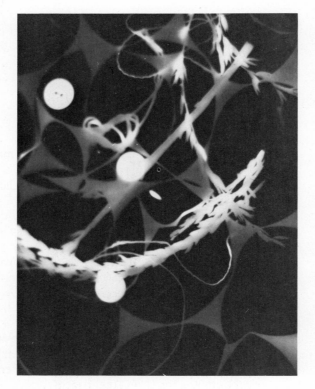

Figure 21-8. Photogram made by a fifth-grader.

Photography, the newest art form represented in this section, relies on the elements of chemistry and light, and it depends upon a light-sensitive paper or film, a light source, and the chemical to develop and fix the image. It is not necessary to have a camera to produce photographic images. In the nineteenth century Delacroix, Corot,

Rousseau, and Millet used the technique of cliches-verres to express their ideas. To do this, the men drew on glass with oil paint; placed photographic paper under the finished drawing; and exposed the glass and paper to sunlight.

Another method of making photographs without a camera was discovered in 1839 by Fox Talbot. The process called a "photogenic drawing" by Talbot was later called a photogram. A photogram was made by placing objects on light-sensitive paper and exposing both of them to a light source. Opaque objects blocked out the light, leaving the paper white; areas which were uncovered were flooded with light and turned black; and transparent objects and shadows of objects became gray.

Although it was possible to take photographs in a studio with a camera obscuro, it was not until 1888 that hand cameras were available for purchase. This type of camera held a roll of film which was coated with light-sensitive silver salts. In the 1920s, small cameras with wide aperture lenses made it possible to take angle shots and to distort images.

EXEMPLARS OF PHOTOGRAPHY

Two of the three works in this chapter are examples of photography without a camera. Both processes are possible to do with children. A photograph made with a camera is also included.

JEAN-BAPTISTE CAMILLE COROT, 1796–1875

Chapter 5 stated that Corot was one of the most notable French landscape painters of the nineteenth century. Less known, but just as important are his drawings, engravings, and cliches-verres.

Corot was intent upon improving his technique and he accomplished this by drawing every evening. In addition to working when the evening mists began to gather, he also liked to work in his studio at Vill-d'Avray early in the morning. At that time of day the mist had not yet been dissipated by the sun. This environment was reflected in his work in the form of silvery light, delicate trees, and misty fields.

He became interested in cliches-verres through his friend Constand Dutilleux, a lithographer. This technique interested Corot in particular, because it allowed him to combine drawing and photography. Although cliches-verres only permitted the making of two or three proofs, he often used this method.

Corot produced cliches-verres in two different ways. Sometimes he painted a scene with oils on a piece of glass and then exposed it and light-sensitive paper to a light source. At other times, he coated a glass plate with printer's ink using a lithographic roller. Powdered talc was sprinkled over the ink to hasten drying; then he drew on the plate with an engraver's needle. When the drawing was finished, he exposed the glass plate and sensitized paper to sunlight. Occasionally, before exposing the plate, he inserted a plate of clear glass between the drawn-on plate and the paper in order to soften the effect.

Corot repeated his subject matter in paintings, drawings, engravings, and cliches-verres. Plate 21-1 is a cliches-verres made about 1858. It is entitled Le Petit Berger ("The Little Shepherd") and is similar to paintings of the same title made by Corot in 1840 and 1850. The works vary in size and there is much less detail in the photograph. In plate 21-1 he was able to concentrate on form and value.

In making this photograph, Corot began by covering the glass plate with ink or paint. Then he scratched out the ground area, trees, leaves,

Plate 21-1. Jean-Baptiste Camille Corot. *Le Petit Berger.* c. 1858. Clichés-verres. The Metropolitan Museum of Art (Mortimer Schiff Fund), 1922.

and the shepherd. Notice how the cross-hatched lines are easy to see in the light area in the foreground. To create the gray areas, Corot used many cross-hatched lines and in the darkest areas the lines are massed together to form shapes. When you consider Corot's method of drawing (see pages 95 to 96), how do you think he went about this work? Where did he establish light and dark areas? Remember that he was taking ink away from a glass plate so the area that was printed white in the photograph was really black on the plate. The black areas on the clichés-

verres were white or scratched out on the glass plate.

Compare this work with Plate 5-1. How do the style and content differ? In what ways can you tell these two works were made by the same artist?

LÁSZLÓ MOHOLY-NAGY, 1895–1946

László Moholy-Nagy, who began his career as a painter, became interested in the effects of light in motion in the 1920s. This interest prompted him to make many cameraless photographs he called photograms. He considered the photogram to be important to the art of photography because both possess the extremes of black and white along with the in-between grays.

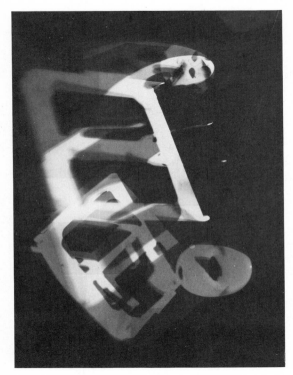

Plate 21-2.   László Moholy-Nagy. *Photogram.* 1929. Shadowgraph, 1 1¾" x 9⅜". Collection, The Museum of Modern Art. Gift of James Johnson Sweeney.

When in 1923 Moholy-Nagy was appointed to the faculty of the Bauhaus, he continued his experiments with photographs. He also worked on ballet and stage designs, typography, layouts, and murals. In 1928, he left the Bauhaus and went to Berlin to design stage sets. Following this, he was a commercial designer in Holland and England until 1937, when he came to the United States to become the Director of the "New Bauhaus" or Institute of Design in Chicago, Illinois. Among the books he wrote, *Vision in Motion* is perhaps his most important writing. It is a summary of his educational philosophy and the foundation for the program of studies of the Institute of Design.

The process of making a photogram is simple. Objects which have unusual shapes, are three-dimensional, or are transparent, translucent, or opaque make interesting photographic compositions. Working in a light-safe room, the objects are placed on the emulsion-covered surface of light-sensitive paper.[1] When the paper and objects are exposed to light the opaque object blocks out the light leaving a white image on the paper. The areas which are not covered by objects are exposed and become black. Shadows of objects as well as transparent and translucent objects become gray. After one or many exposures, the print is developed.

Keeping this procedure in mind, look at the photogram in Plate 21-2. Moholy-Nagy exposed the paper a number of times before developing the images.[2] Before each exposure to light, he rearranged the objects on the paper to create overlapping shapes that give an illusion of depth or movement. The repetition of objects in varying tones of gray gives the feeling of shapes tumbling through a black space. The black area surrounding the objects was created by an exposure to the light source. Some of the objects have crisp edges, while others have fuzzy or blurred borders. How many of these can you find? Notice the variations of gray. Can you see why Moholy-Nagy felt photograms were an important process in the art of photography?

---

[1]Generally, a light-safe room (darkroom) is lighted by a 25-watt ruby bulb. This light will not affect the photographic paper. A regular light bulb can be switched on and off to expose the paper.

[2]When exposing the paper to a light source more than once, some or all of the objects may be moved on the paper to create other images.

DOROTHEA LANGE, 1895-1965

At the age of twenty, while attending the New York Training School for Teachers, Dorothea Lange decided to become a photographer. Arnold Genthe, a photographer, who gave her her first camera and critiqued her first photographs, encouraged this decision. Two years later, she enrolled in a course in basic photography at Columbia University. Upon completion of the course, she set out with a friend to work her way around the world as a photographer. They got as far as San Francisco where she made her home.

Lange worked as a portrait photographer until 1932, at which time she realized the portraits photographed in her studio were not revealing real people. In order to capture their reality she decided to photograph people within the context of their everyday activities.

The people she photographed were not well known, nor were they necessarily good-looking. She rarely had her subjects pose, but preferred to capture fleeting segments of everyday gestures. In Plate 21-3, a common gesture has been stopped by her camera. The title of the photograph simply describes a man stepping from a cable car. We often go through similar motions, or see others doing the same things. What was so extraordinary about this scene that interested Dorothea Lange? Was it the man? The bag he was carrying? Probably, it was all of these everyday, ordinary things that interested her.

A photograph, like any work of art, should be looked at, thought about, and studied. In looking at Plate 21-3, we find the man interesting because he is anonymous. We begin to wonder who he is, where he is going, what he is carrying, how old he is, and where he lives. In addition to the man being anonymous, the street is unknown. Where do you think this street is? Can you tell the time of day or season of the year?

Compositionally, the work is a combination of lines and shapes ranging from white to intense black. The gray pavement, which varies from a

Plate 21-3.   Dorothea Lange. *Man Stepping from Cable Car, San Francisco.* 1956. Photograph. Dorothea Lange Collection, The Oakland Museum.

dark gray to a light gray, is balanced by the dark figure in the upper left-hand corner. The gray edge of the step and the horizontal white lines of the street keep our eyes focused on the man. Upon closer inspection there are a number of triangular and curved shapes repeated throughout the photograph.

Some of her photographs, such as *White Angel Breadline, San Francisco* taken in 1933, or *Migrant Mother* photographed in 1936, have become famous. Her interest in photographing the common man inspired John Steinbeck to write his novel, *Grapes of Wrath.* Lange's photographs of migrant labor in California, along with the social analysis of the situation by Paul Taylor, resulted in building camps for the migrants by that state. Furthermore, she was awarded a Guggenheim Fellowship in 1941 to do a photographic study of the American social scene.

ADDITIONAL EXEMPLARS

Additional exemplars of photography as an art can be found in the work of Ansel Adams, Alfred Stieglitz, Henri Cartier-Bresson, Man Ray, and Thomas Eakins.

PHOTOGRAPHY ACTIVITIES FOR THE PRIMARY GRADES (AGES 6 THROUGH 8)

It is not necessary to have cameras or expensive equipment to share the wonders of photography with children. Only one of the six activities suggested for the primary grades requires the use of a camera, and one activity requires a chemical solution to fix the image.

The materials suggested for the following activities are: index cards, crayons, oil pastels, clear acetate, permanent felt-tipped markers, enamel paint, paper, cameras, black-and-white film, light-sensitive photographic paper, and fixer. A variety of objects that are transparent, translucent, and opaque will be needed for a few of the experiences.

CONCEPTS FOR POSSIBLE DEVELOPMENT

The concepts listed below can be introduced when talking about the photography exemplars:

action shots	light-sensitive paper	subject
aperture	opaque	texture
clichés-verres	pattern	transparent
exposure	posed shots	viewfinder
fixer	printing-out paper	winder
lens	shutter	

SUGGESTED ACTIVITIES

The following activities may be carried out in the classroom or outdoors:

1. Look at the photograph in Plate 21-3. Ask such questions as, "Who is this man?" "Where is he going?" "What is he carrying?" "How old is he?" "Where does he live?" Notice the lines, shapes, and colors found in the photograph.

Following this discussion, have the children look through a 1-inch square cut into a 3-x-5-inch index card. Tell them to pretend their index card is a camera and the hole they look through is the lens. Ask them to look around the classroom, down the hallway, or out the window to focus on some interesting subject. Other subjects can be found outdoors. Have the children use felt-tipped markers, crayons, or oil pastels and paper to draw one of the views seen through the hole.

2. Youngsters are fascinated when their drawings are enlarged and projected onto a wall or movie screen. Black and white or colored drawings may be made on clear acetate with permanent felt-tipped markers. Give each child a piece of transparent acetate the size of the glass on an overhead projector. Tape a piece of paper the same size to one edge of the acetate. The paper is not drawn on, but acts as a background when working on the acetate. Because it is only taped on one edge, the paper may be folded back when the drawing is placed on the overhead projector.

Show the exemplar in Plate 21-3 and discuss the questions suggested in Activity 1. Continue discussing one of the topics below:

Crossing the street   Going to school   Walking along

Following the discussion ask the children to draw on the piece of acetate. Allow time for sharing the drawings by projecting them on the wall or screen.

3. A sun print may be made with printing-out paper and a chemical fixer. The process is as follows. Place the shiny or light-sensitive side of the printing-out paper (Kodak Studio Proof F) up on a counter, table, or windowsill. Make sure that the sun's rays will focus on the paper. If possible, block out the sunlight from the paper while arranging the objects. In the event the children will be working in a sunlit room or outdoors, they will have to work quickly because the paper begins developing as soon as it is exposed.

Arrange transparent and opaque objects on the paper. As it is exposed to light the uncovered areas will turn purple while the covered ones will remain white. In bright sunlight the print will develop in five to ten minutes. But in less sunlight it may take up to thirty minutes for the paper to become deep purple in color. While the paper is developing, it is possible to shift some objects or add others to create gray areas or fuzzy edges.

When the paper is dark purple in color, remove the objects and set the print into a tray that holds the fixer. The fixer is mixed in advance by dissolving five rounded tablespoons of sodium thiosulfate crystals in 32 ounces of cool water.[3] The print should remain in this solution for ten minutes. During that time the dark purple areas will change to a brown color. After a period of ten minutes take a pair of tongs and lift the print out of the fixer. Gently shake any excess solution into the tray. When more than one print is in the tray, lift each paper out separately.

---

[3]These can be purchased at any photo supply store.

Place the print into a water bath for one hour. The rinse can be a dishpan of cool water which is changed five or six times during the hour. If a sink is available, place the pan in the sink. To circulate the water, place a glass tumbler or jar upside down under the faucet. The water will run over into the sink. If a number of prints are being rinsed at the same time, move them periodically so they will not stick together. After an hour remove the print from the bath and blot it with paper toweling.

Before the children begin their sun prints, examine Plate 21-2. Notice and identify the shapes that were repeated. Look at the various tones. Then ask the children to try to capture some of the same things in their prints.

4. When examining the exemplar by Corot (Plate 21-1) with third graders tell them he used the process called clichés-verres. Look at the way in which the trees, leaves, rocks, grass, and shepherd have been drawn with a series of repeated lines. Examine the directions of the lines. Find areas where few lines have been drawn. Talk about the difference in grays between the two areas. Notice where the tree branches are placed in front of the rocks. How did the artist make the branches stand out? After this discussion select one of the topics below:

A helper in our town   Playing   Me and my pet
My room   A trip   My favorite place

Give each child a 7-inch square piece of sprayed acetate and a scratching tool.[4] Dressmaker pins, pen points, a long nail, or a nail file can be used to remove the dried paint. Have the children scratch out their story on the acetate surface. Encourage them to create different dark and light areas by scratching few or many lines. Upon completion, their drawings may be projected onto a wall by placing the acetate on an overhead projector.

5. It is possible to purchase small inexpensive cameras children can operate with little difficulty.[5] Before using a camera they should become familiar with its various parts. When holding the camera up to the eye the photographer looks through a viewfinder to aim the camera. When he wants to catch the image he sees on film, he presses the shutter. The shutter is a mechanical device which opens and closes the aperture or opening in the camera lens. When the aperture is open, light enters the camera and is directed onto the film. The film is moved to the next exposure by the winding mechanism.

In showing the photograph in Plate 21-3, explain that Dorothea Lange used her camera to capture people doing everyday things. For her, it was not always necessary to capture the specific features of a person. What was important was to stop action on a gesture. This candid shot of a man stepping from the step

[4]Spray one side of the acetate with enamel paint.
[5]Inexpensive cameras can be purchased from Workshop for Learning Things, Inc., 5 Bridge Street, Watertown, MA, 02172.

is an action shot because the subject was in motion when the picture was taken. He did not pose for the photograph.

Some possible topics for photo discoveries are listed below:

a) My family and friends. Suggest to the children that they capture candid or posed shots of their family and friends. Encourage the students to photograph typical work or play activities.

b) Animals. Posed and candid shots of dogs, cats, fish, butterflies, and other animals can help children become more observant of their animal friends.

c) Patterns. A series of photographs can be taken of interesting patterns.

d) Textures. The children may be asked to make a series of photographs of different textures.

PHOTOGRAPHY ACTIVITIES FOR THE INTERMEDIATE GRADES (AGES 9 THROUGH 11)

As previously stated, expensive and sophisticated equipment is not needed for photography activities. Materials suggested for the following procedures include clear and colored acetate, enamel paint, window glass, shoe boxes, construction paper, metal foil, black paint, brushes, pins or nails, permanent felt-tipped markers, contact paper, developer, stop bath, fixer, plastic or glass containers, trays, and tongs. Equipment suggested for the activities include cameras and slide projectors.

Only a few of the procedures require a light-safe room and it is possible to turn a regular classroom into a makeshift darkroom by blocking out all light from windows and doorways with dark shades or dark material. Or brown Kraft paper may be taped over windows and doorways to make the room dark. In the darkened room, a safe light source (25-watt red or 60-watt yellow) must be kept on at all times. Depending upon the size of the room, it may be necessary to have more than one safe light. The ceiling lights can be used to expose the photographic paper.

A portable darkroom can be constructed from two refrigerator boxes of the same size.[6] Setting Box A in a horizontal position, remove one of the small ends (1) (see Figure 21-1). Set the box upright so the cutaway end is on the bottom. Then measure 2 inches down from the top on one side and cut the remainder away (2) This is the upper half of the darkroom and needs two holes cut in the top of the box (3) Each hole must be large enough for a cord from a light socket to slip through. One socket is used for a safe light (25-watt) while the second is needed for a 60-watt white bulb. After inserting the sockets, use duct tape or black electrical tape to block out any space around the holes which permit light to come into the box.

---

[6]Darkroom designed and constructed by Josephine Richardson, Art Department, Ball State University.

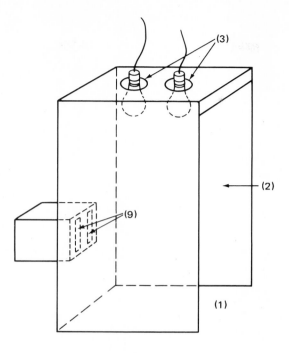

Figure 21-1. Box A—top of darkroom.

To complete the top of the darkroom, two cardboard boxes, one slightly smaller than the other, are taped to the outside of Box A to form an air and light baffle. Taking the smaller one, Box B, measure 3 inches from the bottom on one side and cut a slit (4) (see Figure 21-2).

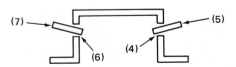

Figure 21-2. Cross section of Box B.

Insert a piece of cardboard at an angle into the slit (5). Cut a slit on the opposite side (6) and insert a cardboard piece (7). Open out the flaps on the top of Box B and tape them to the side of Box A (see Figure 21-3) opposite the cutaway side (8).

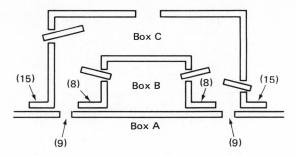

Figure 21-3.   Cross section of Boxes A, B, and C.

Next, measure and cut a 1-inch-wide slit on Box A (9) on either side of the flaps from Box B. These slits allow the air to flow into the darkroom. See Figure 21-3.

On the bottom of Box C (see Figure 21-4), cut a 2- or 3-inch square in the center (10). Then cut a slit on one side about 4 inches from the bottom of the box (11). Insert a piece of cardboard into the slit at an angle. Make sure the cardboard piece projects into the box (12). On the opposite side of Box C, near the box opening, cut another slit and insert a piece of cardboard (13 and 14).

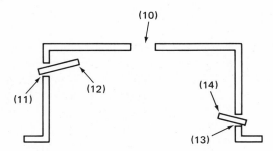

Figure 21-4.   Cross section of Box C.

Then open the flaps on the box top and carefully place Box C over Box B (see Figure 21-3). Tape the flaps to the refrigerator box with duct tape (15).

Next, set Box D in a horizontal position and remove one of the small ends (16). Set the box in an upright position so the cutaway end is at the top (see Figure 21-5). Then measure a 2-inch margin on the top and bottom of one of the sides. Cut away the side leaving the margins (17).

The bottom half of the darkroom will be complete when an air and light baffle has been made from three boxes. First, on the side opposite the cutaway portion, cut a 2-inch square at about eye level (18). Take Box E (see Figure 21-6) and cut the flaps off one end (19). Then take Box G and cut the flaps off both ends

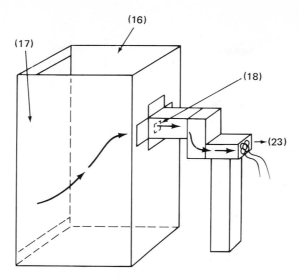

Figure 21-5.   Box D—bottom of darkroom.

(20). Near the top on one side of Box F, cut a hole large enough for the open end of Box E to slide into (21). On the opposite side of Box F, cut a hole large enough for Box G to slide into (22).

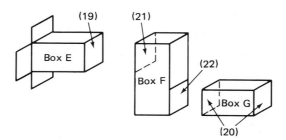

Figure 21-6.   Boxes E, F, and G.

Following this, slide E into F and tape the boxes together. Slide G into F and tape (see Figure 21-5). Open the flaps on Box E, center the baffle over the hole (18), and tape it to the outside of Box D. A support for the baffle may be made from the excess cardboard. In order to circulate the air, place a small electric fan in the opening of Box G (23). Have the fan face out so the air is pulled through the box.

Finally, Box A is lifted up and fitted over Box D. Tape any holes which allow light in the box. Lift up to remove Box A and place a small table inside for a working surface. A holder for the trays of developer, stop bath, and fixer may stand on the table (see Figure 21-7). The darkroom is now ready for use. Each time a student goes into the darkroom, another student must lift up Box A and place it back down on Box D.

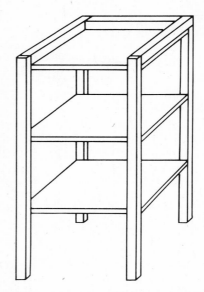

Figure 21-7. Holder for chemical trays.

CONCEPTS FOR POSSIBLE DEVELOPMENT

Along with the concepts mentioned in the primary section, the following ideas should be introduced with the photography exemplars:

angle shot	developer	photogram
camera obscura	distorted image	photographic painting
candid	double exposure	pin-hole camera
contact paper	emulsion-covered surface	still shot
cross-hatch	light-proof box	stop bath
darkroom	light-safe room	translucent

SUGGESTED ACTIVITIES

All of the photography activities suggested for the primary students are suitable for children in grades four through six. It may be helpful to review the procedures in the primary section before presenting the following:

1. Light-sensitive paper can be painted with chemicals to produce photographic paintings. In place of paint, chemical developer is brushed or drawn on the contact paper. The developer should be mixed according to the instructions on the container. If gray tones are desired, dilute the developer with water (1 part developer to various parts of water). Then pour the developer into watercolor pans or small glass jars for the students. An assortment of pens, brushes, and cotton swabs can be used to apply the developer to the paper. One tray filled with stop bath and one containing fixer can be readied before the students begin working (see Activity 2, page 376). Because the paper is exposed to light as the children work, it is advisable to turn off the overhead lights. Suggest that the students begin drawing or painting in one corner of the paper and work toward the center. As the developer is applied to the emulsion-covered surface or the shiny side of the paper, it will begin to darken. When the desired darkness is achieved, dip the corner which has been drawn on into the stop bath. This will stop the solution from developing any further. Remind youngsters to submerge only the corner of the paper which has been drawn upon. Removing the paper from the stop bath, another corner may be worked on. Continue the process until the drawing is complete. Then set the entire sheet in the tray with stop bath for a period of five seconds. Remove the print with tongs, let it drip by holding one corner, and then place it into a tray with fixer for a period of ten minutes. Following this, the print should be rinsed in clear water for one hour, removed, blotted, and laid flat to dry.

   Before the students are given the photographic contact paper, look at the images found in Plates 21-2 and 21-3. Point out tones, shapes, patterns, and textures found in each work. Although their photographic paintings may look more like the Moholy-Nagy photogram it is possible to paint subject matter such as that found in the photograph by Lange.

2. It will be necessary to have a light-safe room for the making of photograms (see pages 378–382). Other necessities such as contact paper, developer, stop bath, and fixer can be purchased from a photo supply store. Kodak Dektol is purchased in powder form and should be mixed according to the directions found on the package. The solution can be mixed in a plastic gallon container and stored in a darkened place. Never pour a used solution into a fresh supply of developer. The second chemical, stop bath, is acetic acid, which comes in a liquid concentrate form and is diluted with water. A small amount of stop bath may be mixed when needed. This solution stops the action of the developer. The last chemical, fixer, dissolves the unexposed emulsion on the paper and should be mixed according to the directions on the package. As with the developer, this solution is stored in a plastic or glass container. Be sure to label the contents of each bottle because the developer and fixer look alike. Also mark the trays that hold the three solutions. Number the trays in the order in which they are used: 1) developer; 2) stop bath; and 3) fixer. Two pair of tongs can be used to handle the prints. One pair can transfer the paper from the developer to the stop bath; a second pair can remove the print from the stop bath and place it in the fixer.

Look at the exemplar in Plate 21-2. Examine the arrangement of shapes, tones, and textures. Ask the students to find places where objects have been moved to create a double exposure. Demonstrate the following process in a light-safe room. Turn off all light sources except the safe light or lights. Take one sheet of contact paper from the package and close the package tightly. With the emulsion surface or shiny side up, arrange objects on the paper surface. When the objects are satisfactorily arranged, turn on the light source. The paper may be exposed to the light from two to eight seconds depending upon the desired degree of darkness. If gray areas, fuzzy edges, or double exposures are desired, shift the objects and expose the paper again.

After completing the exposure or exposures, place the paper (emulsion side up) into the developer. The images will soon appear on the paper. Holding the corner of the paper with the tongs, gently agitate it so the solution washes over it. After approximately 90 seconds, pull the print from the developer. Holding it above the developer, allow the excess solution to drip into the tray. Place the paper into the stop bath for 30 seconds. Remove the print with the second pair of tongs, letting the excess solution drip into the tray. Slip the photogram into the tray with fixer for approximately 10 minutes. The print is then washed in cool water for an hour. It is safe to turn the classroom lights on during this period. If many prints are rinsed at the same time, they should be moved frequently to prevent sticking. See Figure 21-8, at the beginning of the chapter.

In the event that a portable darkroom or a small room is used for the making of photograms, you can describe the process to the students. Some visual aids, with the necessary information on them, may be placed in the darkroom.

3. Although a darkroom or light-safe room is needed to make a clichés-verres print, part of the process may be done in room light. For an explanation of a clichés-verres, see page 371.

For the first part of this exercise refer to Activity 4 on page 377. In place of the topics mentioned in that primary activity, select one of the following for a discussion:

Water images	Self-portrait	Insects
The school yard	Birds and other fliers	

Using pieces of sprayed acetate and nails, pins, or sharp tools, the students may scratch out their pictures. Encourage the use of cross-hatching to create textured areas. After the drawing is complete, the acetate and a piece of contact paper are exposed to a light source. This step must be done in a light-safe room. The emulsion surface of the paper is placed face up on the table. Gently lay the acetate over the paper. Expose both acetate and paper to the light source for a few seconds. To process the print, follow the procedures described in the previous activity.

4. Another kind of clichés-verres may be made by brushing images onto a glass, plexiglass, or acetate surface with opaque paint. The areas painted in will produce white images on the paper, while any unpainted sections will become black in color.

5. A form of the camera obscura or a lightproof box can be constructed from a shoe box, metal foil, black photographic tape, pins, black tempera paint, and a knife. In addition, photographic contact paper is needed and a darkroom with trays of developer, stop bath, and fixer must be set up. To make the pin hole camera, paint the inside of the box with black paint. After the paint dries, cut a small square from one end of the box; tape a piece of metal foil over the hole; then take a pin and poke a hole through the center of the foil. Cover the hole with a small piece of black tape. Take the box into a darkroom and tape a piece of contact paper to the inside of the box opposite the pin hole. Be sure to have the shiny side of the paper facing the hole. If distorted images are desired, tape the paper to three sides of the box. Place the lid on the box and seal it thoroughly with black tape. The camera is now loaded and ready. Ask the children to find an object that has an interesting pattern or texture. Place the subject so that it faces the side of the box with the pin hole. Gently lift the tape to expose the paper inside. Approximately 30 seconds of sunlight should be enough to expose the paper. Next, return to the darkroom and remove the paper from the camera. Print the paper by following the procedures described in Activity 2.

6. Instead of a pin-hole camera, small inexpensive cameras are suggested for this procedure.[7] In presenting this lesson, review the information on the parts of the camera found in Activity 5 on page 377. Examine the photograph taken by Lange, explaining that this work is an example of a candid rather than a posed shot and it exemplifies an action shot rather than a still shot. Consider the angle from which the picture was taken and discuss how objects look different when the point of view is changed. Mention that the objects in the photograph look clear because they were in focus. Continue the discussion by suggesting one of the following for a photo essay.

a) A bug's world. Have the children shoot pictures from a bug's point of view.

b) The neighborhood. Talk about the people and places making up the community in which they live. Suggest that they take candid and posed shots as well as action and still shots.

c) Points of view. Encourage the children to take a roll of film of one object (bicycle, doorway, lamp, shoe, and the like) and have them photograph the item from many points of view.

d) An emotion. Ask the children to take a series of photographs which show happiness, sadness, anger, love, or fear.

---

[7]See footnote 5 on page 377 for sources for inexpensive cameras.

7. Enlarged and projected images can be made by placing small things inside a square pocket of acetate and putting it in a slide projector. Because the contents of the acetate pocket are enlarged, tiny objects may be observed closely.

Before making slides, spend time talking about the transparent and opaque areas in the photogram of Moholy-Nagy. In the event children made photograms, discuss the opaque and transparent areas in their works. Then encourage them to find things which are small, flat, transparent, translucent, and opaque which can be put into a slide pocket.

Show the children how to make a slide by taking a piece of clear acetate that measures 1⅛ inches by 3¾ inches. Fold the acetate in half (lengthwise) and tape up two of the sides. The third side will be taped after things have been placed into the clear pocket. Then the sealed square is inserted into a slide projector and the images are shown.

Things which make interesting slides are bits of tissue paper, cellophane, and colored acetate; spices such as pepper, salt, curry powder, and celery salt; sequins and beads; sewing thread and strings; paper clips and staples; rubber cement, cooking oil, and drops of food coloring; and crumpled plastic. The acetate pocket may also be drawn on with permanent felt-tipped markers. See Figures 21-9 and 21-10.

Figure 21-9. Slide of tissue acetate and netting made in art methods class.

8. Another way to make slides is to use a two-inch square piece of acetate that has been sprayed on one side with enamel paint. After the paint dries the acetate may be inserted into slide mounts which are purchased at a photo supply store. Using pins, needles, and other sharp tools a picture may be etched on the painted side of the acetate.

Before the children begin their slides, look at Plate 21-1. Examine the directions of lines created by Corot as he etched the paint away from the glass surface. Consider the way the artist created texture. Ask them to create texture areas in their slides. Because the slide surface is small, this activity requires patience and the ability to work on a small surface.

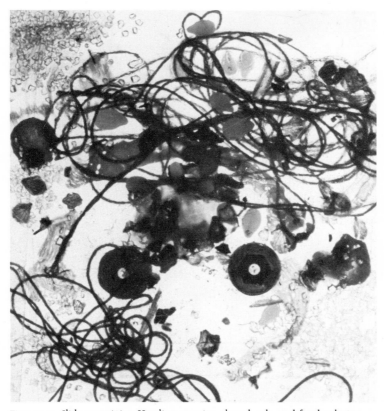

Figure 21-10. Slide containing Vaseline, sequins, thread, salt, and food coloring.

BIBLIOGRAPHY *Chapter 1*

Chapman, Laura H. *Approaches to Art in Education*. New York: Harcourt Brace Jovanovich, Inc., 1978.

Churchill, Angiola R. *Art for Preadolescents*. New York: McGraw-Hill Book Co., Inc., 1971.

Eisner, Elliot W. *Educating Artistic Vision*. New York: The Macmillan Co., 1972.

Eisner, Elliot W., and Ecker, David. *Readings in Art Education*. Waltham, MA: Blaisdell Publishing Co., 1966.

Feldman, Edmund. *Becoming Human through Art*. Englewood Cliffs, NJ: Prentice-Hall, Inc., 1970.

Gaitskell, Charles D., and Hurwitz, Al. *Children and Their Art*. New York: Harcourt Brace Jovanovich, Inc., 1975.

Greenberg, Pearl. *Children's Experiences in Art*. New York: Reinhold Publishing Corporation, 1966.

Hubbard, Guy, and Rouse, Mary. *Art 1–6: Meaning, Method and Media*. 6 Vols. Westchester, IL: Benefic Press, 1973.

Hurwitz, Al, and Madeja, Stanley. *The Joyous Vision: Art Appreciation for the Elementary School*. New York: Van Nostrand Reinhold, Inc., 1976.

Lansing, Kenneth M. *Art, Artists, and Art Education*. Dubuque, IA: Kendall-Hunt Publishing Co., 1976.

Lark-Horovitz, Betty; Lewis, Hilda Present; and Luca, Mark. *Understanding Children's Art for Better Teaching*. Columbus, OH: Charles E. Merrill Publishing Co., 1973.

Linderman, Earl W., and Herberholz, Donald W. *Developing Artistic and Perceptual Awareness*. Dubuque, IA: William C. Brown Co., 1974.

Linderman, Marlene M. *Art in the Elementary School: Drawing and Painting for the Classroom*. Dubuque, IA: William C. Brown Co., 1974.

Lowenfeld, Viktor, and Brittain, Lambert W. *Creative and Mental Growth*, 5th ed. New York: The Macmillan Co., 1970.

McFee, June King. *Preparation for Art*. Belmont, CA: Wadsworth Publishing Co., 1970.

McFee June King, and Degge, Rogena M. *Art, Culture, and Environment: A Catalyst for Teaching*. Belmont, CA: Wadsworth Publishing Co., 1977.

Montgomery, Chandler. *Art for Teachers of Children*. Columbus, OH: Charles E. Merrill Publishing Co., 1968.

Pappas, George. *Concepts in Art and Education*. New York: The Macmillan Co., 1970.

Sawyer, John R., and DeFrancesco, Italo L. *Elementary School Art for Classroom Teachers*. New York: Harper and Row, Inc., 1971.

Smith, Ralph A. *Aesthetics and Problems of Education*. Urbana: University of Illinois Press, 1971.

Wachowiak, Frank, and Ramsay, Theodore. *Emphasis: Art*, 2nd ed. Scranton, PA: International Textbook Co., 1971.

BIBLIOGRAPHY *Chapter 2*

De Tolnay, Charles. *History and Technique of Old Master Drawings*. New York: H. Bittner and Co., 1943.

Goldwater, Robert, and Treves, Marco, eds. *Artists on Art*. New York: Pantheon Books, Inc., 1945.

Hale, Robert Beverly. *Drawing Lessons from the Great Masters*. New York: Watson-Guptill Publications, 1964.

Jones, Edith H., ed. *The Drawings of Charles Burchfield*. New York: Praeger Publishers, 1968.

Kahnweiler, Daniel Henry. *Juan Gris, His Life and Work*. New York: Abrams, Inc., 1946.

Mendelowitz, Daniel M. *Drawing*. New York: Holt, Rinehart and Winston, 1967.

Myers, Bernard. *Understanding the Arts*. New York: Holt, Rinehart and Winston, 1953.

BIBLIOGRAPHY *Chapter 3*

De Tolnay, Charles. *History and Technique of Old Master Drawings*. New York: H. Bittner and Co., 1943.

Goldwater, Robert and Treves, Marco, eds. *Artists on Art*. New York: Pantheon Books, Inc., 1945.

Mendelowitz, Daniel M. *Drawing*. New York: Holt, Rinehart and Winston, 1967.

Myers, Bernard, ed. *McGraw-Hill Dictionary of Art*. New York, 1969.

Myers, Bernard. *The German Expressionists*. New York: McGraw-Hill Book Company, Inc., 1963.

Myers, Bernard. *Understanding the Arts*. New York: Holt, Rinehart and Winston, 1963.

Newman, Thelma R. *Wax as Art Form*. South Brunswick, NJ: Thomas Yoseloff, 1966.

Parmelin, Helen. *Picasso: Intimate Secrets of a Studio*. New York: Abrams, Inc., 1966.

Russell, John. *Seurat*. New York: Praeger Publishers, Inc., 1965.

Watrous, James. *The Craft of Old Master Drawings*. Madison: University of Wisconsin Press, 1957.

BIBLIOGRAPHY *Chapter 4*

Barr, Alfred H. Jr. *Matisse: His Art and His Public*. New York: Museum of Modern Art, 1951.

Bittner, Herbert, ed. *George Grosz*. New York: Arts, Inc., 1960.

De Tolnay, Charles. *History and Technique of Old Master Drawings*. New York: H. Bittner and Co., 1943.

Elgar, Frank. *Van Gogh*. New York: Praeger Publishers, Inc., 1958.

Goldwater, Robert, and Treves, Marco, eds. *Artists on Art*. New York: Pantheon Books, Inc., 1945.

Hammacher, A. M. *The Ten Creative Years of Vincent Van Gogh*. New York: Abrams, Inc., 1968.

Mendelowitz, Daniel M. *Drawing*. New York: Holt, Rinehart and Winston, 1967.

Myers, Bernard, ed. *McGraw-Hill Dictionary of Art*. New York, 1969.

Myers, Bernard. *Understanding the Arts*. New York: Holt, Rinehart and Winston, 1953.

Watrous, James. *The Craft of Old Master Drawings*. Madison: University of Wisconsin Press, 1957.

BIBLIOGRAPHY *Chapter 5*

De Tolnay, Charles. *History and Technique of Old Master Drawings*. New York: H. Bittner and Co., 1943.

Goldwater, Robert, and Treves, Marco, eds. *Artists on Art*. New York: Pantheon Books, Inc., 1945.

Hours, Madeleine. *Jean-Baptiste Camille Corot*. New York: Abrams, Inc., 1972.

Mendelowitz, Daniel M. *Drawings*. New York: Holt, Rinehart and Winston, 1967.

Myers, Bernard, ed. *McGraw-Hill Dictionary of Art*. New York, 1969.

Myers, Bernard. *Understanding the Arts*. New York: Holt, Rinehart and Winston, 1953.

Nagel, Otto. *Kaethe Kollwitz*. Greenwich, CN: New York Graphic Society, Ltd., 1971.

Read, Herbert. *The Philosophy of Modern Art*. New York: Meridian Books, 1955.

Rewald, John. *Gauguin*. Paris: Hyperion Press, 1938.

Rewald, John. *Gauguin Drawings*. New York: Thomas Yoseloff, Inc., 1958.

Watrous, James. *The Craft of Old Master Drawings*. Madison: University of Wisconsin Press, 1957.

BIBLIOGRAPHY *Chapter 6*

Berger, Klaus. *Odilon Redon*. New York: McGraw-Hill Book Co., Inc., 1965.

De Tolnay, Charles. *History and Technique of Old Master Drawings*. New York: H. Bittner and Co., 1943.

Goldwater, Robert, and Treves, Marco, eds. *Artists on Art*. New York: Pantheon Books, Inc., 1945.

Hale, Robert Beverly. *Drawing Lessons from the Great Masters*. New York: Watson-Guptill Publications, 1964.

Mendelowitz, Daniel. *Drawing*. New York: Holt, Rinehart and Winston, 1967.

Myers, Bernard, ed. *McGraw-Hill Dictionary of Art*. New York, 1969.

Myers, Bernard. *Understanding the Arts*. New York: Holt, Rinehart and Winston, 1953.

Watrous, James. *The Craft of Old Master Drawings*. Madison: University of Wisconsin Press, 1957.

Werner, Alfred. *Degas Pastels*. London: Barrie Books, Ltd., 1969.

Wildenstein, Daniel, and Lansner, Kermit. *Degas*. New York: Wildenstein and Co., 1960.

BIBLIOGRAPHY *Chapter 7*

Benesch, Otto. *Rembrandt, Selected Drawings*. London: Phaidon Press, Ltd., 1947.

_____. *The Drawings of Rembrandt*. 6 Vols. London: Phaidon Press, Ltd., 1954–1957.

Bowles, Kerwin. *The Man Who Painted the Sun*. New York: Stravon Publishers, 1951.

Fuchs, Rudolf Herman. *Rembrandt in Amsterdam*. Trans. by Patricia Wardle and Alan Griffiths. Greenwich, CT: New York Graphic Society, Ltd., 1969.

Gardner, Helen. *Art through the Ages*, 5th ed. New York: Harcourt, Brace and World, Inc., 1970.

Janson, H. W. *History of Art*. Englewood Cliffs, NJ: Prentice-Hall, Inc., and New York: Abrams, Inc., 1969.

Kuh, Katherine. *Léger*. Urbana, IL: The University of Illinois Press, 1953.

Lieberman, Alexander. *The Artist in His Studio*. New York: Viking Press, 1960.

Rowley, George. *Principles of Chinese Painting*. Princeton, NJ: Princeton University Press, 1947.

Sewell, John Ives. *A History of Western Art*, rev. ed. New York: Holt, Rinehart and Winston, 1961.

Sirén, Osvald. *Chinese Painting: Leading Masters and Principles*. 7 Vols. New York: Ronald Press, 1956–1958.

Slive, Seymour. *Drawings of Rembrandt*. 2 Vols. New York: Dover Publications, Inc., 1956.

Swann, Peter C. *Chinese Painting*. Paris: Éditions Pierre Tisné, 1958.

BIBLIOGRAPHY *Chapter 8*

Baur, John I. H., ed. *New Art in America*. Greenwich, CT: New York Graphic Society, and New York: Praeger Publishers, Inc., 1957.

Brown, Milton. *Jacob Lawrence*. New York: Whitney Museum of American Art, 1974.

Cummings, Paul. *Dictionary of Contemporary American Artists*, 3d ed. New York: St. Martin's Press, 1977.

Eichmann, Ingeborg. "Five Sketches by Henry Rousseau," *Burlington Magazine*, Vol. LXXII, June 1938, pp. 302–303, 307.

Encyclopedia of World Art, Vol. X, pp. 899–931.

Goodrich, Lloyd. *John Sloan*. New York: The Whitney Museum of American Art, 1952.

Haftmann, Werner. *Emil Nolde: Unpainted Pictures*. Trans. by Inge Goodwin, rev. ed. New York: Praeger Publishers, Inc., 1971.

Huisman, P., and Dortu, M. G. *Lautrec by Lautrec*. New York: The Viking Press, 1964.

Myers, Bernard S. *The German Expressionists: A Generation in Revolt*. New York: McGraw-Hill Book Co., Inc., 1963.

Rich, Daniel Catton. *Henri Rousseau*. New York: The Museum of Modern Art, 1942.

Roh, Franz. *German Painting in the Twentieth Century*. Trans. by Catherine Hutter. Greenwich, CT: New York Graphic Society, Ltd., 1968.

Rose, Barbara. "Georgia O'Keeffe: The Paintings of the Sixties," *Artforum*, Vol. IX, no. 3, November 1970, pp. 42–46.

Scott, David. *John Sloan*. New York: Watson-Guptill Publications, 1975.

Selz, Peter. *Emil Nolde*. New York: The Museum of Modern Art, 1963.

Urban, Martin. *Emil Nolde Landscapes*. London: Pall Mall Press, 1970.

Viola, Jerome. "Georgia O'Keeffe," *McGraw-Hill Dictionary of Art*, Vol. IV. pp. 245–246.

Wilder, Mitchell A., ed. *Georgia O'Keeffe*. Fort Worth: Amon Carter Museum of Western Art, 1966.

Wilenski, R. H. *Modern French Painters*, Vols. I and II. New York: Vintage Books, 1960.

BIBLIOGRAPHY *Chapter 9*

————. *Georges Braque*. Edinburgh: The Royal Scottish Academy, n.d.

Hope, Henry R. *Georges Braque*. New York: The Museum of Modern Art, 1949.

Janis, Harriet, and Blesh, Rudi. *Collage: Personalities, Concepts, Techniques*. Philadelphia: Chilton Company, 1962.

Moulin, Raoul Jean. *Henri Matisse: Drawings and Paper Cut-Outs*. Trans. by Michael Ross. New York: McGraw-Hill Book Co., Inc., 1969.

Mullins, Edwin B. *The Art of Georges Braque*. New York: Abrams, Inc., 1968.

BIBLIOGRAPHY *Chapter 10*

Field, Richard S. *Paul Gauguin: Monotypes*. Philadelphia: Philadelphia Museum of Art, 1973.

Hunter, Sam. *American Art of the Twentieth Century*. New York: Abrams, Inc., 1972.

Janis, Eugenia Parry. *Degas Monotypes*. Cambridge: Fogg Art Museum, 1968.

Marsh, Roger. *Monoprints for the Artist*. London: Alec Tiranti Ltd., 1969.

Peterdi, Gabor. *Printmaking*. New York: The Macmillan Co., 1959.

Rasmussen, Henry. *Printmaking with Monotype*. Philadelphia: Chilton Company, 1960.

Rhys, Hedley Howell. *Maurice Prendergast*. Cambridge, MA: Harvard University Press, 1960.

Taylor, Joshua C. *Learning to Look*. Chicago: University of Chicago Press, 1957.

Wechsler, Herman J. *Great Prints and Printmakers*. New York: Abrams, Inc., 1967.

BIBLIOGRAPHY *Chapter 11*

Hentzen, Alfred. "Rolf Nesch," *Prints*. New York: Holt, Rinehart and Winston, 1962, pp. 39–54.

Hunter, Sam. *American Art of the Twentieth Century*. New York: Abrams, Inc., 1972.

Naylor, Colin, and P-Orridge, Genesis, eds. *Contemporary Artists*. New York: St. Martin's Press, 1977.

Peterdi, Gabor. *Printmaking*. New York: The Macmillan Co., 1959.

Ross, John, and Clare Romano. *The Complete Printmaker*. New York: The Free Press, 1972.

Wechsler, Herman J. *Great Prints and Printmakers*. New York: Abrams, Inc., 1967.

BIBLIOGRAPHY *Chapter 12*

Breeskin, Adelyn. *William H. Johnson 1901–1970*. Washington: Smithsonian Institution Press, 1971.

Dover, Cedric. *American Negro Art*. New York: New York Graphic Society, 1960.

Duncan, David Douglas. *The Private World of Pablo Picasso*. New York: Harper and Row, 1958.

Feinblatt, Ebria, ed. *Picasso: Sixty Years of Graphic Works*. Los Angeles: Los Angeles County Museum of Art, 1966.

Karshan, Donald H. *Picasso Linocuts 1958–1963*. New York: Tudor Publishing Co., Inc., 1968.

Myers, Bernard. *The German Expressionists*. New York: McGraw-Hill Book Co., Inc., 1963.

Parmelin, Helen. *Picasso: Intimate Secrets of a Studio*. New York: Abrams, Inc., 1966.

Rosenblum, Robert. *Cubism and Twentieth-Century Art*. New York: Abrams, Inc., 1960.

BIBLIOGRAPHY *Chapter 13*

Auvil, Kenneth W. *Serigraphy*. Englewood Cliffs, NJ: Prentice-Hall, Inc., 1965.

Biegeleisen, J. I., and Cohn, Max. *Silk Screen Techniques*. New York: Dover Publications, Inc., 1942.

Coplans, Johns. *Andy Warhol*. New York: New York Graphic Society, 1970.

Nalor, Colin, and P-Orridge, Genesis, eds. *Contemporary Artists*. New York: St. Martin's Press, 1977.

Russell, John, and Gablik, Suzi. *Pop Art Redefined*. New York: Praeger Publishers, Inc., 1969.

Shahn, Ben. *The Shape of Content*. New York: Vintage Books, Inc., 1960.

Soby, James Thrall. *Ben Shahn*. New York: George Braziller, Inc., 1963.

Taylor, Joshua C. *Learning to Look*. Chicago: University of Chicago Press, 1957.

BIBLIOGRAPHY *Chapter 14*

Boos, Frank H. *The Ceramic Sculptures of Ancient Oaxaca*. New York: A. S. Barnes and Co., Inc., 1966.

Cailler, Pierre. *Catalog of the Sculptural Works of Andre Derain*. Paris: Galerie Chardin, 1965.

Canaday, John. *Metropolitan Seminars in Art (Portfolio 11: The Artist as a Social Critic)*. New York: Metropolitan Museum of Art, 1959.

Easby, Elizabeth Kennedy, and Scott, John F. *Before Cortes—Sculpture of Middle America*. New York: The Metropolitan Museum of Art, 1970.

International Council of Scholars. *Encyclopedia of World Art*, Vol. 1–15. New York: McGraw-Hill Book Co., Inc., 1959.

MacCurdy, Edward, ed. *The Notebooks of Leonardo da Vinci*. New York: Reynal and Hitchcock, 1938.

Vincent Howard P. *Daumier and His World*. Evanston, IL: Northwestern University Press, 1968.

Wasserman, Jeanne L. *Daumier Sculpture*. Cambridge, MA: Fogg Art Museum, 1969.

Westheim, Paul. *The Sculpture of Ancient Mexico*. Garden City, NY: Doubleday and Company, Inc., 1963.

BIBLIOGRAPHY *Chapter 15*

Friedman, Martin. *Nevelson Wood Sculptures.* New York: E. P. Dutton and Co., Inc., 1973.

Giedion-Welcker, Carola. *Jean Arp.* New York: Abrams, Inc., 1957.

Medina, Jose Ramon. *Marisol.* Caracas, Venezuela: Ediciones Armitano, 1968.

Naylor, Colin, and P-Orridge, Genesis, eds. *Contemporary Artists.* New York: St. Martin's Press, 1977.

Read, Herbert. *Arp.* New York: Abrams, Inc., 1968.

Richter, Hans. *Dada: Art and Anti-Art.* New York: McGraw-Hill Book Co., n.d.

Russell, John, and Gablik, Suzi. *Pop Art Redefined.* New York: Praeger Publishers, Inc., 1969.

BIBLIOGRAPHY *Chapter 16*

De Voe, Shirley Spaulding. *English Papier-Mâché of the Georgian and Victorian Periods.* Middletown, CN: Wesleyan University Press, 1971.

Johnson, Pauline. *Creating with Paper.* Seattle: University of Washington Press, 1958.

Naylor, Colin, and P-Orridge, Genesis, eds. *Contemporary Artists.* New York: St. Martin's Press, 1977.

Ragon, Michel. *Dubuffet.* New York: Grove Press, Inc., 1959.

Rose, Barbara. *Claes Oldenburg.* New York: The Museum of Modern Art, 1970.

Rowell, Margit. *Jean Dubuffet: A Retrospective.* New York: Solomon R. Guggenheim Foundation, 1973.

BIBLIOGRAPHY *Chapter 17*

Bihalji-Merin, Oto. *Great Masks.* Trans. by Herman Plummer. New York: Abrams, Inc., 1971.

Grohmann, Will. *Paul Klee.* New York: Abrams, Inc., n.d.

Hopper, Brizella. *Puppet Making through the Grades.* Worcester, MA: Davis Publications, 1966.

Laude, Jean. *The Arts of Black Africa.* Trans. by Jean Decock. Berkeley: University of California Press, 1971.

Lazzaro, Gualtieri Di San. *Klee*. Trans. by Stuart Hood. New York: Praeger Publishers, Inc., 1957.

Leuzinger, Elsy. *Africa: The Art of the Negro Peoples*. Trans. by Ann E. Keep. New York: McGraw-Hill Book Co., Inc., 1960.

Lommel, Andreas. *Masks: Their Meaning and Function*. Trans. by Nadia Fowler. New York: McGraw-Hill Book Co., Inc., 1972.

Meauze, Pierre. *African Art: Sculpture*. Cleveland and New York: World, 1968.

Ray, Dorothy Jean. *Eskimo Masks, Art and Ceremony*. Seattle: University of Washington Press, 1967.

Riley, Olive L. *Masks and Magic*. New York: Studio Publications and Thomas Y. Crowell, 1955.

Underwood, Leon. *Masks of West Africa*. London: Alec Tiranti, Ltd., 1948.

BIBLIOGRAPHY *Chapter 18*

Baker, Denys Val. *Pottery Today*. London: Oxford University Press, 1961.

Barford, George. *Clay in the Classroom*. Worcester, MA: Davis Publications, 1963.

Brown, Eleese V. "Developmental Characteristics of Clay Figures Made by Children from Ages 3 through 11," *Studies in Art Education*, Vol XVI, no. 3, 1975, pp. 45–53.

Bushnell, G. H. S. *Ancient Arts of the Americas*. New York: Praeger Publishers, Inc., 1965.

Charleston, Robert Jesse, ed. *World Ceramics*. New York: McGraw-Hill Book Co., Inc., 1968.

Cox, Warren Earle. *The Book of Pottery and Porcelain*. New York: Crown, 1970.

"Dipylon Gate, Athens," *McGraw-Hill Dictionary of Art*, Vol. II. 1969, p. 259.

"Dipylon Vase," *McGraw-Hill Dictionary of Art*, Vol. II. 1969, pp. 259–260.

Green, David. *Pottery: Materials and Techniques*. New York: Praeger Publishers, Inc., 1967.

Lassaigne, Jacques. *Miró*. Geneva: Skira, 1963.

Lee, Ruth. *Exploring the World of Pottery*. Chicago: Children's Press, 1967.

Marenco, Ethne K. "Maya," *McGraw-Hill Dictionary of Art*, Vol. I. 1969, pp. 97–101.

Myers, Bernard S. "Miró," *McGraw-Hill Dictionary of Art*, Vol. IV. 1969, pp. 87–88.

Richter, Gisella. *A Handbook of Greek Art*. London: Phaidon, 1959.

Savage, George. *Pottery through the Ages*. London: Cassell and Company, Ltd., 1963.

————. *Sculptures de Miró; Ceramics de Miró et Llorens Artigas*. Paris: Foundation Maeght, 1973.

Soby, James Thrall. *Joan Miró*. New York: Museum of Modern Art, 1959.

Spinden, Herbert. *Maya Art and Civilization*. rev. ed. Indian Hills, CO: The Falcon's Wing Press, 1957.

Supensky, Thomas G. *Ceramic Art in the School Program*. Worcester, MA: Davis Publications, 1968.

Walters, Henry Beauchamp. *History of Ancient Pottery*, Vol. I. London: John Murray, 1905.

BIBLIOGRAPHY *Chapter 19*

Anders, Nedda. *Appliqué Old and New*. New York: Hearthside Press, 1967.

Fowke, Frank Reed. *The Bayeux Tapestry*. London: G. Bell and Sons, Ltd., 1971.

Gibbs-Smith, Charles Harvard. *The Bayeux Tapestry*. London: The Phaidon Press, Ltd., 1973.

Groves, Sylvia. *The History of Needlework Tools and Accessories*. Country Life Books, 1966.

Krevitsky, Nik. *Stitchery: Art and Craft*. New York: Van Nostrand Reinhold, n.d.

Moseley, Spencer; Johnson, Pauline; and Koenig, Hazel. *Crafts Design*. Belmont, CA: Wadsworth, 1962.

Schuette, Marie, and Muller-Christensen, Sigrid. *A Pictorial History of Embroidery*. New York: Praeger Publishers, Inc., 1964.

Schwartz, Marvin D. "Embroidery," *McGraw-Hill Dictionary of Art*, Vol. II. 1969, pp. 344–345.

Stenton, Sir Frank, ed. *The Bayeux Tapestry*, 2nd ed., rev. London: Phaidon Press, 1965.

BIBLIOGRAPHY *Chapter 20*

Albers, Anni. *On Designing*, 2nd ed. Middletown, CT: Wesleyan University Press, 1961.

_____. *On Weaving*. Middletown, CT: Wesleyan University Press, 1965.

Anton, Ferdinand. *The Art of Ancient Peru*. New York: G. P. Putnam's Sons, 1972.

Bennett, Wendall Clark. *Ancient Arts of the Andes*. New York: The Museum of Modern Art, 1954.

Bennett, Wendall Clark, and Bird, Junius B. *Andean Culture History*. New York: American Museum of Natural History, Handbook Series No. 15, 1949.

Harcourt, Raoul d'. *Textiles of Ancient Peru and Their Techniques.* Trans. by Sadie Brown. Seattle: University of Washington Press, 1962.

Held, Shirley E. *Weaving: A Handbook for Fiber Craftsmen.* New York: Holt, Rinehart and Winston, 1973.

Hoffman, Walter James. "The Menomini Indians," *Fourteenth Annual Report of the Bureau of Ethnology,* Government Printing Press, Washington, DC, 1896.

Hoyle, Rafael Larco. *Peru.* Trans. by James Hogarth. Cleveland and New York: World, 1966.

Keesing, Felix Maxwell. *The Menomini Indians of Wisconsin.* Philadelphia, PA: the American Philosophical Society, 1939.

Mason, John Alden. *The Ancient Civilizations of Peru.* Harmondsworth, Middlesex: Penguin Books, Ltd., 1957.

Moseley, Spencer; Johnson, Pauline; and Koenig, Hazel. *Crafts Design.* Belmont, CA: Wadsworth Publishing, 1962.

Rainey, Sarita P. *Weaving without a Loom.* Worcester, MA: Davis Publications, Inc., 1964.

Ritzenthaler, Robert E., and Ritzenthaler, Pat. *The Woodland Indians of the Western Great Lakes.* Garden City, NY: Natural History Press, 1970.

Znemierowski, Nell. *Step-by-Step Weaving.* New York: Golden Press, 1967.

BIBLIOGRAPHY *Chapter 21*

Davidson, Abraham. "History of Photography," *McGraw-Hill Dictionary of Art,* Vol. IV. 1969, pp. 356–357.

_____. "Moholy-Nagy," *McGraw-Hill Dictionary of Art,* Vol. IV. 1969, pp. 97–98.

Gernsheim, Helmut, and Gernsheim, Alison. *The History of Photography from the Earliest Use of the Camera Obscura in the 11th Century Up to 1914.* London: Oxford University Press, 1955.

Holter, Patra. *Photography without a Camera.* New York: Van Nostrand Reinhold, 1972.

Hours, Madeleine. *Jean-Baptiste Camille Corot.* New York: Abrams, Inc., 1972.

The Museum of Modern Art. *Dorothea Lange.* New York: The Museum of Modern Art, 1966.

Moholy-Nagy, László. *Vision in Motion.* Chicago: Paul Theobald and Company, 1969.

Pollack, Peter. *The Picture History of Photography.* New York: Abrams, Inc., 1958.

NAME INDEX

SUBJECT INDEX

DATE DUE

MR 1 6 '03			
AP 1 1 '05			

MAR 11 03